The Body and the State

SUNY series in American Constitutionalism

Robert J. Spitzer, editor

THE BODY
AND THE STATE

۵

Habeas Corpus and
American Jurisprudence

CARY FEDERMAN

STATE UNIVERSITY OF NEW YORK PRESS

Published by
State University of New York Press, Albany

© 2006 State University of New York

For information, address State University of New York Press,
194 Washington Avenue, Suite 305, Albany, NY 12210-2384

Production by Christine Hamel
Marketing by Susan Petrie

Library of Congress Cataloging-in-Publication Data

Federman, Cary, 1963–
  The body and the state : habeas corpus and American jurisprudence /
Cary Federman.
    p. cm. — (SUNY series in American constitutionalism)
  Includes bibliographical references and index.
  ISBN 0-7914-6703-1 (hardcover : alk. paper)
  1. Habeas corpus—United States—History. 2. Habeas corpus—United States.
I. Title. II. Series.

KF9011.F43 2006
345.73'056—dc22

                                                                        2005012801

  ISBN-13: 978-0-7914-6703-9 (hardcover : alk. paper)

10 9 8 7 6 5 4 3 2 1

For Masha,
Mnogo te Volim

Sometimes it seems that there is only one story in American legal thought and only one problem. The story is the story of formalism and the problem is the problem of the subject. The story of formalism is that it never deals with the problem of the subject. The problem of the subject is that it's never been part of the story.

Until Now.

—Pierre Schlag, "Beyond Critique:
Law, Culture, and the Politics of Form"

Contents

Chronology of Habeas Corpus   ix

Introduction: Understanding Habeas Corpus   1

1   Habeas Corpus in the New American State, 1789–1915   21

2   Bodily Inventions: The Habeas Petitioner and the
Corporation, 1886   45

3   Habeas Corpus as Counternarrative: The Rise of
Due Process, 1923–1953   63

4   Confessions and the Narratives of Justice, 1963–1979   95

5   Future Dangerousness and Habeas Corpus, 1982–2002   125

6   Habeas Corpus and the Narratives of Terrorism, 1996–2002   157

7   Conclusion   185

Notes   191

Index   235

Chronology of Habeas Corpus

Definition: Literally, "you have the body." A writ issued by a court to inquire into whether a person is lawfully detained or imprisoned.

Significance: Habeas corpus provides an important avenue of appeal for state prisoners with unresolved federal questions. Upon completing the state appellate process, a prisoner may petition for habeas corpus in a federal district court. This is called a "collateral attack." District court denials can be appealed to federal courts of appeals and then to the Supreme Court.

The history of habeas corpus in the United States can be divided into five periods: 1789 to 1863; 1867 to 1915; 1923 to 1953; 1963 to 1979; and 1986 to the present.

1789–1863. Habeas corpus before the Civil War could not be issued after trial and conviction; it could only be used to question the jurisdiction of a committing court. The key to understanding habeas corpus before the Civil War is not the constitutional prohibition against suspending the writ during times of rebellion (Article 1, section 9), but the Judiciary Act of 1789. The act granted Supreme Court justices and federal court judges the power to issue writs to those held "in custody, under or by colour of the authority of the United States." This meant that only prisoners held under federal law could apply for habeas corpus, thereby excluding state prisoners with federal claims (*Barron v. Baltimore*, 1833). *Ableman v. Booth* (1859) prevented state courts from issuing habeas corpus to federal prisoners and runaway slaves.

1867–1915. In 1867, Congress passed a habeas corpus act intended to reach state prisoners. The act gave the federal courts the power to issue habeas corpus "in all cases where any person may be restrained of his or her liberty in violation of the Constitution." Congress was concerned, however, that the Supreme Court would strike down Reconstruction laws that arose on habeas appeals from state prisoners and subvert Congress' postwar civil rights agenda. In 1868, Congress suspended the Court's appellate habeas corpus jurisdiction, restoring it in 1885. In *Ex parte Royall* (1886), the Supreme Court required state prisoners to exhaust all available means of appeal before attacking their convictions in a federal district court. The Supreme Court continued to defer to state court convictions into the twentieth century. In *Frank v. Magnum* (1915), a case involving mob threats to the defendant during his trial, the Court denied habeas corpus because the state had satisfied the defendant's due process rights of notice and a hearing. The Court, as it had since *Royall*, relied on a conception of due process rooted in the common law tradition and deference to state law.

1923–1953. In *Moore v. Dempsey* (1923), a case like *Frank* that dealt with mob violence at trial, Justice Oliver Wendell Holmes, for the majority, granted habeas corpus and declared that due process cannot be satisfied if a state appellate court rejects a defendant's federal claim without inquiry. *Moore* did not overturn *Frank*, but it linked habeas corpus claims to an expanding notion of due process of law under the Fourteenth Amendment (1868). In *Brown v. Allen* (1953), though the Court denied the defendant's habeas corpus claim, it held that that the federal courts have a duty on habeas appeals to redetermine constitutional claims already decided by a state court.

1963–1979. *Brown* broke the jurisdiction of the state courts to determine final guilt and punishment. In *Fay v. Noia* (1963), the Court, on habeas review, held that a prisoner's failure to comply with state procedural requirements regarding the timing of appeals was not a bar to federal habeas relief. Justice William Brennan held that habeas corpus provides "a mode for the redress of denials of due process of law." For the next six years, the Warren Court used habeas claims to expand the due process rights of the accused and the convicted (*Gideon v. Wainwright*, 1963). But in *Kaufman v. United States* (1969), Justice Hugo Black questioned in dissent whether the prisoner's guilt should be a factor in deciding to grant habeas relief on Fourth Amendment questions. In *Stone v. Powell* (1976), Justice Lewis Powell accepted Black's position and held that nonguilt-related Fourth Amendment habeas claims undermined the states' power to punish convicted criminals. *Stone* was based on the general belief that federal habeas review of state prisoners' claims was unnecessary, provided that the state court had afforded the defendant a full and fair hearing of all federal claims.

1986 to the present. The Rehnquist Court's habeas jurisprudence has been marked by a concern with limiting habeas corpus appeals in the interest of federalism. In *Coleman v. Thompson* (1991), a murder case involving a late state petition for appeal, Justice Sandra Day O'Connor denied habeas corpus and declared, "This is a case about federalism" and the "respect that federal courts owe the States and the States' procedural rules." The Rehnquist Court has also issued important decisions concerning whether newly announced constitutional rules are retroactive on habeas corpus (*Teague* v. *Lane*, 1989; *Penry* v. *Lynaugh*, 1991). These rulings require federal courts to apply to habeas cases legal standards that existed at the time of the original state criminal proceeding. The effect of these decisions is to restrict the linkage between habeas corpus and due process and limit federal habeas corpus relief for state prisoners. In 1996, Congress passed the Antiterrorism and Effective Death Penalty Act, which codified many of the Court's habeas decisions that have been critical of *Fay* v. *Noia* and its progeny. The AEDPA forbids federal courts from overturning state court decisions on habeas corpus unless it is "contrary to, or involves an unreasonable application of, clearly established Federal law." It also imposes a one-year period within which state prisoners can file for federal habeas corpus and restricts second or successive federal habeas appeals. The Supreme Court upheld the act's prohibition of successive petitions in *Felker* v. *Turpin* (1996).

INTRODUCTION

Understanding Habeas Corpus

The Writ of Habeas Corpus is not just a piece of paper, not just a quaint Latin phrase. It was the key to my freedom.
　　　　　—Rubin "Hurricane" Carter, "Keynote Address"

Although it may appear unseemly that a prisoner, after conviction in a state court, should be set at liberty by a single judge on habeas corpus, there seems to be no escape from the law.
　　　　　—Justice Joseph Bradley, *Ex parte Bridges*

The murder was brutal.
　　　　　—*Turner* v. *Murray*

Discourse will become the vehicle of the law: the constant principle of universal recording.
—Foucault, *Discipline and Punish*

THIS BOOK TRACES the history of the writ of habeas corpus and its influence on the development of federal-state relations and capital punishment from 1789 to 2004, when the writ was linked by Congress and the Supreme Court to antiterrorism laws and threats to the peace and security of Americans.

Habeas corpus ("you have the body") is the principal means by which state prisoners attack the constitutionality of their convictions in federal courts. It is "the fundamental instrument for safeguarding individual freedom against arbitrary and lawless state action."[1] Habeas corpus appears in the Constitution under Article I, section 9: "The Privilege of the Writ of Habeas Corpus shall not be suspended, unless when in Cases of Rebellion or Invasion the public Safety may require it." President Abraham Lincoln relied on this clause when he suspended habeas corpus during the Civil War. Although the meaning of the suspension clause is not settled, it is best understood as a "limit on congressional power to restrict judicial inquiry into the lawfulness of executive decisions."[2] This understanding of the writ will be discussed in chapter 6, with an analysis of the cases stemming from Guantánamo Bay, Cuba. But the source of the writ as a procedural device used after conviction by state prisoners is the Habeas Corpus Act of 1867, which gives power to "the several courts of the United States, and the several justices and judges of such courts, within their respective jurisdictions, in addition to the authority already conferred by law [the Judiciary Act of 1789] . . . to grant writs of habeas corpus in all cases where any person may be restrained of his or her liberty in violation of the Constitution, or of any treaty or law of the United States."[3] While it seems that Article I, section 9 regards habeas corpus as a remedy for those detained without trial, the Habeas Corpus Act of 1867 is set up as a federal challenge to state criminal convictions considered unlawful by convicts. Yet the act makes no distinction between presidents arresting citizens and arbitrary state arrests directed at society's weakest and most vulnerable. Like the constitutional clause, the act is silent on the question of habeas corpus as a postconviction remedy. It attacks unlawful confinement in its entirety.

Because of the habeas act, the federal judiciary has the power to inquire into the states' judicial processes and release the prisoner, without regard for the determinations of juries or the feelings of state court judges. The Supreme Court, however, has lacked the constitutional support of a strong central state apparatus that can reach state action and a language with which to base an argument that could set a convict free from state incarceration. Consequently, despite the fact that the 1867 act posed a challenge to the antebellum constitutional structure that remained in place after the Civil War, the Supreme Court rarely granted habeas corpus in the aftermath of the war. Rather, attempting to bolster federal-state comity concerns in the wake of the failure of Reconstruction, the Supreme Court considered federal review of state habeas petitions wasteful of important judicial resources and therefore constitutionally unnecessary. A vocabulary of class and race developed alongside a rhetoric of deference, guilt, and administrative burden, which appeared in case law as the trinity comity, finality, and federalism. After Reconstruction ended in 1877, and electoral competition at the national level increased, both Congress and the Supreme Court abandoned concerns over the legal status of state habeas petitioners, as convicted criminals, blacks, Asians, other minorities and indigents in need of national protection from hostile state courts and juries replaced federal revenue and military officers as the chief petitioners for habeas corpus in the federal courts.

Despite the 1867 act's intentional intrusion into state criminal processes, neither Congress nor the federal judiciary took over the interests or showed any regard for the rights of state prisoners with constitutional claims. In part through a policy of deference to state comity concerns,[4] and in part because the Court had restricted federal habeas corpus relief to extraordinary claims of illegal detention, Supreme Court justices throughout the nineteenth century allowed the state courts to set the constitutional boundaries of what constituted illegal confinements. The nineteenth-century federal judiciary's concerns with property rights permitted the Supreme Court in the twentieth century to reverse Congress' postbellum redirection of federal-state relations. Concerned with limits on judicial capacities in civil rights cases, the Court ignored the increase in the number of habeas petitions coming from racial and ethnic minorities seeking federal relief from the decisions of local juries and rejected calls to reexamine state courts' criminal convictions. In general, the Supreme Court barred granting the writ, provided the state court possessed jurisdiction over the case and the petitioner's guilt was determined within the historic (and limited) meaning of due process.

Habeas corpus is no longer governed by this Reconstruction-era law, passed in the wake of the arrest of federal tax and military officials operating in states hostile to federal power both before and during the Civil War and amid future fears that the states would not protect the rights of newly enfranchised blacks. Habeas corpus is now under the Antiterrorism and Effective Death Penalty Act of 1996,[5] passed one year and five days after Timothy McVeigh and Terry Nichols blew up the Alfred P. Murrah federal building in Oklahoma City, Oklahoma, killing 168 people.

Although the writ has no formal or historical links with terrorism, it is difficult to divorce the connection that Congress has now placed before us: between habeas corpus on the one hand as a threat to federal-state relations and as a "get out of jail" card for convicted criminals and, on the other, as a way to aid terrorists. Justice Antonin Scalia explained the connection between habeas corpus and terrorism in *Rasul* v. *Bush* (2004), where he viewed the granting of the writ as a form of surrender to international terrorism. Justice Scalia relied on Justice Robert Jackson's opinion in *Johnson* v. *Eisentrager* (1950), writing, "To grant the writ to these prisoners might mean that our army must transport them across the seas for hearing. . . . Such trials would hamper the war effort and bring aid and comfort to the enemy."[6]

And so, today, in light of terrorist events conducted by American citizens and foreigners alike, and amid a generalized fear of crime in the streets, the writ of habeas corpus stands accused of setting the guilty free, of opening up the prisons, of preventing the full force of punishment, and of providing the vehicle for Al Qaeda's victory. It is quite an indictment for a rule of law long associated with defending civil liberties against unlawful executive detention, both in the United States and in Great Britain.

In large part because of the writ's historic association with Magna Carta, many scholars consider habeas corpus as a tool of liberty in the fight against governmental oppression. Variously called "the great writ of liberty," a "human right," and "a bulwark" and "palladium" of English liberties, the ancient writ of habeas corpus has achieved a status in American jurisprudence that has surpassed even those rights deemed by the United States Supreme Court to be "preferred" or "fundamental," such as free speech and the right to privacy.[7]

The language of habeas corpus has changed little since the seventeenth century; newspaper editorials still refer to habeas corpus as if the glow of its ancient powers were still visible. But the writ is not an instrument of domestic peace. It upsets power relations between the states and the federal government and between the individual and the state. Even worse, the prompt comes not from an internal domestic problem—the incarceration of federal tax collectors by jealous state officials, as was the case in 1812—but from a convicted criminal, contesting his sentence, perhaps for the second time, perhaps for the third, and perhaps some ten years after the initial conviction first sealed his fate. In many cases, the petition will come from death row. Despite the writ's "extraordinary prestige"[8] among law professors and editorial page writers, habeas corpus has been a source of mostly unrecognized conflict between the states and the federal government.

STUDYING HABEAS CORPUS OVER TIME

Throughout most of its history, habeas corpus in Britain was a pretrial remedy for those detained by order of the king.[9] A judge had the power to command a jailor to appear before a court of competent jurisdiction and justify the reasons for detaining a particular person. But it "would have been intolerable for a person to have the legality of his custody determined conclusively by the first judicial body to hear the matter."[10] There were limits, however, to this method of appeal. Only executive clemency could rectify claims of a miscarriage of justice.[11]

In Anglo-American jurisprudence, habeas corpus is an institutional means to test the proposition that individuals have the right to be free from arbitrary arrests. In Britain, unlike the United States, the procedural question attached to a habeas challenge—"who has the body?"—measured the degree of autonomy the governing institution possessed. Indeed, the British never separated the writ's purpose from national sovereignty. "The Royal courts scarcely would have dared to issue a command 'to have the body' unless there were officers to execute it and some reasonable certainty that subjects of the realm would respect the order or at the least do little to interfere with it."[12] By situating the writ in Parliament in the seventeenth century, the British embedded habeas corpus within the state's sovereign purposes and rejected the idea, later adopted in America, that habeas corpus was a formal process.[13] Until the seventeenth century, the debate over the jurisdictional possession of the bodies of subjects was less a question about procedure and more a question about the autonomy of the British state over civil society and its rivals. By the seventeenth century, Parliament had taken away the king's power to arbitrarily imprison his subjects. The king wanted to control habeas corpus because he recognized that the institution that protects and defends personal liberty gains the favor of the people. Parliament seized habeas corpus because it knew that the institution that controls jurisdiction governs the state. A granted writ altered regime boundaries.

Relying on the common law to mythologize American liberty, U.S. historians have removed the state from habeas' development. In the United States, legal elites have emphasized historically based jurisdictional limitations on federal court power over state prisoners to limit the federal courts' reach into state law. But habeas corpus has not been restricted in the United States simply because the states have traditionally exercised sovereignty over persons in areas of law not specified by the Constitution. That argument is unpersuasive because the same federal judicial system that refused to hear claims from blacks of gross constitutional violations at the state level, such as lynchings and mob violence, did not fail to restrict the states' ability to control interstate commerce in the nineteenth century.[14] Relying on "federalism per se" obscures the changes in federalism's meaning that have developed over time. Indeed, the failure to note the interaction between the institution of federalism and political interests pressing for national solutions to perceived local problems prevents a fuller understanding of how legal change occurs, particularly during a given time frame, when one interest wins and another does not. No matter how powerful federalism's influence has been on restraining centralization in the United States, as a political entity it can never determine final events, because its meaning both shifts over time and within political contexts. As I show in chapter 1, observing jurisdictional niceties before the Civil War did not prevent Congress from altering the states' criminal procedures when it wanted to. Patterning habeas corpus over time allows us to see the shifts in federalism's meaning over time.[15]

In a federal republic with a strong tradition of local civil society and a weak central state, assertions about local sovereignty and legal formality will not be uncommon. Between the Civil War and World War I, the federal courts defined federalism as state sovereignty, not as a dialectic between levels of government.[16] This rigid and ahistorical definition of federal-state relations lies directly in habeas corpus' path from mythic writ to constitutional remedy. By the twentieth century, opponents of legal formalism, such as Oliver Wendell Holmes, were arguing that it was unconstitutional for a state to fail to defend a prisoner's due process rights at trial. By focusing on the due process clause of the Fourteenth Amendment as a means to restrict state behavior,

Holmes and others blurred the line between the powers of the federal government and those of the states. Looking at criminal justice from a pragmatic standpoint, the legal realists believed that habeas corpus enforced the American ideal that no one can be held by a government without an opportunity to be heard. In this regard, one legal fiction (the loss of jurisdiction by a state court because of constitutional impropriety and its replacement by a federal court) replaced another (the states' sacrosanct jurisdiction). But the realists made the point that the reasons for the writ's limitations have more to do with public policy preferences than with mythic associations of the sovereignty of local governments formed in the current of history. Yet, as a matter of law, the Supreme Court's regard for protecting the states' interests against state prisoners' Fourteenth Amendment claims had in fact squeezed barely developed "due process" claims into minimal equations about the respect federal judges owe to state court judgments. Thus, throughout this book, I look at the application of a writ with a statist history that has caused enormous changes in the way rights are structured and applied in a federal republic. The path of a state prisoner's habeas challenge is long and winding, and the fate of those who need its protection most depends all too much on the Supreme Court's excessive regard for state operating procedures and congressional fears of freeing convicted criminals.

THE RHETORIC OF HABEAS CORPUS

As will become clear, I view the Court's reliance on federalism more as a prop than as a substantive reason for restricting habeas corpus. I will show that the Court has had other motives for denying habeas corpus to qualified state prisoners than the preservation of the federal-state structure. A habeas corpus case often involves a murder. It was only a matter of time before the Supreme Court could no longer avoid relying on the character of the habeas petitioner—his crime, his brutality, his effrontery—to make the case for why habeas corpus should be denied. By the middle of the twentieth century, the rhetoric of violence found within a particular case supplanted the Court's federalism rationale. This is my key claim, the one to which I would like to direct my readers' attention.

Long-time American critics of habeas corpus charge that the writ releases the convicted, not on innocence grounds or even for reasons of clemency, but on technical principles of law, in other words, for dubious procedural rules created by the Warren Court that the police did not perfectly observe. The AEDPA largely restricts this possibility by shortening the habeas filing process, preventing multiple habeas applications and requiring federal court deference to state court factfinding (see chapter 6). In principle, however, the writ of habeas corpus allows a solitary federal judge—so many miles removed from the crime scene, and perhaps some ten years after the initial conviction was rendered, after memories have faded and witnesses have either moved away or died—to find a due process violation sufficient enough to overturn the judgment of numerous state judges and twelve jurors. To add insult to injury, habeas corpus interferes with the workings of what Justice Felix Frankfurter once called "our federalism."[17]

Does federalism have significance as an institutional norm outside the context of case law? Is federalism a stable structure whose meaning is readily apparent to students of the law? Or is it a trump card in a constitutional lottery that stops debate and allows for executions to proceed? There is a peculiar mixture in habeas corpus law of the language of federalism with the rhetoric of retribution that, it seems to me, is difficult, but not impossible, to sever.

Death penalty cases tend to emphasize both the functional aspects of the law and its discursive components. In *Furman* v. *Georgia* (1972), Justice William Brennan expressed his disapproval of capital punishment by pointing to a timeless notion of "human dignity," while Justice Lewis Powell, favoring capital punishment, spoke of "brutish and revolting murders."[18] Justice Powell, consequently, emphasized the state of Georgia's historical mission over criminal justice, while Justice Brennan highlighted the death penalty's general brutality and Georgia's historical mistreatment of racial minorities. In *Gregg* v. *Georgia* (1976), which restored the death penalty to the states and overturned *Furman*, the Court relied heavily on the idea that the states could be trusted with the exercise of jurisdiction over convicted criminals, while papering over the problems of majority oppression over minorities. As Justice Potter Stewart wrote in *Gregg*, a "heavy burden rests on those who would attack the judgment of the representatives of the people."[19] Habeas corpus cases, perhaps because they so often involve capital punishment, follow a similar narrative pattern that tries to balance federalism with due process.

Justice Brennan sees the writ as an "unceasing contest" between the power of the state to assert its authority over vulnerable members of the population and the weakness of the prisoner to state his case; Justice Sandra O'Connor sees it as an essential prop of "federalism," if not federalism itself.[20] Justice Thurgood Marshall, like Justice Brennan, worries, in *Vasquez* v. *Hillery* (1986), that denying the writ in the name of upholding procedure would allow form to "triumph over substance"; while Justice Powell, like Justice O'Connor, prefers to set the image of the writ as a merger among three evils: the writ's ability to free the convicted, questions of timing, and the administrative burdens habeas corpus imposes on the states.

> Respondent, a black man, was indicted by a grand jury having no black members for the stabbing murder of a 15-year-old girl. A petit jury found respondent guilty of that charge beyond a reasonable doubt, in a trial the fairness of which is unchallenged here. Twenty-three years later, we are asked

to grant respondent's petition for a writ of habeas corpus—and thereby require a new trial if that is still feasible—on the ground that blacks were purposefully excluded from the grand jury that indicted him. It is undisputed that race discrimination has long since disappeared from the grand jury selection process in Kings County, California. It is undisputed that a grand jury that perfectly represented Kings County's population at the time of respondent's indictment would have contained only one black member. Yet the Court holds that respondent's petition must be granted, and that respondent must be freed unless the State is able to reconvict, more than two decades after the murder that led to his incarceration.[21]

I imagine that any legal remedy so constructed as a weapon against tyranny and a dire threat to the states' criminal justice administrations would provoke more than a few literary flourishes as well as prosaic accounts of the honesty of state court criminal trials. The rhetoric of the defenders and critics of habeas corpus is instructive.

Liberals more than conservatives cast the writ as an absolute protection for individuals against all kinds of governmental actions that may restrict personal liberty. Liberals tend to borrow their view of habeas corpus from Tudor England and Whig history. Many liberals today understand habeas corpus as a simple ordering mechanism, from a federal to a state court, guided, in the words of one constitutional historian, by "the invisible hand of constitutional law."[22] In this view, the state is not important, but the individual is. Because the state's actions against the individual violated a constitutional procedure, the criterion of justice is met, and habeas corpus should flow. But neither entity in this equation is fully realized. The state is the cold monster that interferes with freedom, and the individual is a colorless and neutered "constitutional person" entitled to rights under the Fourteenth Amendment. Hoping that no one would notice the historical and institutional differences between the writ in Britain and the writ in the United States, liberals try to apply habeas corpus as it operated in liberal Britain, that is, directly from one court to another, without causing so much as a ripple in the patterning of American legal institutions.

There are two problems with this view. First, in the United States, a prisoner cannot directly appeal his or her conviction from a state court to a federal court. Habeas corpus is a collateral attack on a state conviction; it attacks the state court's judgment from the side, as it were, not directly. If a federal court issues the writ, the state judgment is not overturned. Second, this Whiggish view that downplays conflict and stresses rights vindication places the writ's failure as a remedy for unjust confinement on the defendant's character as a criminal, not on the state judge concerned with reelection or a criminal justice system hampered by a legacy of legal formalism, racism, and "overproceduralism."[23] Overall, liberals ascribe to the writ a timeless quality and ignore the interests and institutions that have influenced habeas corpus' development and the federal-state structure over time.[24] They ignore the state, but mostly they ignore the subject, the petitioner, seeing him as a vessel that contains individual liberty, without any outside characteristics that may in fact bind him and restrict his movement. They posit a timeless actor, unjustly confined, consuming his way through the Constitution's smorgasbord of rights. But interested actors, like the vague term *interests* itself, matter. "Courts and parties" dominated the nineteenth century, Stephen Skowronek writes, consciously reshaping the design of the American state. "It fell to the courts at each level of government to nurture, protect, interpret, and invoke the state's prerogatives over economy and society as expressed in law."[25] Liberals fail to give individual habeas petitioners their due.

By contrast, conservatives are less concerned with individual liberty than with the problems the writ poses for federalism and innocence.[26] Conservatives reject the exceptional and timeless descriptions of the writ liberals usually rely on, preferring to situate the writ's ideal interpretation from the day after *Ex parte Royall* was decided in 1886 to the day before *Brown* v. *Allen* was decided in 1953. We can call these seventy years the Gilded Age of habeas corpus law, if only to orient our attention to the federal courts' corporate thrust that managed to define habeas corpus not on its terms but by the characteristics of the petitioners unlawfully held. The key to this book, then, lies in chapter 2, which describes the Supreme Court's habeas jurisprudence as a narrative, a story about institutional competency and the vilification of criminals. As I make clear in that chapter, federalism did not apply to all kinds of cases in the Gilded Age. It was largely limited to criminal justice. Federalism had no bearing on property law, corporations, and wealth accumulation, all of which began as local concerns and became national interests because nineteenth-century judges said they were. Federalism only had resonance for crime, habeas corpus, capital punishment. A purely institutional look at habeas corpus would therefore be incomplete. Rhetoric has achieved what institutions have failed to occupy.

Chapter 2 compares two cases decided during the same term: one was a habeas corpus case, in which a prisoner, William Royall, held in prison for a federal offense, asked the Supreme Court for relief and was denied, in the name of deference to lower court decision making (a logic that translated all too easily into the language of federalism); the other was a corporate case, wherein the Supreme Court calls the aggrieved corporation a person under the Fourteenth Amendment and gives federal protection from state interference with its operations. The corporate case achieves victory: it gets into the federal courts. The habeas petitioner does not. Federalism is born.

Because of *Royall* and *County of Santa Clara* v. *Southern Pacific Railroad*, it is understood that federalism is a story the justices tell to restrict (or enlarge) the jurisdictional claims of kinds of persons, hiding the fear they have of releasing criminals, duly convicted in their view, from committing future crimes behind the formalism of state sovereignty. Federalism, in other words, finds itself, by the end of the nineteenth century, embedded within a larger vernacular logic that includes race and capital punishment. To rely on habeas' development solely from an institutional standpoint, to direct the reader's attention to the virtue of state court judgments, and then to reify those decisions by history and tradition and prejudice, without understanding how those judgments were constructed by law and by language, is to come to an incomplete understanding of habeas' history.

Conservatives, then, substitute their own exceptionalist language for restricting the writ. They argue that federal habeas corpus review is not justified as long as state courts are open to appeals, and the Supreme Court has the formal authority to render final judgment of any state court decision. Allowing for some degree of federal oversight in criminal justice (at the Supreme Court level), conservatives nevertheless reject interference from the lower federal courts as unnecessary and unconcerned with comity. The terms of the Constitution of 1787 and the arguments of Gilded Age lawyers fix the site of power at the state level for the rest of eternity. By and large, conservatives regard federal habeas corpus review as a needless intrusion into state and local criminal justice policies. They adopt a functionalist and instrumentalist understanding of the states' criminal justice administration that celebrates convictions done early and fast and castigate relitigation as costly and wasteful of valuable resources, excluding the idea that an unjust confinement (or execution) is a waste of a valuable resource. According to conservative critics of habeas corpus review, such as former Supreme Court Justices Lewis Powell and Sandra O'Connor, the state courts should have final say on the constitutional rights of defendants because, until the Warren Court, that is how justice (and habeas corpus) in the United States was administered. In short, in the opinion of leading conservative jurists, federal habeas corpus review upsets the delicate balance between the state and federal judicial systems that has evolved over time.

The Rehnquist Court's decisions since 1986 have streamlined the rights prisoners have in the context of postconviction relief and redefined and limited their applicability to the most egregious state offenses.[27] For the Rehnquist Court, these restrictions reflect society's concern that crime is on the rise and that criminals should not be set free on judicial "technicalities,"[28] that is, constitutional infractions that do not rise to the level of fundamental challenges to the prevailing constitutional configuration. In insulating the state courts from claims of unconstitutional state behavior, the Rehnquist Court has shielded its narrow interpretation of the writ from any understanding of the racial patterning of American constitutional history. It has frozen federalism's meaning in time, mostly before the 1960s. But even if we are sophisticated enough to no longer "bother to maintain the myth of formal federalism,"[29] the fact is that the Supreme Court today believes that the traditional autonomy given to state courts during the nineteenth century, regarding prisoner appeals, remains functionally valid across time.

The twofold argument this book relies on is a historical-institutional approach to the study of habeas corpus that is not insensitive to the role of narrative. The historical and institutional scope of this book means that I view habeas corpus as operating within a framework that "illuminates how political struggles 'are mediated by the institutional setting in which [they] take place.'"[30] In other words, habeas corpus does not stand outside of politics without reference to context; it is an integral part of American institutional development, politics, and law. I accept that habeas corpus threatens the smooth operation of criminal justice by exposing arbitrary arrests by state governments to the light of federal due process protections. Indeed, it is this entrenched discourse, and not federalism itself, that habeas corpus seeks to break. Because of the Fourteenth Amendment, state procedural infractions of personal liberties have substantive ramifications.[31] Habeas corpus is perforce part of federalism's language because it calls into question a state's judgment of guilt and the sentence of imprisonment or death. But it is the institution of federalism—that peculiar division of governmental authority—and not the relief from unlawful arrest that orients our vision to the problem of habeas corpus.

Without being insensitive to the institutions that shape the law, this work cannot simply offer an institutional look at a judicial concern that attempts to reify rights and challenge state authority. To do so would be to fail to understand habeas corpus as a law that operates within society, on individuals, and against the state's criminal justice apparatus. Habeas corpus is also part of the language of criminal justice and civil liberties. Viewing the writ as a symbol and a sword, prisoners seek its protection from all forms of judicial detention, local and national. Consequently, I pay particular attention not just to the institution of federalism but also to the arguments over federalism that have framed the horizons of habeas corpus. This language is mostly one of restriction. If habeas corpus is to be understood in its totality, then we have to face the fact that narratives of criminal events are as important in shaping the law as institutions. I look, then, at federalism and the writ of habeas corpus as creating a discursive formation regarding imprisonment, punishment, authority, and law.

Viewed from an interdisciplinary lens of history, language, politics, and law, a purely institutional analysis of the great writ is untenable. To be sure, habeas corpus adopts the language of normal constitutional discourse. William Royall's request for a writ of habeas corpus in 1886 is no different, functionally, than William Marbury's request for a writ of mandamus in 1801. They both asserted a claim and asked for a remedy. Writs follow the rules of procedure, but only up to a point. The rules of procedure must be capable of bending, as Chief Justice John Marshall did in *Marbury* v. *Madison*. But habeas corpus is a hubristic writ. It charges the state with offending a norm,

a concept, and a value that the Supreme Court has recognized and even celebrated. It presupposes a more superior knowledge of constitutional law than
the state itself possesses, because it demonstrates a pattern of constitutional
irregularity operating just beneath the constitutional radar. The writ reveals a
breach, not just institutionally but also in language. It exposes a different way
to understand the law, one based on the reality and harshness of the criminal
justice system for those unable to secure quality counsel. Consequently, a writ
designed to allow federal courts to grant state prisoners the ability to overcome state imprisonment must be understood as possessing the ability to dis-
rupt institutional and discursive arrangements. It is no small irony that with
the help of convicted criminals, Supreme Court justices form the language of
the law.

The language of the law, then, does not operate freely. It remains bounded
by institutions but molded according to the needs and interests of prisoners
and state actors. The development of a doctrine of federalism during the last
quarter of the nineteenth century should be seen for what it was: not the spon-
taneous outgrowth of the Constitution's design of the federal-state relationship expressed in language, as if "federalism" explains more about the federal-
state relationship than "comity" (federalism's previous name) did, but a
concerted effort by property-minded justices to reify state criminal justice
practices in light of the Supreme Court's understanding that habeas corpus is
a threat to the states' criminal justice capabilities. Habeas corpus, then, has a
separate power that makes it different from other legal concerns. It has a
rhetorical element that separates it from other judicial directives.

A purely institutional approach to the problem of habeas corpus in
American life leaves us wanting more, by way of explanation, for its overall
failure and limited success, because habeas corpus disrupts more than just
institutional patterns of governance. As a petition for release by a convicted
criminal, the writ latches onto constitutional language that in its form, if not
its substance, celebrates the individual and mitigates state power. The writ
burrows its way through the federal-state judicial apparatus, along the way
picking up vague legal concepts, such as "fundamental fairness," "due
process," and "the incorporation of the Bill of Rights," and then attaches
these ideas to the bodies of state prisoners. If the graft is successful, as it was
during the 1960s, the Court applies the new meaning to the habeas applicant
and sets him free. The writ's discursive function is as encompassing as its
institutional operation. As it makes its way through the marsh of federal-
state relations, it relies on a narrative of justice—free speech—to get out of
jail. The writ means liberty, the freedom to be able to contest a confinement
in a court of law. It stands for bodily integrity against the state's claim to hold
and imprison it. As Justice William Brennan wrote in the seminal habeas
corpus case *Fay v. Noia* (1963), "vindication of due process is precisely
[habeas corpus'] historic office."[32]

Habeas corpus operates both within the structures of federalism (as a form of appeal from a state to a federal court) and without (because it does not recognize the legitimacy of the state court). It operates discursively. It reconfigures constitutional language because it modifies the established understanding of the appellate process that denies state prisoners federal court access. Moreover, it upsets the discourse, created by the Supreme Court, that the federal-state relationship ought not be disturbed on habeas appeals. Not only does the writ challenge the Supreme Court to rearrange criminal narratives, it forces the Court to continually alter federalism's meaning to fit its conception of the proper procedures criminals must obey to get relief in the Supreme Court.

If habeas corpus was simply an ordering device, a way for prisoners to contest their confinements and get out of jail, no story of its history and development would be necessary. We could focus solely on the minutiae of habeas corpus. Was the conviction legitimate? Does the petitioner have standing? Was the state court ruling lawful? In answering these questions, we can locate the moment when the institutional equilibrium was punctuated and return to our study of habeas corpus as nothing more than a minor disruption in American law.[33] But habeas corpus is at the center of a storm in criminal justice. The writ's alterity, its ability to undergo change through the narratives of both petitioners and Supreme Court justices, finds its strength in federalism's alterity, the decade-by-decade manipulation of the boundaries of the federal-state relationship that depends not just on the makeup of the Court but also on its overall view of the rights of prisoners at any given time.[34] In its fullest development, habeas corpus stops justice (as death penalty proponents understand that term) from being done. It prevents prosecutors from describing the accused the way they want; it prevents the police from obtaining confessions using psychological and physical force. In its worst form, it more than just allows the guilty to go free, releasing sex offenders, recidivists, and violent criminals. It can overturn death sentences.

AN OVERVIEW OF THE COURT'S USE OF NARRATIVES

In *South Carolina v. Gathers* (1989), Justice Sandra Day O'Connor, in dissent, wrote, "I would reject a rigid Eighth Amendment rule which prohibits a sentencing jury from hearing or considering evidence concerning the personal characteristics of the victim."[35] Since the 1930s, the justices of the Supreme Court have been introducing crime stories into their opinions. The stories the justices tell are more than just wallpaper; they are legally intertwined within the fabric of the decision. It matters, for example, for the outcome of a decision, whether the defendant was black and the murdered victim and the jury were white. It matters whether a black attorney offers to help a white defendant and is turned away, fearing "an ill effect" on the jury from Georgia. And it matters that that fact does not turn up in the Supreme Court's opinion until eighteen pages into the decision, and in Justice Brennan's dissent.[36]

Narratives are elective affinities; they are the willful inventions of the justices operating under enormous formalist constraints. A narrative is also an ordering device, a way of describing how something has moved from A to B. But we are dealing here with larger issues than my car hitting your car. Habeas corpus narratives often attach themselves to larger structural issues in American law and practice. Indeed, habeas corpus narratives have created both the language of rights and the language of institutional constraints. Because they involve capital punishment and sex offenders, lack of quality counsel and racial biases, police violence and coerced confessions, habeas opinions legitimate themselves "with reference to a metadiscourse,"[37] which is often so much a part of the reader's worldview that the reader does not really notice that the narrative circle has been enlarged (or narrowed, as the case may be), a way of life described that satisfies one's commonsense understanding of the world (the guilty are punished), that places the state and its productive elements at the center of things and elides the plaintive cry of unlawful confinement. As Pierre Schlag has written, "One of the charming things about the rationalist aesthetic (at least, for its practitioners) is that it is extremely flattering to the self. The legal self is endowed with autonomy and self-direction—freed from its context and its objects. Meanwhile the law and the world are laid about before it as a series of 'concepts,' 'propositions,' 'positions,' 'models,' 'theories'— all to be 'chosen' or 'rejected.'"[38]

One can easily find instances of such narrative devices in habeas corpus opinions. Felix Frankfurter, writing for himself (in support of the majority opinion) in *Louisiana* v. *Resweber* (1947), a case involving the failed execution of Willie Francis ("duly convicted of murder") and Louisiana's second attempt to place Francis in the electric chair (the first time was not successful), stated that "this Court must abstain from interference with State action no matter how strong one's personal feeling of revulsion against a State's insistence on its pound of flesh."[39] Such admonitions for federal restraint are common in death penalty and habeas corpus cases. But *Resweber* is significant for another reason, concerning its use of narrative. The majority opinion elides the petitioner's side of the story. His pain is not considered to be a constitutional issue, only the fact that he was not executed is. It fell to Justice Harold Burton, in dissent, and in a footnote, to note Willie Francis' pain: "I saw the electrocutioner turn on the switch and I saw his lips puff out and swell, his body tensed and stretched. I heard the one in charge yell to the man outside for more juice when he saw that Willie Francis was not dying and the one on the outside yelled back he was giving him all he had. Then Willie Francis cried out 'Take it off. Let me breath [sic].' Then they took the hood from his eyes and unstrapped him."[40] The state's brief to the Supreme Court stated nothing more than that the state failed to achieve its goal: "Through a latent electrical defect, the attempt to electrocute Francis failed, the State contending no current whatsoever reached Francis' body, the relator contending a current of electricity did pass through his body; but in any event, Willie Francis was not put to death."[41]

Until the beginning of the twentieth century, neither the victim nor the perpetrator appeared in habeas or criminal cases, but states did. The language of federalism (a language that was unstable until habeas corpus appeared) seeped into the language of rights fairly quickly, at the start of the Supreme Court's habeas corpus jurisprudence in 1886. Before long, habeas cases became treatises, not on the expansion of rights or the protection of the accused or on the abuse of police powers by state officials acting under the color of law, but on protecting the expansive powers of the states to arrest, try, incarcerate, and execute persons, free from federal oversight or meddling. Who has the body? has always been an institutional question, but from the 1880s on, it is clear that it was an institutional question that arose out of the language of crime and punishment, with a particular focus on the criminal body and the death penalty. That body (the corrupt, imperfect, darkened criminal body of the late nineteenth century), the Supreme Court determined, belonged someplace, with the states and in prison, and not out of prison. The context and content of federalism determined the language of prisoners' rights. After 1886, respect for state judgments is the respectable name we give to denials of prisoners' petitions. These denials encapsulate a world of meaning, as Frankfurter's anguished history of federalism in *Resweber* reveals, regarding the fear of releasing convicted murderers.

Habeas corpus has been about federalism since 1886, when the Court denied William Royall's untimely petition, only the concept had not been named. Back then, they called it "federal-state comity." When the Court broke free from that narrative, around 1937—"the switch in time that saved nine," in Henry Abraham's quip describing Justice Owen Roberts' change of constitutional allegiances during Franklin Roosevelt's Court-packing plan[42]—it put in place a counternarrative, invoking what the French philosopher Jean-François Lyotard has called "little stories."[43] These little stories subverted the dominant paradigm that the states had first and last say on the status of criminals in their courts. A purely institutional approach here would have to bracket the Court's language regarding state violence and institutionalized racism and overlook the different patterns of federalism development since 1886. Instead, recognizing the weaknesses of the federalism defense, the New Deal justices invoked stories of extreme violence directed against society's weakest by state officials, altering traditional notions of violence and crime that had hitherto been characterized in case law only individually, not collectively or institutionally.

The justices of the New Deal made constitutional law come alive. They took arid cases involving the Fourth, Fifth, Sixth, and Eighth Amendments and revealed the color, the background, the poverty, the mental state, the numerous confessions under extreme pressure and threat, the excess of light, and the denial of food and drink that got the state the conviction it wanted. To be sure, they mentioned the crimes, and they worried about state law, but they contextualized it, wondering if the Court should turn a blind eye, in the name of respect, deference, federalism, and legal formalities, and whether, therefore, in doing so, they would sustain "an act so arbitrary and so cruel in its operation, considering that life is at stake, that in the circumstances of this case it constitutes a denial of due process in its rudimentary procedural aspect."[44] Not satisfied with mere descriptions of state-sponsored violence, they further explained that the petitioners' weaknesses were contrived weaknesses, constructed through societal norms and legal and medical discourses marred by racism, and categorized the state's case not as strength or heroism but as brutality, violence, usurpation, and indifference. They reversed the constitutional order, inverting the legal topography that had placed the state first and the accused last.

Anyone, however, can use a counternarrative, reactionaries and postmodernists alike. Conservatives on the Court began their counternarrative counteroffensive primarily against the Warren Court, which managed to attach the Fourteenth Amendment's due process clause to amendments Four, Five, Six, and Eight in just eight years. The Warren Court, in other words, institutionalized the stories the New Deal Court justices had told that extended due process in some cases but could not fully capture within the language of the Fourteenth Amendment. In purely institutional terms, the Warren Court disrupted federalism, and conservatives would simply have to wait until the disruption ended, returning the federal-state relationship to the way it has always been. But this is not what happened. The Rehnquist Court's habeas narrative has focused only in part on delinking habeas applications from the Fourteenth Amendment. It has recognized that that language is no longer powerful. Federalism, however important to constitutional law and political scientists, has no resonance with the public as a way to restrict rights, and the Court's habeas decisions were playing directly to the public. Federalism has no moral voice, no sense of indignation. Tales of violence do. Murders do. Brutality does.

The purpose—the "moral judgment"—of victim impact statements, according to Justice O'Connor, is to give the "sentencer a 'glimpse of the life' a defendant 'chose to extinguish.'"[45]

> Helen Schartner was last seen alive in the evening of February 5, 1985, leaving the County Line Lounge in Virginia Beach, Virginia. Her lifeless body was discovered the next day, in a muddy field across a highway from the lounge. Schartner's head had been laid open by several blows with the barrel of a handgun, and she had been strangled with such violence that bones in her neck were broken and finger imprints were left on her skin. An abun-

dance of physical evidence linked petitioner to the crime scene and crime—among other things, tire tracks near Schartner's body were consistent with petitioner's car, and bodily fluids recovered from Schartner's body matched petitioner. He was indicted on counts of capital murder, rape, sodomy, and abduction.[46]

The constitutional question in this case (*O'Dell* v. *Netherland*, 1997) is a technical one, not an interesting one. According to Justice Clarence Thomas, who wrote the majority opinion and the above story, "This case presents the question whether the rule set out in *Simmons* v. *South Carolina*—which requires that a capital defendant be permitted to inform his sentencing jury that he is parole ineligible if the prosecution argues that he presents a future danger—was 'new' within the meaning of *Teague* v. *Lane*, and thereby inapplicable to an already final death sentence."

To understand the case, one should know what *Simmons* held, what *Teague* is about, how the Warren Court muddied the concept of "retroactivity," what the Rehnquist Court thinks of "new meanings" and why that term is important, and whether or not assertions of future dangerousness are tendentious.

To get to O'Dell's case, one has to climb the mountain of Supreme Court habeas corpus decisions. But my questions here are: did Justice Thomas have to describe O'Dell's crime in such detail? Did he have to omit Joseph Roger O'Dell's name, referring to him only as "the petitioner" or as "he," but mentioning the victim's name, not once but several times, detailing her torture, her blood, her bones, her dissection? Couldn't Justice Thomas have described this case as one about federalism, as a threat to the state's ability to punish criminals—as Justice O'Connor did in *Coleman* v. *Thompson* (1991), a death penalty case that turned on the question of whether or not a late filing of an appeal by Coleman's attorney threatened the foundation of federal-state relations? To be sure, the rest of the case is exactly what one would expect. It is dry, formal, baroque, yet tightly argued on both sides. The descriptive narrative does not reappear, but it does not disappear either. O'Dell's murder is what defines *Teague*, explains "new meaning," fills out the *Simmons* decision. O'Dell is a murderer, of the "wanton, vile [, and] inhuman"[47] kind. That is all the jury and we need to know. Federalism is now the narrative known as future dangerousness.

For the Rehnquist Court, what the state did to an individual petitioner is no longer part of the dominant narrative. If sheriffs still handcuff young men to poles and beat them to within an inch of their lives, we do not hear of it.[48] We have moved away from the days of the "rack and screw."[49] These days, to find out why the case you are reading is a habeas case, why, that is, it matters that a state has violated a constitutional right, one has to begin where the majority opinion "tersely ends," the dissent, where, according to Justice John Paul Stevens, "it is undisputed that the conduct of the sentencing hearing that led to the imposition of [O'Dell's] death penalty violated the Due Process

Clause of the Fourteenth Amendment."[50] Thus, we are drawn further into the structures of individual narrative and further away from political and institutional narratives, toward a dissenting counter-counternarrative directed at the Burger Court's counternarrative, which is itself directed at the Warren Court's narratives, and so on.

But for the Rehnquist Court the master narrative lives on. If the petitioner can be shown to have violent tendencies that prison has not cured, then he presents a danger to society upon his release. Juries, as we can see from Justice Thomas' excerpt of the case, are informed of an accused's potential for future dangerousness, which takes on the components of a master narrative. Denying habeas corpus is doing one's duty. In *O'Dell*, the state's prosecutor told the jury:

> We are a society of fair, honest people who believe in our government and who believe in our justice system; and I submit to you there was a failure in the Florida criminal justice system for paroling this man when they did. [He concluded:] [Y]ou may still sentence him to life in prison, but I ask you ladies and gentlemen[,] in a system, in a society that believes in its criminal justice system and its government, what does this mean? . . . [A]ll the times he has committed crimes before and been before other juries and judges, no sentence ever meted out to this man has stopped him. Nothing has stopped him, and nothing ever will except the punishment that I now ask you to impose.[51]

Habeas corpus threatens that judgment. It gives the dangerous classes more than a voice; it gives them a weapon to attack a jury's psychological determination of guilt and dangerousness. It gives the condemned a language to rebut the charges, convictions, misrepresentations in the same terms that were used against them. Habeas petitions turn legal language upside down and with it, the historical evolution of federal-state relations. This was the Warren Court's innovation (see chapter 4). But for the Rehnquist Court, only disciplinary institutions can enforce responsible freedom. Habeas petitioners demonstrate their unwillingness to be governed in such manner. They refuse to remain silent. The petitions themselves mark them as recalcitrant, unwilling to accept their fate. The connection between dangerousness and habeas corpus tells us not just what "we fear the most," but "what we value—and the lengths we are now prepared to go in attempting to reduce such risks to our well-being."[52]

Throughout this book, I have tried to be comprehensive without burdening the reader with the intricacies of habeas law. Yet mere slices of this tale and distillations of its story would not be enough to understand why a writ so beloved in legal language can be so maligned by politicians and Supreme Court justices.

Each chapter of this book presents a new era in federal-state relations and habeas corpus. Chapter 1 situates the writ between feudalism and the modern state. After noting the writ's development in Britain and comparing and contrasting it with the antebellum period in the United States, I then move to a discussion of habeas corpus and federalism from the end of the Civil War to Leo Frank's conviction in 1915.

The Court's multiple definitions of federalism, which surely must match the numerous Eskimo words for snow, have never covered the grand scope of habeas corpus law in its entirety. "Federalism" is a constantly shifting concept that only gains resonance by the type of case that dares use its name. As chapter 2 demonstrates, the introduction of the habeas regime in the 1880s, coeval but never congruent with due process, coincided with the beginning of the industrial revolution, and therewith, the introduction of federal-state comity relations. In one set of cases (habeas corpus, criminal justice, broadly conceived), the Court sided with federalism, with the interests of the states; in the other (corporate, state regulations of industry), it refused even to consider federalism as a legitimate constitutional protection.[53]

Noticing a shift in the Court's late nineteenth-century discourse regarding criminals, property, and federalism, I focus on two cases, one habeas corpus, *Ex parte Royall*,[58] and the other corporate, *County of Santa Clara v. Southern Pacific Railroad*,[59] both decided in 1886. The corporate case is the first to grant corporations federal jurisdiction as "persons" under the Fourteenth Amendment, and the habeas case is the first to deny habeas petitioners federal access. One case extends rights; the other takes them away. One case ascribes personhood to an inanimate object, made up of many animate ones, and the other denies personhood to flesh and blood. One case describes the manly virtues of work and industry, and the other castigates the prisoner as a usurper and constitutionally unworthy. One case assigns to the body beauty and worth and sets it free, and the other denigrates it, shuts it out, imprisons it. One case attributes to the petitioner classically republican virtues of thrift, hard work, fairness, and love of country, and the other removes all semblance of humanity from future habeas petitioners and questions their capacity for accepting constitutional limits. Both cases are of course also about federalism, but only in one case is federalism made an issue.

Chapter 3 places the writ in an era in flux, the New Deal, and extends from 1923 to 1953. During this time, progressive intellectuals attacked the high Court's persistent judicial formalism left over from the nineteenth century. Following the strategy of property holders, habeas petitioners increasingly challenged their convictions on due process grounds. Sometimes they were successful, and sometimes they were not. The New Deal Court gave habeas petitioners some room to maneuver through the federal court system, though not without paying their respects to the state courts.

Chapter 4 discusses the third era of the development of habeas corpus, from 1963 to 1979. It is an era in conflict. The writ's greatest period of expansion by the Warren Court, marked by *Fay v. Noia*, gave way to retraction by the Burger Court's regard for federalism. Chapter 5 discusses the 1980s to 2002. These twenty years brought the writ full circle, back to the legal formalism of the 1920s, first by the Supreme Court, then by Congress, as each institution responded to domestic terrorism and fears of rising crime by cutting back on the rights of death-row inmates to petition for a federal hearing. This chapter also introduces the concept of "future dangerousness" into the habeas mix. Although the concept appears as early as the 1930s, by the 1990s, the Court was in a position to review state laws that allowed juries to determine the future dangerousness of convicted criminals based on storytelling and the conflicting views of medical experts.

Chapter 6 starts with the Antiterrorism and Effective Death Penalty Act of 1996, which restricted the availability of habeas corpus for state prisoners in such manner that it is all but impossible for prisoners successfully to petition for it.[54] It also includes a look at the cases dealing with terrorism that came out of Guantánamo Bay, Cuba. In this chapter, I find that the Court has divided habeas corpus into two components, habeas corpus I and II. Habeas corpus I is the favored discourse, relying on common law traditions and not involving federal-state relations; habeas corpus II is the statutory writ with which this book largely deals. It creates federal-state friction, and the Court is reluctant to celebrate its virtues. The cases coming from Guantánamo highlight these distinctions. Chapter 7 sums up the book.

Without further introduction to the problem of habeas corpus in the United States, it should be clear that the development of habeas corpus has not been evolutionary and disinterested, but episodic, conflict-ridden, and, at times, regime altering. Thus, periodizing habeas corpus helps us to understand how a writ wrapped in the myth of an Englishman's liberty failed in a country similarly entranced by the language of rights. By chopping up the writ into discrete eras, we are better able to concentrate on the subtle shifts in the Court's language, first away from English common law and toward an American conception of legal rules, second, toward a firm foundation in federalism, which allowed the Court to utilize the language of rights and liberty, but to corporate bodies (states and corporations) not persons, and third, away from federalism and toward the character of habeas petitioners, who are always guilty.

Throughout this book, I treat habeas corpus discursively as a means to understand legal change and the political development of civil liberties over time. Prisoners may use the writ for their own ends, but the writ challenges the federal-state structure and the power of state courts to arrest and detain American citizens without further judicial oversight.

ONE

Habeas Corpus in the New American State, 1789–1915

Rights declared in words might be lost in reality.
—*Weems* v. *United States*

THE FIRST SIGNIFICANT era of habeas corpus in American political history
extends from the passage of the Habeas Corpus Act in 1867 through 1915,
when the Supreme Court denied a writ of habeas corpus to Leo Frank, in the
celebrated murder case, *Frank* v. *Magnum*.[1] This chapter reviews this first
period of the Supreme Court's habeas corpus jurisprudence with a brief look
at the writ in the antebellum period. Habeas corpus in the antebellum period
is distinctive (when compared with its postwar history) in terms of its congressionally led expansion across federal-state jurisdictional lines. The use of
federal habeas corpus and removal statutes to interfere with state laws regarding arrest before and during the Civil War mirrors more closely the writ's
English past than its American future.

Sectional differences and party divisions over the extent of federal power
were facts of political life in the antebellum period that, in part, highlighted the
federal government's incapacity to reach state action.[2] One notable but over-
looked example of pre-Civil War sectional stress and party division took the form
of state arrests of federal military and revenue personnel during wartime and the
crisis over tariff collection.[3] State-sanctioned arrests of federal officers (first in the
North, then in the South) capitalized on the inability of state arrestees to appeal
directly to the federal courts for relief from unjust confinement.

During the war of 1812, Massachusetts arrested U.S. custom officers to prevent the federal government from collecting taxes over a war it did not support. In 1815, the thirteenth Congress responded to the arrests of federal revenue officers in New England by passing "An Act to prohibit Intercourse with the Enemy, and for other Purposes." The act allowed federal prisoners held in state jails to remove their cases to the federal judiciary.[4] Section eight of the act allowed for any suit begun in state court against persons "civil or military," who had acted under color of U.S. law pursuant to their duties, to "file a petition for the removal of the cause for trial at the next circuit court of the United States." The law forbade the state courts from further proceedings. The act also allowed for removal after "trial judgment," but it did not apply to criminal trials.

Throughout the tariff and secession crisis of 1833, South Carolina threatened to arrest any federal revenue officer who came to collect revenue from "the tariff of abominations." The main sections of the 1833 act, numbers three and seven, dealt respectively with removal and habeas corpus. Removal was restricted to any time before the state trial began, but it allowed for "de novo" review if no state record existed.[5] The habeas clause granted power to federal court judges, but not to the courts themselves, to grant writs "in all cases of a prisoner or prisoners, in jail or confinement, . . . for any act done, or omitted to be done, in pursuance of a law of the United States." The debate in Congress took several forms: sectional strife, fears of executive power, deference to executive power, state sovereignty concerns, partisan differences, and concerns over the power of the national judiciary.[6]

In 1842, Congress passed an emergency habeas corpus law to allow a foreign national held in a state jail to remove his case to the federal courts (and perforce all similarly situated foreign nationals), to avoid prejudice against him by the local jury. A British naval officer, Alexander McLeod, who boasted that he had killed "a damned Yankee," was arrested upon entering New York harbor. The British government made a formal request for the release of McLeod, and entreated President Martin van Buren to expedite the matter. The president responded that McLeod was held under state law, and neither he nor the federal government had the authority to release him. Teetering on the brink of war,[7] Congress in August of 1842 empowered federal district court judges to issue writs of habeas corpus to foreign nationals, upon removal to a federal court.

The 1842 bill "to provide remedial justice" provoked common fears among states-rights advocates that it would force the states to "surrender a vital part of [their] most cherished and rooted institutions."[8] Charles Ingersoll, a Whig congressman from Pennsylvania, thought the bill would "repeal all the state courts of justice," "unhinge the law, annihilate state jurisdictions, truckle to a mercenary foreign power, [and] humble the United States before the world." He was concerned, moreover, that foreigners would have more appellate rights than Americans (which was largely true). "War," he declared, "would be better."[9] As in 1833, the southern states opposed the expansion of federal habeas corpus powers because they feared the writ would be used to free enslaved blacks.[10] According to William Duker, the Democratic party opposed the 1842 act because they deemed it to be "destructive of state sovereignty in the enforcement of their criminal codes."[11] Despite Ingersoll's claim that "This bill will not be carried by a party vote,"[12] the vote in the Senate was strictly partisan. The Senate voted 27:17 in favor of the bill, with only one Democrat voting with the Whigs. The *Congressional Globe* did not record the House vote, though it noted that several Whigs had voted against, and the majority was small.[13]

Finally, in 1863, Congress passed a habeas corpus act designed to achieve three objectives. The first provision ratified Abraham Lincoln's suspension of habeas corpus in April 1861, which he had done in the name of "public safety." On July 4th of that same year, Lincoln formally notified Congress, in special session, of his actions.[14] The 1863 act[15] ensured that Congress, not the president, had ultimate constitutional authority over the suspension of the writ. Second, the act indemnified federal officers held in state jails (mostly in Kentucky and Delaware) from further prosecution and detention.[16] Third, as with the previous habeas corpus acts, the 1863 act allowed the federal courts to grant habeas corpus following removal from the state courts.[17]

The debate in 1863 ranged between the legality of Lincoln's suspension to the historical meaning of habeas corpus as a writ of liberty, some calling it "a second Magna Carta," and a "great bulwark of English liberties."[18] When the debate got to the matter at hand, indemnifying federal officers, the Republicans turned not to the English law on habeas corpus, but to previous congressional actions to extend habeas corpus jurisdiction, dating back to the removal act of 1815.[19] In passing three habeas corpus statutes over a brief but critical era in American history, Congress overcame the differences that existed between the two parties in the antebellum period, particularly the fears among southern Democrats that habeas corpus, like internal improvements, would lead to the abolition of slavery.[20] In all cases, Congress could have done nothing, either by claiming a lack of constitutional power to reach state action or by relying on historical restrictions on habeas corpus and removal statutes. Congress' novel action in 1815 formed the basis for all later habeas corpus acts of the antebellum period.

Before the Civil War, no court, state or federal, could issue a writ of habeas corpus to a prisoner after conviction. The Judiciary Act of 1789 prevented any "postconviction" appeal process by granting the federal courts the power to issue writs of habeas corpus only to those held "under or by color of the authority of the United States."[21] The language of the act effectively denied state prisoners the right to appeal for habeas corpus after conviction by a state court. Removal statutes, too, were not designed for releasing prisoners from custody. Removal statutes were to be applied only in diversity of jurisdiction claims. Yet a series of revenue and later military crises exposed the federal government's core jurisdictional weakness: the government was incapable, barring extraordinary measures, of removing federal prisoners from state jails. By confronting this limitation through legislation, Congress turned habeas corpus and removal into vehicles for jurisdictional political change.

A focus on history and a focus on jurisdiction produce different responses to similar events. During the same period, the Supreme Court failed to see the writ in the same way as Congress. In *Ex parte Watkins*[22](1836), Chief Justice John Marshall denied habeas corpus because he believed it would have been improper to issue the writ to a prisoner already under sentence of a state court. Removal to a federal court, then, provided an extraordinary means of relief for federal prisoners held in state jails. Ordinarily, removal statutes were used to resolve commercial matters, to prevent local prejudice against foreigners and outsiders. Until 1815, removal had never been used to free United States marshals arrested for collecting revenue from hostile state and local authorities. Removal provided a way around the restrictions on the appellate and habeas processes found in the Judiciary Act of 1789 and maintained by pre–Civil War Supreme Court decisions.[23] Notably, the removal and habeas corpus clauses of the Judiciary Act of 1789 were the only two sections of the act to expand during the antebellum period.[24]

In the absence of a broad, constitutional grant of authority to reach state jurisdictions and alter their laws, such as we find in section 5 of the Fourteenth Amendment, purposeful and periodic congressional overrides of historically sanctioned limitations on the states' power over detainees belies the general characterization of the antebellum state as weak or limited. The enactment of removal and habeas corpus statutes in 1815, 1833, 1842, and 1863 created a "pathway to the states" that helped ease the passage of the Habeas Corpus Act of 1867, which offered state prisoners access to the federal courts.[25] That is, until the 1867 act, the federal courts had only temporary powers to release persons held in state jails awaiting trial. Before the Civil War, the general notion was that federal courts do not serve as courts of appeal for state prisoners. Taken together, however, these congressional acts illuminate a trajectory of developmental interests within Congress that has gone unnoticed in discussions of the antebellum period and of habeas corpus. Pre–Civil War congressional actions were more than just moments of adjustment and change to endogenous and exogenous forces. They were intentionally developmental. The lack of constitutional guidance regarding the meaning of habeas corpus empowered Congress to act as the British Parliament had in 1641 and again in 1679, when it located habeas corpus securely in legislative courts and kept the king's courts at bay. In spite of any perceived historical or actual limitations then in existence, Congress, like Parliament before it, extended the reach of habeas corpus against recalcitrant local or collateral organs of power. The key question is whether Congress could maintain the same level of interest in federal-state criminal justice matters after the Civil War.

HABEAS CORPUS IN THE NEW AMERICAN STATE

At the time of the Constitutional Convention in 1787, the common law tradition on habeas corpus was well established. Dallin Oaks writes that there was a "close conformity" between state legislation on habeas corpus and the Habeas Corpus Act of 1679. Of the twelve states with constitutions in 1787 (Rhode Island relied on its charter), "there were four states with habeas corpus guarantees in their constitutions, eight with none," but none "made any affirmative guarantee of the writ."[26] The assumption was that the constitutional prohibition against suspending the writ, except in times of rebellion, guaranteed its availability at the state level.

Despite the implication that this might mean that federal habeas corpus is always available to state prisoners,[27] habeas corpus in the new republic retained its formal, common law meaning. The usual guide for habeas' connection to the common law is Chief Justice Marshall's opinion in *Ex parte Bollman* (1807).[28] In that case, involving charges of treason against the United States, Chief Justice Marshall wrote "that for the meaning of the term habeas corpus, resort may unquestionably be had to the common law." Commentators omit, however, the crucial second part of that sentence: "but the power to award the writ by any of the courts of the United States, must be given by written law."[29] And yet, despite Chief Justice Marshall's recognition that American law defines habeas' parameters, not the common law operating in isolation from the American experience, sectional concessions in the first Congress prevented Congress from establishing a national criminal law that could reach state action.[30] One of the reasons federal prisoners had such trouble getting out of state jails is because the first Congress had not created federal jails, and it could only request the states to hold federal prisoners with state prisoners.[31] In fact, there were no federal prisons in the United States until the latter half of the nineteenth century.[32] Consequently, throughout most of U.S. history, the control over federal prisoners fell to the state courts, allowing them to exercise supreme jurisdictional authority over all prisoners contesting their confinements on constitutional grounds.[33]

Because of party and sectional divisions in Congress, the framers of the first Judiciary Act did not provide for full, federal court appellate review.[34] From the nation's founding to the latter half of the nineteenth century, federal jurisdiction did not cover the entire spectrum of possibilities intended by the phrase "the judicial power of the United States."[35] As there was no federal criminal law at the time of the Judiciary Act of 1789, the drafters of the

Constitution refused to grant federal district courts the power to hear cases that might subsequently arise under federal law. Congress remedied this with the act of March 3, 1875.[36] In 1889, Congress passed a law allowing federal criminals to appeal their convictions, including capital offenses, directly to the Supreme Court.[37]

The writ's success in the antebellum period against entrenched state interests came about despite these limitations. Short of a show of force, it was the only corrective available to release arrested federal revenue and military officers held in state jails. External crises, such as wars and the threat of war, revealed in part the depth of partisan and sectional divisions plaguing the country. But it was the way in which these divisions manifested themselves that is significant to the development of habeas corpus, that is, through sectional arrests of federal officers and foreigners that forced Congress to turn to habeas corpus as a national solution to a local problem. This development was not inevitable. The framers of the Constitution had understood habeas corpus as a limited and extraordinary writ. With the exclusion of the South at the end of the Civil War, Congress achieved enough partisan support to permanently alter habeas' jurisdiction. Only then—freed from institutional constraints rooted in evolving conceptions of federalism that had limited the central government's authority—did it become the great writ of liberty.

Taken together, the strong congressional responses during these crises altered the politically agreed upon jurisdictional boundaries set in 1789. Each crisis deepened the path for a constitutional-level change.[38] Each resolution of the particular crisis forced the states to give up some degree of their sovereignty over captured persons. The 1867 act codified the budding relationship that prisoners would have with the national judiciary, not the states, under the Fourteenth Amendment. The act thus stands as an example of Reconstruction era liberal statemaking[39] and marks not only a passage of power from state courts to Congress (as an overseer of federal court jurisdiction) but also an apparent disjunction between antebellum and postbellum politics. Nonetheless, once passed, the act ushered in the beginning of a century-long pattern of legislative and judicial forbearance on civil rights. The act, by institutionalizing habeas corpus as a permanent form of judicial relief from unjust state confinement, allowed Congress to turn over control of state prisoners to the federal judiciary. In doing so, Congress was relieved from investing its time in local and state affairs. The Supreme Court did not see the matter differently, either. Rather than having habeas corpus serve as the instrumental means to attack state court convictions, the Supreme Court after the Civil War deferred to state court judgments and forced federal habeas courts to do the same. The "command" of the habeas statute was not fulfilled.

In this chapter I focus on the rise of federalism as the most important structural inhibitor in habeas' history. But I cannot ignore the role of Supreme Court justices in defining this term. The writ in the post–Civil War United

States created not just a language of rights and of protest, but a language of federalism, of deference, of guilt, punishment, and respect for state court finality. It is the state of California, Justice Anthony Kennedy wrote in *Calderon* v. *Thompson* (1998), that "is entitled to the assurance of finality" on habeas challenges, because finality preserves "the federal balance" and protects the states' "good faith attempts to honor constitutional rights."[40] In this case, Justice Kennedy ignored the petitioner's interest in liberty and did not speak of that to which the petitioner was entitled. His opinion is devoid of historical references to the writ's contribution to individual liberty in Britain and of California's violation of Thompson's Sixth Amendment rights. He meant by finality the right of the state to proceed to execution or to close the door to more appeals. Finality as a code word for the administration of the death penalty in habeas corpus cases finds its roots in the Court's late nineteenth-century habeas cases that molded federalism's meaning to conform to the ends of criminal justice. More important, though, is that the desire for finality denies the individual a voice in the judgment of his own fate. Finality elevates jury determinations of guilt and lowers Fourteenth Amendment due process claims. Not unlike today's Supreme Court, cost effectiveness determined full citizenship in the post–Civil War industrial regime, with concerns for personal safety running a close second.

Outside the context of race or property or the protections offered by the Bill of Rights, federalism has no meaning. A common definition of federalism, such as that of Daniel Elazar, that it "represents a synthesis of the Puritan idea of the covenant relationship as the foundation of all proper human society and the constitutional ideas of the English natural rights school of the seventeenth and early eighteenth centuries,"[41] means nothing when placed alongside the daily realities of black life in the nineteenth- and early twentieth-century South. Only by bracketing out lynchings, the forceful denial of the right to vote, and other forms of violence directed at blacks could federalism be thought of as a structure outside of historical circumstances, as the outcome of "reflection and choice,"[42] as an institution that deserves respect for what it is. Federalism's meaning only gains content by the accretion of case law, by the interplay of citizens and state actors challenging state practices, and by the judgments of federal courts determining whether or not it is acceptable for a state to stack the rules "in favor of death."[43]

Federalism is reflexive. It can only refer back to some practice, idea, or challenge to justify its existence. Federalism scholars treat federalism as a given, then propose some sort of reform to make it explainable.[44] But this confuses federalism with the rule of law itself. Federalism is evolutionary; it ripens on the vine of criminal justice case histories. It gets its meaning by saying no to those on the outskirts of political power.[45] By the end of the nineteenth century, in the name of "federalism," or more properly "comity," the justices had granted the states wide powers over criminal justice, but this concern was notably absent from the Supreme Court's discussions of corporate behavior, which flooded the Court's docket during the Gilded Age. Before passage of the habeas act, the Court had not defined federalism.[46] Federal-state comity was the vague composite the Court used to uphold state law or common law practices used by the states regarding arrest or due process. Federalism was born in the aftermath of the collapse of Reconstruction, as a policy instrument to reduce national involvement in civil rights, particularly in light of the expansive language of the Fourteenth and Fifteenth amendments.[47] Federalism's powers over criminals have been shaped neither by the founding generation nor by treatises written by philosophers but by the practical aspects of everyday life: arrest, conviction, sentence; race, class, occupation and status.

The 1867 act, like the due process clause of the Fourteenth Amendment, never reached its full potential in the nineteenth century because neither Congress nor the Court fully accepted the goals behind it. Without congressional prodding, that is, without jurisdictional intervention, the Court's restrictive interpretation of the Habeas Corpus Act proved infallible simply because the historical judgment of the Supreme Court was final.[48] Merging the remnants of British feudalism and the inchoate feelings of devotees of "states' rights" before it became more respectable as "American federalism" into a defense of state sovereignty, the Supreme Court found a way to merge the patterns of congressional weakness and the limitations on congressional intervention of the Supreme Court's jurisdiction into traditional and historic state functions regarding arrest, incarceration, and execution. The creation of a deferential "jurisdiction standard" during the latter half of the nineteenth century for state courts, which allowed the federal judiciary to deny habeas corpus, provided the state court's conviction was not without jurisdiction over the matter, was the Supreme Court's boldest attempt to thwart the goals of the Radical Republicans in Congress, and as a parry, it went unanswered.

In 1886, the same year the Supreme Court first subsumed the meaning of the habeas act within federal-state relations in *Ex parte Royall*, it made corporations persons under the Fourteenth Amendment.[49] Like all historical constructs, this is no accident. In 1884, the Court had refused to apply the Fifth Amendment's guarantee of a grand jury in criminal cases to the states. In 1890, it refused to connect the Eighth Amendment's protection against cruel and unusual punishment to the Fourteenth Amendment's due process clause. As Felix Frankfurter has written, "By 1900 the applicability of the Bill of Rights to the States had been rejected in cases involving claims based on virtually every provision in the first eight Articles" of the Bill of Rights.[50] But in 1897, the Court applied the Fifth Amendment's protection against taking property without due process to the states.[51]

Justices William Douglas and Hugo Black echoed Frankfurter's point about the failure to incorporate the Bill of Rights in the nineteenth century in their dissent in *Wheeling Steel Corporation* v. *Glander*.[52] "Since 1886," they wrote, "the Court has repeatedly struck down state legislation as applied to corporations on the ground that it violated the Equal Protection Clause." Carl Mayer has written, "For the period from 1889 to 1918 attacks upon state statutes were made in 422 cases involving state police power. Fifty-three of these were held invalid, of which the greater number involved the regulation of public service corporations. Only 14 involved legislation affecting the general rights and liberties of individuals."[53] Until the 1960s, the Court had refused to extend federal protection to natural persons in every conceivable state criminal case, but it granted corporations Fourteenth Amendment protections in 1897 (extending the equal protection clause to corporations), in 1889 (due process, Fifth Amendment), in 1893 (due process, Fifth Amendment), in 1906 twice (Fourth Amendment and Fifth Amendment, self-incrimination), and in 1908 (Sixth Amendment),[54] all before such protections were extended to real live human beings. More pointedly, "By 1938 Justice Hugo Black observed with dismay that, of the cases in which the Court applied the Fourteenth Amendment during the first fifty years after [*Santa Clara County* v. *Southern Pacific Railroad* (1886), the first case to apply the Fifth Amendment to corporations] 'less than one-half of 1 percent invoked it in protection of the Negro race, and more than 50 percent asked that its benefits be extended to corporations.'"[55] Between 1873 and 1906, Justices Joseph Bradley, David Brewer, Stephen Field, Samuel Miller, Rufus Peckham, and Chief Justice Morrison Waite all pushed the Court's corporate jurisprudence in the direction of greater acceptance for the corporation's Fourteenth Amendment's due process claims by disparaging the states' use of their police powers, because it was historically limited to the right to contract.[56]

Why deference to federalism in one set of cases and not another? Why make nonhumans persons and deny that criminals are persons for Fourteenth Amendment purposes? These historical dichotomies establish at the least that, because of a strengthened Congress (the antebellum era; the New Deal) or a strengthened Court (the Hughes and Warren Courts), because of economic developments or changed ideologies, because of the intensity of propertied interests and the weaknesses of others to include excluded minorities within the meaning of the word *person* in the Fourteenth Amendment, the meaning of federalism changes over time. Yet the Supreme Court has ignored federalism's fundamental alterity because it treats federalism as if its meaning were transhistorical or timeless, much like it treated corporations in the Gilded Age.

Between 1870 and 1905, when the Supreme Court struck down New York's regulation of bakers' hours in *Lochner* v. *New York* (1905), the Court moved, slowly but inexorably, away from Chief Justice Roger Taney's limited notion of police powers in *Brown* v. *Maryland* (1827) and John Marshall's common law understanding of corporations. In 1870, the Court struck down the Legal Tender Act, in part because the Court believed that it deprived creditors of property without due process.[57] In *Loan Association* v. *Topeka* (1875), Justice Samuel Miller struck down a Kansas law designed to help local industries because it was an unauthorized invasion of the right to private property.[58] In *Munn* v. *Illinois* (1877), the Court upheld Illinois' regulation of grain elevators but not without a visceral dissent from Justice Stephen Field.[59] In *Allgeyer* v. *Louisiana*[60] (1987), Justice Rufus Peckham declared, for a unanimous Court, that a Louisiana law denying out of state corporations the right to do business in Louisiana, without having at least one place of business within the state, to be a violation of the due process clause of the Fourteenth Amendment. And in *Lochner* v. *New York* (1905), Justice Peckham declared, in overturning the New York law regulating hours of work for bakers, "the limits of the state's police powers have been reached."[61]

What is notable is that, as early as 1878, the Court was becoming concerned about the number of state cases pressing for due process relief on property grounds, but it showed no signs of interest in the "problem" of federal-state relations.[62] The 1880s began habeas' path to restriction. With military troops removed from the South, and that region now an integral part of the Union, there was the "appearance of new economic interests in Congress," which once again divided the country by section, and there was pressure to restrict federal judicial power over the states.[63] Rather than striking the habeas act down, the Court, within twenty years of its passage, deemed it incompatible with the workings of a federal republic that by tradition had allowed the states to determine the boundaries of arrest and punishment. The loose language of the habeas corpus act, and a historical occlusion of the due process rights of prisoners beyond state borders, allowed the Court to make the case for federalism by focusing on an abstract notion of liberty that, curiously, never mentioned race or ethnic prejudice as factors in its decisions. The Court declared the states' regulations of health and safety incompatible with individual liberty under the Fourteenth Amendment's due process clause but extorted confessions and the first use of the electric chair by New York state against William Kemmler drew no protection from the Constitution. Motivated by economic and administrative concerns regarding federal court access, the Court in the latter half of the nineteenth century intentionally bifurcated federalism questions by category of privileged personhood and recast the habeas problem. When the Supreme Court decided its first important habeas corpus case in 1886, *Ex parte Royall*, for the first time a Supreme Court narrative spoke of constitutional privileges extended to one class but not another, while other late nineteenth-century cases focused on the historic mission of the states, and still other narratives ignored these concerns and concentrated on economic and administrative efficiency issues.[64]

The introduction of these new narratives limiting federal relief created a criminality/habeas corpus discourse that turned upside down the writ's British legacy. Rather than a writ of liberty that endangered and sought to curtail arbitrary governmental power, habeas corpus threatened the states' administration of justice because it allowed for the release of convicted criminals. Rather than a writ that drew its support from the legislative branch rather than the executive, because that branch was the most willing to act in an arbitrary fashion, and therefore more dangerous to civil liberties, the Supreme Court favored state executive powers over the individual's right to be free from unlawful confinement.

Throughout the nineteenth century, the Court tied rights claims to institutional capacities. Weighing limitations on the Court's time, neither Congress nor the Supreme Court wanted to increase federal remedies for both corporations and civil rights defendants. The courts chose commerce.[65] Sectional and institutional differences also impinged on congressional policy.[66] The House of Representatives supported restrictions on the federal courts; the Senate, regardless of the party in charge, did not. The Senate wanted corporations protected by the federal courts. During a period of congressional inaction to relieve the courts of jurisdictional burdens, the Supreme Court's nineteenth-century rulings on property and habeas corpus helped establish a pattern of legislative forbearance and judicial autonomy that has lasted until the present time.

By creating a forum for the articulation of constitutional rights in federal courts, Congress in 1867 thought it had eliminated the need for congressional intervention and oversight at the state level. In the name of separation of powers, it removed itself from the conflict over citizens' criminal rights and remedies. It removed itself from the important question that lies at the core of habeas corpus law: who has the body? Postwar, illegal detention was strictly a judicial matter, a question of form and of forum, and not a question of national sovereignty. Not surprisingly, waning congressional interest in protecting the rights of the accused after 1877 encouraged federal judicial forbearance as well, and thereafter, the protection of persons from arbitrary arrests remained with the state courts.

THE DEVELOPMENT OF THE
JURISDICTION STANDARD

The Habeas Corpus Act of 1867, passed just four years after Lincoln's suspension of habeas corpus, directed its strongest language not to the problem of containing rambunctious presidential power, but to the likelihood of state recalcitrance in enforcing federal law.[67] Congress' pressing concern in 1867 was not fear of arbitrary executive action, for the end of the Civil War had restored the presidency to its traditional and limited role.[68] Rather, the Radical Republicans were concerned with the ability of the national government to reach state and individual behavior. To Congress, the states were exercising arbitrary executive power, not the national government.[69] The habeas act followed a number of legislative reforms with judicial content, with the Civil Rights Act of 1866 and the Thirteenth and Fourteenth Amendments the most prominent efforts by the Radical Republicans to bring about federal-state changes.[70]

The drafters of the 1867 act did not take into account the questions involving transferring jurisdiction from state to nation, standing, or the baroque patterns of the states' appellate processes.[71] As Laurent Frantz has made clear, "the framers and backers of the Fourteenth Amendment were primarily interested in enlarging the powers of Congress, not those of the federal judiciary, which was looked upon with considerable distrust."[72] They created an arena for change without considering the institutional and political barriers that existed to thwart it. They sought to free the writ from the historical limits of federal-state comity concerns and partisan compromise and focused on the inability of those detained by the states to get federal protection. They assumed that Northern victory and subsequent congressional legislation had eliminated those limitations. They then attempted to prevent those barriers from reappearing with a general law, without regard for judicial capacity.

To implement vertical jurisdictional change, Congress needed the Supreme Court to enforce the notion of one superior jurisdiction presiding over the myriad jurisdictions that had hitherto possessed the primary police powers.[73] This was a formidable task, but not insurmountable.[74] Under the Habeas Corpus Act of 1867, lower federal court judges would have to be the agents for change, not Congress, supervising alterations in state criminal procedures on a case-by-case basis. With their newfound power, they could deny that, in a given case, and as a matter of jurisdiction, a defendant's criminal conviction was no longer constitutionally final at the state level. In effect, during the era when presidents were weakest, Congress needed federal judges to act as national executives. They could not merely be the arbiters of federal-state relations, weighing state concerns equally against those of the federal government. Eliminating unconstitutional confinement requires partisanship, not cooperation. Rather then promoting neutrality between governments, federal judges, armed with the power to remedy any individual's complaint that came before them, would become sentries, looking out for constitutional violations at the state level.

For the Court, deference, forbearance, and federalism fundamentally meant the same thing during the postwar era. Whichever word was invoked, the point was to reject habeas petitions alleging unconstitutional confinements. Postwar national political development on civil rights was incremental and unsuccessful in large part because the battle for control over America's postwar political development was rooted in the formalized language of jurisdictional boundaries. Congress, consumed with questions of economic growth and beset by increased partisanship, fell silent concerning its Fourteenth Amendment enforcement powers.[75] Moreover, the Court, equally consumed with the same concerns, did not just sit back and do nothing. As Charles Warren has written, the Supreme Court "largely eliminated from National politics the negro question which had so long embittered Congressional debates; they relegated the burden and the duty of protecting the negro to the States, to whom they properly belonged; and they served to restore confidence in the National Court in the Southern States."[76] The *Slaughterhouse Cases* (1873), which kept citizenship dual, is the clearest example of the Court's late nineteenth-century formal and jurisdictional methodology. "[P]roperty ownership was viewed as establishing the economic basis for freedom from governmental coercion and the enjoyment of liberty."[77] From that point forward, crimes not related to property remained state concerns throughout the nineteenth and early twentieth centuries.[78]

The Supreme Court developed its defense of states' rights during the suspension of its appellate habeas powers (1868–1885).[79] Through a series of mostly federal cases that began in the 1870s, the Supreme Court, on direct review, frequently denied claims of illegal detention. During this period, however, because of Congress' suspension of the Supreme Court's appellate habeas jurisdiction, the lower federal courts were free to overturn state convictions on habeas corpus without the possibility of Supreme Court review.[80] The federal courts, in fact, had shown some sympathy for due process claims made by state prisoners during the Court's appellate suspension. By 1885, pressure was building in Congress, where the power of the Radical Republicans had already weakened,[81] to restore the Supreme Court's jurisdiction to protect the states from federal intervention.[82]

The pressure to reestablish the Court's jurisdiction was for the benefit of the states, not for civil rights defendants, not for the affirmation of federal law. Riding circuit in 1875, Justice Joseph Bradley tipped off his colleagues and members of the bar to the power exercised by federal court judges in overturning state convictions.[83] Charles Warren, quoting from an 1884 law review article, wrote that the "the federal judges have asserted power 'to annul the criminal judgments of the state courts, and to pass finally and conclusively upon the validity of the criminal codes, the police regulations, and even the constitutions of the states.'"[84] Fearing federal court power over state criminal convictions, and with the hope for a renewed federalism on the horizon, Congress, on March 3, 1885, restored the Supreme Court's appellate jurisdiction on habeas corpus.[85]

A defense of property expanded the federal government's jurisdiction and restricted the states' powers; a fear of race limited the federal government's jurisdiction and expanded the states' powers. The Court began searching for the meaning of federalism after 1875, when Congress increased the jurisdiction of the federal courts.[86] The Act of March 3, 1875, enabled the federal courts to hear cases previously restricted by the 1789 Judiciary Act, which had not bestowed upon the federal courts the complete judicial power mentioned in the Constitution. The Act of 1875, as Charles Warren has noted, granted to the federal courts "for the first time, jurisdiction in all suits arising under the Constitution and laws of the United States."[87] The act increased the classes of cases that could be removed from state to federal court, which led to increased federal judicial oversight of state court decisions.[88]

The Supreme Court created the jurisdiction standard in an 1876 case, *Ex parte Parks*,[89] and relegated an 1873 habeas corpus case, *Ex parte Lange*,[90] to a "special" category of habeas cases.[91] Parks was convicted of forgery. The federal district court denied Parks a writ of habeas corpus. On appeal, Justice Bradley relied on the common law notion of the sanctity of a court's jurisdiction and stated that a superior federal court can only interfere with a lower federal court's ruling "if the inferior court had exceeded its jurisdiction, or was not competent to act."[92] The Court now had its definition of federalism. Merging concerns over what was not yet called "federalism" with simple deference to lower court judgments, the Supreme Court applied the distinction between "superior" and "inferior" courts to the federal-state relationship, with the hierarchical components of that relationship reversed to favor deference toward state cases.

In *Ex parte Siebold*[93] (1880), the Court fixed its eye on the growing problem of federal interference in state police matters. The Court stated that habeas corpus could issue only if the committing court lacked jurisdiction over the prisoner. "An unconstitutional law is void, and is no law. . . . A conviction created under it is not merely erroneous, but is illegal and void, and cannot be a legal cause of imprisonment."[94] The Court gave the federal courts room to issue habeas corpus under certain circumstances but denied habeas corpus in this case, finding the law in question to be constitutional. It was a question not of rights but of the preservation of the federal structure. The Court followed the general rule that the judgment of a court of competent jurisdiction that convicts a defendant, even if constitutional infractions occurred, should stand. *Ex parte Siebold* set the tone for the Court's deferential jurisprudence in criminal justice cases. "[T]hat the nature of sovereignty is such as to preclude the joint co-operation of two sovereignties, even in a matter in which they are mutually concerned, is not, in our judgment, of sufficient force to prevent concurrent and harmonious action on the part of the national and state governments. . . . There is nothing in the Constitution to forbid such co-operation in this case."[95] With this insignificant case lies the peculiar contribution of habeas corpus to the development of federal-state relations. Around a group of cases commonly referred to as "state police powers," the Court in the late 1870s carved out a sphere of sovereignty that the federal courts could not invade, barring exceptional circumstances. Federalism meant deference to state court jurisdiction largely on matters relating to crime, intended for this particular class of cases and not applicable across the constitutional spectrum.[96]

As a response to the formalism of the Supreme Court's property cases, progressive academics in the early twentieth century tried to replace the rigid application of rules with the sociology of law and the sovereign command of the law with an understanding of the interests behind it and to redirect the restraint rooted in principles of comity to the necessity for judicial action in light of political realities.[97] The legal realists' threat to the Court's late nineteenth-century jurisprudence required the justices to develop a forceful defense of federalism to challenge their notions. Instead, the justices obscured the full reach of the federal government's remedial powers. To counteract the centralizing tendencies of a large, commercial nation that was not yet a state but was willy-nilly becoming one, the Court needed to anchor the states' claims for finality in a constitutional doctrine of federalism that was tied historically to the jurisdiction standard or to some notion of federal limits, as outlined in the Constitution.

Lacking a historic referent for such a defense, the Court offered the exhaustion rule. The Court accepted the 1867 act's expansion of federal protection but created a way to work around it. The exhaustion doctrine required habeas petitioners to exhaust all available state appellate opportunities, including applications for certiorari to the United States Supreme Court, before collaterally attacking their convictions in the federal courts. With the exhaustion doctrine, the Court accepted the power of federal habeas corpus jurisdiction, while demonstrating respect for state court procedures by requiring strict adherence to its rules. The underlying idea is that, with sufficient evidence of the petitioner's guilt established at the state level, through years of trial and appeals, a federal court judge will be reluctant to release a prisoner on habeas corpus.

A narrative of character is already apparent within the Court's emerging habeas jurisprudence. It will take some years to develop, as we will see in chapter three. But the exhaustion rule had characterological elements that cannot be denied in that it placed the burden of asking for relief not on the state court but on the petitioner himself. The habeas petition would consist of a narrative of the petitioner's crimes. The Court first used the exhaustion doctrine in *Ex parte Royall* (1886). *Royall* is the first case of significance following the restoration of the Court's habeas appellate jurisdiction.[98] It upheld national supremacy in speech while relegating federal habeas corpus powers to the discretion of the district court judge in fact. In effect, the Court declared a clear policy preference for state sovereignty on habeas corpus by denying that federal habeas corpus was a command. Because *Royall*'s legacy is tied closely to the Court's creation of corporate personhood and the narrative of character of which I have been speaking, which has ramifications for the writ's failure to attach to the Bill of Rights, I discuss *Royall* separately in the next chapter.

THE WEAKNESS OF THE JURISDICTION
STANDARD AND THE RISE OF DUE PROCESS

The first Justice John Marshall Harlan, who supported full incorporation of the Bill of Rights in *Hurtado* v. *California* (1884), found support for federal forbearance on habeas corpus in *Covell* v. *Heyman*[99] (1884). In that case, the Supreme Court justified federal judicial deference by stating that "forbearance . . . is a principle of comity, with perhaps no higher sanction than the utility which comes from concord; but between state courts and those of the United States it is something more. It is a principle of right and of law, and therefore of necessity."[100]

The Court recognized the problem of the jurisdiction standard in a rights-based regime. It limited attacks against state courts in the name of something more powerful than a claim of unjust confinement, the states' sovereignty over criminal justice. But the paradox was clear. In an attempt to redirect the nascent language of the Fourteenth Amendment away from convicted criminals, the Court tried to ground federal-state comity in something more than utility. It was clear from the start that a state court's jurisdiction could be breached. The question, however, was: was federal forbearance necessary in light of an illegal detention claim? The Court had still not worked out a viable definition of federalism, comity, or deference. The Supreme Court could not decide if federalism was a process or if it had substantive value; if it was a means to an end or it was an end in itself; if it was a technical principle to facilitate governance in a large nation or if it was a great principle of democracy.

A search of nineteenth-century Supreme Court cases regarding both property and criminality demonstrates that the Court had not successfully articulated federalism's independent value.[101] Rather, the Court ignored federalism in its contract cases and focused on the liberty of the individual. In its habeas cases, it reversed those concerns, subsuming "rights" claims under the general concerns of comity, finality, and conviction. From the standpoint of individual rights, the exhaustion doctrine was another jurisdictional hurdle for a habeas petitioner to overcome that was not mandated by the habeas statute. Created to protect state court judgments from untimely federal review, the doctrine in fact immunized the states from federal review. But it is a weaker standard than jurisdiction because it lacks constitutional moorings.

The jurisdiction standard and the exhaustion doctrine give the impression that federal habeas corpus review is inappropriate but not unconstitutional. For habeas to be effective, as in property or contract cases that moved from state to federal courts, the Court had to go beyond the mere words of the habeas corpus act and the limitations of the Fourteenth Amendment's history. It had to argue that rights were fungible, that procedure implied substance, that federal supremacy was tied to the claims of due process, that claims of illegal or unlawful detention had substantive meaning within the Fourteenth Amendment that would allow a state prisoner access to a federal court. Of course, the Court did not do this. Yet, perhaps unwittingly, the more substance the Court gave to due process on economic matters, as in *Lochner* v. *New York* (1905), the more it undermined its restrictive stance on habeas corpus. The jurisdiction standard became porous only when the concept of a state's jurisdiction expanded to include events surrounding a trial, such as the quality of a defendant's counsel or mob influence of a jury. The jurisdiction standard weakened with the slow application of the Bill of Rights to the states, driven by property cases. The Court's property jurisprudence paradoxically undermined its restrictive view of jurisdiction for civil rights defendants. In the next section, I discuss the conflict over due process and habeas corpus as an aspect of federal-state development in the nineteenth century.

HABEAS CORPUS AND DUE PROCESS

Habeas corpus has a historical connection with due process. Among seventeenth-century English writers, it was common to link the two from their mutual birth at Runnymeade in 1215. Modern historiography has disproved that connection,[102] but the relationship between them is difficult to sever. It is problematic to separate the function of habeas corpus, a process-oriented writ, from what process is due a prisoner alleging illegal detention.

Institutionally, the prospects for substantive due process in criminal cases were bleak. A limited federal judiciary and sufficient case law to prevent the applicability of the Bill of Rights to the states through the Fourteenth Amendment presupposes a limited scope for due process. Moreover, from 1789 to 1889, prisoners could not challenge their federal convictions in the Supreme Court. Cases involving life or death reached the Court only because of a division of opinion among district courts.[103] This gave the single federal judge enormous power. To remedy this, Congress passed the Act of February 6, 1889, which gave federal defendants the right to appeal to the Supreme Court.[104] The Act of 1889 "restricted resort to the Supreme Court in criminal cases to capital crimes."[105]

On March 3, 1891, Congress passed a bill establishing the circuit courts of appeals.[106] The purpose of that act was to reduce the Supreme Court's docket by creating nine federal courts of appeals, which cut off whole classes of cases the Court had previously been obligated to accept.[107] "The history of latter-day judicial acts," Felix Frankfurter has written, "is largely the story of restricting the right of appeal to the Supreme Court."[108] The Court's smaller docket increased the power of the lower federal courts and helped the Court concentrate on those classes of cases that were pressing on the Court's time, principally commerce and Fourteenth Amendment cases.

The replacement of Chief Justice Morrison Waite with Chief Justice Melville Fuller in 1888 was another significant change concerning the Court's view of due process. In the period from 1890 to 1910, "'the ceaseless accumulation of power' in the National Government became the theme of law writers."[109] Time and again, the Fuller Court prevented state criminal defendants from obtaining federal habeas review.[110] The Court, for example, rejected claims by a black man charged with murder and sentenced to die who alleged that his conviction was unconstitutional on the basis of a biased and all-white jury; by a Japanese subject charged with murder whose lawyer had not been admitted to the state bar; and by a white man charged with murder. Most important, it rejected William Kemmler's novel constitutional claim that New York State's first use of the electric chair was a violation of the Eighth Amendment's "cruel and unusual" clause.[111] A typical decision by the Supreme Court denying habeas corpus during this era stated: "[A] habeas corpus proceeding is a collateral attack of a civil nature to impeach the validity of a judgment or a sentence of another court in a criminal proceeding, and it should, therefore, be limited to cases in which the judgment of sentence attacked is clearly void by reason of its having been rendered without jurisdiction, or by reason of the court's exceeding its jurisdiction."[112] The Supreme Court was still under the standard set forth in *Ex parte Royall* (1886), which limited federal court jurisdiction to issue the writ of habeas corpus to cases of "peculiar urgency" or when a state court blatantly exceeded its jurisdiction.[113] "Upon habeas corpus the court examines only the power and authority of the court to act, not the correctness of its conclusions."[114]

This was the last word on habeas corpus before *Frank* v. *Magnum*. In the early twentieth century, the Court continued to defer to the state courts on due process challenges, such as in *Maxwell* v. *Dow*[115] (1900), upholding a conviction by a jury of eight rather than of twelve. Between *Holden* v. *Hardy*[116] in 1898 and *Twining* v. *New Jersey*[117] in 1908, the Court allowed the states to set their own standards on juries free from the restrictions asked for by defendants on due process claims. Following an 1891 habeas corpus case,[118] the Court held that the Fourteenth Amendment did not interfere with the protection of life, liberty, and property, "nor with the exercise of that power in the adjudications of the courts of a state in administering process provided by the law of the state."[119] By the beginning of World War I, all that could be asked of federal courts in habeas proceedings was that they "carefully inquire into any matter involving the legality of the detention and remand or discharge as the facts may require."[120] To establish a general rule governing habeas corpus would concede the argument for national supremacy. The Court feared unprecedented federal control over the administration of criminal justice in the states.[121]

By the twentieth century, the Court was operating on two discursive levels that were on a collision course. Concerning commercial matters, the Court had given the states little room to maneuver. State defendants seeking federal redress in matters relating to finances had little difficulty getting into federal courts.[122] In criminal cases, particularly habeas corpus, the Supreme Court treated the states as virtual sovereign entities. Federal review was nearly impossible in light of the jurisdiction standard and the exhaustion doctrine. The Leo Frank case pushed those doctrines to their limits but could not penetrate the Court's protections. *Frank* v. *Magnum* laid the basis for all habeas challenges that followed.

THE LEO FRANK CASE

The defense of the jurisdiction standard in *Frank* revealed the difficulties the Court's nineteenth-century property jurisprudence had created for civil rights. By the end of the nineteenth century, the Supreme Court had applied the Fifth Amendment's property clause to the states. Why not the Eighth Amendment's protection against cruel and unusual punishment? Rather than noting a problem of enforcing justice at the state level, the Court assumed that state prisoners were causing federal-state conflict. It is here, then, that we can locate the rise of the Court's linguistic methodology regarding habeas appeals. The basis for the exhaustion rule was not jurisdictional but personal. The burden was on habeas petitioners to establish a reason why the federal courts should even consider overriding a state court decision. The exhaustion doctrine assumed federal-state comity; the habeas corpus act did not. The Court recast the problem.

From early on, the Supreme Court clearly saw the administrative difficulties of habeas corpus. Granting the writ redirects authority from the states' executive branches to the national judiciary. But beyond making overtures to federal-state harmony, the Court never stated what benefit protecting federalism and denying claims of illegal detention would bestow on individuals. At best, a case for federal forbearance was made "in recognition of the fact that the public good requires that those [federal-state] relations be not disturbed by unnecessary conflict between courts equally bound to guard and protect rights secured by the Constitution."[123]

By acknowledging the threat posed by individual rights claims and the due process clause of the Fourteenth Amendment to the jurisdiction standard, the Court made its defense of comity more difficult. It created the problem of the interests of justice versus the interests of federalism. If a right was in question, why was a remedy not at hand?[124] The Supreme Court's task was to reconcile the protection of rights against competing structural concerns, in light of its own attempts to minimize state interference in individuals' lives on economic matters.

In 1913, accused of murdering Mary Phagan, Leo Frank was tried, convicted, and sentenced to death in Atlanta, Georgia. A motion for a new trial was filed on the day his sentence was imposed. Two months later, Frank's attorneys amended their motion to include one hundred and three grounds for error, such as an unfair trial, a biased jury, disorder inside and outside the courtroom that disrupted the trial, and inadmissible testimony. In February 1914, the Georgia Supreme Court affirmed the trial court's judgment of conviction and denied the motion for a new trial.

Leo Frank operated a pencil factory in Atlanta. Although born in Texas, he was a New Yorker living in the South, was educated at Cornell University and was Jewish. During the first quarter of the twentieth century, the post-Reconstruction South was industrializing, and there was local resentment over the influx of "foreigners" and the sight of women and children working in factories. The Leo Frank case operated against this backdrop.[125]

During Frank's trial, a mob outside the courtroom shouted anti-Semitic epithets and chanted for his death.[126] The Georgia Supreme Court did not find sufficient evidence that the mob in any way influenced the jury's decision.[127] After conviction, the Georgia Supreme Court denied a writ of error to have the judgment reviewed by the Supreme Court. Frank next applied to individual Supreme Court justices, all of whom denied his petition.

Having exhausted his state's remedies, Frank petitioned the U.S. district court for a writ of habeas corpus, arguing a denial of due process protection at trial and a loss of jurisdiction by the trial court, as it had failed to maintain peace and good order during the trial. The district court rejected Frank's plea for habeas corpus. On appeal, Justice Mahlon Pitney, for a 7:2 majority, denied Frank's claims.

Frank's attorneys made five procedural points in defense of their client.[128] Justice Pitney responded with three points of his own. First, to grant Frank habeas corpus, it must appear "that he is held in custody in violation of the Constitution." Second, regarding the jurisdiction standard, Pitney held that habeas corpus could not be issued to correct errors in law. And third, the limits of due process circumscribed the power of habeas corpus to overturn a state court conviction.

Twining v. *New Jersey* (1908) was the final word on due process up to this point. *Twining* tried to strike a balance between individual rights claims and the preservation of the federal order. "Whenever a new limitation or restriction is declared, it is a matter of grave importance, since, to that extent, it diminishes the authority of the state, so necessary to the perpetuity of our dual form of government, and changes its relation to its people and the Union."[129] But *Twining* did not solve the problem, and the imbalance remained. As for due process, the Court rooted its understanding of that historic phrase in the common law.[130] Justice William Moody, writing for the Court in *Twining*, refused to inquire into the meaning of an individual right to due process. Unlike *Lochner* v. *New York*, decided just three years earlier, the Court in *Twining* defined due process procedurally, not substantively. "The essential elements of due process of law, are singularly few though of wide application and deep significance," the Court held. Due process requires "that the court which assumes to determine the rights of parties shall have jurisdiction." And finally, "given a court of justice with jurisdiction and acts, not arbitrarily but in conformity with a general law, upon evidence, and after inquiry made with notice to the parties affected and opportunity to be heard, then all the requirements of due process, so far as it relates to procedure in court and methods of trial and character and effect of evidence are complied with."[131]

Following *Twining*'s formalism and respect for state court jurisdiction, the Court in *Frank* believed that it had no choice but to deny habeas corpus to Frank. Notice and a hearing, or an opportunity to be heard, the Court stated in *Frank*, "according to established modes of procedure, is due process in the constitutional sense."[132] There is no doubt that Frank had had his day in court. But was it a trial in form only? This was the crucial question that the Supreme Court did not answer. Frank's attorneys argued that the trial court had lost its jurisdiction over the case by failing to control the mob and by not dismissing two jurors before the trial who were openly biased against Frank. Yet the Court maintained that "the writ of habeas corpus will lie only in case the judgment under which the prisoner is detained is shown to be *absolutely void* for want of jurisdiction in the court that pronounced it."[133] It is not clear if "absolutely void" adds anything to the Court's previous standard.

The Court in *Frank* accepted that "due process of law guaranteed by the Fourteenth Amendment has regard to substance of right, and not to matters of form and procedure," without acknowledging that the jurisdiction standard was effectively undermined in the process. Moreover, the Court also accepted that the 1867 act empowered federal courts and judges in a habeas challenge "to look beyond forms and inquire into the very substance of the matter,"[134] while at the same time failing to acknowledge that its decision in *Frank* was based on the formalism of the law of jurisdiction.

Until *Frank* v. *Magnum*, the Supreme Court was silent concerning the connection between due process and the appellate stage of a criminal procedure. Before *Frank*, the Court had ruled that the Fourteenth Amendment did not require appellate review in criminal cases.[135] With *Frank*, the Court could no longer ignore the significance of the appellate process in a criminal adjudication. The appellate process was an extension of the state's jurisdiction over the prisoner. Consequently, appellate courts had to conform to the rules governing jurisdiction and due process that applied to trial courts. "This is not a mere matter of comity," Justice Pitney wrote. "This rule stands on a much higher plane, for it arises out of the very nature and ground of the inquiry into the proceedings of the state tribunals, and touches closely upon relations between the state and federal governments."[136]

The appellate process, then, was a significant addition to any defendant's due process rights. As Justice Pitney acknowledged, "the petition contains a narrative of disorder, hostile manifestations, and uproar, which, if it stood alone, and were to be taken as true, may be conceded to show an environment inconsistent with a fair trial and an impartial verdict."[137] The purpose of appellate review is to defend a defendant's due process rights and to inquire into the truthfulness of the petition's narrative. But Frank's understanding of the trial does not impress Pitney. Frank's narrative is a legal formality which Pitney finds to be of a lower order than the trial court's verdict. Frank's narrative, despite its important claims, does not remove the trial court's jurisdiction, which remains the foundation for the Court's deference policy. Pitney then switches the burden of appeal from the state to the petitioner. "The narrative has no proper place in a petition addressed to a court of the United States except as it may tend to throw light upon the question whether the state of Georgia, having regard to the entire course of the proceedings, in the appellate as well as in the trial court, is depriving appellant of his liberty and intending to deprive him of his life without due process of law."[138] Frank's petition, Pitney finds, is "only a reiteration of allegations that appellant had a right to submit, and did submit, first to the trial court, and afterwards to the supreme court of the state, as a ground for avoiding the consequences of the trial."[139] Appellate review, for Pitney, does not add anything of substance to a petitioner's narrative; indeed, it subtracts from it by drawing attention to the reason for the appeal in the first place: Frank's murder of Mary Phagan. Mere reiteration of the petitioner's narrative of events by an appellate court has no power to break the deference that the Supreme Court is required to show to state courts.

Once again, the Court tried to create a comity standard that was more than a mere formality. But the Court expressed nothing more than a preference not to disturb federal-state relations or the judgment of the trial court. The *Frank* case was the Court's most formidable challenge to the formalism of the jurisdiction standard and it lacked a satisfactory response to meet that challenge. Without admitting as much, the Court's *dicta* from its commerce cases about the primacy of individual rights had undermined its decisions on habeas corpus.

Justices Oliver Wendell Holmes and Charles Evans Hughes dissented on the grounds that the jurisdiction standard could no longer contain a substantive plea of illegal detention. Holmes pointed to an unresolved jurisdictional issue that the majority did not consider, namely, that "the loss of jurisdiction is not general, but particular, and proceeds from the control of a hostile influence."[140] For Holmes, however, the argument for habeas corpus was even stronger. Habeas corpus, he wrote, "cuts through all forms and goes to the very tissue of the structure. It comes in from the outside . . . and opens the inquiry whether they have been an empty shell."[141]

The practical problem with Holmes' metaphor was that while it denied that the states had any constitutional jurisdictional foundation to hold someone unlawfully detained, it continued to stress that habeas corpus was an extraordinary remedy, not part of the constitutional fabric. Coming in from the outside meant that other courts in different situations could close the door to habeas' entreaties. Holmes proposed no structural revision of Georgia's criminal justice system or of federal habeas corpus. As a practical matter, Holmes' colleagues in the majority realized that Holmes' description would only bring more habeas cases before the Court. This is why the dissent in *Frank* was so radical. A jurisdiction standard based on forbearance wants to preserve federal-state relations as they existed in the post-Reconstruction era, not to contribute to the enmity that lies dormant between the two judicial systems. Holmes' dissent and metaphor (whatever its limitations) were ill-suited to the limited demands on the judiciary in the era of legal formalism.

As the Court came to accept a more expansive definition of federal jurisdiction over the states, it reluctantly confronted an expanded definition of due process. The Court met the expansion of rights against the states with an increase in one's duties toward the Court. The Court did not negate those claims, it accepted them, with the concession that individual conditions be attached to each state petitioner's habeas challenge. Any violation of these regulations (which the defendant may be unaware of prior to his suit) would result in denial of the writ. A high standard of individual behavior had subtly replaced the jurisdiction standard. A narrative of personal behavior was in the making. The *Frank* decision was just the beginning of the enactment of judicial barriers to habeas challengers.

CONCLUSION

Throughout the first wave of habeas jurisprudence, the Court relied on a policy of comity between state and nation. But it was not an impenetrable doctrine. The purpose of the comity standard was to mitigate federal involvement in light of the nationalist intent of the Habeas Corpus Act of 1867, which had broadened the Court's powers over state prisoners. By deferring to state court decisions, the Court hoped to facilitate governance in a large nation, not to increase the trend toward centralization.[142]

To be sure, the command of the writ operated against the Supreme Court's policy of deference to the state courts, if only because habeas corpus has a historic connection to due process of law. The development of substantive rights through due process violations threatened the necessity of federal restraint and the legitimacy of a federal state that was decentralized by legal category. By the twentieth century, the jurisdiction standard, which was designed to protect the states, could no longer do so. Evolving conceptions of due process from property cases ate into the state courts' criminal justice jurisdiction and forced the final determination of a prisoner's status into the federal courts. The jurisdiction standard and the exhaustion doctrine could only delay what the command of the habeas corpus statute sought to obtain, that is, federal review of state court convictions. The Leo Frank case embodied all of these concepts, and it should be clear how mired in contradiction the Court's decision was. The final case of the jurisdiction era is in fact the first case of the due process era that follows. The protection of the individual at trial becomes the new ground for habeas challenges.

TWO

Bodily Inventions

The Habeas Petitioner
and the Corporation, 1886

When we see a culture self-consciously defining bodies, it is
already in trouble.

—Hyde, *Bodies of Law*

KINDS OF PERSONS

LURKING WITHIN VICTORIAN respectability was the dangerous individual. In
1885, Louis Vivet was diagnosed as the first male multiple personality.
Regarding the discovery of new forms of mental illness in the late nineteenth
century, Ian Hacking suggests that these innovations were not only scientific.
A "feature of a new mental illness is that it embeds itself in a two-headed way
in a culture,"[1] producing two versions of the same thing: one healthy, the other
ill. Hacking's point is that to stabilize the two-pronged entity being observed
it is necessary to separate the idealized image of the self-as-rationalist from
the deviant, such that both versions become understood, explainable, and clas-
sifiable. These scientific classifications then become part of legal language. By
bracketing the context of this other self's emergence within the binary distinction of a pure and impure self, an ahistorical self emerges, which the law
quickly and neatly comes to possess. By setting one self against the other, the

law brings a greater unity to these two selves. A picture emerges; a grid is produced; a person is attached to a body.

The aim of this chapter is to mark the formal point of emergence in U.S. law of two kinds of persons, the corporator, or the one who has vested interests in a corporation, and the criminal, by focusing on the positive forms of the production of personhood by the Supreme Court in 1886. It was, after all, also in 1886 that Robert Louis Stevenson wrote in *Dr. Jekyll and Mr. Hyde* that "man is not truly one, but truly two."[2] With the birth of the corporation, we see the rise of the criminal, a split personality.

County of Santa Clara v. Southern Pacific Railroad[3] and *Ex parte Royall*[4] provide the first two instances in American jurisprudence of the judicial measurement and classification of legal personalities by extralegal signs of health and illness. The emphasis on legal discourse as a producer of selves is designed to shed light on the way in which such discourse is tied to the wider rationalities of government, principally the monitoring of behavior through technological advances made during this era that first captured the image of the criminal, both in photographs and in fingerprinting, then refracted it through the image of the corporator, who comes to us through legal changes made throughout the nineteenth century to ease transcontinental business operations. First in March and then in May 1886, the Supreme Court fashioned the criminal body in *Ex parte Royall*, the first significant habeas corpus case following the end of the Civil War and Reconstruction, then shaped corporate personhood in *County of Santa Clara v. Southern Pacific Railroad*.

The simultaneous constitutional appearance in 1886 of corporate and criminal bodies began the important process of normalizing judicial proceedings for two different (but not altogether dissimilar) types of persons. The *Santa Clara* decision created the norm: it reinforced the hitherto unstated idea that corporations are persons under the Fourteenth Amendment and therefore worthy of constitutional protection. *Royall* provided the exception: it denied criminals seeking federal remedies for unlawful confinement by state courts on habeas corpus the same national privileges afforded corporations. At the institutional level, these two cases advanced a zero-sum jurisdictional argument of individual liberty versus states' rights. What the Supreme Court gave to one petitioner in terms of access and respectability, it denied to the other. Both cases therefore fed off each other. The "privileged norms" of corporate personhood were "reinforced by the reaction against the transgressor."[5]

Created by the justices of the Supreme Court at the beginning phase of the advent of the transnational corporation and the rise of widespread underworld criminality, the simultaneous creation and denial of legal personhood served as an accommodation for the lower federal courts to changing social patterns caused by the industrial revolution and advances in corporate structures, the emancipation of slaves, Asian immigration, and general population growth. The Supreme Court's purpose in these two cases was to design a way to disperse newly emergent and conflicting interests in particular directions. But the Court did not create each subject before it by adding or subtracting from the biological givens of the petitioners. Rather, it created a language and set of norms around each subject as a constitutional reality, filling in their characteristics, objectifying their behavior, and channeling the given realities of corporate and criminal personhood in different legal directions, one up, and the other down. By creating the body corporate and the criminal body during the same term, the Supreme Court embedded within the meaning of the Constitution the kind of legal person it found suitable to offer legal redress within the vague concept of 'person,' as outlined in the Fourteenth Amendment. The result, as Phillipa Rothfield has written in a different context, "is that the body comes to be understood *through* discourse, not outside of it. So the body which is being introduced can be described as a *discursive body*, not as an anatomical given."[6]

For the first time in American constitutional law, the legal person takes shape not simply as a bearer of traditional English liberties, with all that that implies regarding personal autonomy, but as a corporate "person," who is not dissimilar to the bearer of traditional English liberties, yet is structurally different. The Court corporealizes the corporate subject to subject him to a specifically American constitutional analyses, to his legal benefit. After 1886, corporations gained access to the federal courts, and though the Court does the same discursive trick with the criminal in *Royall*, it constructs to deconstruct, it does not afford him similar protections; quite the opposite. The Supreme Court denied state criminals access to the federal courts until the 1960s. This legal unveiling, this autopsy on legal twins, one stillborn, conceals as much as it reveals about the status of criminals in the United States in the nineteenth century. The composite photograph of the corporator and the criminal in 1886 reproduced selves as much as it suppressed them.

Before these two historic cases, state and federal courts in the United States had largely subsumed personal characteristics within developing case law, emphasizing the importance of deeply structural concerns to the overall health of society, such as the right to protect contracts, judicial and economic efficiency, local autonomy, law and order, the meaning and limits of fundamental rights, and the merits of harmonious relations between the states and the federal government. "[T]here was no ordinary individuality, no autonomy, no discrete body, prior" to these two cases in American law.[7] But with the passage of the Fourteenth Amendment in 1868, and the concomitant "release of individual creative energy to the greatest extent compatible with the broad sharing of opportunity for such expression,"[8] William Royall and the Southern Pacific Railroad corporation became constitutional realities, not persons as such, but kinds of persons, with constitutional rights and privileges that only gained meaning by their attachment to legal conceptions of embodied personhood.

Rather than bringing unity to the Court's conceptions of federal-state relations or individual liberty, by the end of the nineteenth century these two cases had created a schism. On the one hand, it is *Ex parte Royall*, not *County of Santa Clara*, that forced the Supreme Court to develop a federal-state comity doctrine in the 1890s to accommodate the number of cases coming from the states alleging economic discrimination and violations of criminal procedures under the due process clause of the Fourteenth Amendment. State criminal defendants in the United States did not have access to the federal courts (that is, they had no right to a federal hearing despite allegations of federal, constitutional violations at the state level), with few exceptions, until the Warren Court era (1953–1969). On the other hand, *Santa Clara*, not *Ex parte Royall*, created the legal atmosphere for the federal supplanting of state business laws in the last decade of the nineteenth century, "as an ever-growing number of firms extended business operations across state lines."⁹ Where *Royall* celebrated federalism and state sovereignty, *Santa Clara* castigated those ideas as oppressive. Where *Santa Clara* venerated individual liberty and federal protection, *Royall* looked to ancient liberties and respect for federal-state comity. Legal personhood emerged here, amid the formal splitting of the constitutional body into a psychic duality, one criminal, the other corporate.

Viewing these cases as more than creations of jurisdictional boundaries, I suggest that *Santa Clara* and *Royall* are discursive and disciplinary attempts to formulate truths about persons (or types of legal men) by connecting the images of personhood evolving during nineteenth-century capitalism to subjects jurisdictionally, and to the techniques and levels of governance of a federal republic, thereby creating a hierarchy of rights and privileges within the law that forced changes not just in the economy but also in social relations as well.¹⁰ These two cases are united not by abstract notions of the "liberty of the individual" (disguised as a corporation) or the virtues of a decentralized federal republic for the administration of the criminal law (but not for economic development) but by the fact that the Supreme Court created a set of truths about corporate and criminal persons at the end of the nineteenth century, by constructing a set of legal distinctions based on the individual petitioner's status and ranking within American society.

From this point forward, from a constitutional perspective, one's self in the nineteenth century is constituted by how one conducts oneself within the matrix of forces operating within the legal system and civil society. Taken together, these two cases bring about greater judicial certitude in weighing future constitutional claims regarding property and criminality. As a result, the application of the Bill of Rights to the states splits in 1886, based on what kind of person petitions for the Fourteenth Amendment's due process protections. With each future case, courts will attribute to every legal subject an identity within the social and moral fabric of nineteenth-century life. In the fabrication of these constitutional persons, the Supreme Court produced what

Michel Foucault calls "domains of objects and rituals of truth."[11] With *Royall* and *Santa Clara*, we find the Supreme Court, for the first time, giving kinds of persons a solid foundation, not simply in law but also in science—a descriptive table upon which all types of men can be analyzed.[12]

To pursue this line of inquiry, the aim of this chapter is not to take "man as he really is," in the manner of Enlightenment philosophy and Whig history, lest every man be viewed as a merchant[13] or every subject be thought of "in its empty sameness throughout the course of history."[14] Nor is my purpose to provide a historical analysis of the development of corporate personhood.[15] Rather, my intention is to focus on the Supreme Court's creation of a legal distinction in 1886 that is "formed gradually within the structures of the body."[16] As Alan Hyde makes clear, "multiple constructions" of the body are "already immanent in law."[17] Corporate and criminal selves emerge within the shifting sands of case law and through the discursive constructs of corporations and criminality, in an effort to deny and admit various persons entry into federal courts. It is the discursively constructed subject who directs the course of constitutional law from the Gilded Age on, and not the logic of constitutional interpretation or the political structure of a decentralized and federal state.

WHO HAS THE BODY?

Habeas corpus is a writ designed under the common law to allow any judge the power to free any person unlawfully committed. It relates the subject's desire for freedom to the spheres of governmental power. A writ of habeas corpus, technically in U.S. law not an appeal but functionally so, shatters the functionalist's desire that justice done once is justice done forever. The key inquiry in a habeas attack—who has the body?—requires an independent judicial framework to investigate how the numerous layers of government that seeks to control criminal bodies function. Habeas corpus is the archeologist's spade; it cuts through the legal formalities that have accumulated over time that protect state court decisions from being overturned on appeal and that keep prisoners in prison. Operating within the density of American legal structures—federalism and the separation of powers—the writ erupts, and the solitary prisoner, perhaps after years on death row, asks the law to recognize the pain of imprisonment, the wrong of the conviction, the unconstitutionality of the arrest.

Despite the Supreme Court's high regard for the legitimacy of state court criminal convictions, the writ presupposes a centralized judicial power that can enforce the command "to have the body" over rival departments of government and jurisdictions. If "the prison seizes the body of the inmate,"[18] habeas corpus allows the inmate to seize it back. In shifting political operations from the local to the national level, the criminal body, formally hidden behind prison bars and layers of legal norms, classification schemes and regulations, enters the political realm as a contested site for further legal observation, classification, and review. But habeas corpus is not just an appeal; it is a call for liberation from unjust confinement, biased juries, inept lawyers, and politically motivated state judges. By accusing the state of acting illegally, the habeas petitioner aligns himself with the national over the local, with reason over prejudice, with law over vengeance.

The heart of the Supreme Court's decision in *Ex parte Royall* is that the Court read the habeas act not as an unconditional command to set unlawfully confined prisoners free but as presenting release from state confinement as one option for judicial resolution among others, including deference to state court judgments, subject to future constitutional considerations. In doing so, the Court set aside the body of the prisoner and redirected the argument to an institutional conflict between the federal government and the states over which level of government ought to maintain possession over the body of the prisoner.[19] In an effort to restrict prisoners' future access to federal courts, and thereby prevent an infusion of claims by minorities about unjust treatment by state officers, *Ex parte Royall* buried the prisoner's body within a structural concern for corporate rights and privileges.

The Court in *Royall* held that federal courts, as a matter of discretion but not of law, and in the absence of exceptional circumstances, did not have to assume jurisdiction over a case that had not yet been litigated. The decision also implied that state court determinations of guilt deserved lower levels of scrutiny from federal courts on habeas appeals and that state court decisions should be final, pending "extraordinary circumstances."[20] More substantively, *Royall* denied the applicability of the Bill of Rights to habeas petitioners in cases dealing with capital punishment, poor counsel, racial and ethnic discrimination, and biased juries. As Paul Bator, a noted habeas corpus critic, wrote in 1963, after *Royall*, "subsequent cases held that habeas should be denied while a prisoner seeks to vindicate his federal rights in the state appellate courts and through state postconviction procedures. And still another line of cases established that even after all state remedies were exhausted, habeas corpus should be denied and the prisoner put to his writ of error in the United States Supreme Court."[21] *Royall* did more than set limits on federal court access for convicted criminals. It rendered the live body of the prisoner invisible to the law and substituted the healthy and productive body politic. Society, *Royall* declared, has no interest in expanding habeas corpus' jurisdiction. By preventing habeas petitioners from gaining entry to federal courts, *Royall* began the law's turn, in the latter half of the nineteenth century, toward a more detailed governance of criminals in prison and under state law. *Royall*'s legacy has less to do with a defense of federalism than with vilifying the prisoner's body by casting it as a usurper of the federal structure, a drain on valuable constitutional resources, a terrorist and a threat to the body politic.[22] *Ex parte Royall* is not concerned with William Royall's body but with future imprisoned bodies, who will not be white, male, and well educated, as William Royall was.

THE ROYALL BODY

In 1886, white-collar criminality became visible to American society when Thomas Byrnes, the New York City chief of detectives, published his rogues' gallery of "free-enterprise villainy."[23] Byrnes' book, *Professional Criminals of America*, is a collection of pictures and running commentary on forgers, swindlers, bank robbers, confidence men, pickpockets, sneaks, and shoplifters. Byrnes was the product of the Gilded Age: his book has no pictures of murderers. He considered white-collar criminality a business that posed a threat to the good, honest men of Wall Street. But white-collar criminality was a profession without legal imprimatur: it was the flipside of the respectable careers. By seeing criminals as the negation of the real and trustworthy men who worked for their livelihood, Byrnes was able to break into the criminal underworld by using business techniques. He relied on treaties and informers to keep thieves outside of New York City and infiltrated criminal groups by using undercover police officers. In doing so, he helped collapse the distinction between law abiders and law breakers. White-collar criminals were by definition fakers, confidence men who changed their identities as they moved from city to city.[24] Criminals were dangerous to polite society because their crimes "depended on anonymity, ambiguity of identity, and the fluidity of lines that separated strata and classes in the population."[25] Byrnes taught the police to be the same.

Byrnes relied on photographs to track criminals, but the problem of discerning the "real criminal" and the "true self" amid fakery and deceit was not confined to the New York City underworld. Earlier in the decade, various states, mostly in the South, had begun enacting laws to protect themselves against the fraud and forgery of government-issued bonds. William L. Royall, a former Confederate soldier and attorney who had argued numerous bond cases before the Supreme Court in the 1880s, challenged Virginia to uphold its agreement to pay back bonds at their full, pre–Civil War value. Royall was not a forger; he belonged to a politically conservative movement ("the Funders") of aristocratic planters and businessmen who wanted Virginia to honor its debt to creditors, most of whom were British.[26] Another group, the "Readjusters," made up of somewhat less conservative middle-class whites and newly emancipated blacks, wanted Virginia to repudiate or minimize its debt to help pay for infrastructure costs, such as education. In 1882, the Virginia legislature passed such an act; the following year, it passed another act to prevent fraudulent bonds by having juries determine their authenticity.[27] In a further effort to protect against fraud, the legislature required the licensing of bond salesman and lawyers. Royall refused to be licensed, sold some bonds, and got himself arrested. Although Royall argued in court that Virginia's laws violated the contract clause of Article I, section 10, of the Constitution, he wrote in his memoirs that the Readjusters had let "negro blood in the body politic."[28]

Royall's place in the 1886 corpus of cases dealing with imprisoned bodies lends itself to a study of the shifts in bodily representation taking place on the Supreme Court during the Gilded Age. *Ex parte Royall* is not just about forgery; it is a case about an imprisoned (white) body set against a free black man's body. Corporate personhood and imprisoned bodies are linked in the Court's jurisprudence in 1886 by accident of the docket. But the larger point I want to make is that the two kinds of bodies that occupied the Court's time in 1886 are inseparable, because each became a site for disciplinary tactics based on similar legal rationalities, designed to channel subjects in particular directions within society and the judicial apparatus, as well as for techniques and procedures necessary for the production of law at the turn of the century.

The law and the social sciences in the Gilded Age had created techniques for classifying various kinds of persons that produced ways of seeing subjects, which then rationalized these visions into a purposive symmetry of cultural norms and common values, for example, "white" and "colored," "health" and "illness," "authentic" and "fake," the "normal" and the "pathological." Once stabilized and categorized as such, these productive and unproductive selves were then classified in law according to their worth or appearance. Moreover, advances in statistical thinking in the late nineteenth century helped create mathematical norms that could be applied to human behavior and legal categories, which aided the development of a taxonomy of personal characteristics.[29]

The splintering of the corporate body by the midnineteenth century into levels of corporate governance forced a reconception of corporate ownership and personhood into a private versus a public self, expressions that played themselves out in the medical-juridical literature in terms of averages and norms.[30] Heightened awareness of statistical techniques and of their manipulation made it easier for the legal profession to distinguish between kinds of persons and kinds of things, that is, between "legitimate" businessmen and counterfeiters. The discovery of statistical techniques for use in anthropometry, for example, was intended as an applied science, a kind of circulatory knowledge that would use the body as its drawing board. Information about forgeries or the descriptions and activities of immigrants made its way through the body politic by means of technology and legal rules.[31]

Law in the nineteenth century had acquired "an increasingly particularistic character laying down detailed rules and procedures for a host of specialised areas of activity."[32] The state itself got involved in developing procedures for knowledge production. "A corpus of knowledge, techniques, 'scientific' discourses is formed and becomes entangled with the practice of the power to punish."[33] We can see the inventions of photography and finger-printing not as neutral and harmless creations for the suppression of crime, but note their use and appropriation for criminal statistics and tracking by agents of the state. State functionaries produced "documents, practices, and institutions" in such ways as to collapse "the distinction between 'identity' and 'identification.'"[34] Allan Sekula has written that some nineteenth-century photographers applauded "the adoption of photography by the police, arguing that convicted offenders would 'not find it easy to resume their criminal careers, while their faces and general aspects are familiar to so many, especially to the keen-sighted detective police.'"[35] Photographing criminals was neces-sary to fix the image of the criminal in popular opinion, because so many criminals "dressed[ed] up to their business."[36]

By the end of the nineteenth century, the regulation of prisoners takes on subtle, classificatory schemes, aimed specifically at the body, its shapes, marks, and protuberances. The law relies on photographs and fingerprints, phrenol-ogy, anthropometry, and eugenics to explain the subject's identity.[37] The cor-porate person becomes the photographic obverse of the criminal, the one who, unlike the entrepreneur, poses a threat to the economic well-being of fami-lies.[38] Rather than lazy and shiftless, with features that mark him as a crimi-nal, the capitalist is a "self-made man," who emphasizes "time more insistently than anyone" and who practices "more rigorously than men of any previous age the self-denial of conventional pleasures today in return for power and wealth tomorrow."[39]

William Royall was not immune to this double-sided discourse. On the one hand, this former Confederate soldier associated himself with the nation, with honor, with the business class, his English ancestors, the Constitution, and the rule of law. On the other hand, he placed himself on the side of hygiene and against racial pollution. In court, he pressed, as no one had before, for national, constitutional procedures for habeas corpus petitioners, to free his body from his home state's criminal laws, which, he thought, unjustly confined him. Yet in his memoirs, his imprisoned legal body is less important than the color of his skin. Royall projects his body into the discourse about governmen-tality taking place on multiple levels in Gilded Age America. He reifies his state's (white) traditions, raises the specter of "black blood" infiltrating the (white) body politic of Virginia, and moves away from the formal, legal description of the imprisoned body he offered in court. He shifts his argument toward a cultural and overtly racial construction of his body and the law. The Supreme Court avoids this kind of language, to be sure, focusing solely on Roy-all's claim for preconviction relief from confinement on a writ of habeas cor-pus. But within the same term, the Court found it necessary to distinguish between two kinds of bodies suitable for federal review, one productive, the other degenerate; the one potentially white, the other potentially black.

In 1886, the Supreme Court created, within the particular sociohistorical context of the corporate reconstruction of American capitalism, the type of subject who is acceptable to a legal discourse first learning to integrate capitalist economic language into its vocabulary. By constructing two different kinds of subjects in 1886, one free and protected by the federal government, the other imprisoned and subject to each state's laws and customs, the Supreme Court produced a whole new body of law, with techniques for criminal adjudications and insights into the ways to assess who is and who is not a (constitutional) person.

THE CORPORATE BODY

Corporations were created as persons in the era of criminology's turn to, and concern with, the measurable body.[40] But the invention of a corporate anatomy linked with the healthy body was not a sudden discovery in 1886. Gilded Age writers had struggled to find the proper nomenclature for all kinds of bodies. *Corporator*, a corporation organizer or stockholder, first came into use in 1784, long after the word *corporation* had been invented (the fifteenth century). Not surprisingly, "vernaculars had devised words for the extremities of human appearance—for harelips, protruding ears, or hooked noses—but lacked vocabularies for the 'normal.'"[41] The Industrial Revolution in Britain occurred without "industrialists."[42] Between the last quarter of the eighteenth century and the middle of the nineteenth, neologisms sprouted up in Britain and France to characterize the new occupations that surrounded the factory. According to François Crouzet, the "'industrialist' . . . did not emerge before the 1860s." A "large merchant-manufacturer could give out work to hundreds, even to thousands of people . . . but he was not an industrialist. . . . [H]e is the man who owns and operates the factory." "[M]anufacturer," Crouzet writes, "was used indiscriminately to mean either workman or master and more usually meant the former." By 1816, a manufacturer "designated a handloom weaver, as well as the owner of a workshop where weavers were gathered." But at the same time in Britain, "a calico printer was not a 'manufacturer,' because the word implied an owner or capitalist." "'Engineer' made its appearance in advertisements in Manchester newspapers from 1772 onwards, as applied to engineering firms; but it is another ambiguous word, and 'engine-maker,' 'machine-maker' or 'tool-maker' designated more explicitly the head of such firms."[43]

The multiple descriptions of emerging classes of workers and owners during the industrial era point to the inability of leading scientists and jurists to identify satisfactorily the place of these various classes within the legal culture. By midcentury, a technology of the self was underway. Crouzet describes a time just prior to the law's colonization of legal personhood. But the need to track criminal excess, called "recidivists" in French since 1844 (recidivism is first used in English in 1886), forced the criminal's body into view as a durable object of measurement. By 1886, then, the year of our two cases, Byrnes' book of criminal photography, *Dr. Jekyll and Mr. Hyde*, and recidivism, the criminal or deviant type is stabilized both in pictures and in words, his features reduced to specifications based on the size and shape of his ears, nose, head, and feet; the loops, arches, and whirls of his fingerprints are classified into some thirty-two different categories. The criminal is now a type of person produced by various natural and discursive elements operating within and against the body, in and around 1886. But there is no simple procedure for defining kinds of persons; the discourse over the body is itself unstable. Because "discipline is a technique, not an institution,"[44] a technology of the self is in constant operation.

Despite the flux in meaning, the Supreme Court in 1886 imposes on the corporation a new representation of the normal understanding of the new American man, the bodily expression of male power, the individual self liberated from the constraints of the past and "the molestations of society or the state."[45] The Supreme Court aids the corporate body in rejecting its former master, the state and its charter, in the name of a higher justification, legally speaking, due process, but in fact, efficiency of operation and control over resources within its domain. The corporation can now resist the state in order to exercise a minority leadership over society itself.[46] It is now the construct of a well-placed, self-interested enterprising group of persons willing to stake their lives and livelihood for economic success. As such, the corporation meets the requirements of the "balanced character," that psychological trait necessary (and applied only to elite white males) for the emerging commercial economy of the late nineteenth century.[47] Recognizing the legal significance of this shift in the corporation's meaning and structure, courts found it necessary to link the creation of corporate personhood with the analytics and technologies of power that had formed an integral part of the social and legal construction of corporate personhood in 1886.

IMPERSONATING THE BODY

For the United States Supreme Court in 1886, the idea that the corporation is a person, for Fourteenth Amendment purposes, was sufficiently plain to warrant this economical declaration: "The court does not wish to hear argument on the question whether the provisions in the Fourteenth Amendment to the Constitution, which forbids a State to deny to any person within its jurisdiction the equal protection of the laws, applies to these corporations. We are all of the opinion that it does."[48]

The traditional notion of the corporation—that is, the one beginning in English corporate law and extending through Chief Justice John Marshall's

tenure on the Supreme Court (1801–1835) and beyond—regarded the corporation as an artificial creation of the state, dependent upon its resources.
According to Marshall's opinion in *Dartmouth College* v. *Woodward* (1819),
which established the classic theory of the corporation, "A corporation is an
artificial being, invisible, intangible, and existing only in contemplation of law.
Being the mere creature of law, it possesses only those properties which the
charter of its creation confers upon it, either expressly, or as incidental to its
very existence."[49] The corporate body is not autonomous because the state is
not yet ready to cast it off; at this time, state charters explicitly limit the individual corporation's legal capacities.

Chief Justice Marshall based *Dartmouth* on *Bank of the United States* v.
Deveaux[50] (1809), where he relied on what came to be called the "creature theory" of the corporation, that is, that the corporation is a mere invention of
state legislative enactments. What is important here is that Marshall main-
tains that the state's "body" was indivisible, preventing the corporation from
being the kind of person who gets into a federal court.

> That invisible, intangible, and artificial being, that mere legal entity, a cor-
> poration aggregate, is certainly not a citizen; and, consequently, cannot sue
> or be sued in the courts of the United States, unless the rights of the mem-
> bers, in this respect, can be exercised in their corporate name. If the corpo-
> ration be considered as a mere faculty, and not as a company of individuals,
> who, in transacting their joint concerns, may use a legal name, they must be
> excluded from the courts of the union.[51]

Until the latter half of the nineteenth century, as *Deveaux* demonstrates,
the corporation was not a vehicle for private enterprise but of state development. As such, courts did not regard it in individualist terms. "Personification
meant very little when a charter specified the powers of a corporation and the
general rule was to construe charters strictly."[52] The typical corporation in the
early nineteenth century was a "device of mercantilist policy,"[53] connected to
the state's interest in economic development, in some cases charitable and
municipal corporations, in others transportation, communication, and
finance. Even up to the 1880s, "the corporation was primarily conceived of as
a legal device by which to extend public power to private individuals."[54] Legal
writers construed the early-nineteenth-century corporation as a form of state
production, or as a "socially useful instrument of economic growth."[55]

General incorporation laws emerged between 1845 and 1880, partly
because of an increase in popular hostility to the perceived injustice of special
privileges that incorporation generated and partly because "a steady stream of
small profits from corporate organization made it economic to lobby for revisions in the corporation laws rather than to achieve immediate incorporation
by paying a large initial amount."[56] Incorporation laws also gave corporations

greater legal protections against hostile state laws, by allowing corporations doing business in one state seeking to do business in another to obtain federal redress in national courts. The corporate self emerges through these transformations, not simply as a productive self or even as an autonomous self, but as a model self for a developing middle-class population to emulate. According to Mark Barkelay and Rogers Smith, "By making the corporate form almost universally available, the government would no longer be a source of immoral services to special interests but would once more be encouraging private endeavors by all that would include not only increased efficiency but equal opportunities for all conscientious Americans to obtain through their own thriving businesses."[57]

The Taney Court's *Bank of Augusta* v. *Earle*[58] (1839) provides the link between the Marshall Court's state-centered views of corporations and Justice Stephen Field's corporation-as-person jurisprudence that we find at the end of the century. In *Augusta*, an Alabama citizen had refused to honor a Georgia bank's bills of exchange. He claimed that the bank was a foreign (i.e., non-Alabamian) business and had no right to contract in a sovereign state other than its own. The bank claimed protection under the privileges and immunities clause of Article IV of the Constitution. Chief Justice Roger Taney, Marshall's successor, writing for the Court, held that corporations, though not enjoying all the rights of persons under the Constitution, do have the right to conduct business in other states if no state law prohibits them from doing so. "In its twin aspects," J. Willard Hurst has written, "*Bank of Augusta* v. *Earle* mirrored the tensions of mid-nineteenth-century public policy toward the legitimacy of the corporation."[59] On the one hand, denying corporations federal constitutional status played into the sense of "distrust of the corporation which underlay insistence that only a positive act of a sovereign might confer corporate status." On the other hand, *Bank of Augusta*'s bow toward federal comity was a recognition of the fact that "almost any businessman who wanted corporate status could get it. . . . There is at least as much concern for the federal balance as there is concern for the corporation in the policy brew of *Bank of Augusta* v. *Earle*."[60] By 1884, it was clear to a number of members of the bar that the "fiction of the 'legal person' ha[d] outlived its usefulness, and [was] no longer adequate for the purposes of an accurate treatment of the legal relations arising through the prosecution of a corporate enterprise."[61]

If, by the second half of the nineteenth century, the state no longer constituted the legal basis for corporations, what did? Persons, in the form of stockholders and interest bearers, began to make their appearance. "A successful theory," Gary Mark writes, "had to recognize the functional economic autonomy of the corporation, derived initially from the corporators and thereafter from the effective operation of the entity by its management."[62] But just as with criminals, it is not the corporate person as such in which the law is interested. It is the body and its productive forces. A technology of the body materialized in the midnineteenth century just as the corporation began to break away from the state. Late nineteenth-century technological changes in corporate structures necessitated disciplinary changes within factories, which affected working bodies and the legal relationship the corporation had with the state. "The major, publicly traded large-scale corporation constituted a new type of property" by fundamentally altering the relationship of "rights, entitlements, and obligations bundled with ownership of productive enterprise."[63] The new corporation separated out this bundle of rights, creating a hierarchy of corporate persons: an owner of the factory, a middle-level manager, and a worker. But disciplinary interventions were also increased, including "the right of authority over others participating in using the factory (an entitlement), and obligations to pay debts incurred in production."[64] The rise of boards of directors further diversified control within corporations while increasing the autonomy of corporations against the state. As William Roy states, "the socialization of ownership created by intercorporate stock ownership and common stockholders came to operate in tandem with the socialization of authority forged by shared directors, solidifying relations at the social as well as the individual level."[65]

The creation of a corporate bureaucracy by midcentury necessitated the birth of a corporate governing mentality. Middle managers at Chicago B & Q Railroad, for example, had the power to "discipline their subordinates," determine take home pay, and further careers and had "significant financial responsibility." Most of all, they were "conscious of the role they played in changing the society in which they lived."[66] Not only will these middle-level executives soon exercise considerable influence within the corporation, but they will become part of it; their output will be measurable.[67] According to Olivier Zunz, "the middle-level executive is not simply a stage in an organizational flow chart, but a specific person in a specific social circumstance whose degree of independence and whose part in a larger 'business' culture can be assessed."[68] The law does not modestly gaze at the middle-level manager; it forms his personhood, values his output, shapes his worldview. As Louis Galambos demonstrated in his study of the professional engineer, after 1880, the engineer "was already devoted to modern, corporate values—he stressed the role of group activity, the need to control emotions and remain neutral, the necessity of universal standards and highly specific definitions of responsibility."[69]

Justice Stephen Field's jurisprudence marks the shift in the conception of legal bodies in the nineteenth century. His dissents in the *Slaughterhouse Cases* (1873) and in *Munn v. Illinois*[70] (1877) express a desire to modify the perception of persons as passive and law-abiding to efficient users of constitutional rights and privileges. In the *Railroad Tax Cases*,[71] Field, riding circuit in California, made it clear that the Fourteenth Amendment protects not corporations as persons, but the persons who are part of the corporation. Field held in the *Railroad Tax Cases* that the truth of the corporation was the interests of the corporators. Field obscured the issue of the plurality of persons who constitute the corporation by asking in the singular, "Is the defendant, being a corporation, a person within the meaning of the Fourteenth Amendment, so as to be entitled, with respect to its property, to the equal protection of the laws?" But he answered in the plural: "Private corporations are, it is true, artificial persons, but with the exception of a sole corporation, with which we are not concerned, they consist of aggregations of individuals united for some legitimate business."[72] Field defined these aggregations as doing the stuff of civilization not as a unity, a corporation, but as discrete entities, as corporate persons. The following quote from the *Railroad Tax Cases*, lengthy but necessary, is an excellent example of how "the interests of the corporation become instead the interests of its members."[73] Note, also, that Field relies on the third-person plural, not the third-person singular, to make his point that it is the members of the corporation, and not the corporation itself, who deserve constitutional protection.

They engage in commerce; they build and sail ships; they cover our navigable streams with steamers; they construct houses; they bring the products of earth and sea to market; they light our streets and buildings; they open and work mines; they carry water into our cities; they build railroads, and cross mountains and deserts with them; they erect churches, colleges, lyceums, and theaters; they set up manufactories, and keep the spindle and shuttle in motion; they establish banks for savings; they insure against accidents on land and sea; they give policies on life; they make money exchanges with all parts of the world; they publish newspapers and books, and send news by lightning across the continent and under the ocean. *Indeed, there is nothing which is lawful to be done to feed and clothe our people, to beautify and adorn their dwellings, to relieve the sick, to help the needy, and to enrich and ennoble humanity, which is not to a great extent done through the instrumentalities of corporations.* . . . It would be a most singular result if a constitutional provision intended for the protection of every person against partial and discriminating legislation by the states, *should cease to exert such protection the moment the person becomes a member of a corporation.* We cannot accept such a conclusion. On the contrary, we think that it is well established by numerous adjudications of the supreme court of the United States and of the several states, that whenever a provision of the constitution, or of a law, guaranties to persons the enjoyment of property, or affords to them means for its protection, or prohibits legislation injuriously affecting it, the benefits of the provision extend to corporations, and that *the courts will always look beyond the name of the artificial being to the individuals whom it represents.*[74]

Although Field buried at the bottom of this corporate photomontage the bodies of corporate persons, the subjects of the law, those getting due process, they are not invisible to the law. As John Flynn has written, "Mesmerized by laissez-faire, classical economics and an absolutist view about the rights of property, Field converted the concept of corporate personhood into a tool for ruling out of consideration competing value choices."[75] Yet this power to exclude is not negative; it produced a particular kind of knowledge about corporate and imprisoned bodies that privileged the former at the expense of the latter. Field, after all, imprinted the corporate body into the foundation stone of federal rights, the Fourteenth Amendment. Lawyers were now free to lift the mask of corporate personhood and see what is real, the "stockholder," and what is not, the "criminal." These constitutional subjects are made actual only by the elision of those denied constitutional protections during this era, those the Constitution does not see—emancipated blacks, immigrant Asians, the poor, the hanged, the imprisoned; those, in short, who are not members of a corporation. This "ruse of discourse,"[76] which marries the nineteenth century's focus on the utility of the subject with premodern communitarianism, conceals kinds of subjects only by highlighting others.

In *Santa Clara*, the Supreme Court held that corporate bodies seeking autonomy from state regulations could be classified as property (and therefore as persons) for Fourteenth Amendment purposes. In *Royall*, the Supreme Court said that prisoners seeking federal relief were not entitled to federal protection, barring "exceptional circumstances." *Santa Clara* regards the due process clause of the Fourteenth Amendment as the privileged place for historically constituted rights, without which the body would have no order or discipline or personhood. The *Santa Clara* decision anchored the modern self in the highest legal concept the nation (prejudicially and parsimoniously) had to offer, thereby creating a struggle for national recognition among various other kinds of persons. *Santa Clara* created the autonomous, sovereign self. *Ex parte Royall*, by contrast, enforced a disciplinary understanding of the body, calling for monitoring, self-regulation, and judicial, as well as self, restraint. Without the Fourteenth Amendment, Southern Pacific Railroad is a corporation, and William Royall is a criminal. Each represents a degenerate or imperfect form of personhood in late nineteenth-century America. With the Fourteenth Amendment, Southern Pacific Railroad is a person, and William Royall is not a law breaker. The Court could abide by the former but not the latter, so it made the corporation a real person, while relegating the criminal to the states' criminal justice systems.

CONCLUSION

Creating corporate persons and denying state habeas applicants access to federal review produced a binary calculus within American law of "authentic" versus "counterfeit" and "the real" versus "the forged." Through these twofold

oppositions based on the petitioner's legal condition (the aggrieved corporation; the convicted felon) and personal characteristics (the upright citizen, the
degenerate person), the Court stabilized the differences between criminals
and corporators, creating the means to classify the motivations of actors seeking access to the federal courts in 1886 and beyond.

Eighteen eighty-six, then, marks the beginning of a judicial turn toward
the surveillance of bodies for the purpose of classification. It denotes the
beginning of the recognition by legal elites of the body's capacity to produce
healthful and dangerous things simultaneously and of the perception of bodies as resources, some of which promote, some of which exploit, governmental services. The *Santa Clara* decision did not just declare corporate personhood, it was

> the product of an ideological elite seeking to impose its values on society
> during a time of revolutionary economic change through an institution
> whose role as a branch of government was changing dramatically. The
> Court's role was shifting from a subservient branch of government in eco-
> nomic policy making to that of the principal branch of government in defin-
> ing both economic policy and the role of government in implementing the
> policy defined.[77]

This discursive struggle for a particular truth about what the law and its relationship to corporations provides excludes by definition other notions of truth
about what the law and its relationship to persons who challenge the criminal
law provide. Read together, *Santa Clara* and *Royall* form a kind of master-
slave dialectic. But there is no synthesis, no recognition of the other as one's
self. *Santa Clara/Royall* creates, indeed embeds in American legal consciousness, a binary distinction between two kinds of selves at the dawn of their
birth, the one industrious, the other injudicious. As the following chapters will
show, this narrative turn will influence the Court's understanding of federalism and of habeas corpus for many years.

THREE

Habeas Corpus as Counternarrative

The Rise of Due Process, 1923–1953

Not until comparatively lately has much attention been given to
the way in which criminals are produced. It was with them much
as it was at one time with lunatics: to say of the former that they
were wicked, and of the latter that they were mad, was thought
to render any further inquiry superfluous. It is certain, however,
that lunatics and criminals are as much manufactured articles as
are steam-engines and calico-printing machines, only the
processes of the organic manufactory are so complex that we are
not able to follow them. They are neither accidents nor anom-
alies in the universe, but come by law and testify to causality.
—Maudsley, *Responsibility in Mental Diseases*

THIS CHAPTER ANALYZES the development of habeas corpus within the context of a legal system still restrained by, but no longer beholden to, a nineteenth-
century understanding of federalism.[1] What began as a defense of federal-state
comity rooted in institutional constraints and constitutional traditions now
turned its attention to narratives of violence, directed in part at examining the
states' manner of obtaining confessions but pointed mostly in the direction of
the habeas petitioner's established guilt, his behavior toward the court, his racial
background, and his previous record of violence. This chapter, then, analyzes
habeas corpus as federalism began to weaken as a jurisdictional device designed

to thwart federal habeas review, and narratives of violence made their appearance. Neither side achieved victory, but the casting aside of the jurisdiction standard, and the introduction of stories of state-sanctioned violence toward outcast minorities, changed the tenor of habeas corpus throughout this era.

Freed during the first quarter of the twentieth century from relying exclusively on the states' determination of guilt to restrain prisoners from contesting their sentences in federal courts, the Supreme Court, during habeas' second wave, turned toward vilifying criminal bodies, focusing on their guilt and the threat that their habeas petitions posed to the integrity of the states' criminal justice apparatuses. Perhaps because of the extent to which the accuracy and validity of various states' criminal justice institutions had been called into question by the persistence of lynching and torture during the Jim Crow era, the emphasis on the demands for judicial restraint turned increasingly toward the prisoners themselves, their bodies and behaviors, in particular, their ability to maneuver through the jurisdictional maze placed in their path by the Supreme Court during the latter half of the nineteenth century. No longer capable of sending habeas petitioners back to the state courts because the grand tradition of state deference demanded it, the Court turned to rejecting habeas petitions on more intricate grounds, notably, issues of timing, as in *Daniels* v. *Allen* (1953), where the Court upheld North Carolina's rejection of an appeal filed one day late, because, it said, "A period of limitation accords with our conception of proper procedure."[2]

By the late 1920s and early 1930s, the Court's defense of property rights through a substantive reading of the due process clause of the Fourteenth Amendment had unintentionally opened the door for convicted criminals (and criminal syndicalists, anarchists, and Communists as well) to contest their state sentences in collateral habeas proceedings. But the Hughes Court (1930–1941) was not in a position to do for criminal defendants what the Warren Court (1953–1969) would do some thirty years later: apply amendments Four through Eight directly to state petitioners via the Fourteenth Amendment. Rather, a new though more enigmatic judicial discourse entered into the Court's criminal jurisprudence during the 1930s, one largely based on moderate extensions of constitutional protections to hitherto excluded persons that was intent on managing that risk.[3]

The method adopted by the Court was to turn the spotlight onto the states' criminal justice procedures and bring into the conversation the stories of abuse inflicted by agents acting under color of state law. Regardless of the technicalities involved in habeas petitions by the late 1940s, which are discussed later in this chapter, the discursive emphasis shifts away from the constitutional dignity of state criminal institutions and toward developing new strategies for incorporating the Bill of Rights, based in part on institutional means but also on storytelling. This era is marked by the appearance of narratives of violence replacing dissertations on federal-state comity relations.

Relying less on institutional factors that had performed the dual function of simultaneously repressing and liberating rights for almost a century, the Court's discourse, from the Progressive era to midcentury, was specifically directed at the anatomies, morphologies, and physiognomies of criminal defendants and their potential for future dangerousness if released on habeas corpus. Operating in the twilight of substantive due process for corporations, the Court focused on juridical and administrative symbols to discern who is eligible for constitutional protections. Discourses, as Alan Hunt and Gary Wickham remind us, "put in place a set of linked signs."[4] By the 1930s, habeas petitions turn into due process stories. As it did for property in the nineteenth century, due process opens up the tap of narrative. The difference is that now the convicted habeas petitioner is the new sign of the new era in constitutional jurisprudence, not the corporation.

Ashcraft v. *Tennessee* (1944) is the Supreme Court's first opinion in the modern era that clarifies the lines I am discussing, regarding the split between narratives of violence that are used to give a voice to the accused and a continued reliance on a nineteenth-century narrative of federal structures. In *Ashcraft*, Justice Hugo Black garnered a majority of the Court for the proposition that "if Ashcraft made a confession it was not voluntary but compelled."[5] *Ashcraft* came on the heels of a number of Supreme Court cases, from the early 1930s through the early years of World War II dealing with coerced confessions, most of which were decided unanimously or with near total unanimity in favor of the defendant. *Ashcraft* reveals the break in that pattern. Justice Robert Jackson dissented, beginning his opinion as if the state of Tennessee were on trial, not Ashcraft. "A sovereign state is now before us," he wrote, "summoned on the charge that it has obtained convictions by methods so unfair that a federal court must set aside what the state courts have done."[6] Justice Jackson lamented the passing of the time when the Court would regularly give the state the "benefit of a presumption of regularity and legality."[7] Instead, during the dawn of the personal narrative that operated under the banner of the Fourteenth Amendment, the petitioner occupies center stage, his identity formed in part by his own plea for relief, as well as the Court's impressionistic constructions of legality, only peripherally rooted in established constitutional norms. The petitioner's growth is the state's retraction. Due process remains a zero-sum game. The last case of this chapter, *Brown* v. *Allen* (1953), not unlike *Ashcraft* in some respects, will pursue this argument further.

CONSTRUCTING THE CRIMINAL

Law is not the only discipline concerned with the manufacture of identities, but it plays an important role in contributing to the development of discursive practices within which our knowledge of social life is contained. Narratives of violence can both perpetuate and undermine the status quo. Formal legal reasoning that functions as narrative, for example, the retelling of crimes for the purpose of justifying confinement, can produce "hegemonic tales—stories that reproduce existing relations of power and inequity."[8] However, Rosemary Coombe sees the social constructivist vision as a counternarrative, devoted to the "provisional, fluid, strategic, and contested identities constructed in contexts mediated by law."[9] Supreme Court opinions function from both sides of the narrative divide.

Operating with a concern for future dangerousness long before that term became fashionable, late nineteenth- and early twentieth-century judicial discourse literally created kinds of legal persons, separated only by the Court's understanding of who qualifies for Fourteenth Amendment protection. Within the fin de siècle legal community, the law viewed itself not as an isolated and idealistic discipline but as part of the larger project of modernist social science, whose principal task is to obtain knowledge. State and federal courts during the Gilded Age, for example, were confronted with innovative jurisdictional and administrative challenges to the many new laws relating to forms of property confiscation, the appearance of fraud, the regulation of industry and working hours, and criminal behavior punishable by new forms of execution.[10] Forced to adapt (and therefore classify) these new forms of knowledge, the judiciary created constitutional types out of the language of the due process clause of the Fourteenth Amendment. In turn, these decisions, over time, created legal images of what kinds of persons qualified for constitutional protection under the Fourteenth Amendment's due process clause and what kinds did not. Ostensibly for reasons of economy, the courts created a catalog of persons out of the Fourteenth Amendment, the property privileged and the criminally undeserving. As I discussed in the previous chapter, the corporator, or the one with vested financial interests in a corporation, was produced by a number of federal court cases that equated property with due process and industriousness with the Constitution. Once the federal courts protected property by invoking the Fourteenth Amendment, they constructed an image of the holder of property, the kind of person, that is, who is worthy of constitutional protection. This constitutional fabrication of corporate personhood was not to be seen as a usurpation of the nation's resources, despite the fact that both criminals and corporators in the late nineteenth century were making similar claims about the content of state laws. Rather, corporate personhood bestowed national rights on entities that could successfully prove that due process applied to them, because their success was related to, if not substantively tied into, the very meaning of what it is to be a person, constitutional or otherwise.

However, criminals had no reserve fund that they could spend in courts or legislatures. Lawrence Friedman says that criminals were "men at the bottom of the heap."[11] Criminals, after all, did not create steam engines or bridges; they stole them or slept under them. Stamped as threats to public safety, destroyers of public morals and order, criminals were easily categorized as dangerous and in need of confinement. In large part, cases involving the writ of habeas corpus that came out of the 1930s and 1940s provide the linguistic framework around which the discourse of dangerousness emerged. The reason has do to with the Court's creation of a hierarchy of concerns regarding both the problem of recidivism and the need for deference to state court findings of guilt over the concerns (expressed by the convicted) for rectifying constitutional improprieties. The criminal type developed in the latter half of the nineteenth century by virtue of the fact that the Fourteenth Amendment did not recognize the accused as a constitutional person. (In constitutional language, the Fourteenth Amendment did not yet incorporate the criminal procedure amendments of the Bill of Rights.) Juries, trial records, prosecutors, and medical professionals defined the criminal's "personhood" for him or her. Consequently, any person attacking a conviction was, constitutionally speaking, already beneath the law.

In the last decades of the nineteenth century, images of the potential for criminal irresponsibility emerged largely out of habeas corpus cases because habeas cases involved thick narrative descriptions of already convicted criminals contesting the grounds of their confinement on relatively novel constitutional arguments (for example, the applicability of the Fifth or Eighth Amendments to the states). Recognizing the potential for endless appeals that could undermine state justice systems and overrun the federal courts, late nineteenth-century habeas jurisprudence was attuned to the problem of what would later be called "societal costs." In *Moore* v. *Dempsey* (1923), a case discussed in depth later in this chapter, Justice James McReynolds, writing in dissent, argued against granting habeas corpus to six black men convicted of murder in the first degree, because, he wrote, "If every man convicted of a crime in a state court may thereafter resort to the federal court and by swearing, as advised, that certain allegations of fact tending to impeach his trial are "true to the best of his knowledge and belief," and thereby obtain as of right further review, another way has been added to a list already unfortunately long to prevent prompt punishment."[12] The habeas petition brings forth the criminal; it establishes her identity, marks her crime, exposes her temerity and in the process, facilitates both the assessment of the potential for future dangerousness and the narrative construction of the criminal as a persistent pest and a commandeer of constitutional language.

Justice Jackson's concurring opinion in *Brown* v. *Allen* (1953) is a trenchant description of the lost language of federalism-based constitutional adjudication that arose at midcentury as a result of a habeas petition that challenged not only the state's conviction but also its ability to render a fair judgment. Brown's habeas petition alleged that North Carolina's jury system was historically biased against blacks and remained so. The Court disagreed with Brown's restatement of the facts of North Carolina's history of racial exclusion on juries and denied his challenge. But the majority opinion is muddied by the Court's willingness to look into Brown's charges, thereby questioning the state's presentation of facts as well as its jurisdiction over the case. Concurring in the Court's decision to deny to Brown (and two other petitioners) the writ of habeas corpus, Justice Jackson mourned the loss of a determinate language by which the Court could uphold a conviction for rape. The Court's dominant narrative, as presented by Justice James Byrnes, is as follows.

> This situation confronts us. North Carolina furnished a criminal court for the trial of those charged with crime. Petitioners at all times had counsel, chosen by themselves and recognized by North Carolina as competent to conduct the defense. In that court all petitioners' objections and proposals whether of jury discrimination, admission of confessions, instructions or otherwise were heard and decided against petitioners. The state furnished an adequate and easily-complied-with method of appeal. This included a means to serve the state of the case on appeal in the absence of the prosecutor from his office. Yet petitioners' appeal was not taken and the State of North Carolina, although the full trial record and state on appeal were before it, refused to consider the appeal on its merits.
>
> The writ of habeas corpus in federal courts is not authorized for state prisoners at the discretion of the federal court. It is only authorized when a state prisoner is in custody in violation of the Constitution of the United States. That fact is not to be tested by the use of habeas corpus in lieu of an appeal. To allow habeas corpus in such circumstances would subvert the entire system of state criminal justice and destroy state energy in the detection and punishment of crime.[13]

Despite the easy-going formalism of Justice Byrnes' statement, that habeas corpus must be denied because respect for state law means upholding swift and effective punishment, there is more to this case than meets the eye. Justice Jackson's opinion in *Brown*, which closes out this chapter, sees beneath the formalism upon which he himself relies, and offers a critique of habeas corpus based on the petitioner's crime and the problem that habeas corpus poses to the federal judiciary, both of which will form the basis for the battle over habeas corpus in the 1960s.

Habeas petitioners appear dangerous in this era, then, partly because of their crimes, partly because of their potential for future crimes, but most of all, because of their linguistic struggle to force the Court to apply constitutional protections to them as it did to property holders. They ask the Court to respect and grant them the same privileges and immunities, the same equal protection, the same due process as was given to the inventor of the steam engine. Convicted criminals as habeas petitioners do not challenge the law as an abstraction. Rather, they call into question the language of the law that justifies distinctions between persons, which is exactly what disturbs Justice Jackson, because it reconfigures the framework within which judges determine who is and who is not a person, who is and who is not guilty, and who has the body and who does not. The habeas petitioner, in an effort to keep open the constitutional space given to the convicted by the Habeas Corpus Act of 1867—the space that allows the convicted to be a constitutional person, protected by federal courts—must rely on constant critique of the law rather than demonstrations of remorse,[14] because the law always already presumes "nonpersonhood" in habeas criminality. For the courts, the habeas petitioner operates without clean hands; his (legally valid) conviction being the reason for his appeal, the habeas challenge is seen as a threat to the very purpose of punishment.[15] Habeas corpus allows the convicted criminal to separate guilt from procedural infractions that, he or she might argue, produced the guilt in the first case. A habeas petition does more than prevent and delay justice, it subtracts from its justification; it creates doubt.

The Hughes Court's increasing dependence on narratives during the 1930s represents a discursive shift away from the states' institutional support for their criminal justice goals. The objective of this chapter, then, is to analyze the Supreme Court's role in producing these characterizations by focusing on a number of key cases that spanned the Court's movement away from restrictions on habeas corpus to the opening up of federal habeas avenues. I will focus on the narratives of violence produced by Supreme Court decisions, in particular, the way in which criminals are constructed, criminality structured, and appeals denied.

COUNTERNARRATIVES OF VIOLENCE

The purpose of early twentieth-century narratives of crime was to shed light on the problem of civil liberties in a federal republic. By the 1930s, the Court began introducing more detailed storytelling into its decisions. The reason is rooted in the structural concerns in which midcentury justices were engaged. Hitherto excluded by the twin grand narratives of the nineteenth century, a reliance on federal-state comity and the protection of property, the subject of American constitutional law, the criminally accused, had historically been covered over by these larger institutional interests. As Felix Frankfurter wrote in *Screws* v. *United States*: "Observance of this basic principle [federalism] under our system of Government has led this Court to abstain, even under more tempting circumstances than those now here, from needless extension of federal criminal authority into matters that normally are of state concern and for which the States had best be charged with responsibility."[16] But in an effort to gain acceptance for the idea that the Fourteenth Amendment applied to the states through the various amendments of the Bill of Rights, the Supreme Court offered up narratives that were often detailed descriptions of violence committed against minorities to extort confessions.[17] These narratives were not designed to upset federal-state relations; but it was understood that they would cause institutional friction because so many of the confessional narratives involved white police officers extracting confessions from illiterate or semieducated black men through violence and intimidation that took place in forbidding surroundings.

The New Deal Court's twofold concern was to serve as a counterbalance to the state's demonstration of a recalcitrant suspect who is already guilty, while at the same time trying to maintain the boundary between legitimate and ill-considered federal intervention in criminal justice. Thus, to take one exemplary case, in *Ward* v. *Texas*[18] (1942), the Court held that extorted confessions were unconstitutional, despite the fact that it could not but acknowledge that "[e]ach State has the right to prescribe the tests governing the admissibility of a confession."[19] Ward, who was black, killed a white man. But the "[p]etitioner's contention that he was beaten, whipped and burned by Sheriff Sweeten just before the confession was made, however, was squarely denied" by the police. The Court supplied the narrative.

> All of the officers involved asserted that [Ward] had not been mistreated, with the exception of the slap by [officer] Redfearn. Sweeten's explanation of how the confession was obtained was: "We just talked that confession out of him. It took us 20 to 30 minutes to get that confession." And one of the patrolmen who took petitioner to the jail in Athens stated: "We just talked to him to get that statement. Yes sir, we just sweet talked him out of it." Several witnesses who were not officers testified that they had examined petitioner's body and found no bruises or burns. Only the sheriff of Titus county corroborated petitioner's charges. He testified that when petitioner was back in the Gilmer jail several days after the confession, "I saw some marks on his neck and shoulders and arms that appeared to be cigarette stub burns. Yes sir, they were fresh. There were several of them on his body."[20]

Respect for federalism clearly pervades the Court's opinion, but it is also clear that the Court could no longer concern itself with the niceties of federal-state comity relations. Justice Byrnes relied on the Court's more liberal due process decisions of the past three decades to provide Ward with a remedy.

> This Court has set aside convictions based upon confessions extorted from ignorant persons who have been subjected to persistent and protracted questioning, or who have been threatened with mob violence, or who have been

unlawfully held incommunicado without advice of friends or counsel, or who
have been taken at night to lonely and isolated places for questioning. Any
one of these grounds would be sufficient cause for reversal. All of them are
to be found in this case.[21]

At times during the New Deal Court, the justices used descriptions of violent
behavior to reinforce the criminal's dangerous past and potentially dangerous
future.[22] But overall, the use of thick descriptions of violence during this era
against outcast minorities (both state sanctioned and otherwise) had a twofold
purpose that benefited the habeas petitioner.

The first relates to the problem of knowledge that is produced by the
struggle between law and the social sciences over determining the boundaries
of the legal self. It is to some degree a question of regulation. The administrative power of government in this regard "consists in the deployment of
social scientific knowledge to the end of societal normalisation."[23] The passage
from law to norm effaces the legal subject's individuality. In terms of the legal
structuralism we are encountering in the 1930s, the author of the state's violence—the criminal—is canceled out and replaced by a functionalist narrative
favoring harmony between federal and state jurisdictions. It is thus no accident that not once in *Brown* v. *Allen* is Brown's first name mentioned. The
Court consistently calls him "petitioner, a Negro." Concerns for institutional
integrity surround the criminal and deny his personality, his legal standing as
a person. To be sure, the Court's structuralist narrative is also a humanist one:
it presupposes that the world is explainable and that language can capture that
reality. What the Court does for added effect, as it were, is to announce that
only it can describe that reality, not the convicted criminal.

Knowledge of crime gets filtered through institutions and the mechanisms
of political power. By invoking constitutional amendments, habeas petitioners
follow the patterns of accepted legal language and practice. But the language,
particularly "equal protection" and "due process," is sufficiently vague as to
undermine any conception of determinate legal understanding that we all
share. Yet by the 1930s, the Court begins to accept the prisoner's tale, thereby
upsetting the structuralist paradigm of a closed-off system that denies individuality. The prisoner on death row is the isolated element in the system, who
now has an avenue for his protest. The Supreme Court institutionalizes the
prisoner's story in a legal narrative before doing so constitutionally.

In telling tales about lynchings, beatings, and indiscriminate violence
against outcast minorities that the state courts had ruled did not violate constitutional norms, midcentury narratives of violence from the Supreme Court
demonstrated before the entire federal government (and to a lesser extent, the
general public) the way in which minorities were being treated at the local
level, by pointing not just to the maltreatment of blacks by whites living in particular areas of the country but also to the failure of the states (and presumably

Congress) to take responsibility for the protection of civil rights.[24] These opinions, written by the more progressive justices on the New Deal Court, such as Black, William Douglas, Frankfurter, Wiley Rutledge, and Frank Murphy, contested the narrative orthodoxies of previous Courts that had celebrated federalism and punishment as the twin objects of law, while ignoring the subject's plea. They formed counternarratives to the Court's overall image of criminality as inherited deviance. The idea is that these counternarratives are not merely poignant but that they point to the limits of raw instrumentalism and legal functionalism inherent in the Court's pre-New Deal jurisprudence. Larger issues of systemic state-authorized violent behavior toward racial minorities, and the inabilities of minorities to have their convictions overturned by state appellate courts, become factual bases for critical inquiry into state criminal justice procedures. Institutionally, these stories serve as the reason for reversing the constitutional construct of deference to state police powers. By telling stories of state-sanctioned violence, criminals become persons entitled to due process of law. But more important, from the standpoint of social science and law, patterns and knowledge about race and crime emerge out of these stories, revealing the failure of the states and the federal government to act on the levels of violence going on in the streets and back roads of urban and small-town America.

In fact, the legal realists could not contain these stories within their own formalistic understanding of law, because narratives of violence cut through their institutional and legal determinism. Narratives of lynching and of coerced confessions, by virtue of their exposé of state police practices, revealed the problem of judicial resolution along purely institutional lines. What purpose was served by alleviating the individual injustice in *Powell* v. *Alabama*, for example, without addressing the entrenched problem of black-white relations and its effect on the right to counsel? For liberal New Dealers, the point of entry into the story is what the state has left out of its judicial narrative: the beating, the denial, the abuse of basic criminal procedures, all of which called into question the stability of the institutions the legal realists sought to protect. For conservative justices, by contrast, the point of entry is the creation of the victim: the murder itself. On the New Deal Court, these two narratives were somewhat in tension; on the Rehnquist Court, the latter narrative becomes dominant.

In an institutional sense, these New Deal narratives can be seen as forms of reconnaissance; they speak to the problem of how national elites acquired access to information about legal, social, and economic events in a highly complex, fragmented, and separated system of criminal justice and how that knowledge got disseminated. For the midcentury liberal justices on the Supreme Court, storytelling unified the constitutional universe of state-sanctioned violence against minorities by making clear the connection between the abstraction "due process of law" and the demands of observing proper criminal procedures in the modern era. By using the language of rights hitherto applied only to property owners, these justices created a clearing for federal judicial intervention on broadly conceived civil rights questions, if not immediately then in the future.[25]

Deference to state court criminal opinions may be justified by conceptions of functionalism, the importance of maintaining structural efficiency in a splintered and patchwork political system, and the desirability of punishment, as Justices Sandra Day O'Connor and William Rehnquist often argue,[26] but the creation of such policies in relation to claims usually made by outcast minorities points not to the strength of this kind of institutional logic but to the personal unwillingness of national actors to apply knowledge (and extend political power) learned from events below. The power, in other words, is already there, as the narratives reveal, and corporations benefitted from it for more than fifty years. Resistance to legal change based on knowledge gained from facts, and individual pleas for justice that describe personal horror at the hands of the police without reaching the law, reifies the status quo; it is the denial of institutional and personal autonomy. Narratives fill in the knowledge gap that functionalists disregard. Narratives are acts of transgression, but up to a point, and no further.

Narratives open up a window, but often they do not provide a resolution to actually existing contradictions. Thus, in looking at criminal case law in particular as a source for legal and political knowledge, in that it presents Supreme Court justices as social actors concerned about political, economic, and racial configurations in society, the personal weaknesses of the justices, fostered by institutional overlap and the inherent inconsistencies of the federal state to act against individual and state-sponsored violence directed at minorities, are demonstrated. Judicial storytelling that does not rise to the level of a judicial order, along the lines of school busing or prison reform, is phantom knowledge, white noise that has yet to turn into a clear signal for reform.

In *Culombe* v. *Connecticut* (1961), for example, Felix Frankfurter spent so much time going over Connecticut's abuse of Arthur Culombe, a "33-year old illiterate mental defective of the moron class who was suggestible and subject to intimidation," that Earl Warren categorized Frankfurter's majority opinion overturning Culombe's conviction as "in the nature of an advisory opinion"[27] and stated in his concurrence that he would wait for another case before expounding on the constitutional problems of such police tactics sanctioned by state courts. Narratives are not useless, but their value can easily be ascribed a lower order within a tightly wound federal-state criminal justice system that searches relentlessly for short-term conclusions. Narratives of state-sanctioned violence accumulate facts, take into consideration interests, and expose society's fault lines. But from a policymaking standpoint, they can fail to accomplish their goal if all the dusty volumes of U.S. Reports amount to nothing more than a "deep grave under an enormous sand pile of social knowledge."[28]

The result of the New Deal Court's reversing the constitutional calculus of protecting certain kinds of subjects based on personal characteristics, particularly concerns related to morality and immorality that were themselves linked to property holding, subverted historically and constitutionally sanctioned beliefs about governmental limits and undermined the stability of the existing federal-state relationship. In effect, this is related to the second, more pragmatic purpose in highlighting detailed, graphic imagery of violence against minorities: to demonstrate the effects on actual persons of not applying the Fourteenth Amendment's due process clause to the states. Throughout the nineteenth century, the Court's silences regarding petitioners' narratives reinforced the absence of a constitutional complaint. States and individuals acting under color of state law got away with murder, not because the Court could find no breach of the law, but because the Court could not find the person harmed by law. Narratives of violence spread knowledge and tell us who the petitioner is and what happened to him or her.

As the nineteenth century drew to a close, the "murderer grew in stature; the meaning of murder, its metaphysics, was no longer evident in the event but in its main actor."[29] Michel Foucault locates the turn toward the criminal body in European penology from the "first congress on Criminal Anthropology (1885) to Prinz's publication of his *Social Defence* (1910)."[30] It should come as no surprise that the United States duplicated this pattern. Between Charles Guiteau's assassination of President James Garfield in 1881 and Leon Czolgosz's assassination of President William McKinley in 1901, medical writers increasingly turned to various technological and statistical advances to match personal identities to criminal typologies. Fears of the pollution of the social body merged with the fear of the body itself.[31] The McKinley assassination in particular drew the attention of medical professionals to the problem of immigration, the rise of anarchism, and the vices of city life. Overall, these two assassinations shook the medical and legal professions out of their search for the moral causes of insanity and violence; the problem was deeper and, at the same time, more on the surface. Criminology turned toward the body.

Recognizing that murderers come to us with a "maximum of consequences [but with] a minimum of warning, the most effects and the fewest signs,"[32] American scientists and forensic criminologists began to map the human body to find the sources of deviant criminal behavior. Following Garfield's assassination, the *American Journal of Insanity*, for example, explicitly turned toward the body and its various types in an effort to bring scientific clarity to the problem of insanity and dangerousness. Relying on new developments in forensic sciences, such as fingerprinting and anthropometry, the editors of the journal were now free to ignore the problem of "moral insanity" that had plagued nineteenth-century psychology. They began publishing numerous articles that focused on the study of jaws, brain sizes, and palates, all testifying to the important link between physical traits and the potential for crime.[33] As the fear of criminal, racialized, and foreign influences within the United States grew from the last quarter of the nineteenth century to the first quarter of the twentieth, and as press reports about murder trials increasingly focused on the unexplainable motives of criminal defendants who killed children or women or parents and siblings, the penal-medical apparatus turned to fingerprinting, anthropometry, and phrenology to assess the "stigmata of degeneration" and mark the future dangerousness of the native born as much as of aliens and immigrants.[34]

The courts, following developments in the natural sciences, increasingly embedded dangerousness within the criminal's body, which was replete with unread signs. Anthropometry mapped the body, searching for navigational patterns that could make the body speak the truth of its criminal history. If the anthropometrist found a match between one person's file and another, the criminal came into view, like a photograph,[35] and was given a name, first an offender, then a recidivist. With a healthy reliance on statistics, the law did not simply name the pathological condition; it also constituted the criminal. The contours of one's head or hands and feet, the size and shape of one's extremities, the predilections toward vagabondage or talkativeness or silence—all were sediments of one's character, layers to be dissected by a forensic criminologist until a self emerged, ready for punishment.

Brown v. *Mississippi* (1936) represents both a structural and a discursive turning point in constitutional law and the discourse about dangerous bodies. In *Brown*, Chief Justice Charles Evans Hughes shifted the focus of the story of a coerced confession case from the conclusion (the state had denied Brown his due process rights) to the events that led up to the conviction in question.

The crime with which these defendants, all ignorant negroes, are charged, was discovered about 1 o'clock p.m. on Friday, March 30, 1934. On that night one Dial, a deputy sheriff, accompanied by others, came to the home of Ellington, one of the defendants, and requested him to accompany them to the house of the deceased, and there a number of white men were gathered, who began to accuse the defendant of the crime. Upon his denial they seized him, and with the participation of the deputy they hanged him by a rope to the limb of a tree, and, having let him down, they hung him again, and when he was let down the second time, and he still protested his innocence, he was tied to a tree and whipped, and, still declining to accede to the demands that he confess, he was finally released, and he returned with some difficulty to his home, suffering intense pain and agony. The record of the testimony shows that the signs of the rope on his neck were plainly visible during the so-called trial. A day or two thereafter the said deputy, accompanied by another, returned to the home of the said defendant and arrested him, and departed with the prisoner towards the jail in an adjoining county, but went by a route which led into the state of Alabama; and while on the

way, in that state, the deputy stopped and again severely whipped the defendant, declaring that he would continue the whipping until he confessed, and
the defendant then agreed to confess to such a statement as the deputy
would dictate, and he did so, after which he was delivered to jail. . . . Further
details of the brutal treatment to which these helpless prisoners were subjected need not be pursued. It is sufficient to say that in pertinent respects
the transcript reads more like pages torn from some medieval account than
a record made within the confines of a modern civilization which aspires to
an enlightened constitutional government.[36]

Brown represents a significant discursive turn from structure to subject in
Supreme Court criminal jurisprudence. The *Brown* opinion could not have
been possible without the nineteenth-century's reliance on the scientific study
of criminals. This is what makes Chief Justice Hughes' dicta so extraordinary.
He highlights the criminal's body, but not as a subject of derision. He turns
Brown's body into a constitutional remedy. It is a carrier of rights and not of
stigma. In opening up a space for the individual criminal defendant to appear
in a Supreme Court case, particularly a lynched black man, the Court recon-
figured the body of all future Fourteenth Amendment petitioners, from
(white) property owners to (minority) criminal defendants.

FEDERALISM AND FINALITY

Unlike the exhaustion doctrine, which is a prophylactic device designed to
protect the state courts from ultimate federal review, the jurisdiction standard
was rooted in the formal division of governmental authority between state and
nation, a division that did not allow for the introduction of storytelling. Thus,
if the Court avoided categorizing the criminal in anthropological terms, it is
because it could rely on jurisdictional support, which was historically based in
the language of the Constitution. The Court in *Frank* v. *Magnum* had relied
prominently on the jurisdiction standard. *Frank* demonstrated how the Court
subordinated concerns over changing social patterns in the undeveloped
twentieth-century South to the legal remnants of antebellum America. The
beginning of the New Deal did not change these jurisprudential patterns.

The years just before and after the New Deal form an intermediate era in
habeas' growth, a period of flux in the Constitution's development toward individual rights that denies easy categorization. The redundant "dual federalism" of
the nineteenth century became the uncertain "cooperative federalism" of the
1940s but without any discernable impact on the development of constitutional
rights. Elites, resigned toward the structural constraints on rights seemingly
embedded in the Constitution, failed to protect minorities from majoritarian
enmity in the name of federalism. Centralization remained an economic concept.

On an institutional level, the claim that what applies to the federal government applies, more or less, to the states challenged federalism concerns during this era. Justice Wiley Rutledge, one of the most liberal members of the New Deal Court, viewed the purpose of the writ of habeas corpus extra-institutionally, "not only to determine points of jurisdiction . . . and constitutional questions, but whenever else resort to it is necessary to prevent a complete miscarriage of justice."[37] Not until Justice William Brennan joined the Court were such views again held. Justice Rutledge was not bound by functional considerations of prison capacities, balancing tests, and jurisdictional formalities, as so many justices in the nineteenth century were. To Rutledge, "considerations of economy of judicial time and procedures, important as they undoubtedly are, become comparatively insignificant" in the face of an unconstitutional detention.[38] From 1923 to 1948, when Congress codified habeas corpus,[39] the Court grappled with jurisdictional and exhaustion problems in habeas cases without resolution. Changing members of the Supreme Court alleviated some of the jurisdictional burdens imposed on state prisoners, but these new justices failed to address the more direct question of finality: which level of government has ultimate say regarding the freedom of the individual? Specifically, in regard to habeas corpus after *Frank* v. *Magnum*, the question to be considered is: "Under what circumstances should a federal district court on habeas corpus have the power to redetermine the merits of federal questions decided by the state courts in the course of state criminal cases?"[40]

The Aftermath of Frank *v.* Magnum: *Due Process Reconsidered*

On appeal from the federal court for the eastern district of Arkansas, which had rejected the petitioners' habeas corpus claims of unlawful detention, *Moore* v. *Dempsey* arrived at the Supreme Court in 1923.

For their participation in a racial "insurrection" near Elaine, Arkansas, the state sentenced six blacks to death.[41] Approximately 5 whites had been killed, while the number of blacks killed has been estimated to be as high as 250.[42] Altogether, the all-white grand jury initially indicted 122 blacks. After the trial, 11 were sentenced to death, and 54 were given prison terms, none exceeding 21 years. The police later apprehended a twelfth man who was also sentenced to death. For appellate purposes, the state divided the men into two groups of 6. The state granted one group a new trial and subsequently released them because of constitutional defects.[43] The second group provides us with some insight into the habeas corpus process before the due process revolution of the 1960s.

One year after the conviction of the six in 1920, they lost their appeal in the Arkansas supreme court. Like Leo Frank's case, a mob outside the courtroom dominated the trial, demanding "justice" from the court in lieu of lynching. Frank Moore's court-appointed attorney did not ask for a change of venue or for separate trials for the six defendants. Indeed, "there is no record that any of the attorneys asked for a continuance to put together a defense."[44] The trial lasted three-quarters of an hour, and the all-white jury deliberated for five minutes before returning with a guilty verdict. At no time did the state supreme court conduct an inquiry into the truth of the allegations of mob domination. An execution date was set for June 10, 1921, but was stayed pending the outcome of further appeals.[45]

Did the state provide Moore with an adequate opportunity to raise his constitutional allegations in the state appellate process? If not, then a federal habeas judge was empowered by law to investigate the facts of the case. Justice Oliver Wendell Holmes wrote the 7:2 decision in favor of the defendants' claims and reversed and remanded the case. On remand in the state court, the six were released.

Citing his dissent in *Frank* v. *Magnum*, Holmes held that a trial dominated by a mob violated the due process clause of the Fourteenth Amendment. A federal judge cannot "escape the duty of examining the facts when if true as alleged they make the trial absolutely void."[46] On the one hand, Holmes was constrained in part by Justice Mahlon Pitney's decision in *Frank*, which declared that due process is satisfied in habeas corpus cases if the state provides "notice, and a hearing, or an opportunity to be heard, before a court of competent jurisdiction, according to established modes of procedure."[47] On the other hand, Holmes held, "It is certainly true that mere mistakes of law in the course of a trial are not to be corrected [by habeas corpus]. But if the case is that the whole proceeding is a mask . . . [then nothing] can prevent this Court from securing to the petitioners their constitutional rights."[48] Holmes thought that this concern for procedure was lacking in *Moore*, and it provided him with a way around the institutional restrictions *Frank* had bestowed on the Court's habeas jurisdiction. If the proceedings were a mask for the power of local elites, and the procedural violations had substantive weight, then Holmes would have to discern the real issue from what had been obscured and couch it in constitutional terms sufficient to ground the granting of the writ within the legal tradition of respect for state criminal jurisdictions. A counternarrative of events would have to replace the trial court record as the source for judicial knowledge regarding the application of constitutional principles. But Holmes did not open up a second front, in terms of addressing both the race riot that spurred the police to arrest only blacks from Elaine or the racialized component of the judicial proceedings. He recounted the facts "as they are admitted in the demurrer," more or less in a straightforward manner. Indeed, he wrote, "it will be understood that while we put it in narrative form, we are not affirming the facts to be as stated but only what we must take them to be."[49]

But in his last sentence in the recapitulation, he asserted, as if the demurrer itself made it clear, that "there never was a chance for the petitioners to be acquitted; no juryman could have voted for an acquittal and continued to live in Phillips County and if any prisoners by any chance had been acquitted by a jury he could not have escaped the mob."[50] This is the crux of Holmes' burden in questioning the state's proceedings as a mask for mob justice, and he does not spend much time discussing it. Holmes' subtlety is quite different from what we will see in later cases, and it may be the reason that *Moore* is often considered an exception in habeas cases to the general proposition (held until *Brown* v. *Allen* in 1953) that courts do not look behind the record on habeas appeals.

Moore did not create a constitutional revolution regarding habeas petitioners;[51] it did not spur the Court to reconsider the limits of habeas corpus. Nor did *Moore* stir up much discussion among legal elites concerning the problem of protecting minorities against racial hatred. More concerned with "reds" than "blacks"[52] during the 1920s, neither the Court, the Congress, nor leading intellectuals thought the Elaine riots pointed to a pervasive problem in American criminal justice. Holmes' counternarrative was a minor interruption in the Court's overall approach to habeas corpus cases. Inasmuch as "Ensuring minimal federal procedural safeguards for defendants constituted a second front on behalf of blacks oppressed by the administration of criminal law during the age of segregation,"[53] *Moore* corrected only the problem of procedural injustice in this particular case. Habeas corpus remained contingent on federalism's meaning, itself a judicial contingency. *Moore* did not constitute a front, but a beginning. As such, it left open the question, what remedies are available for state prisoners seeking federal collateral relief?[54]

After 1916, federal review of state court decisions was not available as of right, provided the federal question involved was not the validity of a treaty or a federal statute.[55] Moreover, changes in the Judiciary Acts of 1916 and 1925 allowed the Court to choose the kinds of cases it could accept on petitions for certiorari. A state defendant who challenged his detention on procedural grounds could only find relief by way of a writ of certiorari from the Supreme Court, which the Court was free to deny. The states' traditional lack of adequate postconviction relief allowed state appellate court decisions to remain the final judgment on state prisoners' claims.[56]

The problem of what remedies were available to state prisoners raising federal constitutional issues after conviction during the 1930s goes to the heart of the debate over criminal justice in the federal system. But with the jurisdiction standard crippled by due process considerations that were slowly seeping into petitions for relief, the Court went in search of yet another standard to retard state prisoners' claims. It came up with the "adequate and independent state ground" rule. In other words, what is the "adequate state ground" that would keep the case out of the federal courts, and what behavior by the state would "shock the conscience" of the Court into overturning a state conviction?[57]

The basis for the adequate state ground rule, which prevents a federal court from deciding a case because of an overwhelming presence of state issues, is to limit potential friction between federal and state judicial systems.[58] As in the nineteenth century, the Court gave substance to a procedure designed to shore up federalism, not protect civil rights. In *Herb* v. *Pitcairn* (1945), the Court noted:

> This Court from the time of its foundation has adhered to the principle that it will not review judgments of state courts that rest on adequate and independent state grounds. . . . The reason is so obvious that it has rarely been thought to warrant statement. It is found in the partitioning of power between the state and federal judicial systems and in the limitations of our jurisdiction. Our only power over state judgments is to correct them to the extent that they incorrectly adjudge federal rights. And our power is to correct wrong judgments, not to revise opinions.[59]

This was, however, a selective policy. For Curtis Reitz, the 1867 habeas act was federalism's trump card because it began the "process for the vindication of federal rights."[60] "The state ground is not independent," according to Reitz, "if the state court, apprised by the Supreme Court that it erred on the question of federal law, would alter its views of the state law issue as a result." "The test of adequacy," he noted, "is a matter exclusively of federal law."[61] But this is only true as a matter of form; neither the institutions designed to protect federal rights nor the language that was necessary to carry through the commands of such institutions were in place by the 1930s, not to say 1867. Quite simply, relying on the adequate and independent state ground rule prevents federal remedies from being applied. State institutions remained unmolested, and the language of rights as deserts continued intact.

THE SUPREME COURT RELATES
DUE PROCESS TO HABEAS CORPUS

The Supreme Court related due process to habeas corpus largely through detailed narratives of violence built into the recapitulation of trial records. Thus, the constitutionality of lynching "becomes accountable in view of stories told about it."[62] Constitutional heuristics revolving around the body of the prisoner replaced narratives of the state as the cornerstone of political activity. Change will come first because Frank Moore has a lawyer, then second because the Court is solicitous of his argument, then third because it finds a way to adapt due process to the habeas claim, but only so far. It is in fact quite possible, as Michael Klarman suggests,[63] that the Court sided with black defendants in cases such as *Moore* and the "Scottsboro Boys" case because it sensed that whites were not opposed to extending constitutional protections in cases such as these, which is to say, in limited fashion. But surely it is equally important to note how unique the Court's turn toward narrative was in these cases. In this regard, the Court did not try to gain acceptance from the public for the constitutional expansion of civil rights during the mid-1920s. Rather, by introducing lengthier narratives about state-sanctioned local violence, the Court hoped that these stories would influence public opinion and open up the possibility of incorporating the Bill of Rights. The rise of these peculiar judicial narratives, "entwined with questions of authority and legitimation,"[64] particularly in regard to the Court's knowledge of state violence against blacks, set up a new, less formal way to view constitutional law that was free to ignore public opinion yet operate within formalist legal boundaries.

As if the narratives themselves were pushing for expansion, the idea of applying the procedural amendments of the Bill of Rights to the states gained currency throughout the 1930s, as the Court accepted more cases from petitioners with "no social status," from "lowly environments," and with no "class or family" as allies.[65] Both the willingness of certain justices to apply the Bill of Rights to the states and the reaction to incorporation that it spurred influenced the development of the writ and gave the impetus to prisoners seeking to break the hold of the state courts over criminal justice. By the 1930s, due process of law, *per legem terrae*, came to mean in its application, *the* law of the land. It presupposed a national judiciary in a national state.

An example of the historical development from federal deference to local administration to a national standard of law is the first Scottsboro case, *Powell* v. *Alabama*[66] (1932). The story of the "Scottsboro Boys" is probably better known than the Court's decision, which, though it granted the boys their petition for a right to counsel, did not extend that right to all petitioners similarly situated. Yet the Court did, in limited fashion,[67] establish a Sixth Amendment right to counsel in a state case. *Powell* held that *Hurtado* v. *California* (1884), which had restricted the applicability of the Bill of Rights to the states, to be "not without exceptions."[68] Justice George Sutherland argued against the claims of Alabama that inquiry into the meaning of due process required a judge "to ascertain what were the settled usages and modes of proceeding under the constitutional and statutory law of England before the Declaration of Independence, subject, however, to the qualification that they be shown not to have been unsuited to the civil and political conditions of our ancestors by having been followed in this country after it became a nation."[69] Sutherland held that the formalism of *Hurtado* and the Court's historical reliance on preconstitutional rights that limited the application of the Bill of Rights was secondary to the national protection of rights that "are of such a nature that they are included in the conception of due process of law." *Powell* is the twentieth century's *County of Santa Clara* decision; it recognized, albeit in limited fashion, the criminal as a constitutional person. The narrow reach of *Hurtado* "must yield to more compelling considerations whenever such considerations exist."[70]

We see here what is becoming a not uncommon narrative in Supreme Court opinions during the late 1930s. The desire by individual justices to break away from the common law and begin establishing a purely American understanding of legal concepts. We saw this in *Ex parte Royall* in regard to habeas corpus. To do this in *Powell*, Sutherland relied extensively on the trial record, which, unlike *Moore*, was replete with blatant constitutional infractions, including intimidation, misinformation, and a rush to judgment without the provision of counsel ("The record indicates that the appearance [of the attorneys] was rather pro forma than zealous and active"[71]). But Sutherland also began a critique of the historical legacy of the common law on American institutions. "In England, a person charged with treason or felony was denied the aid of counsel, except in respect of legal questions which the accused himself might suggest."[72] For Sutherland, however, "If recognition of the right of a defendant charged with a felony to have the aid of counsel depended upon the existence of a similar right at common law as it existed in England when our Constitution was adopted, there would be great difficulty in maintaining it as necessary to due process."[73]

Yet *Powell*, like *Moore*, was only a start, and a false one. Against Chief Justice Charles Evans Hughes' expansive reading of due process in *Brown v. Mississippi* (1936), Justice Benjamin Cardozo, in *Palko v. Connecticut* (1937), cataloged what behavior is "implicit in the concept of ordered liberty" and what is not.[74] Cardozo, too, offered his own understanding of the Constitution's reach, rooted in part in the American practice of deference to state laws and in part on a fair amount on his own notions of the law's limits, and avoided classifying the Fourteenth Amendment's protections. Along with freedom of thought and speech, he included "the concept of due process," which prevents condemnation of the accused except after trial, and the requirement that the trial "must be a real one, not a sham or a pretense."[75] He also added the right to counsel in capital cases because it is "essential to the substance of a hearing."[76] But Cardozo denied Palko's claim to Fifth Amendment protection in a state case and thereby created an accommodationist line with opponents of incorporation. His view, in the long run, was not principled but impressionistic and heartfelt, something Justice Jackson will accuse the more liberal justices of in *Brown v. Allen*.

Building on Cardozo's claim that the right to counsel may in fact be part of the concept of "ordered liberty," the Court extended the right to counsel in federal cases in *Johnson v. Zerbst*[77] (1938), a noncapital federal habeas corpus case. In *Zerbst*, the petitioner, indicted for counterfeiting, was unaware he had a right to counsel. A federal court twice denied his petition for habeas corpus, the second time after a hearing. The Supreme Court reversed the denial of habeas corpus and remanded the case to the federal court to determine whether the petitioner had waived his right to counsel.[78] "The scope of inquiry in habeas corpus proceedings has been broadened—not narrowed—since the adoption of the Sixth Amendment."[79]

Justice Hugo Black, who wrote the majority opinion in *Zerbst*, built his case on the Court's *Frank*, *Moore*, and *Mooney* v. *Holohan*[80] decisions. The "rudimentary demands of justice" (citing *Mooney*) must be protected by a court of law, lest that court lose its jurisdiction over the prisoner (citing *Frank*). Such demands now include that counsel be present during interrogation and at trial.[81] Black also emphasized that a federal habeas judge cannot simply confine his inquiry to the "proceedings and judgment of a trial court." The petitioned court has the power to inquire into the subject matter presented "as it relates to jurisdiction and to examine facts outside the record."[82] Black read the case as if narratives of justice were custom-built into habeas appeals. But as we will see in the next chapter, narratives are historically constructed rather than innate. They can be used to expand and retract rights. The Supreme Court ruled similarly in two identical federal habeas corpus cases, *Walker* v. *Johnston*[83] (1941) and *Waley* v. *Johnston*[84] (1942), which put an end to the jurisdiction standard. These three federal habeas cases were subsequently applied to the states.[85]

We have here an increasing reliance on American narratives of violence, rooted in peculiar American practices, such as lynching and the legacies of slavery. In *Chambers* v. *Florida*[86] (1940), Justice Black, inching toward the full incorporation view he later espoused in his dissent in *Adamson* v. *California*,[87] stated that the Fourteenth Amendment "requires" the states to conform to "fundamental standards of procedure in criminal trials."[88] He wrote: "[L]aw enforcement methods such as those under review are [not] necessary to uphold our laws. The Constitution proscribes such lawless means irrespective of the ends. . . . Due process of law . . . commands that no such practice as that disclosed by this record shall send any accused to his death."[89] Along with *Chambers*, the Court continued to apply the due process clause of the Fourteenth Amendment in habeas cases against claims of coercion and mob-dominated courtrooms, such as in *Lisenba* v. *California*[90] (1941) and *Hysler* v. *Florida*[91] (1942). But in both cases, with Justices Black and William Douglas dissenting, the Court upheld the defendants' conviction and denied habeas corpus.

DEFINING HABEAS CORPUS

During the 1940s, the status of federal habeas corpus had become technical and confusing, but an emphasis on procedures marks the study of habeas corpus from this point on. This section emphasizes the function of habeas corpus, the use of the writ as a personal tool to reconstitute rights, to bring about a prisoner's release from unconstitutional confinement, irrespective of jurisdictional concerns. In particular, the question is what is required of the habeas petitioner as he makes his way through the state appellate process to bring about his release? This section focuses on three important habeas corpus cases, *Wade* v. *Mayo*[92] (1948), *Darr* v. *Burford*[93] (1950), and *Brown* v. *Allen*[94] (1953).

The Basis for the Exhaustion Doctrine

In 1948, Congress codified the Supreme Court's habeas corpus jurisprudence.[95] The legislation required state prisoners to exhaust the available remedies offered at the state level and the Supreme Court before proceeding to the federal courts for relief. The legislation largely codified restrictive nineteenth-century Supreme Court practices, making some revisions in the common law practice of habeas corpus.[96] Although there was some uncertainty regarding whether the exhaustion rule was designed to be a bar to or a basis for federal habeas review,[97] the Court in the late 1940s obstructed the habeas petitioner's path to the federal judiciary.

The process of exhausting remedies, which dates to *Ex parte Royall*, includes appealing to the state's appellate courts following conviction. Following denial of review, a state petitioner then applies for a writ of certiorari to the United States Supreme Court to review the federal claim adversely decided by the state trial court and upheld on appeal. The application for certiorari is not part of the legal requirements of the habeas corpus statute. A certiorari application is the link between the state and federal courts and functions as the Court's imprimatur that state prisoners have satisfied all requirements at the state level.

Ex parte Hawk[98] (1944) is the classic exhaustion case of the 1940s. The decision formulated explicit rules and conditions for state prisoners seeking habeas relief in the federal courts. The petitioner in *Hawk* alleged, among other charges, that he was denied counsel and that perjured testimony had been admitted against him.[99] The Supreme Court refused to rule on the merits of the case because the petitioner had not exhausted his state remedies.

> Ordinarily an application for habeas corpus by one detained under a state court judgment of conviction for crime will be entertained by a federal court only after all state remedies, including all appellate remedies in the state courts *and in this court* by appeal or writ of certiorari, have been exhausted. . . . [I]t is a principle controlling all habeas corpus petitions to the federal courts, that these courts [i.e., federal courts] will only interfere with the administration of justice in the state courts only "in rare cases where exceptional circumstances of peculiar urgency are shown to exist." To this, some courts have added the intimation that when the writ is sought by one held under a state conviction the only remedy ordinarily to be had in a federal court is by way of application to this Court.[100]

The Supreme Court during the 1940s saw no reason for federal intervention in the ordinary course of events following a state's criminal trial. "Where the state courts have considered and adjudicated the merits of [a] contention, and this Court had either reviewed or declined to review the state court's decision, a federal court will not ordinarily re-examine upon a writ of habeas corpus the questions thus adjudicated."[101]

By the middle 1940s, however, habeas petitions began to increase, though the number of petitioners released during the same period actually decreased.[102] In 1941, the number of state prisoners filing habeas corpus petitions in federal district courts strictly on federal questions was 127. By 1949, that number had reached 583.[103] Between *Brown* v. *Allen* (1953) and *Fay* v. *Noia* (1963), petitions to the federal courts continued to rise, reaching 9,000 by 1969, and 10,000 by 1989.

Despite a disproportionate number of habeas petitions coming from Illinois, the number of habeas petitions in the 1940s remained small in proportion to the total prison population, growing to a mere 2.4 percent of the prison population by 1947–48. Yet Congress responded to protests from members of the federal judiciary and the legal community seeking to prevent habeas petitioners from inundating the federal courts by passing legislation designed to restrict access. This was done not in the name of restricting the writ, but of preventing habeas corpus from becoming the "plaything of penitentiary inmates [seeking] to accomplish temporary vacation visits to the federal courts," in the words of Louis Goodman, a United States district court judge at the time.[104]

The Court did not mean to eliminate habeas corpus as a remedy for state prisoners. The criteria for federal intervention were the minimal due process violations cited in *Moore* and *Mooney*.

> When resort to state court remedies has failed to afford a full and fair adjudication of the federal contentions raised, either because the state affords no remedy [citing *Mooney*], or because in the particular case the remedy afforded by state law proves in practice unavailable or seriously inadequate [citing *Moore*], a federal court should entertain [a] petition for habeas corpus, else [the petitioner] would be remediless. In such a case [the petitioner] should proceed in the federal district court before resorting to this court by petition for habeas corpus.[105]

The Role of Certiorari and the Exhaustion of Remedies

Wade v. *Mayo* (1948), *Darr* v. *Burford* (1950), and *Brown* v. *Allen* (1953) close out this chapter and raise the question of certiorari and the exhaustion of remedies in the context of individual rights.

Wade v. *Mayo* is the first serious break in the Court's effort to restrict access to the federal courts. Prior to *Wade*, the Court had held that applications for certiorari were required before attacking one's state conviction in a federal court and after exhausting one's state remedies. The Habeas Corpus Act of 1867 was silent on such methods. Unlike the federal courts, which are congressional creations, the Supreme Court considers itself part of the federal system. Certiorari review is "part of the state procedure for purposes of habeas corpus."[106]

Wade was sentenced to five years in jail. The state court had denied his request for counsel. Rather than applying for certiorari with the Supreme Court, Wade attacked his conviction in federal court. Under Florida law, "a defendant who is denied counsel in a non-capital case . . . may attack the constitutionality of such treatment either by the direct method of an appeal from the conviction or by the collateral method of habeas corpus."[107] Wade chose the latter course and thereby satisfied the state's exhaustion rule. The Supreme Court upheld Wade's bypass of certiorari review of his federal claims, noting that habeas corpus is available to state prisoners in the federal courts "to prevent an unjust and illegal deprivation of human liberty" and therefore should not be burdened by jurisdictional formalities that interfere with federal supremacy.[108]

The dissenting justices, Chief Justice Fred Vinson, Robert Jackson, Harold Burton, and Stanley Reed, who wrote the dissent, constituted a conservative bloc of justices on habeas corpus and criminal justice issues on the Vinson Court (1946–1953). They did not deny the importance of collateral relief to unearth a constitutional violation that may have occurred at trial or on appeal, but collateral relief, they held, is an extraordinary remedy that fosters the view that the state courts are not doing their job and that federal courts exist as appellate courts for unsatisfied convicted criminals. This the minority denied. Perhaps federal-state conflict is inherent in our "partly federal, partly national" system, the dissent noted, but it is nowhere written that such friction is to be encouraged in the name of validating what they considered to be technical points of constitutional law.

"Collateral attack may be needed," the Harvard law professor Paul Bator wrote in a seminal antihabeas corpus article in 1963, "but the need for appeal does not prove it; federal habeas corpus remains to be justified even if we concede the necessity for direct Supreme Court review of federal questions in state cases."[109] The dissent in *Wade* saw an application for certiorari to the Supreme Court as a way to maintain "[r]espect for the theory and practice of our dual system of justice."[110] According to Justice Reed, as long as habeas corpus is a discretionary writ, the need to impose limitations on its acquisition "is reinforced by considerations of practical administration,"[111] the latest code-word for the protection of states' rights. For the dissenters, to bypass Supreme Court review is to make an unwarranted assumption that the state courts "deliberately deny to the individual his rights under the federal Constitution."[112]

Not surprisingly, Wade's victory was short-lived. In *Darr v. Burford*[113] (1950), the Supreme Court affirmed a denial of a petition for habeas corpus

by a state prisoner who had failed to exhaust his state remedies by not applying for a writ of certiorari in the Supreme Court from the state court's denial
of habeas corpus. Justice Reed, who dissented in *Wade*, wrote the 5:3 decision
in *Darr*. (Justice Douglas took no part.)

The majority opinion in *Darr* viewed an application for certiorari to the
Supreme Court as a necessary prop of federalism. The dissent viewed certiorari not only as of no legal significance, but as a procedure that fostered a
"meaningless multiplication of steps in the legal process."[114] *Darr* sought to
correct "whatever deviation" *Wade* had created in the "established rule" from
Royall (1886) to *Hawk* (1944) that comity concerns, including a petition for
certiorari to the Supreme Court, be respected.[115] The Court saw the *Hawk*
rule, that is, the exhaustion of state remedies through certiorari appeals, not as
a byzantine trap, but as a contribution "towards expeditious administration,
since it raised the constitutional issue in a federal forum immediately, without
the necessity of a second trial court proceeding and the compilation of a second record."[116]

But is an application for certiorari and almost certain denial a necessary
principle of federalism? The Court held that it is. "Such a rule accords with
our form of government. Since the states have the major responsibility for the
maintenance of law and order within their borders, the dignity and importance of their role as guardians of the administration of criminal justice merits review of their acts by this Court before a prisoner, as a matter of routine,
may seek release from state process in the district courts of the United
States."[117] Justices Frankfurter, Black, and Jackson dissented in *Darr*. Frankfurter and Black saw no reason to tie a denial of certiorari to a determination
of the merits of the case or to require Supreme Court review before applying
for habeas corpus in the federal courts when the 1867 act imposed no such
obligation on a defendant. While it is certainly true, Frankfurter wrote, that
this "seemingly technical problem of jurisdiction concerns the relation of the
United States and the courts of the United States to the states and the courts
of the states,"[118] he saw no reason to equate certiorari review with a fundamental principle of federalism. "The denial [of certiorari] means that this
Court has refused to take the case. It means nothing else."[119]

The 1948 congressional revisions of the criminal code[120] concerned the
rights and responsibilities of habeas petitioners and the state and federal court
judges who hear their pleas. Section 2254 is of particular interest because it
not only grants federal judges and Supreme Court justices power to issue
habeas corpus to those "in custody in violation of the Constitution or the laws
of the United States," but it also allows a judge to deny habeas corpus "unless
it appears that the applicant has exhausted the remedies available in the courts
of the state."[121] The historical and revisionary note attached to the statute
reads: "This new section is declaratory of existing law as affirmed by the
Supreme Court (see *Ex parte Hawk*)."

Frankfurter, who dissented in *Darr*, insisted that the new legislation did not codify *Hawk*. He stressed that applications for certiorari to the Supreme Court by state prisoners were not remedies "available in the courts of the state." The 1948 legislation relied on *Hawk*, Frankfurter noted, because *Wade* had not yet been decided.[122] Under 2254(c): "An applicant shall not be deemed to have exhausted the remedies available in the courts of the state . . . if he has the right under the law of the state to raise, by any available procedure, the question presented." But John J. Parker, who was not only the chief judge of the United States Court of Appeals for the fourth circuit in 1948 but also the chairman of the Judicial Conference Committee that drafted the habeas corpus sections of title 28, thought differently, and his view carried more weight than Frankfurter's. "The effect of this last provision is to eliminate, for all practical purposes, the right to apply to the lower federal courts for habeas corpus in all states in which successive applications may be made for habeas corpus to the state courts."[123] The Judicial Conference wanted to abolish, so far as possible, what it deemed "abuse of the writ."[124] The purpose of the 1948 reforms was to "give precision and definiteness to the rule [of exhaustion] and prevent attempts to have the lower federal courts review state court proceedings where there are no special circumstances justifying departure from the ordinary practice."[125]

The difficulty here lies in the definition of what is ordinary. If 2254(b) and (c) had not been passed, or the revisor's notes had taken into consideration *Wade* v. *Mayo*, presumably a habeas petitioner could have gone to the federal courts after the state's highest court had denied relief.[126] But the passage of 28 U.S.C. 2241–55 made the vindication of a state prisoner's rights in the federal courts more difficult. The last case of this chapter, *Brown* v. *Allen*[127] (1953), highlights the changes brought about by the 1948 reforms and will introduce the reader to the complexity of habeas corpus law as we enter the Warren era in the next chapter.

An Act So Cruel

Brown v. *Allen* builds on the legacies and ambiguities of *Hawk*, *Wade*, and *Darr* but is in fact closer to *Ashcraft* v. *Tennessee* in that it further exacerbated the split the Court was experiencing regarding federalism and the uses of counternarrative. *Brown* v. *Allen* is three cases rolled into one[128] and has two majority opinions, one regarding the claims alleged by the petitioners (which the Court denied) and another regarding whether federal district courts should give effect to the Court's denial of certiorari, such that the district courts are free to infer that the Court viewed the writ unfavorably. Perhaps not surprising to Court watchers, Felix Frankfurter wrote both a majority and a minority opinion in *Brown* (the first denied that certiorari mattered, the second dissented from the Court's denial of relief). Overall, *Brown* is a contrapuntal mess. Here is Justice Black's summary of the cases, written in dissent: "The four petitioners in these cases are under sentence of death imposed by North Carolina state courts. All are Negroes. Brown and Speller were convicted of raping white women; the two Daniels, aged 17 when arrested, were convicted of murdering a white man. The State Supreme Court affirmed and we denied certiorari in all the cases. These are habeas corpus proceedings which challenge the validity of the convictions."[129]

Brown was arrested in North Carolina for rape and found guilty. He was sentenced to death. A timely petition to quash the indictment was denied. Brown alleged that blacks had been discriminated against in the selection of the grand and petit juries. He also stated that his confession was coerced and therefore unconstitutional. These issues were fully litigated at trial and not questioned on appeal. The North Carolina Supreme Court affirmed the conviction. The U.S. Supreme Court denied certiorari. Brown then appealed to the federal courts for habeas corpus. The district court dismissed the application and the court of appeals affirmed. The Supreme Court affirmed the district court's decision,[130] with Justice Stanley Reed writing the majority opinion.

As noted, there are two opinions at work in *Brown*: one by Justice Reed and another by Justice Frankfurter. Frankfurter garnered a majority for the proposition that a district court should not give weight to the Supreme Court's previous denial of certiorari. On the merits of the case, though, Frankfurter, with Black and Douglas, dissented. The majority held that the defendants' rights had not been violated.

Although the Court upheld the conviction of Brown, Speller, and the two Daniels, it did so by rejecting the merits of the federal claim that had previously been adjudicated by the state court. That is, it was immaterial to the Supreme Court that North Carolina had provided Brown with an adequate judicial process to test his conviction. Reliance on state procedures that were in accordance with due process had been the reason why *Frank* v. *Magnum* upheld the state court conviction and *Moore* v. *Dempsey* overturned the state court conviction. For almost one hundred years, the sovereign jurisdiction of the state court was the anchor of a habeas corpus attack.[131] In *Brown*, this security is missing. The new ground became the linguistic formulation of due process tied to criminal persons, and the issue was whether or not there was an underlying constitutional error that had contributed to the petitioner's conviction.

In all three cases covered in *Brown*, the district courts held that if there had been a constitutional violation at the state level, then the Supreme Court would have accepted the cases on certiorari. Certiorari was "designed to permit [the Supreme Court] to keep within manageable proportions . . . the business that is allowed to come before [it]."[132] But by questioning the state's recapitulation of the facts, the Court in effect questioned the state's ultimate power to determine guilt and inflict punishment.

The issue of federalism here is subtle but important. An application for certiorari increases the length of the habeas corpus process and makes access to the federal judiciary difficult.[133] For the majority, it reinforced the nineteenth century's habeas jurisprudence, by making the states "the real guardians of peace and order within their boundaries."[134] But Frankfurter had looked at the statistics on habeas corpus from the 1940s up to *Brown* (1953) and found that of the 3,702 applications for habeas corpus in the seven years prior to *Brown*, only 67 had been granted.[135] Contrary to Justice Jackson's concurring opinion, Frankfurter demonstrated that federal review did not lead to federal usurpation of states' rights.

Frankfurter saw the role of the federal judiciary in habeas corpus jurisprudence as more benign and the law governing habeas corpus as more categorical than his more conservative brethren. "Our problem arises," Frankfurter stated, "because Congress has told the District Judge to act on the those occasions, however rare, when there are meritorious causes in which habeas corpus is the ultimate and only relief and designed to be such."[136] He stated, "The complexities of our federalism and the workings of a scheme of government involving the interplay of two governments, one of which is subject to limitations enforceable by the other, are not to be escaped by simple, rigid rules which, by avoiding some abuses, generate others."[137]

The essence of a habeas attack lies not with any indignity done to the state judge's decision but with the right of citizens to be free from illegal detention. Although Justice Jackson disapproved, the Habeas Corpus Act of 1867 suggests that the determination of guilt by a state court is never final. The statutory codification of 1948 modified that goal in the name of federalism and finality, but it did not end it. For Jackson, then, concurring in the Court's opinion to uphold the convictions, the habeas act had created an impressionistic palette by which the justices could color any constitutional attack, even one that was already adjudicated not once but twice. He directed his comments to the proper source. "The generalities of the Fourteenth Amendment," he wrote, "are so indeterminate as to what state actions are forbidden that this Court has found it a ready instrument, in one field or another, to magnify federal, and incidentally its own, authority over the states. . . . It must prejudice the occasional meritorious application to be buried in a flood of worthless ones."[138] But is not the purpose of a habeas attack to expose the conflict over the exercise of state power and assert the individual's right to be free from arbitrary and reckless arrest, and not, as Paul Bator alleged, the state judge's "inner sense of responsibility" that is apparently destroyed by federal collateral review?[139]

"Finality and justice," Daniels' attorneys, O. John Rogge and Murray Gordon, wrote some years after their case was decided, summing up the problem of habeas corpus in the 1950s, "are frequently incompatible,"[140] and it is these two big ideas that divided the Court in *Brown*. The 1948 codification of the habeas statute gave the state courts some measure of protection for their fact-finding techniques, but it denied that a state court judgment should be final and determinative of a prisoner's guilt or innocence. The question, then, is: at what point is justice done and how do we know it? This is the theme pursued by Justice Robert Jackson's concurrence in *Brown*.

Justice Jackson was troubled by the "generalities of the Fourteenth Amendment" because, he thought, it led to judicial impressionism. "A manifestation of this," he wrote, "is seen in the diminishing respect shown for state court adjudications of fact"[141] by the federal courts on collateral attack. Although the Court upheld the convictions, Jackson saw the effect of *Brown* v. *Allen* as detrimental, not just to the states' criminal justice procedures but also to law and language itself. "Whatever has been intended, this Court also has generated an impression in much of the judiciary that regard for precedents and authorities is obsolete, that words no longer mean what they have always meant to the profession, that the law knows no fixed principles."[142]

And here we get to the heart of the matter. The movement away from a jurisdictional defense of the states in habeas cases leads to a tectonic shift in constitutional law, a falling off of the scales that had encrusted habeas jurisprudence for almost one hundred years. This shift away from state sovereignty opened up the role of narratives of violence unrestrained by tradition, by law, and by language. By removing jurisdiction as a defense of states rights, *Brown* exposed federalism as a metaphor, as a literary description of the way things were. The amputation created habeas petitioners as performers before the stage of the law courts. And the actors, Jackson feared, were not union but free agents, uninhibited as to their claims because they sit in prison and on death row. For Jackson, habeas narratives are without foundations; they are inherently impressionistic, prolix, redundant, event-laden. They turn the Constitution on its head. They reverse the usual equation that sets the state as the determiner of guilt and the accused or prisoner as the one who must bear that responsibility, in silence. For Jackson, narratives built upon stories of state violence for the purpose of reversing the flow of constitutional law—especially on collateral attack—lack self-restraint, the very source of the Court's habeas corpus jurisprudence since 1886.

What is driving Jackson's opinion in *Brown* is that the Court has invested too much intellectual time and energy defending the states' right to determine the outcome of a criminal trial, from start to finish, conviction to execution. *Brown* v. *Allen* disturbs that notion and with it, rationality, reason, and personal responsibility. "It really has become necessary," Jackson wrote, "to plead nothing more than that the prisoner is in jail, wants to get out, and thinks it is illegal to hold him. If he fails, he may make the same plea over and over again."[143]

Justice Jackson is the first to notice (apart from William Royall himself) that habeas corpus is a language game that allows a purely subjective understanding of right and wrong, crime and punishment, the limits of federal and state powers, to determine the outcome of a trial. It is pure contingency. Worse, for Jackson (which sets his opinion apart from *Royall*), is that the author of that game is a convicted rapist. He then tries to swim upstream, to get ahead of what's coming, to reify the Court's historic language of denial—federalism—by removing its rough outer edges and anchoring it in something permanent, fixed: justice, respect, finality—but for whom? His concurrence, not surprisingly and unfortunately, is devoid of a narrative regarding North Carolina's legacy of mistreatment of blacks. Unlike Frankfurter, no frail defender of federalism himself, Jackson fails to see an injustice in North Carolina's denial of the Daniels' petition for appeal, which their attorney served one day late, and resulted in a death sentence. His defense of federalism as smooth administration creates an overarching umbrella that covers the phrase *due process of law* in a protective blanket of shade, as nineteenth-century courts had done, but that also had silenced the victim of state abuse and denied the habeas petitioner's personhood. Moreover, to be sure, he fails to see the Court's defense of federalism as itself a narrative, created by the Court in the nineteenth century as a counternarrative to the Court's nationalist defense of property. His defense of federalism exists within brackets. He sees federalism as a story about small government, but not slavery; as a defense of localism, but not lynching; as the conductor of the administration of things, but not as the cruel taskmaster that denies applications for appeals one day late.

Because Jackson thought federal-state relations had worsened over the years, he believed that finality of litigation was necessary in habeas cases. He sees federalism is a brake, a method of stopping constitutional change from being imposed by courts of law. Paul Bator built on Jackson's narrative by making finality itself the form of justice in a federal republic. Bator's attack on habeas jurisprudence was a naked defense of state power and institutional norms, established before the Civil War. For Bator, neither the judicial system nor federalism exists to establish the "ultimate truth" about a defendant's claims. "A procedural system which permits an endless repetition of inquiry into facts and law in a vain search for ultimate certitude implies a lack of confidence about the possibilities of institutional justice that cannot but war with the effectiveness of the underlying substantive claims."[144] For Justice Jackson, the incorporation of rights through the due process clause of the Fourteenth Amendment had not brought the United States any closer to what constituted justice than before incorporation began. "[R]eversal by a higher court is not proof that justice is thereby better done."[145] He went on to say, "There is no doubt that if there were a super-Supreme Court, a substantial proportion of our reversals of state courts would also be reversed. *We are not final because we are infallible, but we are infallible only because we are final.*"[146] Jackson suggested that in a federal system, finality is necessary to protect the great writ from itself, lest truth be a casualty of habeas corpus attacks. "The writ has no enemies so deadly as those who sanction the abuse of it, whatever their intent."[147]

But Larry Yackle has seen through Jackson's criticism of impressionism by pointing out that there is more than just a tinge of nihilism in this view.[148] The Court evades its responsibilities to protect individual rights claims through forbearance from federal review because it believes that deference, not individual liberty, is a constitutional principle.

Dissenting in *Brown*, Frankfurter questioned whether an excessive regard for formalism on a habeas challenge involving life and death was the best policy for the Court to pursue. In *Daniels v. Allen*, the companion case decided with *Brown*, the petitioners had filed an appeal one day after the deadline for such appeals had passed. The Supreme Court upheld the lower court's denial of relief. For Frankfurter, the respect for finality had reached its limit. "The decisive question is whether a refusal to exercise a discretion which the legislature of North Carolina has vested in its judges is an act so cruel in its operation, considering that life is at stake, that in the circumstances of this case it constitutes a denial of due process in its rudimentary procedural aspect."[149] By denying the writ because it is not a substitute for appeal, the Court returned habeas corpus to the nineteenth century. For Frankfurter, this was a "jejune abstraction." He concluded his dissent by noting that habeas corpus is not a curse on a federal republic but "is necessary to prevent a complete miscarriage of justice."[150]

CONCLUSION

Habeas corpus is a jurisdictional problem in a nation of jurisdictions. From 1867 to about the time *Frank v. Magnum* was decided in 1915, habeas corpus' reach was limited by the Supreme Court's creation of a jurisdictional foundation that protected state governments from federal intervention. The new ground of due process to challenge illegal detentions hinted at in *Frank*, revealed in *Moore*, and then debated in the extraordinary number of habeas corpus and due process cases the Court decided between 1923 and 1953, not only altered the rights afforded to prisoners but also affected the responsibilities jurisdictionally assigned to the states and the federal government by the Court's decisions.

The expanded use of habeas corpus by state prisoners contesting their detentions in the federal courts paralleled the slow incorporation of the Bill of Rights into the Fourteenth Amendment. This was not an accident. Until *Frank* and *Moore*, a state court's jurisdiction over a prisoner was reasonably safe from federal intervention. Only a blatant misuse of the trial court's jurisdiction, for example, imposing a punishment greater than is required by law, could result in a prisoner's release by habeas corpus. The era under review in this chapter saw the jurisdictional ground of state sovereignty punctured by due process claims that affected the trial court's jurisdiction enough to question the state's sovereign right to detain a convicted criminal.

The exhaustion doctrine, created in the first era of habeas jurisprudence, was held, in the second, to include not only completing the state appellate process but also an application to the Supreme Court for certiorari before attacking the state conviction in federal court. The reason was that Supreme Court review of state court decisions was considered to be in the best interests of federal-state comity. By the 1940s, that view was held to be a hindrance to habeas petitioners, and the defense of federal-state comity was deemed slight. Finally, in *Brown* v. *Allen*, Justice Frankfurter garnered a separate majority opinion for the view that the federal courts should not rely on denials of certiorari as opinions of the Court denying the merits of a habeas petitioner's claims.

Brown, however, barely settled the complexity of a habeas corpus challenge. The decision in *Brown*, which upheld the denial of habeas corpus to petitioners accused of rape and murder, established that the federal courts can redetermine the issues involved in a habeas appeal. If the decision in *Brown* was restrictive, its opinion was in the spirit of Justice Holmes' in *Moore*. The inability of the Court to defend the primacy of the state court's jurisdiction over criminal justice, and its willingness to allow federal courts to consider settled issues as open questions, opened the door to the Supreme Court's more liberal habeas policy in the 1960s. Despite the enormous institutional thrust of the Court's habeas decisions throughout this era, it is undeniable that, from this day forward, narratives will play a key role in deciding the fate of habeas corpus petitioners.

FOUR

Confessions and the
Narratives of Justice, 1963–1979

Once again the Court is confronted with the painful duty of sitting in judgment on a State's conviction for murder, after a jury's
verdict was found flawless by the State's highest court, in order to
determine whether the defendant's confessions, decisive for the
conviction, were admitted into evidence in accordance with the
standards for admissibility demanded by the Due Process Clause
of the Fourteenth Amendment. This recurring problem touching
the administration of criminal justice by the States present in an
aggregated form in this case the anxious task of reconciling the
responsibility of the police for ferreting out crime with the right
of the criminal defendant, however guilty, to be tried according
to constitutional requirements.

—*Culombe* v. *Connecticut*

Offenses frequently occur about which things cannot be made
to speak.

—*Culombe* v. *Connecticut*

A SUDDEN RISE in habeas' success and a precipitous decline in its status as a
means to check unlawful confinement mark this third era in the writ's
jurisprudence. The purpose of this chapter is to understand how these events
occurred. To many observers, the Supreme Court in the 1960s broke the ad

hoc pattern of selectively incorporating the Bill of Rights, begun with *Palko* v. *Connecticut*[1] in 1937. Justice Benjamin Cardozo had spoken in *Palko* of the "concept of ordered liberty," which he presumably thought implied a more elevated yet narrower conception of rights applicability than the more straightforward language of due process and equal protection found in the Fourteenth Amendment. Cardozo rejected Palko's Fifth and Fourteenth Amendment claim that for Connecticut to try him twice for the same offense because the first time the state had failed to get a death sentence had any place in a double jeopardy case. But the phrase turned up in the Fourth Amendment case *Wolf* v. *Colorado*[2] (1949), in which Felix Frankfurter wrote that the right to be secure in one's home and among one's personal effects is part of *Palko's* calculus. *Mapp* v. *Ohio*[3] (1961) carried over part of the logic of ordered liberty, applying not just the right to privacy from *Wolf* but also the exclusionary rule from *Weeks* v. *United States*[4] (1914) to the states. For Frankfurter, though, dissenting in *Mapp*, only privacy fell within the concept of ordered liberty, and not the nuts and bolts of the Fourth Amendment's language. Frankfurter continued Cardozo's legal subjectivism and nineteenth-century understanding of the limits of institutional reform. *Wolf's* strength, Frankfurter wrote in dissent in *Mapp*, was precisely its regard for federal-state comity.[5]

Closer analysis of the incorporation debate, then, reveals that the Warren Court's break with precedent is bracketed by the decade itself and therefore quite limited. The "revolution" in criminal justice procedures enacted by the Warren Court certainly put a dent in the idea that federalism was a doctrine to be upheld in every instance, as *Mapp*, *Gideon* v. *Wainwright*[6] (1963), and *Miranda* v. *Arizona*[7] (1966) demonstrate. Among these incorporation cases, the language of civil rights forced the Court to drift away from institutional structures that prevent federal redress and gravitate toward individual case histories and the inclusion of narratives of injustice perpetrated by states against individuals. In this regard, the 1960s truly disrupted the past.

The purpose of this chapter is to cover the two main strands that occupied the Court's habeas jurisprudence—federalism and narrative—as it shifted gears away from relying exclusively on institutional supports, such as state sovereignty claims to restrict the writ, and toward greater reliance on narratives and confessions. The 1960s, building on the Court's jurisprudence of the 1930s, opened up a space for a strange development in habeas and criminal justice jurisprudence. By admitting to the weakened condition of federalism following *Brown* v. *Allen* (1953), the Court in the 1960s could demonstrate that individual lives were being harmed by state criminal justice procedures and a restricted habeas corpus jurisprudence. The Court could thus hold, throughout the 1960s, that habeas corpus exists to cut through the forms of injustice that unlawfully put people in prison, "however guilty," as Frankfurter wrote in *Culombe* v. *Connecticut*,[8] they may be. But at the same time, as we will see in the 1970s, the Court put much emphasis on the habeas petitioner's guilt, both jury determined and by personal confession, whether through subtle or unsubtle means of persuasion. Narrative reveals itself to be a tool of the justices of the Supreme Court and not justice itself. The conflict between the 1960s and 1970s, between the Warren and Burger Courts, is less over who has the body and more over who gets to determine the legal meaning of the imprisoned body's plea for release.

Until the 1960s, as each habeas corpus era ended, the Supreme Court had decided a habeas case that, although restrictive and in accordance with previous principles of federal-state comity, nonetheless set the tone for a more liberal understanding of the writ in the next decade. Justice Oliver Wendell Holmes' dissent in *Frank* v. *Magnum* (1915) influenced *Moore* v. *Dempsey* (1923), and Justice Frankfurter's dissenting opinion, along with parts of the majority opinion in *Brown* v. *Allen* (1953), led the way to *Fay* v. *Noia* (1963),[9] which established the primacy of individual rights claims over state jurisdictional restrictions on habeas appeals. The end of the 1960s broke that pattern and reversed it.

Looking back, the pattern of rights development in the twentieth century holds to a mildly progressive path in which expanding concentric circles made up of due process decisions enveloped habeas corpus from 1886 to the end of the 1960s. There was, after all, an assumption held among Warren Court justices that justice has a teleology, a known language, a set design. One only has to search for, and then connect, the form with the content, the rights with the amendments, and justice is done. Thus the full effect of Justice Hugo Black's jurisprudence, beginning in *Adamson* v. *California* (1948): rights without amendments are meaningless, and vice versa. A constitutional configuration can therefore be discerned among Warren Court justices that demonstrates the slow expansion of constitutional rights to larger and larger classes of Supreme Court petitioners: first property holders, then speech advocates, then, in rapid succession, the Fourth (1961), Eighth (1962), Sixth (1963) and Fifth (1966) Amendments.

By the end of the 1960s, as the expansion of rights reached its peak, it showed signs of exhaustion. The Supreme Court's discourse in the 1960s, more so than in the 1930s and 1940s, increasingly focused on the fear of releasing criminal defendants, which raises the question: can rights be foundational, when, in fact, it seems more likely that rights have a melting point— that they rely on the patience of Supreme Court justices?[10] The cases that defined the amendments (and it was not the other way around) seemed, by the end of the 1960s, to have lost their adhesiveness to the very same amendments that they had built up and made part of the discourse of civil liberties. (One speaks, after all, of one's First Amendment rights, not of *Gitlow* v. *New York*, despite the fact that the First Amendment was useless before it.)

By the end of the 1960s, the arguments for expanding prisoners' rights no longer stuck. One could no longer say that one was denied a right guaranteed by a particular amendment based on a previous ruling. The timing of the ruling mattered; the guilt of the petitioner mattered; the effect the Court's decision would have on the states' administration of justice mattered. The amendments no longer meant what the Warren Court said they had meant or had required them to mean. Prisoners' rights, refracted once again through the lens of federalism, became fungible, assignable, indeterminate, but only because the Warren Court's consensus that the Fourteenth Amendment trumped states' rights had eviscerated in light of crime stories told by Burger Court justices.

It is the unfulfilled promise of Reconstruction that allowed rights to be traded for security, for patterns of justice, for respect for the victim, for the way in which crime stories were told. The Warren Court's habeas decisions had reversed almost one hundred years of narrow applications of the statute governing prisoners' habeas corpus rights. With *Fay* v. *Noia* (1963), "a habeas petitioner could successfully attack his conviction collaterally despite the fact that the 'new' rule had not even been suggested in the original proceedings."[11] But from the end of the 1960s on, one had to demonstrate the context of the right's denial in time, according to certain procedures. Notably, as the 1960s came to an end, the Supreme Court, in *Desist* v. *United States* (1969), refused to apply *Mapp*'s holding to cases decided before December 18, 1967.[12]

Fearing administrative complications arising from the creation of new (or as Earl Warren stressed in *Miranda*, "innovative") constitutional rights, the Court, even as it was expanding the rights of the accused, remained convinced that the best course of action on habeas corpus cases is deference to the doctrine of federalism. Even more directly, in *Kaufman* v. *United States*[13] (1969), decided the same day as *Desist*, Justice Hugo Black asked in dissent whether innocence is irrelevant to a petitioner's constitutional claims, particularly as they arise in habeas petitions, a question that gained prominence among Nixon appointees on the Burger Court.[14]

With Burger's elevation to chief justice, the Court's spotlight on unlawful convictions dimmed. The incorporation debate was practically over by 1969, when the Supreme Court overturned *Palko*.[15] That same year, Earl Warren retired, and habeas' usefulness as a protection against unlawful state arrest was put in doubt by John Marshall Harlan's dissents in *Fay* and *Desist* and Black's dissent in *Kaufman*. Like other dissents at the end of preceding decades, Black's dissent in *Kaufman* set the parameters for habeas debates in the 1970s and 1980s, whether it was proper to release a prisoner on habeas when his guilt was not in question. By the 1970s, jurisdiction as an absolute bar to a defendant's claims was out, but in its place the Court imposed a test of each habeas defendant's moral character, focusing on confessions and determinations of guilt, setting the tone for the explosion of behavioral and characterological criminal narratives by the Supreme Court in the 1980s and 1990s. In institutional terms, the Burger Court's emphasis on the "new federalism"[16] required a return to a pre-*Moore* v. *Dempsey* (1923) standard on habeas corpus. Justice Lewis Powell, for example, was "unwilling to assume" that there exists "a general lack of appropriate sensitivity to constitutional rights in the trial and appellate courts of the several states." State courts, like federal courts, have a constitutional obligation "to safeguard personal liberties to uphold federal law."[17]

Institutional support for the states' criminal justice practices remained in the foreground of Supreme Court concerns in habeas cases, but the justices' language in denying relief increasingly relied on less structured discourse. The justices were less interested in wanting to know the state's reason for detaining an individual and were more concerned with what remedy the habeas petitioner/convicted criminal was entitled to and at what point the petitioner's conviction became final. *Fay*, then, serves not only as a bridge between past and present but also as a clear break in any ostensible pattern of restrictive Supreme Court decisions. *Fay* obscured the jurisdiction standard without eliminating it. Brennan's decision broke with the past and forced the Court to confront it.

THE 1960s: INDIVIDUAL RIGHTS
IN AN INSTITUTIONAL CONTEXT

Federalism textbooks speak of the "backlash against centralization" that began in the late 1960s, as the "centralization of power in distant Washington, D.C." alienated voters longing to "exercise control . . . over the policies that would determine their quality of life."[18] Crime, too, in the 1960s became a national question and a measurement of the quality of life,[19] largely on the strength of habeas corpus' ability of attach itself to important due process concerns relating to capital punishment. But habeas corpus was never the federal bulldozer its critics have made it out to be. Indeed, without patterning habeas corpus, the impression is that during the 1960s centralization won and that the institutions of government became impervious to change through individual conflicts with state institutions. This is not the case, as the analysis of habeas corpus in the 1960s will reveal. Focusing not only on arrests but also on *who has the body* deepens our understanding of constitutional politics and legal change.

Prior to *Fay*, the only rights the Supreme Court had incorporated under the Fourteenth Amendment's due process clause were the right to just compensation of property taken by the state,[20] the First Amendment freedoms of speech, press, and religion,[21] and the Fourth Amendment protection against unreasonable search and seizure.[22] In *Robinson* v. *California*[23] (1962), the Warren Court applied the Eighth Amendment's prohibition against cruel and unusual punishment against the states. In 1963, along with *Fay*, *Townsend* v. *Sain*, and *Sanders* v. *United States*[24] (all habeas cases), the Supreme Court decided *Gideon* v. *Wainwright*, also a habeas case, which established a Sixth Amendment right to counsel.

Shortly thereafter, the Court decided *Malloy* v. *Hogan*[25] (1964), which brought the Fifth Amendment protection against self-incrimination within the Fourteenth Amendment's purview. In 1966, *Miranda* v. *Arizona* established the right against self-incrimination and required counsel at custodial interrogations, if requested. *Klopfer* v. *North Carolina*[26] (1967) established the right to a speedy trial. *Pointer* v. *Texas*[27] (1967) established the right of a defendant to confront witnesses, and *Washington* v. *Texas*[28] (1967) enforced the right to a compulsory process for obtaining witnesses. As the Warren Court came to a close, *Duncan* v. *Louisiana*[29] (1968) established the right to an impartial jury, and *Benton* v. *Maryland* (1969), which prohibited a defendant from being put twice in double jeopardy by a state court, overturned *Palko* v. *Connecticut* (1937).[30]

At the end of Earl Warren's tenure as Chief Justice in 1969 the rout of state court criminal procedures was seemingly complete. The Court had cast aside all habeas corpus administrative hurdles and incorporated almost all of the criminal procedural aspects of the Bill of Rights. In his survey of federalism cases by the Warren Court in 1970, Philip Kurland wrote that "federalism is dead and the Supreme Court has made its contribution to its demise."[31] Kurland's Nietzschean bravado focused on the alteration under Chief Justice Warren of the Supreme Court's traditional role as a protector of property and a guardian of decentralization. Kurland argued that the Warren Court had subsumed all manner of cases—labor, race, and crime—under the rubric of the Fourteenth Amendment's centralizing force. According to Kurland, the Court's "essential role has been to act as a centripetal force, to modify the Constitution in order to sustain the enhancement of national authority and the despoliation of state power."[32] Rather than stand within that tradition, the Warren Court helped increase the "trend toward centralization."[33] By reinterpreting the major provisions of the Bill of Rights to comply with the due process demands of "fundamental fairness,"[34] the Court's criminal justice cases created a constitutional revolution in due process.

This is the standard history of the era. My purpose is to be more discerning regarding the nuances of the Court's criminal justice jurisprudence, by including analyses of habeas corpus cases that focus not just on the constraints of federalism but also on the uses to which federalism has restricted the applicability of constitutional rights to prisoners. Throughout this text, I have insisted that federalism be understood as a linguistic construct of Gilded Age lawyers, looking to separate corporations from criminals. Law can meet the challenge of an institution whose meaning shifts every decade or so, but it is pointless to make federalism the very ground of the law in habeas or capital punishment cases. Rather than accepting the legal order as something made tangible by the existence of penal institutions, I see the law as supplying an ambiguous foundation regarding federal-state questions, because, particularly in federalism's case, the meaning of the term is too soft to supply guidance.

Would *Ex parte Royall* really have disrupted federal-state relations more than *Santa Clara* or *Lochner* did? Federalism informs legal consciousness because it is part of the law's language that classifies persons, constructs relationships, and disperses responsibilities.[35] At best, federalism supplies the Court with a variety of tropes or heuristic devices with which the justices can discern the limits of the Constitution's applicability to the states, but only after a crime has been committed. Because of a historic lack of federal control over criminal justice, the idea that the states can control their populations through the instruments of crime and punishment, operating under minimal standards of due process, informs the Court's view that habeas petitions attack federalism. But it is not federalism that prevents habeas' success; it is the uses to which it is put. My aim, then, is to cast a more critical eye on the course of the Court's shift away from foundational concerns, such as federalism, and toward confessional narratives in the 1970s. Considerations of federalism and a reliance on the common law have forced habeas corpus onto a more deferential path regarding individual rights than other criminal justice concerns. Yet habeas corpus is very much about the "institutional logic of political disruption,"[36] even if the disruption comes not from institutions but from convicted criminals writing petitions from prison.

Studying habeas corpus in the 1960s provides a different lens with which to observe the weaknesses of the Supreme Court's incorporation debate and the inconsistent judicial patterning of centralization over time. Although the writ is an aspect of the criminal law that affects the arrest, incarceration, and rehabilitation stages of confinement, most Supreme Court opinions have stressed that the writ can operate only within the context of a rigid understanding of federal-state relations, governed by conceptions of institutional logic, deference, and respect for local decision-making powers. Such, for example, are the opinions of Justices Powell, Burger, and Rehnquist, in *Schneckloth* v. *Bustamonte*[37] (1973), who express their "grave doubts"[38] about William Brennan's broad understanding of the federal courts' habeas corpus capabilities in *Fay* v. *Noia*. Powell, Burger, and Rehnquist declared that habeas corpus undermines "the values inherent in our federal system of government"[39] by exacting "costs" on the system, in terms of burdening "limited judicial resources," by failing to respect "the necessity of finality in criminal trials," thereby heightening the "friction between our federal and state systems of justice," which destroys "constitutional balance upon which the doctrine of federalism is founded."[40] Federalism for them has an intrinsic worth that legitimates their understanding of the purposes of punishment, rather than being the result of competing interest-group politics over crime and punishment.

Yet Powell, Burger, and Rehnquist aimed their guns in the wrong direction. The paradigm they focused on was undermined not by Justices Brennan and Warren in the early 1960s but during the age of legal realism, by Justices Frankfurter, Black, Douglas, Rutledge and Murphy, in case after case that relied on the Fourteenth Amendment to overturn a state court conviction. But for the torture or trickery of the defendant, the state's case would have been upheld, on the very grounds that Powell, Rehnquist, and Burger upheld such cases in the 1970s. Moreover, but for Justices Frankfurter, Black, Douglas, Rutledge and Murphy, we would never have known about those stories. They would be historical relics, part of the states' archives but not part of due process of law. The problem of habeas corpus in American jurisprudence is that too often, the habeas petitioner's story is left out or included only in the dissent. Thurgood Marshall's dissent, in *Johnson* v. *Massachusetts*[41] (1968), could not have been possible without the New Deal justices' help. Thus, it fell to Justice Marshall to let us know that, though the facts of the case were not in dispute, the petitioner had a "sixth-grade education and an I.Q. of 86," that he confessed after spending "eight hours" in "police custody," that he was never "advised of his right to remain silent or his right to consult with an attorney," or that at "the time of his arrest petitioner was bleeding from a cut an inch or an inch and one-half long on the side of his head," and that "two weeks after his arrest and confession, petitioner underwent a brain operation for a sub-dural hematoma; the surgeon who operated on him testified that the hematoma 'could have been there anywhere from one to two weeks.'"[42]

By the mid-1930s, a kind of anarchy of constitutional interpretation had gained prominence among various justices regarding not just the ends of the Constitution but also the means, the ways in which decisions were made in (non-) conformity with constitutional rules. From the closing days of the Progressive era, the Court began looking beneath the states' records, prompted by individuals who were lynched, lied to, stamped with cigarettes, frightened, denied counsel, and beaten up. The justices on the Court in the 1960s simply picked up where the justices of the 1930s had left off. Yet, in response to similar cases, the 1970s Court turned its gaze away from such stories and toward the view that habeas corpus is a criminal justice tool, a way of preventing the release of convicted criminals, and left concerns over the demise of federalism to the backdrop of the story, a ready prop if all else fails.

The Burger Court met the Warren Court head on. The Court's narratives from the 1930s had sufficiently impaired the institutional support of the states' criminal justice apparatuses, by noting in individual cases the degree to which the confessions of the convicted had been coerced yet admitted into trial and relied on by state prosecutors.[43] In *Brown* v. *Mississippi* (1936) and *Thomas* v. *Arizona*[44] (1958) for example, it was confessions extorted through lynching; in *Ashcraft* v. *Tennessee* (1944), it was intensive police interrogation "with one five minute pause"; in *Rochin* v. *California*[45] (1952), it was the police pumping the accused's stomach for drugs; in *Culombe* (1961), as described at the outset of this chapter, it was through a "suction process" of intense interrogation that drained Arthur Culombe of his "capacity for freedom of choice";[46] in *Leyra* v. *Denno*[47] (1954), it was continual questioning over four days until Leyra confessed, and so on. But in retelling these tales without tying them directly to the Constitution, these narratives increased the level of surveillance of prisoners, heightened the regard for prisoners' anatomies, and fostered a more direct concentration on legal controls over prisoners' bodies. *Leyra*, in fact, is a good example of the sheer malleability of constitutional narratives. For every Justice Black or Frankfurter, sensitive to the nuances in law, language, and politics, there is a Justice Harold Burton, a Stanley Reed, or a Sherman Minton, who, writing in dissent in *Leyra*, began with this recapitulation of events: "This petitioner was charged with murdering his parents by beating the life out of them with a hammer. No one claims that he has a defense to the charge. It is contended, however, that his conviction was obtained in accordance with due process of law. He has already had two trials."[48] For constitutional good or ill, members of the Court, by the late 1960s, had come to recognize that the bodies of habeas petitioners contained narratives of their lives, and not just stories of state-sponsored injustices. Storytelling, like the determination of a voluntary confession, is an amphibian.[49] It belongs to no one.

Placing habeas corpus within the criminal law is the clearest example of the Burger Court's unwillingness to accept the Warren Court's application of the Bill of Rights to the states, but the surest sign that it accepted the Warren Court's demolition of federalism as the prop for the antihabeas advocates. To be sure, the Burger Court's decisions explain habeas corpus as it had existed in the nineteenth century—as an exceptional remedy, part of an exceptionalist enterprise—with the added feature that it frees criminals, or, more tendentiously, hammer-wielding murderers. The Burger and Rehnquist Courts once again viewed habeas corpus as a corrective to state court decisions that had to be reacclimated to the federal-state structure, only this time they added descriptions of the petitioners' behavior, which in fact overtook, as the reason for denial, the broad, historically based arguments of federalism's defenders. The second half of this chapter discusses the Burger Court's discursive attack against the Warren Court.

Justice Brennan adopted a novel approach to overcome the nineteenth century's structural prohibitions on habeas attacks. In *Fay* v. *Noia* (1963), in an attempt to break free of the Court's overbearing reliance on state court institutions, Brennan isolated the writ from the jurisdictional considerations of federal-sate comity the Court had imposed on individual petitioners since the end of Reconstruction and focused instead on the harm done to the individual defendant. Like the cases the Court reviewed during the first four decades of the twentieth century, Brennan played the discursive card by emphasizing not just the petitioner's story (the isolated element) but also the institutional mercilessness done to one person by protecting a state's legal tradition. Noia's story, in fact, was not of the same medieval character as that of Leyra, Culombe, or Chambers. *Fay* is a narration of state-sanctioned habeas corpus cruelty, created by a century of federal judicial decisions more attuned to "states' rights" than to individual rights.

In fact, Brennan was not tone deaf to the federalism debate. By isolating a habeas petitioner's claim of illegal detention from a state court's conviction, on the idea that habeas "comes in from the outside,"[50] Brennan hoped to ease federal-state tensions. The problem in *Fay* is that the petitioner, Noia—intentionally or not—had bypassed the state's appellate procedures and went directly, that is, following conviction, but many years later, to the federal courts. In doing so, he put himself above and beyond the "values of comity between state and nation."[51]

Rather than focusing on New York's institutional pain and feelings of hurt, as Justice Harlan had in *Aschraft*, Brennan stressed not Noia's hubris but that of New York. The emphasis laid down by Brennan was on what Abraham Sofaer has called the "isolation principle."[52] Justice John Marshall Harlan, who dissented in *Fay*, wanted to adhere to a modified jurisdiction standard, which would have protected the state courts from the kind of relief for which Noia was asking. Brennan, isolating the respondent Noia's claims from the institutional competency of the state court—in an effort to save the state court from institutional correction—viewed anything short of federal review on a claim of coercion leading to the possibility of the death penalty as federal abdication. Because, Brennan wrote, "In Noia's case the only relevant substantive law is federal—the Fourteenth Amendment. . . . Habeas lies to enforce the right of personal liberty; when that right is denied and a person confined, the federal court has the power to release him. Indeed, it has no other power; it cannot revise the state court judgment; it can act only on the body of the petitioner."[53]

During the Burger Court years, a majority formed that latched onto the weaknesses of Brennan's argument, particularly his underestimation of the judicial community's regard for state courts, and exploited his reliance on telling Noia's unfortunate story. Focusing mostly on the crimes of habeas petitioners, and secondarily on the apparent damage federal habeas corpus did to the legitimacy of state court decisions, the Burger Court embarked on a retrenchment of federal power over state prisoners following these two tracks. The first part of this chapter discusses the writ under the Warren Court and its expansion as a due process tool for state prisoners. The second part discusses the backlash against federal habeas corpus power under the Burger Court by focusing on habeas cases arising from confession stories.

A Prisoner's Dilemma: Fay *v.* Noia

Fay v. *Noia* is the first case of the contemporary habeas corpus debate. For the first time, the Court decided that the "[f]ederal courts have *power* under the federal habeas statute to grant relief despite the applicant's failure to have pursued a state remedy not available to him at the time he applies."[54]

In 1942, Charles Noia and two others were convicted of felony murder in the course of a robbery in Brooklyn, New York. Their signed confessions were the only evidence against them. Noia's two companions, Santo Cominto and Frank Bonino, appealed their convictions in state court and lost. Noia did not appeal. Cominto and Bonino subsequently pursued federal habeas corpus proceedings and won. The federal district court ruled their confessions had been coerced and unconstitutionally admitted into evidence. The presumption was that Noia, had he filed along with Cominto and Bonino, would have met a similar fate.

Noia, buoyed by his friends' success, appealed for habeas corpus in federal court. The court found his confession coerced but denied habeas because of his failure to exhaust his state remedies. The court of appeals reversed and ordered Noia discharged, pending a retrial without the confession admitted as evidence.

The question before the Supreme Court was "Under what circumstances, if any, the failure of a state prisoner to comply with a state procedural requirement, as a result of which the state courts decline to pass on the merits of his federal defense, bars subsequent resort to the federal courts for relief on habeas corpus."[55] In a 6:3 decision, the Court upheld the court of appeals' decision to release Noia.

Under *Fay*, the individual habeas applicant no longer had to abide by every formality imposed by the states and sanctioned by the Supreme Court before applying for federal habeas corpus. Instead, a habeas applicant is to be accorded "every reasonable presumption against waiver of federal rights."[56] The Court dismissed the adequate and independent state ground rule, applied to habeas corpus in *Daniels* v. *Allen* (1953), as another jurisdictional fiction that thwarted the command of the habeas statute. The Court in *Fay* distinguished the writ of habeas corpus from other forms of appeals because its sole purpose is to free those unconstitutionally confined, not to overturn state court convictions. Brennan turned explicitly to the writ's English past and linked it with the language of individual rights in an American context. Although concerned with avoiding unnecessary conflict between layers of judicial proceedings, that concern had to be subordinated to the statutory command of the writ, Brennan thought, which requires federal judges to "determine the facts, and dispose of the matter as law and justice require."

Brennan's opinion in *Fay* dealt with three related concerns: deliberate bypass, the adequate and independent state ground rule, and federalism. A deliberate bypass, which constitutes a "waiver"[57] of one's federal claims, is "an intentional relinquishment or abandonment of a known right or privilege." Although Noia's bypass of his state appellate remedies was deliberate—he feared a death sentence on retrial—the *Fay* majority did not consider Noia's actions a "deliberate bypass" as that term is understood. The defendant, in close consultation with his attorney, must "understandably and knowingly" forgo "the privilege of seeking to vindicate his federal claims in the state courts."[58] Brennan thought that Noia's choice was "not merely tactical": "His was the grisly choice whether to sit content with life imprisonment or to travel the uncertain avenue of appeal, which, if successful, might well have led to a retrial and death sentence."[59] Brennan held that although a federal habeas judge, in his discretion, could deny relief to a defendant who had deliberately bypassed the state court, this "grant of discretion," he wrote, "is not to be interpreted as a permission to introduce legal fictions into federal habeas corpus."[60] Moreover, a state court finding of waiver cannot stand as a bar to an independent determination of the issue by a federal court, "for waiver affecting federal rights is a federal question."[61]

Fay was a departure from the general rule that a claim not raised at trial constitutes a forfeiture of one's federal remedies. This is why *Fay* was controversial. The adequate and independent state ground rule, first stated in *Herb v. Pitcairn*[62] (1945), was designed to protect a state court from Supreme Court review if that decision sufficiently rested on state law.[63] The adequate and independent state ground rule fit well with other lawyerly inventions (Brennan's "fictions") that promoted federalism, such as the jurisdiction standard,[64] which prevented constitutional questions from being raised on habeas, provided the state court had jurisdiction over the case, and the "exhaustion doctrine,"[65] which required petitioners to complete all available remedies in the state courts first, before applying for federal habeas corpus. The Court's underlying rationale in devising these standards was ostensibly its commitment to harmony between court systems and a desire to minimize federal intervention on state criminal matters. But by attaching a linguistic wallop to these structural inhibitors—the defendant's established guilt—the Burger Court virtually rendered federal supervision of state court criminal decisions nonexistent.

Reacting to the legal realists' emphasis on process and institutional competency, Brennan held in *Fay* that habeas corpus does not operate against state procedures but on individual claimants.[66] Brennan denied that habeas corpus can "come in from the outside," because, for Brennan, the writ is not the wind beating against the closed window that is the federal structure of rights enforcement. It lives within the walls of the regime and attaches itself to the inhabitants. Brennan's opinion in *Fay* destroyed the Court's hierarchy of constitutional values, with the criminals roaming the bottom, and the Sheriff Screws of the world inhabiting the top. He viewed habeas corpus the same way Hugo Black viewed constitutional rights: as linguistic constructs that we carry on our person and that define the legal limits of our bodies. For Brennan and Black, these rights come first, and the job of the justice is to make sure the institutions that protect rights have the power and the will to do so. Rights violations may "shock our consciences," as Frankfurter wrote in *Rochin v. California*, but it is not our consciences that rectify the wrong. Wrongs are wrongs as they become structured through language. Institutions do that; they make distinctions between form and content. Brennan's isolation principle, therefore, should not be seen for what it was not: an attack against rigid legal formalism. Rather, for Brennan, habeas corpus directs all institutions engaged in criminal justice administration to track down and produce the live body of the person being unlawfully held, and to set him free if his case is justly made. He reversed the Court's previous ordering of the path of the law that flowed toward the states. The "essential difference," Brennan wrote, between direct and collateral review "is that the Supreme Court, on direct review, can only reverse the case and remand it to the state courts. It cannot secure the prisoner's release directly, and it is from this deficiency in its power that the problem arises of advisory opinions or invasion of the state's legal preserve. Since the federal habeas court does not function under any such limitation on its power, it is confronted by no such dilemma."[67] The adequate and independent state ground rule, then, is inappropriate to federal habeas proceedings because its purpose is purely institutional, not individual. As Curtis Reitz has succinctly stated, "the habeas corpus statute was not designed to express a relationship between federal and state judicial proceedings."[68]

But this is more true in Britain, which has a unitary form of government, than in the United States, which does not. Consequently it is more true in theory than in practice. In the United States, habeas corpus insinuates itself within the federal-state relationship because the states have had historic control over the arrest and punishment of persons, a fact that the Court only got around to interfering with in the 1930s. Ignoring the institutional conflict in the pattern of habeas' development does a disservice to the writ and the place of individual rights in American history. Isolating a habeas petitioner's complaint from the pattern of state-sponsored discrimination that exists against minorities, which the major political parties refuse to address, solves individual problems but perpetuates systemic ones. To be sure, it releases the federal government's power to remedy state-sanctioned unlawful detentions. But from a critical perspective, it tolerates pervasive, institutional illegality so that federal-state relations can continue without increased friction. It releases individuals, but binds the institutions that hold them tighter together.

Brennan's use of constitutional history and the language of individual rights as progressive tools against unconstitutional state action, and his focus on the individual subject's harm, were intentionally designed to demonstrate the individual aspects of the habeas tradition. It was an attempt to delink habeas corpus from the history and cause of federal-state comity by celebrating it as a "writ of liberty" tied by tradition to the movement for individual dignity. His habeas opinion adopts the grand narrative of the modern legal tradition, that of the individual's emancipation from institutional slavery. As such, he stressed the need for federal, not state, determinations of unlawful custody. *"Ex parte Royall,"* Brennan wrote, "stemmed from considerations of comity rather than power, and envisaged only the postponement, not the relinquishment, of federal habeas corpus jurisdiction."[69] Brennan freed the writ from the structural problems of the incorporation argument and concentrated, instead, on the crucial bond between federal review of prisoners' constitutional claims and habeas' "historic" purpose as a check on arbitrary state authority. In emphasizing Noia's situation as the cause for relief—caught as he was between the Scylla of present punishment (based on an extorted confession) and the Charybdis of a possible death penalty—Brennan wanted to show that habeas corpus and due process are historically coupled as agents opposed to arbitrary executive authority and together prevent restraints on individual liberty. Without stressing Noia's crime, he focused his attention on the fact that Noia was a "victim of unconstitutional state action."[70] Avoiding getting caught up in political questions of jurisdictional supremacy between rival governmental powers, Brennan draws our attention to the injustice of a rigid legal system that can find no outlet for those unlawfully committed to prison. In other words, Brennan stressed that because habeas operates solely on the question of whether or not someone is illegally detained, its primary concern cannot be the institutional competence or incompetence of the state courts.[71] As such, by releasing habeas from institutional concerns, he invited narrative tales into the habeas corpus decision-making process. By stripping the writ of its institutional accouterments, he announced that the habeas petitioner has no clothes, just a claim. Moreover, for Brennan, that claim is but a reflection of the person making it, a rhetorical device that will reflect—in the mirror of justice held by conservative Supreme Court justices—on the claim's quality, its applicability, resonance, and constitutionality.

The question in all federal habeas corpus applications from state prisoners is whether or not the petitioner is being held "in custody under or by color of the authority of the United States."[72] To determine the legality of a prisoner's confinement, a habeas court will often require an evidentiary hearing. According to the habeas statute (28 U.S.C. 2243):

> A court, justice or judge entertaining an application for a writ of habeas corpus shall forthwith award the writ or issue an order directing the respondent to show cause why the writ should not be granted, unless it appears from the application that the applicant or person detained is not entitled thereto. . . . When the writ or order is returned a day shall be set for hearing, not more than five days after the return unless for good cause additional time is allowed.

The question in *Townsend* v. *Sain*,[73] a companion case to *Fay*, was whether the district court was required "to hold a hearing to ascertain the facts which are a necessary predicate to a decision of the ultimate constitutional question."[74] The Court in *Townsend* relied heavily on the narration of events, particularly because this case involved a drug addict given a truth serum (disguised as relief for withdrawal pains) by a police physician to secure a conviction. Chief Justice Earl Warren, however, made an even stronger case for adopting a more narrative, literary approach to such cases than Brennan in *Fay*. "The function on habeas is different," he wrote. "It is to test by way of an original civil proceeding, independent of the normal channels of review of criminal judgments, the very gravest allegations. . . . Simply because detention so obtained is intolerable, the opportunity for redress, which presupposes the opportunity to be heard, to argue and present evidence, must never be totally foreclosed."[75]

Warren put the individual's own story, "the opportunity to be heard," at the front of the habeas challenge. He readied the habeas petitioner for speech, something denied him since 1886. Whether intentionally or not, Warren elided Brennan's discovery of isolation. To situate habeas corpus outside the governing structures of federal-state comity, as Brennan did, created yet another judicial fiction, as Holmes had in his dissent in *Frank v. Magnum*. Warren grafted habeas corpus onto the federal system, embedding it within the structures of criminal justice, placing the petitioner's testimony at the beginning of the equation. Habeas corpus for Warren is the very ground upon which arrests and convictions stand. The opportunity to be heard, a fundamental right within criminal justice, is habeas' mission. Warren linked the writ's historic thrust with a far more radical understanding of habeas corpus than any Supreme Court justice ever did: the writ allows the prisoner to rearrange the terms of debate regarding the conviction, placing himself at center stage and putting the state on trial. The opportunity for the petitioner (now a victim of the state's criminal justice system, in which the federal government is complicit) to be heard and to redress the state's narrative of events gains primacy of place over silence, deference, respect.

Since *Brown v. Allen*, the federal courts had struggled with Frankfurter's guidelines on the necessity of holding evidentiary hearings.[76] Between *Brown* and *Townsend*, developing case law had accepted Frankfurter's broad language.[77] But Warren believed that the guidelines in *Brown* had outlived their usefulness, and *Townsend v. Sain* provided him with the opportunity to correct Frankfurter's dicta.

Townsend and *Fay* both sought to end the debate over federal collateral review. Warren rejected the *Brown* standard for determining the admissibility of a confession because that standard was based solely on the ability of the accused "to make a narrative of past events or of stating his own participation in the crime."[78] Warren thought this was incomplete. The aggrieved individual is too weak to rebut the state's more dominant narrative. Indeed, even a subjective retelling of events could prove insufficient to establish innocence. The Court needed to provide the means by which the convicted could speak in his own voice, aided by the Court's authority, encasing the petitioner's narrative in the proper legal language. In Charles Townsend's case, the state court hearing, which determined the facts of the case, never noted that Townsend was forced by the police to ingest "hyoscine," a so-called truth serum, to induce his confession. Townsend, in fact, was a nineteen-year-old heroin addict at the time of his conviction, suffering from the pains of withdrawal. These facts could only be determined by an independent evidentiary hearing conducted by a federal judge.[79]

Warren supplies the facts of the case.

> The undisputed evidence adduced at the trial-court hearing on the motion to suppress showed the following. Petitioner was arrested by Chicago police shortly before or after 2 a.m. on New Year's Day 1954. They had received information from one Campbell, then in their custody for robbery, that petitioner was connected with the robbery and murder of Jack Boone, a Chicago steel-worker and the victim in this case. Townsend was 19 years old at the time, a confirmed heroin addict and a user of narcotics since age 15. He was under the influence of a dose of heroin administered approximately one and one-half hours before his arrest. It was his practice to take injections three to five hours apart. At about 2:30 a.m. petitioner was taken to the second district police station and, shortly after his arrival, was questioned for a period variously fixed from one-half to two hours. During this period, he denied committing any crimes. Thereafter at about 5 a.m. he was taken to the 19th district station where he remained, without being questioned, until about 8:15 p.m. that evening. At that time he was returned to the second district station and placed in a line-up with several other men so that he could be viewed by one Anagnost, the victim of another robbery. When Anagnost identified another man, rather than petitioner, as his assailant, a scuffle ensued, the details of which were disputed by petitioner and the police. Following this incident petitioner was again subjected to questioning. He was interrogated more or less regularly from about 8:45 until 9:30 by police officers. At that time an Assistant State's Attorney arrived. Some time shortly before or after nine o'clock, but before the arrival of the State's Attorney, petitioner complained to Officer Cagney that he had pains in his stomach, that he was suffering from other withdrawal symptoms, that he wanted a doctor, and that he was in need of a dose of narcotics. Petitioner clutched convulsively at his stomach a number of times. Cagney, aware that petitioner was a narcotic addict, telephoned for a police physician. There was some dispute between him and the State's Attorney, both prosecution witnesses, as to whether the questioning continued until the doctor arrived. Cagney testified that it did and the State's Attorney to the contrary. In any event, after the withdrawal symptoms commenced it appears that petitioner was unresponsive to questioning. The doctor appeared at 9:45. In the presence of Officer Cagney he gave Townsend a combined dosage by injection of 1/8–grain of phenobarbital and 1/230–grain of hyoscine. Hyoscine is the same as scopo-

lamine and is claimed by petitioner in this proceeding to have the properties of a "truth serum." The doctor also left petitioner four or five 1/4–grain tablets of phenobarbital. Townsend was told to take two of these that evening and the remainder the following day. The doctor testified that these medications were given to petitioner for the purpose of alleviating the withdrawal symptoms; the police officers and the State's Attorney testified that they did not know what the doctor had given petitioner. The doctor departed between 10 and 10:30. The medication alleviated the discomfort of the withdrawal symptoms, and petitioner promptly responded to questioning.[80]

The next day, Townsend awoke at a desk with a pen in his hand. He "signed his name believing that he was going to be released on bond," but was later told that he had confessed.[81]

Warren required a hearing even if the state trier of facts "presents a situation in which the 'so-called facts and their constitutional significance [are] . . . so blended that they cannot be severed in consideration.'"[82] Federal review implies federal independence; more than that, it marks a shift away from local and biased narratives to national, presumably less biased assertions of truth. "The federal court cannot exclude the possibility that the trial judge believed facts which showed constitutional deprivation of constitutional rights and yet (erroneously) concluded that relief should be denied. Under those circumstances it is impossible for the federal court to reconstruct the facts, and a hearing must be held."[83]

Brennan in *Fay* and Warren in *Townsend* viewed habeas corpus not just as a substantive right but as a counternarrative for justice. For Warren, habeas corpus is a "test by way of an original civil proceeding, independent of the normal channels of review of criminal judgments."[84] Warren placed habeas corpus within the network of narratives that question American criminal justice practices. The presumption on Warren's part is that the federal investigation would function as a way to arrive at a determination of events that are counterfactual to the state's punitive narrative. That which the state ignores, elides, covers over, habeas corpus opens up, signifies, renders unconstitutional. It was an enormous task, but one that, Warren thought, the Court was required to do. Habeas corpus, then, does not simply tell the side of the petitioner (or the murderer or rapist); it decenters the entire history of criminal jurisprudence by inhabiting a complex of alternative voices, which, above ground and in the open, are provided a space to compete against the state's more dominant narrative of violence, brutality, and the extinguishing of life.

The more conservative members of the Warren Court refused to tap around the effects of a habeas writ. The decisions in *Fay* and *Townsend* thrust habeas corpus into uncharted waters, they said. Without the ground of jurisdiction to prevent federal usurpation of traditional state functions, habeas corpus could become a question of power between the state and federal courts, and the state courts would always lose.[85] Although Justice John Marshall Harlan admitted in *Fay* that *Brown* v. *Allen* "substantially expanded the scope of inquiry on an application for federal habeas corpus,"[86] he immediately shifted his argument to *Daniels*, decided along with *Brown*, where the petitioner was denied relief and sentenced to death because of a procedural error by his own lawyer, and found that decision to be "wholly consistent with established principles in the field of habeas corpus jurisprudence,"[87] and indeed it was.

The weakness of Harlan's argument in *Fay* is that he tried to reestablish some kind of jurisdiction standard over habeas corpus cases in light of the Court's increasing concern for individual rights. Harlan exalted nineteenth-century procedures over the protection of constitutional rights without acknowledging that that emphasis could also undermine respect for national criminal justice institutions. Neither Harlan nor any other of *Fay*'s critics had an alternative to Daniels or Noia's plight, which is what Brennan and Warren intended. So high was Harlan's regard for federalism that Daniels and Noia's imprisonment (and death) was better than the Court's acknowledgment of institutional error at the state level. What Harlan wanted to do was to deny a federal forum to habeas petitioners to reinforce state rules whose purposes were purely instrumental to keeping prisoners in prison, regardless of the degree or depth of the constitutional claims. Rather than impose a burden on the state governments to prove that the detention was constitutional, conservatives on the Court wanted to deter criminal defendants from a federal hearing. Fundamentally, they viewed with suspicion the application of federal remedies to alleged constitutional violations at the state level on postconviction. To Harlan, habeas corpus did not operate from the "isolation" principle but as a collateral method to incorporate rights.

At the end of the 1960s, another discourse entered in against habeas corpus: fear of continued incorporation and application of the Bill of Rights to a larger group of petitioners, this time self-confessed criminals. *Fay*, therefore, was in danger of being diluted because it had not gone far enough. *Fay* and *Townsend* had not successfully tied habeas corpus to the due process clause of the Fourteenth Amendment. Nor was there any way to institutionalize the need for narratives of state-sanctioned violence within habeas or incorporation cases, particularly in the direction Chief Justice Warren had wanted. Prisoners' bodies, after all, are not neutral vessels. They contain scripts of their past crimes. *Townsend* gave petitioners the right to speak for themselves, but their crimes were never far from their pleas for relief. For this reason, from this weakness, Brennan and Warren were not successful in moving state criminal justice procedures away from formal procedures and toward substantive protections. Relying on the isolation principle forced Brennan to ignore the structure of the states' criminal justice procedures, except on a case-by-case basis. Consequently, Brennan made an unintended alliance with conservative justices to salvage the institutional remnants among habeas corpus, due process, and federalism. Unfortunately for the liberals, as long as due process remained constricted, not part of the Bill of Rights as Justice Black had intended in *Adamson* v. *California*, and habeas corpus independent of institutional considerations, the door remained open to limiting the reach of habeas on procedural grounds in the name of federal-state comity and selective incorporation. By the end of the 1960s, there was not enough support on the Court to free habeas corpus from procedural and guilt-related concerns, to do what Brennan and Warren had wanted.[88] But the door was also open for an attack on *Fay*, and Justice Black, in dissent in *Kaufman*, took advantage.

Kaufman v. *United States* is significant for two reasons. First, it is the last important case of the 1960s to defend a liberal interpretation of habeas corpus on the grounds of *Fay*. Second, Justice Black's dissent laid the basis for the Court's most significant restriction on habeas corpus in American history, in *Stone* v. *Powell* (1976).

Kaufman is a federal case, and its relevance for federal-state development is slight but not insignificant. Kaufman was tried and convicted in federal court in Missouri for armed robbery. He pleaded insanity. The court of appeals affirmed his conviction. Kaufman then filed a federal habeas corpus petition (section 2255 for federal prisoners), alleging that the finding of sanity was based on unlawfully seized evidence. This claim was rejected in an evidentiary hearing.[89] The court of appeals, in affirming, held that a habeas attack on a search and seizure claim is not proper. The Supreme Court reversed.

In *Kaufman*, the government argued that invoking the exclusionary rule on habeas corpus would not serve the purpose of the Fourth Amendment, since the petitioner's guilt had already been established at trial. The government believed that a search and seizure claim, unlike a denial of effective counsel or self-incrimination, is peculiar to the habeas process. In no way does it impugn the "integrity of the factfinding process." The purpose of excluding evidence seized during a search incident to arrest is to "deter Fourth Amendment violations by law enforcement officials."[90] Habeas corpus, a postconviction remedy, comes too late for that. But Brennan viewed *Kaufman* as an attack on *Fay*, because to uphold the federal district court's ruling would vindicate finality over individual rights. "There is no reason to treat federal trial errors as less destructive of constitutional guarantees than state trial errors, nor to give greater preclusive effect to procedural defaults by federal defendants than to similar defaults by state defendants. To hold otherwise would reflect an anomalous and erroneous view of federal-state relations."[91]

It is here that *Kaufman*'s relevance to the Burger Court appointees becomes clear. The dissent in *Kaufman* represents a break in the Court's post-*Brown* v. *Allen* or *Fay* v. *Noia* jurisprudence. It openly reorients the discussion over habeas corpus away from structures and toward individual behavior by bringing in the question of established guilt. Rather than setting a precedent for more openness toward habeas petitioners, the dissent in *Kaufman* reversed course. As Justice Black wrote in dissent in *Kaufman*, and Justice Lewis Powell reiterated in a majority concurrence in *Schneckloth* v. *Bustamonte* (1974), "For unlike a claim of denial of effective counsel or of violation of the privilege against self incrimination, as examples, a claim of illegal search and seizure does not impugn the integrity of the fact-finding process or challenge evidence as inherently unreliable; rather, the exclusion of illegally seized evidence is simply a prophylactic device intended generally to deter Fourth Amendment violations by law enforcement officers."[92] For Powell and Black, the evidence seized, regardless of constitutional improprieties, proves the habeas petitioner's guilt, and it only does a disservice to the workings of federalism to contest those findings after conviction.

The push, then, from the beginning of the 1970s, is toward greater reliance on narratives driven by images of the initial conviction. Thus, whereas Justice Brennan's majority opinion in *Kaufman* begins rather prosaically, stating that the petitioner "was tried and convicted in the District Court . . . on charges of armed robbery of a federally insured savings and loan association,"[93] Black's dissent fills in the gaps, the way Warren's narrative in *Townsend* had against the state. "Petitioner Kaufman was convicted of robbing a federally insured savings and loan association while armed with a pistol. Part of the evidence against him was a revolver, some of the stolen traveler's checks, a money-order receipt, a traffic summons, and gasoline receipts."[94] Brennan was concerned with upholding the exclusionary rule and defending *Fay*'s habeas corpus ruling. Black was far more troubled by Kaufman's character and his failure to assert "either at his trial or in this proceeding" that "he had not actually physically committed the robbery with a pistol, and despite the fact that this plainly reliable evidence clearly shows, along with the other evidence at trial, that he was not insane."[95]

Justice Black's dissent in *Kaufman* was a sign of his frustration at the Warren Court's understanding of habeas corpus. For Black, the Warren Court favored speech that was only directed at state institutions and state agents. Personal confessions of guilt were not part of Warren's understanding of the relationship between habeas corpus and free speech. Black desperately wanted Kaufman to speak, to admit his guilt, though it is unlikely that Justice Black would have changed his vote had Kaufman declared himself guilty.[96]

For Black, speech *was* necessary: a petitioner must establish a "constitutional claim that casts some shadow of a doubt on his guilt."[97] Black blamed more than just the decision in *Fay* for Kaufman's reticence. He blamed the Warren Court's habeas corpus jurisprudence. Kaufman's unwillingness to examine himself, to admit to the Court his guilt, struck Black as more than a slap in the face. It represented the legal system's distortion of important procedures designed to get the truth from convicted criminals without having to endure judicial repetition.

Black was alone among the dissenting justices in relying on guilt as a defense against unconstitutional confinement; but his argument had some force, and with the replacement of key Warren Court members by President Richard Nixon, Black's argument on innocence soon replaced Brennan's emphasis on individual rights. The next section, discussing the 1970s, consists not only of attacks on *Fay*'s reading of habeas corpus but also includes its virtual overthrow as well.

THE 1970s: THE TURN
AGAINST THE WARREN COURT

"Our function," Justice John Marshall Harlan II wrote in *McGautha v. California* (1971), "is not to impose on the States, *ex cathedra*, what might seem to us a better system for dealing with capital cases. Rather, it is to decide whether the Federal Government proscribes the present procedures of these two States in such cases. In assessing the validity of the conclusions reached in this opinion, that basic factor should be kept in mind."[98] What should be a death penalty case is in fact a federalism case and the first case of the 1970s to bring in the defendant's character as a source for judicial determination.

McGautha and its companion case, *Crampton v. Ohio*, are about each state allowing juries to determine punishment without any governing standards. The Supreme Court affirmed the convictions, largely on deference grounds, over objections that the unitary structures of the guilt and punishment phases did not allow the juries to consider "mercy." But that is not "its defect," Justice Douglas wrote in dissent.

> It has a constitutional infirmity because it is not neutral on the awesome issue of capital punishment. The rules are stacked in favor of death. It is one thing if the legislature decides that the death penalty attaches to defined crimes. It is quite another to leave to judge or jury the discretion to sentence an accused to death or to show mercy under procedures that make the trial death oriented. Then the law becomes a mere pretense, lacking the procedural integrity that would likely result in a fair resolution of the issues. In Ohio, the deficiency in the procedure is compounded by the unreviewability of the failure to grant mercy.[99]

Douglas' attack against the Court's opinion was only tangentially based on conceptions of mercy. Rather, he tied Ohio's and California's procedures, which prohibited the juries from showing "sympathy" to the accused, to the inability of the defendants to speak for themselves, to be heard before a jury regarding the history of their lives, thereby discursively connecting *McGautha*'s and *Crampton*'s claims with Warren's opinion in *Townsend*.

But the attack on *Fay* and its progeny, which began in earnest during the mid-1970s, had two prongs, one institutional, the other discursive: the

guilt-innocence standard of *Stone* v. *Powell* (1976) and the cause and prejudice rule of *Wainwright* v. *Sykes*[100] (1977). By 1970, two opposing problems
could be isolated regarding *Fay's* effect on habeas corpus. To the left, *Fay*
had not gone far enough.[101] To the right, the problem with *Fay* was that it
had gone too far in subordinating state criminal procedures in the name of
federal supremacy. *Fay's* high standard in establishing "waiver" drew particular criticism from conservative quarters.

Judge Henry Friendly of the United States Court of Appeals for the Second Circuit began the attack on *Fay* by packaging a defense of federalism
within a larger category of determining the guilt or innocence of habeas petitioners. His 1970 article, "Is Innocence Irrelevant? Collateral Attack on Criminal Judgments,"[102] prosaically argued that it was inconceivable that the *Fay*
majority had allowed Noia to obtain federal review, "since the state ha[d] not
deprived [Noia] of anything to which he [was] constitutionally entitled."[103]
The emphasis on what kind of relief a habeas petitioner is "constitutionally
entitled" formed the basis for Friendly's proposal that "convictions should be
subject to collateral attack when the prisoner supplements his constitutional
plea with a colorable claim of innocence."[104] Friendly would have granted federal review provided the habeas petitioner could demonstrate "a fair probability that, in light of all the evidence, including that alleged to have been illegally admitted (but with due regard to any unreliability of it) and evidence
tenably claimed to have been wrongly excluded or to have become available
only after the trial, the trier of the facts would have entertained a reasonable
doubt of [the petitioner's] guilt."[105]

The Paths to Restriction: Guilt and Federalism

In 1970, the Supreme Court decided three cases known collectively as the
Brady trilogy. These cases dealt with the question "whether and to what extent
an otherwise valid guilty plea was motivated by a prior coerced confession."[106]
One wonders if the introduction of habeas cases tied to coerced confession
cases, at the start of a new decade, is merely fortuitous or the outgrowth of a
system that had so intertwined habeas corpus and confession cases that it was
no longer tenable, in light of *Fay* v. *Noia* and *Townsend* v. *Sain*, to stifle the
relationship between the writ and the right to speak freely regarding one's
conviction. Regardless of the source, the combination of coerced confession
cases coming to the Court on habeas corpus during the 1970s certainly presents an interesting problem. This surge of language and of confession forces
us to look closely at these cases and to cast a more suspect eye on the Court's
defense of federalism as the reason for restricting federal habeas corpus. It
seems clear that the focus on confessions and the restrictions on habeas corpus are related, insofar as the Court had come to rely on the guilt of the petitioners to establish the grounds for habeas denials.

That a guilty plea is a grave and solemn act to be accepted only with care and discernment has long been recognized. Central to the plea and the foundation for entering judgment against the defendant is the defendant's admission in open court that he committed the acts charged in the indictment. *He thus stands as a witness against himself* and he is shielded by the Fifth Amendment from being compelled to do so—hence the minimum requirement that his plea be the voluntary expression of own choice.[107]

The *Brady* trilogy weakened the evidentiary hearing requirements established in *Townsend* v. *Sain,* by placing the burden of the waiver of one's right to appeal in state courts, and consequently the ground for an evidentiary hearing, on the defendant and his counsel.

The question of the validity of the plea remains the same: was the plea a voluntary and intelligent act of the defendant? As we have previously set out, a plea of guilty in a state court is not subject to collateral attack in a federal court on the ground that it was motivated by a coerced confession unless the defendant was incompetently advised by his attorney. For the respondents successfully to claim relief based on *Jackson* v. *Denno,* each must demonstrate gross error on the part of counsel when he recommended that the defendant plead guilty instead of going to trial.[108]

Warren's attempt to open up the habeas challenge to alternative voices, to connect the basic functions of due process with the "right to speak for one's self," as Douglas mentioned in *McGautha,*[109] with the federal government's support and supervision, was now reversed. In *McMann* v. *Richardson,* part of the *Brady* cases, the Court held that the defendant must demonstrate "gross error" by his counsel to clear the waiver standard.[110] "A conviction after a plea of guilty normally rests on the defendant's own admission in open court that he committed the acts with which he is charged."[111]

In *Tollet* v. *Henderson,*[112] a 1976 case, the Court denied habeas corpus to a twenty-six-year-old black man with a sixth-grade education who had confessed to a murder, first without benefit of counsel, then again on advice of counsel. When Henderson appealed the state's ruling in federal district court in the 1960s, alleging, for the first time, that there were no blacks on his jury in Nashville, Tennessee, in 1948, his counsel admitted, in a "sworn affidavit," that he had not known that blacks had been systematically excluded from Tennessee's juries.[113] Justice William Rehnquist, writing for the Court, held that "after a criminal defendant pleads guilty, on the advice of counsel, he is not automatically entitled to federal collateral relief." He continued: "The focus of federal habeas inquiry is the nature of the advice and the voluntariness of the plea, not the existence as such of an antecedent constitutional infirmity. . . . If the prisoner pleads guilty on the advice of counsel, he must demonstrate that the advice was not 'within the range of competence demanded of attorneys in criminal cases.'"[114] The effect of the Burger Court's redirection of habeas corpus was to reverse the relation between the individual habeas petitioner and the state established by the New Deal Court in *Chambers* v. *Florida* (1940). There, the Court was sensitive to the various ways state officials obtain confessions. "The rejection of petitioner Woodward's first "confession," given in the early hours of Sunday morning, because it was found wanting, demonstrates the relentless tenacity which 'broke' petitioners' will and rendered them helpless to resist their accusers further. To permit human lives to be forfeited upon confessions thus obtained would make of the constitutional requirement of due process of law a meaningless symbol."[115] The Burger Court wanted speech to be confessional, not confrontational, as the Warren Court made it out to be in *Fay* and *Townsend*. *Fay* and *Townsend* made the petitioner speak in a way that focused judicial attention on the patterns of bias within state court criminal systems. The paradox of the Burger Court's jurisprudence is that the petitioner's confession and guilty plea stand as the very ground upon which the Court is willing to uphold the conviction—the same petitioner who is a dissembler of facts and a thief of language. The guilty plea represents a break in the constitutional proceedings of habeas applicants, because "a guilty plea, like any surrender of fundamental constitutional rights, reflects the unfettered choice of the defendant."[116] Consequently, the emphasis on the petitioner's speech and action (up until the conviction) engages the interests of the state in a way never before seen. After that "break," which is the petitioner's own doing, the Court continuously reiterates, the *Brady* trilogy and *Tollett* lead to the conclusion that the habeas petitioner has no right to speak.

> We thus affirm the principle in the *Brady* trilogy: a guilty plea represents a break in the chain of events which has preceded it in the criminal process. When a criminal defendant has solemnly admitted in open court that he is in fact guilty of the offense with which he is charged, he may not thereafter raise independent claims [i.e., on habeas corpus] relating to the deprivation of constitutional rights that occurred prior to the entry of the guilty plea.[117]

These four cases go deeper than even Justice Douglas anticipated in his dissent in *McGautha*. The *Brady* trilogy and *Tollett* not only announced the unexceptional claim that a guilty plea constitutes a waiver of federal rights but also the exceptional constitutional doctrine that guilty pleas waive rights "not yet known, or knowable, at the time the pleas were accepted."[118] By turning the basis of a habeas appeal away from state action and toward the individual's confessed guilt and then tightening that new direction in criminal jurisprudence by preventing criminal defendants from becoming habeas petitioners—by making their claims illegitimate at the point of conviction—

the effect was to weaken the abilities of habeas petitioners to contest their confinements in federal courts.

The confession, for Black and Powell, is the centerpiece of the federal courts' reason for rejecting the habeas petition. They, along with other Burger Court justices, accepted the habeas petitioner's confession without showing any interest in having a federal court determine whether the confession was coerced. We are not even ten years removed from *Miranda* v. *Arizona*, and the Court no longer had an interest in revisiting Earl Warren's conditions for establishing the constitutionality of a confession. In *Miranda*, the Court did more than just rehash the facts of the case. Chief Justice Warren spent much time trying to get the lower federal courts and the state courts to understand that confessions do not occur because of a desire on the part of the criminal defendant to express herself. Rather, confessions occur in specific places that are suited to making the defendant speak. Warren wrote, "It is obvious that such an interrogation environment is created for no other purpose than to subjugate the individual to the will of his examiner."[119]

The confession, then, is not speech, as the Burger Court made it out to be, but a "a way of saying, yes, all is gone now, there is almost nothing left now, even this voice, the sounds I am making, no longer form my words but the words of another."[120] By allowing the confession from the police station to determine the guilt of the person, all the way through the legal process, up to the Supreme Court, is, in fact, a way to point out that the individual confession is not something unmediated, but in fact, a "ritual that unfolds within a power relationship, for one does not confess without the presence (or virtual presence) of a partner who is not simply the interlocutor but the authority who requires the confession, prescribes and appreciates it, and intervenes in order to judge, punish, forgive, console and reconcile."[121] But recognizing this and acknowledging it are two different things. Because of the pressures put on federalism by federal court redeterminations of confessions, which could occur years after the initial confession, the Burger Court refused to acknowledge the confession as anything less than an admission of guilt. Rejecting Frankfurter's point in *Culombe* that voluntariness is an amphibian, the Court saw confessions in simpler, straightforward terms. But as Peter Brooks has pointed out, to accept the confession of a criminal defendant is to admit to doubt; it is a conclusion reached based on not really knowing what occurred behind closed doors. By the mid 1970s, the Supreme Court decided that it could live with the "ambiguities of confession." Confessions, Brooks writes, are "too useful to give up."[122]

However messy the Court's reliance on narratives had become, it still had to shore up its defense of federalism. In 1968, Lloyd Powell was arrested in Nevada on vagrancy charges. In a search incident to his arrest, the police discovered a gun and traced it to a shooting in California. Upon extradition, California convicted Powell. In 1971, Powell filed for habeas corpus, alleging that the vagrancy law was unconstitutionally vague; that the police officer lacked probable cause to detain and later search Powell; and that all evidence obtained by the search was unconstitutionally admitted as evidence against him. The district court denied Powell's plea, but the court of appeals reversed.[123] The Supreme Court reversed.

Though much of *Stone* v. *Powell* turned on the role of the exclusionary rule, the crux of the case was whether or not state prisoners could invoke a Fourth Amendment search and seizure claim on habeas. Black, dissenting in *Kaufman*, had written that "[t]he purpose of the exclusionary rule . . . does not include, even to the slightest degree, the goal of insuring that the guilt-determining process be reliable."[124] Justice Powell and five other justices held that, because the evidence illegally obtained by the police and used against the defendant at trial is not only "reliable," but also "often the most probative information bearing on the guilt or innocence of the defendant,"[125] the petitioner could not be granted his request to deny the admissibility of the evidence used against him.

Powell thought Brennan's expansive understanding of the scope of the writ unpersuasive.[126] On Fourth Amendment claims, Powell held that there was no historical guidance at all concerning habeas corpus. Rather than retreating into history, Powell was liberated from it. He could now argue that habeas corpus is inconvenient to the inner workings of "our federalism" because his focus is on the petitioner's established guilt. We thus search in vain in *Stone* for the historical aspect of the Court's traditional federalism claims. The issue in *Stone* turned not on the meaning of the common law, federalism, or on habeas' historic legacy, but on balancing the costs of releasing the guilty against the benefits of allowing for collateral attack in all cases of unlawful detention. This is the peculiar contribution of the Burger Court to habeas corpus. *Stone* v. *Powell* sets habeas corpus free from its historic mission to rectify arbitrary executive action and placed it firmly within the grasp of the criminal law, as defined by reductionist and formalist justices. The Burger Court saw no reason to allow state prisoners to challenge their convictions on habeas in search and seizure cases as long as the prisoner "has been afforded the opportunity for full and fair consideration of his search-and-seizure claim at trial and on direct review."[127] Habeas corpus is an equation of justice, not justice itself.

Powell's attack on the legacy of *Fay* in *Stone* was twofold. On the one hand, he wanted to bring to habeas corpus an innocence standard as a way to diminish the number of appeals from prisoners alleging constitutional violations, not touching their guilt, but effecting the constitutionality of their convictions. On the other hand, he wanted the Court to shed the image it had of the state courts as hostile to civil rights.[128] Both goals present enormous difficulties in understanding habeas corpus.

The basis for the innocence standard was partly rooted in the nature of Fourth Amendment claims. The Court denied that the exclusionary rule was a constitutional protection for citizens. It is a means to prevent, not repair, constitutional infractions. "Its purpose is to deter—to compel respect for the constitutional guaranty in the only effectively available way—by removing the incentive to disregard it."[129] On the assumption that the defendant has either waived his right to the search, or his counsel did not object to the evidence submitted at trial, the Burger Court maintained that there is a preponderance of evidence in such cases suggesting sufficient guilt to ward off collateral attack.

Justice Powell admitted that one difficulty with the innocence standard was that it has no basis in habeas corpus' history. So he edited that out of his considerations and cast habeas corpus as a crime problem tied to a federalism problem. To be sure, Powell had to overcome the argument that a federal district court had the power to release a defendant found to be unlawfully detained. The standard for release is the illegality of the custody, not the defendant's guilt. Truth, Frankfurter held in *Rogers* v. *Richmond*[130] (1961), is not the operative criterion in a habeas challenge; it is whether or not a prisoner is being detained "in violation of the Constitution."[131]

Yet *Stone* v. *Powell* does not read the habeas act that way. It was an expression of anger at the perceived rising tide of habeas applications by state prisoners. But the challenge of *Stone* is not with the number of habeas petitions; it is with the constitutional burdens placed on state and federal courts to respect individual autonomy. According to Charles Weisselberg, federal evidentiary hearings did not inconvenience the federal courts during the 1970s. In summarizing his findings, Weisselberg stated: "[W]hile the absolute number of habeas corpus petitions filed by state prisoners continues to rise, the rate of filings per state prisoner continues to fall. The district courts afford evidentiary hearings to state prisoners in an exceedingly small proportion of cases. The 'presumption of correctness' contained in the 1966 [habeas corpus] amendments have sharply curtailed the incidence of evidentiary hearings."[132] It is difficult to square the fears and the judgment expressed in *Stone* with reality. But the Court, throughout the remainder of the 1970s, and well into the 1980s and 1990s, continued to restrict access to the federal courts on habeas corpus using a number of doctrines not formally required of habeas petitioners.

"Cause and Prejudice": The End of Fay v. Noia

Justice Potter Stewart, writing for the Court in *Francis* v. *Henderson* (1976), officially signaled the Court's willingness to return habeas corpus to the standard set forth in *Ex parte Royall* in 1886. Stewart denied that federal habeas courts could ignore "considerations of comity and concerns for the orderly administration of criminal justice." Such concerns, he wrote, "require a federal court" "in some circumstances" "to forgo the exercise of its habeas corpus power."[133] Next, he held that "considerations of comity and federalism require that [the federal courts] give not less effect to the same clear interests when asked to overturn state criminal convictions."[134] Then, in a conclusion that was all too neat, Stewart held that to overcome the contemporaneous-objection rule, a petitioner must not only demonstrate "cause" for his failure "to challenge the composition of the grand jury before trial" but also demonstrate "actual prejudice" from the ruling.[135]

By the end of the 1970s, a majority of justices on the Supreme Court were convinced that the individual benefits of *Fay* did not outweigh its costs to society. In *Wainwright* v. *Sykes* (1977), Justice Rehnquist established that *Fay*'s deliberate bypass test denigrated "contemporaneous-objection rules" designed by the states to encourage challenges at trial, rather than years later on federal habeas proceedings. Rehnquist determined, against all evidence, that *Fay* encouraged "sandbagging." That is, he believed that defense attorneys intentionally did not bring up potentially salient judicial points in state courts so that they could raise them later in a federal habeas court, which, it was alleged, would be more hospitable to claims against state procedures.[136] *Fay*, in short, according to Rehnquist, fostered the notion that the state court trial is not a "decisive and portentous event."

The Court in *Wainwright* v. *Sykes* created the "cause and prejudice" standard to counteract *Fay*'s denigration of finality and the view that state court trials do not deserve respect. *Sykes* was an attempt to roll back *Fay*, not eliminate federal habeas corpus jurisdiction. Rehnquist accepted *Brown* v. *Allen*'s assertion that claims decided by state courts are open to *de novo* reconsideration at the discretion of the federal habeas judge.[137] But he rejected *Fay*'s assertion that unresolved issues can be relitigated at the federal level. The central irony of *Sykes* is that if a defendant raises his federal claim in a state court and loses, he can raise the claim again in a federal court. But the Court will bar any federal claim if the defendant's attorney errs and fails to raise a claim in a state court. Yet there is no irony in *Sykes*' outcome. *Sykes* imposed a burden on underpaid and overworked criminal defense attorneys and let the ramifications of their errors fall on the criminal defendant.[138]

Neither *Sykes* nor *Henderson* officially overruled *Fay*, but both fundamentally ignored it. *Fay* had rejected the adequate and independent state ground rule on habeas attacks and substituted the deliberate bypass standard. Nevertheless, Rehnquist in *Sykes*, relying on the Reconstruction era case *Murdock* v. *Memphis*[139] (1875), stated, "it is a well-established principle of federalism that a state decision resting on an adequate foundation of state substantive law is immune from review in the federal courts."[140]

Brennan had based *Fay* on three principles. One, that the habeas corpus statute required full federal review of state prisoners' claims with few strings attached. Two, that federal rights were better protected by federal courts than by state courts. And three, that despite the deference normally accorded state court decisions, it was deference and not a want of power that had prevented the federal courts, prior to *Fay*, from exercising their jurisdiction.[141]

Sykes, along with *Davis* v. *U.S.*, *Stone*, and *Francis* struck at Brennan's opinion by arguing that rights, not institutions, were fungible. Relying on Paul Bator's influential 1963 article on finality, the Court's conservative members held up habeas attacks to the light of effective procedure and institutional competence. Under this ahistorical and functional approach, the Court reinstated some of the procedural hurdles from the nineteenth century. Moreover, the Court instituted a new criterion, the default principle, to cut off federal review to those whose lawyers had failed to object to particular claims at trial. *Sykes*, then, cut to the very heart of a habeas attack. Not only did it force habeas petitioners to raise all possible claims in state courts, else their claims be forfeited, but it also benefited the state courts because it allowed the federal courts to ignore claims that the state courts did not hear. Recognizing the resource and time constraints imposed on defense attorneys, *Sykes* limited the number of federal claims made since the application of the Bill of Rights to the states in the early twentieth century, by forcing all issues to be addressed at trial. The Court made this point knowing that many habeas petitioners proceed either without counsel or with lesser quality court-appointed attorneys.[142]

CONCLUSION

As most habeas petitions are filed *pro se*, that is, by the habeas petitioner himself or by counsel that is less than adequate,[143] *Sykes* created a burden on habeas petitioners that few could meet. In large part, the problem with federal habeas corpus jurisdiction is a lack of institutional will to correct constitutional problems. For example, criminal defendants were extended the Sixth Amendment's right to counsel protection in *Gideon* v. *Wainwright* in 1963. Habeas petitioners have no such right.[144] *Fay* could have eliminated once and for all the arguments of the Burger Court by making a larger claim about the due process issues involved in a habeas attack.[145] Or the Warren Court could have tied every habeas decision to a procedural right, thus remedying quality of counsel problems on habeas petitions. What are most procedural default problems, if not attorney error?

Searching through these weaknesses, by the mid-1970s the Court had found a way to restrict *Fay's* reach. In light of the liberalization of federal habeas jurisdiction that occurred in the 1960s, a large number of petitions reached the federal courts asking for review. Apart from the commonsense observation that not all of the petitioners were innocent, it was also apparent that many petitions were downright frivolous or constitutionally vague. Justices Powell and Rehnquist (though not speaking for the Court), relying on *Stone* for innocence and *Sykes* for "cause and prejudice," and default, stated in

Rose v. *Mitchell*[146] (1979) that if the Court was to extend "the writ to cases in which guilt of the incarcerated claimant is not an issue, at least we should weigh thoughtfully the societal costs that may be involved [in releasing the petitioner on habeas corpus]."[147] At the end of the 1970s, a functional approach to federal-state relations, as well as to individual rights claims, had replaced the Warren Court's concern for the fundamental issue of illegal incarceration. In the next chapter, the development of the Court's "cause and prejudice" standard further complicated the habeas process by imposing tighter restrictions on state prisoners' constitutional claims. If the Court abandoned federalism during the 1960s, it reappeared in the 1980s as a forceful narrative restriction on the movement of state prisoners through the federal system.

FIVE

Future Dangerousness and Habeas Corpus, 1982–2002

This Court is forever adding new stories to the temples of constitutional law, and the temples have a way of collapsing when
one story too many is added.

—Miranda v. Arizona

Each chapter of this book is a study of change within time. But the
changes in habeas jurisprudence during the 1980s are distinctive from other
decades. The Rehnquist Court linked habeas corpus with growing fears that
the writ was responsible for releasing the violently guilty. Indeed, by the
1980s, the Court had formally abandoned relying almost exclusively—as it
had up to the 1960s—on jurisdictional constructions designed to force the
federal courts to defer to state court judgments in the name of the smooth
operation of criminal justice. The Court, from the final years of Warren
Burger's tenure as chief justice (1969–1986) to William Rehnquist's elevation to that position in 1986, was engaged in a struggle to define the habeas
petitioner by his crime and his potential for future dangerousness. A punitive rationality, always present in habeas corpus cases, rose to the surface
during the 1980s as the justification for habeas denial. Even the cases most
often associated with imposing jurisdictional restraints on habeas petitioners in the name of federalism, *Teague* v. *Lane* (1989), *Penry* v. *Lynaugh*
(1989), and *Coleman* v. *Thompson* (1991), reveal the Court's more imminent
concern that to grant the writ would be to release the guilty. A narrative of

events, quite often in all of its brutality, replaced the institutional logic and narrative value of federalism.

Yet the change on the Rehnquist Court, away from a strict reliance on federalism and toward narratives of violence, is really an alteration of terminologies rather than of functions, an addition to the Court's peculiar jurisprudential geography of preventing petitioners from getting from point A to point B. The 1980s, then, force us to confront the Court's mirror to history— a history of the present, written in the language of the past, but updated for one's reading pleasure. We will now know not just what the habeas petitioner is charged with; we will read what he has done, and how often, and with how much force. We will have his level of intelligence and motives explained by justices and medical experts, all while the petitioner—in whose name the case makes history—remains unnamed, inert, silent. But we will meet the victim's family, feel their loss, experience their pain, hear their words, relive their agony. The unnamed respondent (or defendant or petitioner, as the criminal appears in various guises) will be executed because a jury has determined that she is guilty, as the law requires. The 1980s, then, mimic the 1880s in this regard, except for the fact that we will no longer read quaint descriptions of murder, such as Justice Frank Murphy's in *Lee* v. *Mississippi* (1948): "Petitioner, a 17-year old Negro, was indicted by a grand jury in Mississippi on a charge of assault with intent to ravish a female of previous chaste character."[1] Instead, we are confronted with Chief Justice Rehnquist's more lurid and indicting description in *Sawyer* v. *Whitley* (1992):

> In 1979—13 years ago—petitioner and his accomplice, Charles Lane, brutally murdered Frances Arwood, who was a guest in the home petitioner shared with his girlfriend, Cynthia Shano, and Shano's two young children. As we recounted in our earlier review of this case [*Sawyer* v. *Smith*] . . . petitioner and Lane returned to petitioner's home after a night of drinking and argued with Arwood, accusing her of drugging one of the children. Petitioner and Lane then attacked Arwood, beat her with their fists, kicked her repeatedly, submerged her in the bathtub, and poured scalding water on her before dragging her back into the living room, pouring lighter fluid on her body and igniting it. Arwood lost consciousness sometime during the attack and remained in a coma until she died of her injuries approximately two months later. Shano and her children were in the home during the attack, and Shano testified that petitioner prevented them from leaving.[2]

Rehnquist's description, in fact, is not as instructive and explicit as Justice Anthony Kennedy's in *Sawyer* v. *Smith* (1990), Sawyer's first time at the Supreme Court. Kennedy's description manages to be more informative and reticent at the same time. But here he names the petitioner:

Over 10 years ago, petitioner Robert Sawyer murdered Frances Arwood, a visitor in the New Orleans, Louisiana, residence petitioner shared with his girlfriend, Cynthia Shano. On September 29, 1979, petitioner and his accomplice Charles Lane arrived at the residence after a night of drinking. They argued with Arwood and accused her of giving drugs to Shano's children. For reasons that are not clear, petitioner and Lane struck Arwood repeatedly with their fists and dragged her by the hair into the bathroom. There they stripped the victim naked, literally kicked her into the bathtub, and subjected her to scalding, dunkings, and additional beatings. Petitioner left Lane to guard the victim, and apparently to rape her, while petitioner went to the kitchen to boil water to scald her. Petitioner kicked Arwood in the chest, causing her head to strike the tub or a windowsill and rendering her unconscious. The pair then dragged Arwood into the living room, where they continued to beat and kick her. Petitioner poured lighter fluid on the unconscious victim, particularly her torso and genital area, and set the lighter fluid afire. He told Lane that he had done this to show "just how cruel he could be." There were further brutalities we do not recount. Arwood later died of her injuries. Petitioner was convicted and sentenced to death for the crime by a Louisiana jury in September 1980. At issue in this case are remarks made by the prosecutor in his closing argument during the sentencing phase of the trial.[3]

The legal subject is once again (as he was in the nineteenth century) clearly defined by the type of case he presents, by the level of violence, by his status within society, but not his name. The Court's historic elision of the habeas petitioner's full personhood means that rights are attached at the level of a jurisdictional split between federal and state courts, which recognizes, contrary to the plain language of the Fourteenth Amendment, two kinds of persons, representing two kinds of institutional solutions, two kinds of rights, two kinds of applications for relief.

In general, prior to the 1980s, macro-level societal changes created institutional adjustments in federal habeas corpus law. For example, alterations in the nineteenth-century economy forced appellate restrictions on criminal defendants because of limited judicial capacity to deal with due process claims coming from aggrieved corporations. Between the New Deal and the Warren Court, changes in the Supreme Court's agenda, away from property concerns and toward "fundamental fairness" demonstrated a higher regard for individual rights than for federal-state concerns. This transformation, by lore attached to *U.S. v. Carolene Products'* footnote 4,[4] had as its source the social and intellectual movements of the early twentieth century that had prompted federal courts to apply the Bill of Rights to the states, to stem racial injustices that were being ignored by state courts and legislatures.[5] The Court's midcentury narratives of lynching added weight to the incorporation debate by focusing judicial attention on the actual effects federal judicial deference had on petitioners' lives. Lynching narratives and detailed stories of coerced confessions became part of Supreme Court opinions in such manner that for some justices, it was inconceivable to attach rights without saying something about the quality of mercy relieved.

In cases such as *Ashcraft* v. *Tennessee, Chambers* v. *Florida, Brown* v. *Allen,* and *Culombe* v. *Connecticut,* tales of violence enveloped constitutional law, giving form and content to the vagaries and generalities of the Fourth, Fifth, Sixth, Eighth and Fourteenth Amendments. What had been the exclusive preserve of corporate clients and the propertied opened up to a variety of litigants who had previously been on the other side of the law: the brown, the black, the poor, the disenfranchised. New Deal justices made narrative retellings of state-sanctioned violence against minorities adhere to the amendments, like moths to a flame, as if without these narratives the Bill of Rights itself would atrophy and revert to the inert state it was in prior to the Fourteenth Amendment.

The amendments, then, are themselves storytellers, and the justices merely spin narratives of justice into constitutional prohibitions. One thinks, therefore, not just of *Mapp* v. *Ohio* connecting the Fourteenth Amendment to the Fourth, but of Dollree Mapp placing the search warrant in her bosom in an act of defiance; of Danny Escobedo,[6] handcuffed and left standing in an interrogation room for four hours until he confessed to a crime he did not commit; of the drifter Clarence Gideon handwriting his own habeas corpus petition; and of the "Scottsboro Boys" huddled around their attorney, instead of thinking prosaically about the link between the Fourth, Fifth and Sixth Amendments to the Fourteenth. For the New Deal justices and for the members of the Warren Court, the amendments have more than legs—staying power—they tell narratives of injustice.

The problem—for the liberals on the Court who began telling stories, that is—was that the persons associated with the amendments had guide maps attached to their stories that allowed the Court to navigate their constitutional intricacies in multiple directions. For the itinerant Clarence Gideon was also a hustler, and Ernesto Miranda was, at the least, "a seriously disturbed individual with pronounced sexual fantasies."[7] In habeas cases, we are not dealing, after all, with the unconvicted innocent. The Rehnquist Court demonstrated that the Warren Court's narratives were foundations built on sand. The amendments do not tell stories; lawyers do. If the New Deal justices had made the amendments vessels for the aggrieved, the hurt, and the silent, Rehnquist Court justices, too, could tell stories, of brutal and violent murders, of the use of hammers, fists, guns, intimidation, rape, volunteered confessions and legitimate professions of guilt, and of butchery and acts of evil, which they then linked to the audacities of habeas corpus petitioners and their quest for constitutional relief from unlawful confinement. Stories of violence stick to constitutional amendments like flies to flypaper, indiscriminately.

The Court during the Burger and Rehnquist years restricted the writ's application against unlawful confinement without a prompt from any outside source except vague concerns about "crime in the streets," which became the ground upon which judgments were made and counter-counternarratives spun. The Court's narratives during the 1970s and 1980s became more focused on the petitioner's guilt, his violence, and his potential for future dangerousness than ever before. Perceptions outpaced reality. Under the Rehnquist Court, habeas corpus took on a life of its own.

A NARRATIVE OF FEDERALISM

There are two narratives at work during the 1980s regarding reigning in habeas petitions: one, the Burger Court's return-to-federalism jurisprudence, and two, the Rehnquist Court's focus on future dangerousness, respect for victims, and concerns over crime control. (In all, these seemingly disparate concerns are connected by a grand narrative of crime control.) Attention to the power of the federal government regarding its reach into state criminal matters is never far from the Court's criminal jurisprudence. But by the time that Justice Rehnquist became chief justice in 1986, the Court was willing to rely on federalism as a narrative, not a jurisdictional prop, only when the criminal narrative itself was insufficient to support a denial of a claim. Extended retellings of crime facts are rare in Supreme Court opinions, but it is within these exceptional stories that the violent criminal emerges.

The Burger Court's commitment to federalism was based on a procedural and functional approach to substantive claims of illegal detention that attempted to undo what *Fay* v. *Noia* had accomplished.[8] The Burger Court's administrative response to the increasing frustration it felt by habeas corpus petitions alleging constitutional infirmities was *Wainwright* v. *Sykes'* "cause and prejudice" test.[9] A regard for federal-state comity,[10] and the immunization of state court decisions from individual attacks, called "finality,"[11] drove the Burger Court to create a way to deny habeas review if the prisoner had not complied with a state's contemporaneous-objection rule. The exception to this rule, which allowed a federal court to grant relief, was if the defendant could offer "cause" for his default of state claims at the time of his trial and demonstrate actual "prejudice" resulting from the outcome.[12]

In the sections that follow, I will briefly focus on the Burger Court's reliance on federalism that was rooted in part in the procedural rules of nineteenth-century federal-state habeas jurisdiction[13] and then more fully discuss the Rehnquist Court's turn toward future dangerousness as a narrative prop to keep habeas petitioners behind bars. Unlike *Brown* v. *Mississippi*, that pivotal

1936 case that introduced a lynched black man not as the criminal subject but as the state's victim, the Court in the 1980s and 1990s relied on the states' narratives of arrest and confinement to define the constitutional parameters of petitioners' claims. These concerns have virtually put an end to the right and ability of state prisoners to contest their convictions in federal courts. In *Rose v. Lundy*[14] (1982), for example, the Supreme Court reintroduced the exhaustion doctrine, first developed in *Ex parte Royall* (1886), and in *Engle v. Isaac*[15] (1982) the Court further refined the "cause and prejudice" standard. By the end of the 1980s, in *Teague v. Lane*[16] and *Penry v. Lynaugh*,[17] the Court increased the burdens placed on habeas petitioners through a nonretroactivity doctrine. Ordinarily, the Court's decisions have applied retroactively, allowing convicted criminals to retry their cases in light of subsequent constitutional changes. *Teague* and *Penry* greatly restrict that possibility. But as these difficult cases show, the Court's concern with federalism was a secondary matter. These cases, and a few others like them, stressed the petitioner's guilt as the primary reason for denying relief.

Legally Guilty Persons: The Redefinition of "Cause and Prejudice"

The Burger Court was convinced that *Wainwright v. Sykes'* "cause and prejudice" standard "will not prevent a federal habeas court from adjudicating for the first time the federal constitutional claim of a defendant who in the absence of such an adjudication will be the victim of a miscarriage of justice."[18] In Justice William Brennan's words, this benign understanding of the "cause and prejudice" standard "exhibits the notable tendency of keeping prisoners in jail without addressing their constitutional complaints."[19] *Engle v. Isaac* tested Brennan's prediction.

The Court in *Engle* consolidated three cases from separate trials in Ohio. Isaac, Hughes, and Bell were tried and convicted on various assault charges; all three claimed self-defense. Ohio law placed the burden of proof on the defendants. At no point did the various defense lawyers object to this burden.

Ten months after the trial, the Ohio Supreme Court, in *State v. Robinson*, overturned the law and placed the burden of proof on the prosecution. Relying on *Robinson*, Isaac appealed in state court. The court rejected the claim on pre-*Robinson* grounds. Because Isaac did not object at trial to the instructions, his silence constituted a waiver of his rights. The federal district court rejected Isaac's plea for habeas corpus because Isaac had failed to show cause for his waiver and prove prejudice. The court of appeals reversed this decision. Justice Sandra Day O'Connor, writing for the Supreme Court, reversed the court of appeals. She could not find any deprivation of Isaac's constitutional rights.[20]

The Court returned to the costs federal habeas review imposes on state courts. According to O'Connor, "liberal allowance of the writ . . . degrades the prominence of the trial." Habeas corpus, she suggested, "may diminish [the "sanctity of state court procedures"] by suggesting to the trial participants that there may be no need to adhere to those safeguards during the trial itself." O'Connor also rejected the idea that habeas corpus may be a just resolution to an unconstitutional arrest or trial because the "passage of time, [the] erosion of memory, and [the] dispersion of witnesses may render retrial difficult, even impossible." Finally, O'Connor argued that the "Great Writ [of habeas corpus] imposes special costs on our federal system. The states possess primary authority for defining and enforcing the criminal law. In criminal trials they also hold the initial responsibility for vindicating constitutional rights. Federal intrusions into state criminal trials frustrate both the states' sovereign power to punish offenders and their good-faith attempts to honor constitutional rights."[21]

In recognition, no doubt, of the weakness of the federalist metaphor for judicial restraint in 1982, O'Connor turned the "cause and prejudice" test into a defense of institutional comity and finality, without ever mentioning that habeas corpus exists to cut through jurisdictional infighting and wars against absolute claims on the movement of bodies. "Where the basis of a constitutional claim is available," she wrote, "and other defense counsel have perceived and litigated that claim, the demands of *comity* and *finality* counsel against labeling alleged unawareness of the objection as *cause* for a procedural default."[22] After determining that the attorney in *Engle* was competent, she returned to abstract federalism concerns to fill in the "cause and prejudice" standard. She rejected the plea to replace "cause and prejudice" with a "plain-error inquiry."[23] Plain error, she wrote, applies to direct review. "Federal habeas challenges to state convictions, however, entail greater finality problems and special comity concerns." "Cause and prejudice," she concluded, "take their meaning from the principles of comity and finality."[24]

So there it is: "cause and prejudice" is not an innovation of late twentieth-century justices concerned with the erosion of federal-state comity. Nor is it an application of inventive reconceptions based on years of refining the role of the states in a federal republic. Instead, it is a rewording of late nineteenth-century federalism, then called "comity." The problem, quite obviously, with this application of nostalgic judicial language, is that *Engle* did not settle the question of how much process is due a state prisoner sentenced to death or how much finality is to be accorded a state court's determination of guilt. Instead, the Court took note that the number of state prisoners had climbed throughout the early 1980s.[25]

Engle is an example of the Court's habeas decisions during the early 1980s that tried to limit habeas appeals in the interests of finality and comity, without expressly defining those terms. The problem was twofold: (1) that regard for these interests came at the expense of state prisoners' due process rights, which the Fourteenth Amendment explicitly protects; and (2) that the Court's inability to define "cause" and "prejudice" and "finality" and "comity" was a clear sign that the metaphors and similes of federalism had reached their natural, linguistic limit. Federalism could only be "like" "cause and prejudice" or comity and finality; but those terms could never enhance our understanding of governmental limits. O'Connor's defense of federalism in *Engle* is without the conviction that the states are sovereign entities and that the federal government has no business interfering in state criminal matters. The reason is that O'Connor cannot say that. There is too much water under that bridge. Instead, defenses of federalism from the Burger and Rehnquist Courts increasingly stressed the "costs" of federal habeas review and relied on abstract appeals to the writ's ability to "undermine the values inherent in out federal system of government,"[26] without ever giving any content to those concerns, for example, explaining why habeas corpus is a "cost" that the nation cannot afford, or offering examples of how weighing the states' concerns against the individual's right to be free from unlawful confinement protects society. The writ of habeas corpus, a historic safeguard against arbitrary governmental action, was again in the middle of a contest between the exercise of executive power by the states (considered arbitrary by liberals and authorized by conservatives) and the requirements of due process at the national level that limits that power through rules determined by national courts of law.

After almost ten years of trying to define and apply "cause and prejudice," the Court was unable to do so, but it was not ready to give up, either. The purpose of the "cause and prejudice" standard was not to bar federal habeas corpus review. A court could issue a writ to a prisoner who could demonstrate his innocence.[27] That, at least, was the view until the Court decided, in 1986, *Kuhlmann* v. *Wilson,*[28] *Murray* v. *Carrier,*[29] and *Smith* v. *Murray.*[30] According to Justice Harry Blackmun's dissent in *Herrera* v. *Collins* (1993):

> Beginning with a trio of decisions in 1986, this Court shifted the focus of federal habeas review of successive, abusive, or defaulted claims away from the preservation of constitutional rights to a fact-based inquiry into the habeas petitioner's guilt or innocence [Justice Blackmun then cites the three cases mentioned above]. In striking this balance, the Court adopted the view of Judge Friendly that there should be an exception to the concept of finality when a prisoner can make a colorable claim of actual innocence.... Having adopted an "actual innocence" requirement for review of abusive, successive, or defaulted claims, however, the majority would now take the position that a "claim of 'actual innocence' is not itself a constitutional claim, but instead a gateway through which a habeas petitioner must pass to have his otherwise barred constitutional claim considered on the merits."... *The only principle that would appear to reconcile these two positions is the principle that habeas relief should be denied whenever possible.*[31]

In *Kuhlmann,* "the respondent," Wilson, and two others had robbed a taxi garage and fatally shot the dispatcher. Wilson turned himself in four days after the incident, admitted to witnessing the robbery, but denied knowledge of the crime and involvement in the robbery and murder. After arraignment but before trial, the police placed an informant, Benny Lee, in Wilson's prison cell. Wilson incriminated himself to Lee, who in turn told the police. Following an evidentiary hearing but still prior to trial, the court suppressed a motion regarding the prison cell "confession."[32] After trial, the court sentenced Wilson to twenty years to life for murder and up to seven years for possession of a weapon. After filing unsuccessfully in the state courts, Wilson filed for federal habeas corpus in 1973. He claimed that the police had used his statements to Lee in violation of his constitutional right to counsel. The district court denied the writ, and the court of appeals affirmed.

In 1980, the Supreme Court decided *United States* v. *Henry,*[33] which applied the ruling in *Massiah* v. *United States*[34] (1964) to postconviction cases. *Massiah* held that a statement "deliberately elicited" from the accused to jailhouse informants by electronic eavesdropping violated the Sixth Amendment. Because of *Henry,* Wilson then filed a second habeas corpus petition in federal district court, which denied the writ. The court of appeals overruled the denial. Wilson had successfully argued that the intervention of *Henry* was a sufficient ground to file a second petition. The Supreme Court disagreed and reversed the court of appeals.[35]

Justice Lewis Powell, writing for a plurality, again refused to view habeas corpus as an equitable form of relief. Powell saw the Court's task as a "weighing of interests" between finality and equitability.[36] Section 2244(a) of the habeas statute governs finality. Powell, however, relied on the 1966 amendments to section 2244 (subsections (b) and (c)), which hold that "after an evidentiary hearing . . . or after a hearing on the merits of an issue of law," a federal judge "need not" entertain a second petition "unless the application alleges and is predicated on a factual or other ground not adjudicated" at the previous hearing or trial. Powell held that section 2244(b) introduces "a greater degree of finality of judgments in habeas corpus proceedings."[37]

Because "the abuse of the writ"—the continual reapplication for federal habeas review for no other purpose than to set aside one's conviction—has clearcut implications for state courts, Powell saw no reason not to tie finality to a claim of innocence. A "prisoner," he wrote, "retains a powerful and legitimate interest in obtaining his release from custody if he is innocent of the charge for which he was incarcerated. That interest does not extend, however, to prisoners whose guilt is conceded or plain."[38] This was the reason why the Court denied Leonel Torres Herrera his habeas petition. Herrera had argued that he was "factually innocent"; that is, he claimed that he did not commit the crime for which he was sentenced. But the Court argued, to the contrary, that Herrera had been found "guilty beyond a reasonable doubt" and is a "legally guilty person."[39] As the Supreme Court tendentiously noted in *Herrera,* "in the eyes of the law, petitioner does not come before the Court as one who is 'innocent,' but, on the contrary, as one who has been convicted by due process of law of two brutal murders."[40] Powell concluded *Kuhlmann* by stating that the "ends of justice" in *Sanders* v. *United States* (1963) require that federal courts can entertain a second petition "*only* where the prisoner supplements his constitutional claim with a colorable showing of factual innocence,"[41] which is not what *Sanders* says.

As Powell equated the "ends of justice" with the meaning of federalism by pushing for an innocence standard on habeas corpus, his counterpart, Justice Sandra Day O'Connor, tried to shore up a defense of the states along more practical lines. As a former state court judge, O'Connor had a high regard for the ability of state court judges to protect federal rights. In a 1981 law review article she wrote: "State judges in assuming office take an oath to support the federal as well as the state constitution. State judges in fact rise to the occasion when given the responsibility and opportunity to do so. It is a step in the right direction to defer to the state courts and give finality to their judgments on federal constitutional questions where a full and fair adjudication has been given in the state court."[42]

According to O'Connor, the purpose of the "cause and prejudice" standard is twofold. On the one hand, the "cause and prejudice" standard serves to deter an attorney's intentional abandonment of a constitutional claim in the state courts. On the other hand, "cause and prejudice" imposes costs on superseding finality claims in the name of promoting federal constitutional rights. O'Connor viewed the "cause and prejudice" standard as a way to reduce the sense of frustration state court judges feel when a federal habeas judge issues the writ. In *Murray* v. *Carrier* (1986), she held that relitigating a "defaulted" claim "gives state appellate courts no chance to review trial errors, and 'exacts an extra charge by undercutting the state's ability to enforce its procedural rules.'"[43] Cause for a procedural default related to attorney error must turn, she wrote, "on whether the prisoner can show that some objective factor external to the defense impeded counsel's efforts to comply with the state's procedural rule."[44]

O'Connor gathered a majority of justices in *Carrier* to support her rejection of *Fay's* deliberate bypass standard.

> We hold that counsel's failure to raise a *particular* claim on appeal is to be scrutinized under the "cause and prejudice" standard when that failure is treated as a procedural default by the state courts. Attorney error short of ineffective assistance of counsel does not constitute cause for a procedural default even when that default occurs on appeal rather than at trial. To the contrary, cause for a procedural default on appeal ordinarily requires a showing of some external impediment preventing counsel from constructing or raising the claim.[45]

O'Connor's expansive reading of the "cause and prejudice" standard subordinated the "miscarriage of justice" and the "ends of justice" concerns of the habeas statute to the Court-created "cause and prejudice" standard.[46] Yet she was "confident" that "victims of a fundamental miscarriage of justice could meet the cause-and-prejudice standard"[47] and held that habeas corpus will always be available to those who are "actually innocent." *Carrier*, however, holds that procedural infractions that conceivably could lead to a determination of not guilty, had they been properly raised at trial or on appeal, will not be given due consideration by a federal habeas court out of respect for state court determinations of guilt, which led Justice John Paul Stevens, writing in dissent in *Smith* v. *Murray*, a case, unlike *Carrier*, that dealt with the death penalty, to write that the "cause and prejudice" standard was now a "rigid bar to review of fundamental constitutional violations" which has no basis in the habeas statute: "the [cause and prejudice] standard thus represents judicial lawmaking of the most unabashed form."[48]

At the end of the Burger years, the Court had developed a successful two-pronged strategy to defeat *Fay*'s deliberate bypass standard. Both prongs seriously undermined the Warren Court's extension of the Bill of Rights to state prisoners seeking collateral review. The Court developed one prong in *Wainwright* v. *Sykes*, focusing on "cause and prejudice." The second prong built on Justice Black's dissent in *Kaufman* v. *U.S.* (1969) and Justice Powell's opinion in *Stone* v. *Powell* (1974). Those cases required habeas petitioners to demonstrate factual innocence to achieve relief. The first prong was rooted in promoting federalism; the second, in reversing the perception that habeas frees the guilty. The habeas statute requires neither test.

In the next two cases, *Teague* v. *Lane* and *Penry* v. *Lynaugh*, the Court succeeded in imposing yet another hurdle in the way of habeas petitioners by issuing guidelines as to what constitutes a new law and when that law can be applied retroactively to the benefit of state petitioners. *Teague* v. *Lane* and *Penry* v. *Lynaugh* bring to a close the Supreme Court's attack on *Fay*, while opening the door to discursive attempts to put a lid on habeas petitions in general.

Reassessing the Writ: Rights and Retroactivity in the Rehnquist Court

Retroactivity restricts federal judges' power to apply the procedural protections of the Bill of Rights to state habeas petitioners. The effect of the retroactivity doctrine was an indirect challenge to the Warren Court's application of the Fourteenth Amendment's due process clause to the states. Summarizing the difficulties of retroactivity for petitioners, Hugo Black wrote in *Linkletter* v. *Walker* (1965) that

> Linkletter, convicted in the state court by use of "unconstitutional evidence," is today denied relief by the judgment of this Court because his conviction became "final" before *Mapp* was decided. Linkletter must stay

in jail; Miss Mapp, whose offense was committed before Linkletter's, is free. The different treatment of Miss Mapp and Linkletter points up at once the arbitrary and discriminatory nature of the judicial contrivance utilized here to break the promise of *Mapp* by keeping all people in jail who are unfortunate enough to have had their unconstitutional convictions affirmed before June 19, 1961.[49]

By creating an entire discourse by which the justices could determine a petitioner's constitutional worth around timing, type of crime, and extent of remorse, the Court drew a circle around the most important rights of the Warren era and cast them off from the writ's historical purposes. It then filled in the space created by the gap that separated habeas corpus from the Bill of Rights by invoking the petitioner's past as a source for not reconsidering the constitutional issues. The debate over habeas corpus in the 1990s, is, as it was during the 1930s and 40s, a debate over the effects of full incorporation.

The foundation for the Court's retroactivity doctrine is *Mapp* v. *Ohio*[50] (1961), which applied the federal exclusionary rule to the states. The Court applied the new rule established in *Mapp* to completed cases pending direct review to the Supreme Court at the time *Mapp* was decided.

In *Desist* v. *United States*[51] (1969) and *Mackey* v. *United States*[52] (1971), Justice John Marshall Harlan, a persistent critic of incorporation and the Warren Court's post-*Brown* v. *Allen* habeas jurisprudence, called for a new approach to retroactivity. *Desist* and *Mackey* involved Fourth Amendment issues, an area of law the Court would later eliminate from postconviction claims. Harlan argued that the Court should apply new rules retroactively to direct review cases but not to collateral attacks.[53] According to Harlan, not applying retroactivity protects the state courts from collateral attack many years later. As Justice O'Connor stated in *Teague*, "Application of constitutional rules not in existence at the time a conviction became final seriously undermines the principle of finality which is essential to the operation of our criminal justice system."[54]

Harlan created two exceptions in *Mackey* that could allow the Court to apply new rules retroactively to cases accepted on collateral attack. First, the Court could apply a new rule retroactively if it places "certain kinds of primary, private individual conduct beyond the power of the criminal law-making authority to proscribe." Second, the Court could apply a new rule retroactively if it requires the observance of "those procedures that . . . are 'implicit in the concept of ordered liberty.'"[55]

Harlan wanted to return the Supreme Court's habeas jurisprudence to the period before *Brown* v. *Allen*. After *Brown*, he wrote, habeas cases constituted "an indefensible departure both from the historical principles which defined the scope of the 'Great Writ' and from the principles of federalism which have formed the bedrock of our constitutional development."[56] To Harlan, regard for federalism required a scaled-down version of habeas corpus, one known to the Court by nineteenth-century code words of deference and respect. Reversing both the founders' understanding of habeas corpus and that of the thirty-ninth Congress, the "primary justification" for the writ, he wrote in *Mackey*, is to deter state court constitutional violations, not to set individuals free from arbitrary or unconstitutional confinement.[57] Harlan then concluded that in most cases, the preservation of the state's case against the defendant will outweigh any benefits prisoners may gain seeking retroactive effect of a new constitutional rule.

In *Teague v. Lane*, a plurality of the Court led by Justice O'Connor agreed to "refuse to announce a new rule in a given case unless the rule would be applied retroactively to the defendant in the case and to all others similarly situated." To O'Connor, the benefit of this approach lay in the "principle that habeas corpus cannot be used as a vehicle to create new constitutional rules of criminal procedure unless those rules would be applied retroactively to *all* defendants on collateral review."[58] In *Penry v. Lynaugh*,[59] the Court applied its nonretroactivity doctrine to capital cases.

Teague and *Penry* represent a radical approach to habeas corpus and death penalty cases rarely seen in Supreme Court opinions. *Teague* is the Court's most forceful effort to restrict the availability of habeas to state prisoners seeking relief in cases decided after conviction. Moreover, *Teague* affected a shift in the Court's understanding of habeas corpus. Until this point, the Court had struck a balance between the protection of procedural and individual rights issues and respect for finality. Even the Burger Court had failed to garner a majority for the view, announced in *Penry*, that a federal court cannot grant an evidentiary hearing to a petitioner sentenced to death if the outcome would be the creation of a new rule.[60]

Retroactivity poses a problem for the Court because "once a new rule is applied to the defendant in the case announcing the rule, evenhanded justice requires that it be applied retroactively to all who are similarly situated."[61] Common law jurists considered all new rules announced by courts to apply retroactively. The modern positivist conception of law rejects the Blackstonian common law view of judges as passive objects and focuses more on the administration of law. Consequently, as the Supreme Court declared in *Linkletter*, "the Constitution neither prohibits nor requires retrospective effect."[62] Although the Supreme Court has long relied on common law rules to restrict the Bill of Rights to the states, particularly on habeas corpus, the Court decided in *Teague* that it had the power to decide whether a case can be applied retroactively, and if so, whether its retroactive status should be limited to direct review or collateral attack. The test is purely functional, and retroactivity is a function of administration. As we have already seen, the Court considered collateral attacks on state court convictions to involve costs to state judiciaries and society that are not worth the benefits.[63]

Teague allowed for the application of new rules only under narrow circumstances. According to Justice O'Connor, "[A] case announces a new rule when it breaks new ground or imposes a new obligation on the states or the federal government. To put it differently, a case announces a new rule if the result was not *dictated* by precedent existing at the time the defendant's conviction became final."[64] Contrary to previous Court holdings, *Teague* holds that the "federal courts should treat retroactivity as a threshold question and decide that issue *before* the Court reaches the merits of the case."[65] "Retroactivity is properly treated as a threshold question. . . . Thus, before deciding whether the fair cross section requirement should be extended to the petit jury, we should ask whether such a rule would be applied retroactively to the case at issue."[66] O'Connor allowed for two exceptions to the general rule of nonretroactivity. First, she accepted Harlan's claim that a new rule should be applied retroactively if it places "certain kinds of primary, private individual conduct beyond the power of the criminal lawmaking authority to proscribe."[67] Second, a new rule should be applied retroactively "to those new procedures without which the likelihood of an accurate conviction is seriously diminished."[68] To state the matter succinctly, "unless they fall within the exception to the general rule, new constitutional rules of criminal procedure will not be applicable to those cases which have become final before the new rules are announced."[69]

O'Connor's definition cast off Harlan's second exception on retroactivity, which was based on *Palko v. Connecticut* (1936). Justice Benjamin Cardozo had argued in that case that rights falling within the "concept of ordered liberty" deserved constitutional protection, which at the time of *Palko* meant the First Amendment but not the criminal procedure amendments. O'Connor rejected that view and turned to the accuracy of the state court conviction. Although *Benton v. Maryland*[70] (1969) had overturned *Palko*, which denied persons the protection of the Fifth and Fourteenth Amendments on double jeopardy, O'Connor understood *Benton* to have overruled *Palko*'s *dicta* as well. "Reviving the *Palko* test now, in this area of law, would be unnecessarily anachronistic."[71] Attempting to move constitutional law forward, beyond the vagaries of Cardozean subjectivity, O'Connor could not help looking back for guidance. She held that "the classic grounds for issuing the writ" are (1) mob violence (*Moore v. Dempsey* [1923]); (2) use of known perjured testimony (*Mooney v. Holohan* [1935]); and (3) coerced confessions (*De Meerlerr v. Michigan* [1947]).[72] Not one of these cases was decided after *Brown v. Allen* (1953).

O'Connor's decision in *Teague* cannot be understood apart from her willingness to recast the purpose of habeas corpus as a deterrent to unconstitutional state court procedures, rather than as a remedy for unconstitutional confinement. The adoption of a high definition of "new law"; the preference for deciding new law questions before reaching the merits; the blanket approach to nonretroactivity on collateral review; and the movement away from a *Palko-*

based jurisprudence, which accepts rights as developmental, to a *Stone* v. *Powell* innocence standard, which restricts rights in the name of institutional respectability, serves to turn away state petitioners seeking federal relief. *Teague*, however, was not the Court's final word on shutting off habeas corpus.

The Court decided *Penry* v. *Lynaugh* (1989) four months after *Teague*. Unlike *Teague*, Justice O'Connor managed to obtain a fifth vote. Also unlike *Teague*, the Court in *Penry* applied *Teague*'s language to capital cases. The question in *Penry* was whether the petitioner, John Paul Penry, "was sentenced to death in violation of the Eighth Amendment because the jury was not instructed that it could consider and give effect to his mitigating evidence in imposing its sentence." Penry was mentally retarded.[73]

In a federal habeas corpus application, Penry asserted that his sentence violated the Eighth Amendment because the trial court had failed to instruct the jury on how to consider mitigating factors. At a competency hearing, Penry's IQ was found to be 54. Nevertheless, the jury determined that Penry was competent to stand trial. They then found him guilty, rejected his insanity defense, and sentenced him to death. Penry claimed that the execution of a mentally retarded person was cruel and unusual punishment. The district court denied his habeas petition. The court of appeals affirmed the conviction but noted that Penry's mitigating circumstances had not been given full effect. The court also rejected the argument that the execution of a mentally retarded person was cruel and unusual under the Eighth Amendment.

Teague held that the Supreme Court must determine, as a threshold matter in cases on collateral attack, whether granting relief would create a new rule. If so, the next inquiry was whether the petitioner could meet the two exceptions that would permit the Court to issue the writ. On the basis of the finality concerns expressed in Justice O'Connor's plurality opinion in *Teague*, the Court applied *Teague*'s holding on retroactivity to Penry. To understand how *Teague* works, it is useful to go behind the *Penry* case.

Penry's conviction became final on January 13, 1986, when the Supreme Court denied certiorari. Penry believed that two Court cases, *Lockett* v. *Ohio*[74] (1978) and *Eddings* v. *Oklahoma*[75] (1982), could benefit his cause. Penry argued that when mitigating circumstances are given, Texas juries must "upon request, be given jury instructions that make it possible for them to give effect to that mitigating evidence in determining whether a defendant should be sentenced to death."[76] In other words, Penry was not seeking a new rule as defined by *Teague*.

The Supreme Court had upheld the Texas death penalty statute in *Jurek* v. *Texas*[77] (1976). Penry relied on *Jurek*'s assumption that questions submitted to the jury allowed the introduction of mitigating circumstances. When the Court restored the states' death penalty statutes in 1976 it required the states to determine death sentences on an individual basis. It also held that juries should consider the circumstances of the event leading up to arrest.[78] Underlying *Lockett* and *Eddings* is the principle that punishment should be "directly related to the personal culpability of the criminal defendant."[79]

The Court in *Penry* remanded the case for resentencing, because Penry's second claim did not establish a new rule and because the questions that govern the imposition of a death sentence did not allow the jury to consider Penry's mental abilities and childhood trauma. Penry's second contention was that the execution of a mentally retarded person violates the Eighth Amendment. The Court thought Penry's complaint that the execution of a mentally retarded person was cruel and unusual required a new rule.[80] To avoid this problem, the Court held that the Eighth Amendment does not preclude the "execution of any mentally retarded person of Penry's ability convicted of a capital offense simply by virtue of [his] mental retardation alone."[81] Texas had argued that "there is insufficient evidence of a national consensus against executing the retarded, and that existing procedural safeguards adequately protect the interests" of defendants such as Penry.[82] At no time prior to Penry's conviction had the Court announced a rule denying the states the right to execute an insane person. To do so in *Penry*, a case accepted on collateral attack, "would impose a new obligation on the states and the Federal Government."[83]

As noted, O'Connor adopted part of Harlan's view on exceptions to retroactivity. She understood Harlan to include in his description substantive matters guaranteed by the Constitution "regardless of the procedures followed."[84] She then noted that *Ford* v. *Wainwright* (1976), which prohibited the execution of the insane (but decided after Penry's conviction), and *Coker* v. *Georgia*[85] (1977), which prohibited the execution of rapists, placed a certain class of individuals "beyond the state's power to punish by death" and thereby constituted a new rule.[86] Penry's claim that the Eighth Amendment prohibits the execution of the insane (but that is insufficient by itself because of *Teague*'s retroactivity rule), and therefore is a substantive matter (thus meeting Harlan's first prong), should qualify as part of Harlan's exceptions.

It is here that we can see the Rehnquist Court's upcoming break with federalism and the turn toward narrative as a foundation for denying review. Personal culpability sneaks into the Court's habeas language just as the Court is trying to establish a new ground for denying habeas claims in the name of federalism. But that argument is now visibly strained. *Teague* and *Penry*, despite the appearance of federal-state comity issues, are really about habeas defendants taking advantage of legal opportunities not available to those who appeal to the Supreme Court directly following rejection by a state's highest court. The Court in these two cases sets out to make habeas corpus claims about innocence and not state neglect of federal constitutional liberties. O'Connor denied Penry's logic not by redefining Harlan, but by redefining Penry. She concluded that the execution of Penry, a person with a mental age of seven, was not prohibited by the Eighth Amendment because Penry was declared competent to stand trial; because he had consulted with his attorney and understood the proceedings against him; and because the jury had rejected his insanity defense.[87]

The application of *Teague*'s doctrine, that new rules will not be announced on collateral review, to *Penry*, a capital case, means that a person may be lawfully executed by a state despite a legitimate constitutional claim, because the Court had not announced a new rule before the petitioner's conviction had become final. After *Penry*, whether a defendant achieves relief may not be a matter of law, but of chance.

Summary of the 1980s

In *Sawyer* v. *Smith*[88] (1990), Justice Anthony Kennedy wrote that:

> The principle announced in *Teague* serves to ensure that gradual developments in the law over which reasonable jurists may disagree are not later used *to upset the finality of state convictions when entered.* This is but a recognition that the purpose of federal habeas corpus is to ensure that state convictions comply with the federal law in existence at the time the conviction became final, and not to provide a mechanism for the continuing reexamination of final judgments based upon later emerging legal doctrine.[89]

Disregarding *Brown* v. *Allen* and the Warren Court's habeas decisions, *Sawyer* v. *Smith* is the logical outcome of the Supreme Court's habeas cases from the end of the nineteenth century through *Frank* v. *Magnum* (1915).

The retroactivity doctrine and the new rule standard developed in *Teague* and subsequent habeas cases were the Court's foremost attempts since the end of Reconstruction to insulate state court decisions from federal review. The elevation of the new rule criteria over consideration of the merits of a claim has enabled the Court to deny relief without addressing the seriousness of the defendant's claimed violations of constitutional law. Federalism is considered the ground upon which such claims are denied. But is that accurate? Has not the Court in fact only used federalism as an institutional means to prevent what it sees as an assault not just on state courts but on justice itself? (Does not this question apply to both nineteenth- and twentieth-century conceptions of federalism?) Moreover, the threat to justice comes, for the Rehnquist Court, from the criminal himself, from his "culpability," his "future dangerousness," and from his petition for a hearing to reevaluate the terms and conditions of his confinement that is nothing short of an attack on state law, state procedures, and state power. Willing to rely quite heavily on the very visible formalities of state police powers, the Rehnquist Court imposes silence on the prisoner. *Teague* and *Penry* lead to that conclusion. And yet, when the accused is silent, or when his will is overborne by stress, by deprivation, by state violence, or by subterfuge, and he speaks—through law—who will be midwife to his thoughts, to his pleas for relief? As Peter Brooks writes, "the process of inference can only be a narrative one."[90]

A NARRATIVE OF VIOLENCE:
FUTURE DANGEROUSNESS

Writing in dissent in *Atkins* v. *Virginia* (2002), a case in which the Supreme Court struck down a Virginia law allowing for the execution of the mentally retarded, Justice Antonin Scalia thought it necessary to begin with a "brief restatement of the facts that are abridged by the Court but important to understanding this case."

> After spending the day drinking alcohol and smoking marijuana, petitioner Daryl Renard Atkins and a partner in crime drove to a convenience store, intending to rob a customer. Their victim was Eric Nesbitt, an airman from Langley Air Force Base, whom they abducted, drove to a nearby automated teller machine, and forced to withdraw $200. They then drove him to a deserted area, ignoring his pleas to leave him unharmed. According to the co-conspirator, whose testimony the jury evidently credited, Atkins ordered Nesbitt out of the vehicle and, after he had taken only a few steps, shot him one, two, three, four, five, six, seven, eight times in the thorax, chest, abdomen, arms, and legs.[91]

Note that Scalia is not satisfied with a simple recapitulation of events. We have traveled far from the days when petitioners ravished young females and were described solely by their age and color of their skin. Instead, Scalia offers a true counternarrative to the majority's elision of the facts of the case. More than just telling the whole story, Scalia fashions Atkins' identity, creating what Rosemary Coombe calls a "paradigmatic subjectivity" by inscribing his legal personality within the body of the victim.[92] At first, Scalia dramatizes the shooting not just by reference to the number of times the gun went off, but sequentially, heightening the drama of the experience. He notes that Atkins shot Nesbitt not once but eight times, the force of repetition implicating Atkins' sanity and responsibility. Scalia then locates each bullet as it pierces Nesbitt's body. Eight bullets enter five body parts. We can almost see the homicide taking place, as if Scalia were filming the murder. Scalia becomes Scorsese. He directs our eye to the continual loop of violence from which Atkins cannot escape. This is who Atkins is, Scalia tells us. The reiteration of violence reverberates throughout this case, and Scalia reminds the Court that narratives of violence form an integral part of the criminal law in aiding the meting out of punishment. Above all, Scalia does this without acknowledging his own role as the author of the criminal's subjectivity.

One of the Rehnquist Court's earliest forays into character construction is *Thompson v. Oklahoma*[93] (1988), a case, like *Atkins*, in which Scalia thought the Court had left out too much regarding Thompson's participation in a crime. Here is the full statement of facts from Justice John Paul Stevens, who wrote the opinion:

> Because there is no claim that the punishment would be excessive if the crime had been committed by an adult, only a brief statement of facts is necessary. In concert with three older persons, petitioner actively participated in the brutal murder of his former brother-in-law in the early morning hours of January 23, 1983. The evidence disclosed that the victim had been shot twice, and that his throat, chest, and abdomen had been cut. He also had multiple bruises and a broken leg. His body had been chained to a concrete block and thrown into a river where it remained for almost four weeks. Each of the four participants was tried separately and each was sentenced to death.[94]

For Stevens, the question of Thompson's age was relevant to the type of punishment chosen by the state. He constructs a strict constitutional calculus, weighing the defendant's age against constitutional law and practice. He downplays the facts of the case because, for him, the constitutional question of the state's right to execute a minor has pride of place over the crime Thompson committed. Like Justice Brennan in *Fay v. Noia*, it is the Constitution's vulnerability about which Stevens is concerned. The execution of minors violates constitutional norms; it is excessive. In editing out the gruesome facts, Stevens concentrated on Thompson's age, his status as a minor, and the state's role in increasing the permissible range of executable persons. To buttress his narrative rejecting the state's expansive view of punishment, Stevens supplied six appendices at the end of his opinion detailing how a majority of states in a number of categories restrict fifteen year olds from various activities, such as driving, voting, and marrying. He noted that the Court since *Gregg v. Georgia* (1976) had restricted the application of capital punishment, not broadened it. His larger narrative links in the reader's mind the limits placed on minors regarding everyday activities with the limits of punishment under the due process clause of the Fourteenth Amendment. Stevens' more formalized narrative elides the brutal facts of the case, though he notes that the facts are brutal, and instead focuses on the petitioner's constitutional status and the delicate relationship that exists between minors and the state. In doing so, he garners three other justices (O'Connor concurred separately) to form a plurality opinion denying Oklahoma the right to execute Thompson.

Justice Scalia, dissenting, is less concerned with Oklahoma's "rights" and with federalism in general. He scoffs at the petitioner's age as a reason to limit constitutional discourse. His dissent turns on what Stevens left out.

> I begin by restating the facts since I think that a fuller account of William Wayne Thompson's participation in the murder, and of his certification to stand trial as an adult is helpful in understanding the case. The evidence at trial left no doubt that on the night of January 22–23, 1983, Thompson brutally and with premeditation murdered his former brother-in-law, Charles Keene, the motive evidently being, at least in part, Keene's physical abuse of Thompson's sister. As Thompson left his mother's house that evening, in the company of three older friends, he explained to his girlfriend that "we're going to kill Charles." Several hours later, early in the morning of January 23, a neighbor, Malcolm "Possum" Brown, was awakened by the sound of a gunshot on his front porch. Someone pounded on his front door shouting: "Possum, open the door, let me in. They're going to kill me." Brown telephoned the police, and then opened the door to see a man on his knees attempting to repel blows with his arms and hands. There were four other men on the porch. One was holding a gun and stood apart, while the other three were hitting and kicking the kneeling man, who never attempted to hit back. One of them was beating the victim with an object 12 to 18 inches in length. The police called back to see if the disturbance was still going on, and while Brown spoke with them on the telephone the men took the victim away in the car.[95]

I cite this at length (and Scalia is not finished recounting the facts) to emphasize two important points about the Rehnquist Court's criminal jurisprudence. Whereas *Brown* v. *Mississippi* (1936) was the first case that brought in the body of the victim of a crime to expand the protections of due process, *Thompson* is the Rehnquist Court's first case to bring in the perpetrator of the crime as a way to restrict those protections. The second point is in regard to the Court's use of narratives. In focusing on what is being said, who is saying it, and more important what is not being said, it becomes clear that the Court is constructing a discursive regime regarding constitutional means and ends and leaving concerns over federalism off to the side. Scalia's only point in his recapitulation is to demonstrate that, fifteen years old or not, Thompson was in full control of his emotions at the time he killed Charles Keene. The state's right to execute a minor, though important, is clearly subordinate to Thompson's brutality.

The Rehnquist Court's narratives are harsher, more descriptive, and more character driven than before.[96] At best, federalism is useful but not determinative of the outcome of the case. Scalia continues his narrative of Thompson's crime.

Several hours after they had left Thompson's mother's house, Thompson and his three companions returned. Thompson's girlfriend helped him take off his boots, and heard him say: "[W]e killed him. I shot him in the head and cut his throat and threw him in the river." Subsequently, the former wife of one of Thompson's accomplices heard Thompson tell his mother that "he killed him. Charles was dead and Vicki did not have to worry about him anymore." During the days following the murder Thompson made other admissions. One witness testified that she asked Thompson the source of some hair adhering to a pair of boots he was carrying. He replied that was where he had kicked Charles Keene in the head. Thompson also told her that he had cut Charles' throat and chest and had shot him in the head. Another witness testified that when she told Thompson that a friend had seen Keene dancing in a local bar, Thompson remarked that that would be hard to do with a bullet in his head. Ultimately, one of Thompson's codefendants admitted that after Keene had been shot twice in the head Thompson had cut Keene "so the fish could eat his body." Thompson and a codefendant had then thrown the body into the Washita River, with a chain and blocks attached so that it would not be found. On February 18, 1983, the body was recovered. The Chief Medical Examiner of Oklahoma concluded that the victim had been beaten, shot twice, and that his throat, chest, and abdomen had been cut.[97]

Because for Scalia Thompson's "motive" is superficial—Scalia understands motive by events described by the police—Scalia, in the manner of nineteenth-century structuralist criminologists, does not shy away from ascribing a motive to Thompson's action that is developed by police reports or the scientific gazes upon the defendant. But he fails to mention that that motive could cast Thompson in a more favorable light. Keene possibly abused Thompson's sister. This, at least, could make Thompson sympathetic. But for Scalia it has the opposite effect. Thompson's cruelty and boastfulness wash over his more pressing motive of saving his sister from an abuser. Scalia then drives the narrative to its bloody conclusion. He ends the narrative by noting that the victim, the silent body in this constitutional story, had been shot twice, cut up, and dumped into a river.

The turn toward including the victim in Supreme Court crime narratives for purposes of restricting defendants' claims dates to *Booth* v. *Maryland* (1987), when the Court first confronted a state's use of a victim impact statement in a death penalty case. Victim impact statements describe "the severe emotional impact of the crimes on the family" and set "forth the family members' opinions and characterizations of the crimes and of the petitioner."[98] Justice Scalia dissented in *Booth*, partly because he felt the Constitution is silent on the question of victim impact statements but also because he saw good reason for bringing into the Court's criminal discourse the value of the victim's life as an assessment for the overall punishment of the perpetrator. Clearly, articulating arguments for the state's right to punish is no longer as powerful an argument as letting the family of the victim speak.

In *Payne v. Tennessee*[99] (1991), Pervis Tyrone Payne was convicted of first-degree murder and assault with intent to commit murder in the first degree. He was sentenced to death for the murders and, for good measure, up to thirty years for assault. In closing arguments, the prosecutor stated: "You saw the videotape this morning. You saw what Nicholas Christopher [the son of the deceased] will carry in his mind forever. When you talk about cruel, when you talk about atrocious, and when you talk about heinous, that picture will always come into your mind, probably throughout the rest of your lives."[100] In *Booth* and again in *South Carolina v. Gathers*[101] (1989) the Supreme Court held that the Eighth Amendment prohibits statements made during the sentencing phase "except to the extent that [they] relate[ ] directly to the circumstances of the crime."[102] The reason given is because of the possibility that sentencing decisions could be made arbitrarily, in violation of the Court's narrowing of sentencers' discretion in *Lockett v. Ohio*, and because of the defendant's inability to rebut those statements.

Payne reversed those two decisions, opening a constitutional space not just for the families of victims to speak of revenge in the name of the victim, but for the Court to reemphasize that it is the perpetrator's behavior (and not the law) that is responsible for the punishment. A technique of power that focuses on the murderer's body, actions, and behavior replaces the formalized display of state power. The law "operates more and more as a norm"[103] and less like an instrumental display of sovereignty. *Payne* hides the power of the law, its ability to punish and execute, behind the voices of the victim's family, who speak for the law. The law does not kill; Payne does. The law is an expression of Payne's action and the victim's grief. Strategic considerations regarding social and individual control mark the Court's late twentieth-century criminal jurisprudence.

The death penalty itself plays both an instrumental and a symbolic role in dealing with criticisms of crime. The victim's body becomes the authentic voice of law and order: silent and resilient. "By turning the victim into a 'faceless stranger at the penalty phase of a capital trial,'" Chief Justice Rehnquist wrote for the Court, "*Booth* deprives the State of the full moral force of its evidence and may prevent the jury from having before it all the information necessary to determine the proper punishment for a first-degree murder."[104] Like *Brown v. Mississippi*, the victim's body is brought in to make a constitutional point; but unlike *Brown*, the purpose is to close off the defendant's due process rights, to silence her claim.

The telling of particularly brutal narratives, such as in *Atkins* and *Thompson*, attempts to create an unbreakable link between the act of violence and the potential for future dangerousness, which become important components in the assessment of a habeas petitioner's claim. Habeas corpus can no longer be considered a "writ of liberty" operating without context as to who is being released, an abstraction of law that justifiably releases the unlawfully detained. Habeas corpus is now criminality, and if some Court narratives unwillingly construct victims of crime,[105] they also willingly construct the perpetrators. The Supreme Court is dependent on the public's fear of danger for its habeas and capital punishment decisions. If you let his man go, he will kill again, wound again, rape again.[106]

Arave v. Creech[107] (1993) is a case about the indeterminacy of language that finds in statutory ambiguities a way to construct criminality through a narrative of violence that ties conceptions of dangerousness to the public's abstract understanding of criminals as persistent threats to public safety. In *Arave*, the Court confronted statutory language that narrowed death eligible defendants to those who commit murder with an "utter disregard for human life." The Idaho statute defined "utter disregard" as the product of a "cold-blooded, pitiless slayer." While in prison, Thomas Creech killed David Jensen, but the facts of the killing are in dispute. Nevertheless, Justice O'Connor, who wrote the majority opinion, considered the murder "chilling"[108] and therefore within the statutory language to execute Creech. Apart from the legal concerns regarding the language of death eligibility, the case centered on the meaning of "utter disregard for human life." The federal court of appeals, hearing the case on a habeas petition, held that "utter disregard" and "cold-blooded pitiless slayer" created a subjective test, which did not clarify the law's intent, but rather "merely emphasize[d] it."[109] O'Connor and a majority of the justices disagreed with the court of appeals and turned to *Webster's Third International Dictionary* to support her argument that the "phrase 'cold-blooded, pitiless slayer' refers to a killer who kills without feeling or sympathy. We assume that legislators use words in their ordinary, everyday senses, and there is no reason to suppose that judges do otherwise."[110]

Turning to the way in which federal and state courts can determine a murderer's utter disregard for human life, O'Connor wrote, "The terms 'cold-blooded' and 'pitiless' describe the defendant's state of mind: not his mens rea, but his attitude toward his conduct and his victim."[111] Motive, again, is determined by one's surface actions, not by a psychological inquiry into one's state of mind. Reconceptualizing "utter disregard" as an attitude and a conscious way of acting, and not as a (more psychologically complex) "state of mind," means that the Court now has a plain meaning that any person with a dictionary and a modicum of common sense can easily understand. O'Connor's opinion breaks down the hierarchies of legal language that exist between the average person's understanding of crime and punishment and the legal technicalities and complexities caught up in legal jargon of protecting the accused. The law, when it wants to, can be radically egalitarian. A judge (no less than any other lay person or juror) can determine a murderer's attitude by considering if the murder was "especially heinous, cruel, or depraved" or if the perpetrator "relishes the murder, evidencing debasement or perversion," or "shows an indifference to the suffering of the victim and evidences a sense of pleasure" in the killing. The Idaho statute, according to O'Connor, "defines a state of mind that is ascertainable from surrounding fact."[112]

Without narratives (re-)written by the justices, we would be forced to confront only "subjective" narratives—habeas petitions that perform the function of permanent critiques of legal and police administration offered by convicted criminals—that the Court clearly finds unacceptable. If not for the Rehnquist Court's counternarratives, we would lose sight of both the ends of justice and the reason for punishment in the first instance. For Scalia, the Court's (counter-) narratives of violence reinforce the moral culpability of criminals precisely because they control the "surrounding facts." The facts as presented allow for a taking of accounts. They cast (or recast) criminals as responsible moral agents (even with elements of mental disease) and regard the infliction of punishment as a legal necessity, a matter of personal responsibility, without which the law would have no purpose or function.

A Narrative of Embodied Punishment

> In Texas, capital cases require bifurcated proceedings—a guilt phase and a penalty phase. If the defendant is found guilty, a separate proceeding before the same jury is held to fix the punishment. At the penalty phase, if the jury affirmatively answers three questions on which the State has the burden beyond a reasonable doubt, the judge must impose the death sentence. One of the three critical issues to be resolved by the jury is "whether there is a probability that the defendant would commit criminal acts of violence that would constitute a continuing threat to society." In other words, the jury must assess the defendant's future dangerousness.[113]

Estelle v. *Smith* introduced the concept of "future dangerousness" into Supreme Court discourse. This was not the Supreme Court's first use of the term,[114] but this case launched the Court down a path to further refinements and reclassifications of the concept. What is interesting about how future dangerousness entered into legal discourse is that Dr. James Grigson, the psychiatrist who used the term to describe Ernest Benjamin Smith's behavior, implied that it was Smith's body language that brought forth the concept.[115] Not unlike psychiatry in the nineteenth century, it was the trained medical gaze upon his body that revealed Smith's condition. Smith's body told the tale of his dangerousness, measured the depth of his violence, and revealed society's weakness. According to the Supreme Court: "Dr. Grigson drew his conclusions largely from the respondent's account of the crime during their interview, and he placed particular emphasis on what he considered to be respondent's lack of remorse. Dr. Grigson's prognosis as to future dangerousness rested on state-ments respondent made, and remarks he omitted, in reciting the details of the crime."[116] What did Smith's body say and not say? Smith, whose only other previous conviction was for marijuana, did not commit murder. Smith was tried and convicted for murder arising from his participation in an armed rob-bery of a grocery store that resulted in the death of the store's owner. Smith's accomplice killed the store owner. Dr. Grigson relied on Smith's "mannerisms, facial expressions, attention span, or speech patterns"[117] to determine Smith's potential for future violence. After Smith described how his friend, Howie, had shot the store owner, Smith, according to Dr. Grigson,

> walked around over this man who had been shot—did not . . . check to see
> if he had a gun nor did he check to see if the man was alive or dead. Did not
> call an ambulance, but simply found the gun further up underneath the
> counter and took the gun and the money. This is a very—sort of cold-
> blooded disregard for another human being's life. I think his telling me this
> story and not saying, you know, "Man, I would do anything to have that man
> back alive. I wish I had not just stepped over the body." Or you know, "I wish
> I had checked to see if he was all right" would indicate a concern, guilt, or
> remorse. But I did not get any of this.[118]

The Court's use of Dr. Grigson's narrative describing Smith's disregard for conventional understandings of remorse, as well as the focus on his peculiar body language, which circumscribed the victim but did not come into contact with it, is part of the Court's strategy to portray dangerousness as embedded within the criminal, by reference to "abnormal" body language, if not within the formalized language of criminal justice and psychiatry itself, the binary classifications of behavior. The effect is to obviate the law's violence, lessen its cruelty, and shift the gaze away from the failure of the law to rehabilitate, transform, and modify the criminal's behavior. Nineteenth-century criminol-ogy, anthropometry in particular, made the body speak through the measure-ment of deviance by way of normality—"the morbid anatomy of insanity"[119] brought forth the truth of one's self. Modern criminology (of which anthro-pometry is a part) makes the body speak not only through formal language, confession, and the reconstruction of events but also through omissions, movement, silences, and gaps. Silence becomes a form of cleverness, of polit-ical deviousness, the kind often associated with far-left political movements.[120] Thus, Smith's lack of remorse sets the boundaries for the outcome of his pun-ishment. Dangerousness is determined first by the profusion of speech, the confession, then within this altered medical-juridical space, by silence, move-ment, omissions.

By the end of the 1980s, the Rehnquist Court had successfully combined a number of ideas culled from the nineteenth century and modern criminology regarding crime control with the habeas challenge, such that petitions for habeas corpus were—from the start—practically doomed to failure. Federalism is background noise for this Court's overriding concern, which is getting the convicted to death row. To be sure, a posthumous haze surrounded the writ, emitting the faint sounds of the Warren Court's criminological legacy. But the hum of due process was all too often drowned out by Rehnquist Court justices' descriptions of brutality.

For the Rehnquist Court, federalism's bloom was off the rose. This is not to say that the Court devalued federalism. Federalism still performed its function: in a line of cases culminating with *Coleman* v. *Thompson* (1991), the Court put federalism concerns front and center of a habeas challenge. It is not, strictly speaking, that federalism fell out of favor or that its utility was no longer apparent, although these are, in part, accurate descriptions of the Court's understanding of federalism's role in criminal justice and habeas corpus cases. Rather, federalism was insufficient as a discursive form of restraint, as a means toward crime control, and it was inadequate as a way to express moral outrage. Only moral outrage, whether that of Scalia or the victim's family, can express moral outrage. The Court's opinions dealing with the death penalty and federalism had been too dry, too formal, too complex, too reminiscent of nineteenth-century jurisprudence that kept largely to the facts and respected the boundaries of civility. Habeas corpus by the late 1980s and early 1990s was a fight over crime control and the death penalty,[121] and Justices Scalia, O'Connor, Thomas, and Kennedy were not shy about saying so.

A Discourse on Dangerousness

In *Ramdass* v. *Angelone*[122](2000), *Shafer* v. *South Carolina*[123](2001), and *Kelly* v. *South Carolina*[124] (2002), the Supreme Court created a small treatise by which legal scholars could read the Court's thoughts on future dangerousness, habeas corpus, and the general purposes of punishment. This trilogy of cases stands for the self-evident proposition that "evidence of dangerous 'character' may show 'characteristic' future dangerousness."[125]

In *Simmons* v. *South Carolina*[126] (1994), which provides the backdrop for these cases, Justice Harry Blackmun, writing for the majority, declared:

> This case presents the question whether the Due Process Clause of the Four-teenth Amendment was violated by the refusal of a state trial court to instruct the jury in the penalty phase of a capital trial that, under state law, the defendant was ineligible for parole. We hold that, where the defendant's future dangerousness is at issue, and state law prohibits the defendant's release on parole, due process requires that the sentencing jury be informed that the defendant is parole ineligible.[127]

In response to the jury's question: "Does the imposition of a life sentence carry with it the possibility of parole?"[128] the trial judge told the jurors that they are not permitted to consider either parole or parole eligibility. The jury was thus in a position to assume that if Simmons was not sentenced to death, he could perhaps be set free at some future time. This was false, but the jury was not instructed otherwise. During closing arguments, the prosecution stated that a vote for death would be a "response of society to someone who is a threat. Your verdict will be an act of self-defense."[129]

In *Jurek v. Texas* (1976), the Supreme Court allowed Texas to consider future dangerousness because such concerns touch upon "all sentencing determinations made in our criminal justice system."[130] In *Simmons*, the Court noted that considerations of future dangerousness would be "inappropriate"[131] during the guilt phase of the trial because juries must convict on the facts and not on speculation. At the sentencing phase, however, the Court saw a responsibility, on the part of the jury, to consider the "defendant's character, prior criminal history, mental capacity, background, and age,"[132] as well as potential for future dangerousness. The Court held in *Simmons* that state courts cannot prevent juries from knowing that a defendant may or may not be parole eligible, because "it is entirely reasonable for a sentencing jury to view a defendant who is eligible for parole as a greater threat to society than a defendant who is not."[133] The state's legal system, then, was in the position of (i) creating linguistically the concept of future dangerousness for the jury and thereby influencing the way it thinks about the outcome; (ii) allowing the jury to consider dangerousness based on prosecutorial assertions (and psychiatric evaluations) of the defendant's character and history, both of which are molded by the state prosecutor's explanation of events; and (iii) setting up a choice for the jury to determine whether the defendant is a future threat based on the defendant's criminal and psychiatric history or is better off dead.

In *Ramdass*, Bobby Lee Ramdass and his accomplices shot and killed a store owner, Mohammed Kayani, at close range. "Petitioner," Justice Kennedy wrote, typically refraining from using Ramdass' full name, "stood over the body and laughed. He later inquired of an accomplice why the customers were not killed as well."[134] As Kennedy said, this crime "was no isolated incident." After being released from prison for a robbery conviction, Ramdass killed a man in Alexandria, Virginia, and then robbed a Pizza Hut, "abducting one of the victims. Four days later, petitioner and an accomplice pistol-whipped and robbed a hotel clerk."[135] Later that month, Ramdass shot another man, who survived, and, on the same day as the shooting, robbed a Domino's Pizza.

"To demonstrate Ramdass' evil character and his propensity to commit violent acts in the future, the prosecutor used Ramdass' prior criminal conduct."[136] The state of Virginia pressed for Ramdass' execution, arguing that his "future dangerousness" was an aggravating circumstance. Ramdass, Virginia argued, "would commit criminal acts of violence that would constitute a continuing serious threat to society," and Ramdass "could not live by the rules of society 'either here or in prison.'"[137] The jurors wanted to know whether if they sentenced Ramdass to life in prison he would be eligible for parole. The trial judge denied the request, saying that the jurors "are not to concern [them]selves with what happens afterwards."[138] The jury sentenced Ramdass to death.

Ramdass contested the judge's ruling that the jury was not to consider whether Ramdass was parole eligible or not. Ramdass' three prior convictions for murder and robbery prevented him from ever becoming parole eligible thus potentially saving him from the death chamber. However, his conviction for the Domino's Pizza robbery had not been rendered final by the state court. (Technically, the decision could be overturned.) In other words, he had been found guilty of robbing the pizzeria, but the court had not entered the judgment, which makes this case all too familiar. Both *Brown* v. *Allen* and *Coleman* v. *Thompson* allowed habeas petitioners to die because of judicial technicalities that have no merit. In any event, Ramdass was guilty of only two offenses, not three; therefore, at the time of his death sentence for the murder of Kayani, he was eligible for parole after twenty-five years. This peculiar and convoluted story has the effect of determining dangerousness solely by the number of convictions, which is not how the Court understands dangerousness, except when it wants to. The construction of dangerousness, like habeas corpus, runs through a crooked path.

The crux of the case is an ironic one. "Petitioner's proposed rule [that the Domino's Pizza conviction be included as a charge against him, thus rendering him parole ineligible with a potential life sentence] would require courts to evaluate the probability of future events where a three-strikes law is the issue."[139] The Court rejected Ramdass' logic to avoid future "litigation on a peripheral point,"[140] but it allowed Virginia to assess Ramdass' future dangerousness, his "evil character"[141] and thereby sentenced him to death, based on his prior convictions, which no more and no less determined Ramdass' future behavior. "[P]ermitting the State to argue the defendant's future dangerousness," Justice Stevens wrote in dissent, "while simultaneously precluding the defendant from arguing his parole ineligibility, does tend to 'impe[l] the jury toward voting for the death sentence.'"[142] The Court's "peripheral point" is Ramdass' death sentence.

In *Shafer*, the South Carolina Supreme Court held that the decision in *Simmons*, requiring jury notification of a defendant's parole eligibility, was not applicable in the present case. The U.S. Supreme Court overturned that decision, holding that when "a capital defendant's future dangerousness is at issue, and the only sentencing alternative to death available to the jury is life imprisonment without the possibility of parole, due process entitles the defendant 'to inform the jury of [his or her] parole ineligibility.'"[143] The Court ruled similarly in *Kelly* v. *South Carolina*.

In *Kelly*, the prosecutor began the case by saying, "I hope you never in your lives again have to experience what you are experiencing right now. Being some thirty feet away from such a person. Murderer."[144] A psychologist called in to testify for the state argued that there was evidence of Kelly's "sadism" at an early age, and that he had "an inclination to kill anyone who rubbed him the wrong way."[145] At sentencing, the prosecutor again used colorful language to describe Billy Kelly—"the butcher of Batesburg," "bloody Billy," and "Billy the Kid"[146]—and concluded that "murderers will be murderers. And he is the cold-blooded one right over there."[147] All of this was said without the prosecutor formally bringing up the concept of future dangerousness.

The Supreme Court dismissed the idea that future dangerousness was not at issue in this case, but the story is more interesting than that. The South Carolina court assumed it could bracket the state's vivid descriptions of Billy Kelly, thereby not bringing in future dangerousness, lest they trip the Supreme Court's due process radar from *Simmons*. The state Supreme Court thought there was a distinction between future dangerousness and examples of Kelly's "character and characteristics."[148]

The error in trying to distinguish *Simmons* this way lies in failing to recognize that evidence of dangerous "character" may show "characteristic" future dangerousness, as it did in *Shafer* and *Kelly*. This, indeed, is the fault of the state's more general argument, that evidence of future dangerousness counts under *Simmons* only when the state "introduc[es] evidence for which there is no other possible inference but future dangerousness to society. Evidence of future dangerousness under *Simmons* is evidence with a tendency to prove dangerousness in the future; its relevance to that point does not disappear merely because it might support other inferences to be described in other terms."[149] But as Justice David Souter wrote in *Kelly*, future dangerousness is an issue because the state "raised the specter" of future dangerousness, despite the fact that "future dangerousness" was never uttered.[150] No doubt catching a cue from previous Supreme Court rulings, where the Court has highlighted the petitioner's brutality but relied on federalism to deny habeas corpus, South Carolina tried to have it both ways. It refrained from invoking the concept of dangerousness, but, at the same time, called Kelly "dangerous" "bloody," a "butcher," and likened him to a "notorious serial killer."[151]

In attempting to balance the jury's responsibility to see through society's risk "actuarialism,"[152] that is, allowing the jury to decide how safe it will feel on the streets if the defendant is one day released, with the scientific community's larger concerns regarding the normalization of individuals, the South Carolina court was "rendering free individuals predictable."[153] Dangerousness performs an important discursive criminological function. It does not emerge out of the various stages of personality development or arise out of the institutional logic of federalism. Rather than viewing the body as passive, dangerousness thrusts the body forward, beyond institutional constraints. The discourse of dangerousness is Scalia's "one, two, three, four, five, six, seven, eight." It is performativity, not judgment or experience. It fills in the gap that separates crime from punishment by distributing the body's potential for violence more evenly along the grid of punishment; it clarifies the judicial waters muddied by due process and federal-state comity concerns. It creates an individual ready for punishment. It explains motive, remorselessness, encirclement, laughter, and silence. It is an aid to the jury, which rarely gets to consider alternatives to that stark dichotomy, crime and punishment. Future dangerousness disaggregates the dangerous classes and focuses its gaze on the "dangerous individual,"[154] now made whole by the scientific discourse of the penal law, as found in *Kansas* v. *Hendricks* and Justice Scalia's repetition of gun shots. The problem is that the writ of habeas corpus, strategically designed to limit the state's power in relation to the individual since the seventeenth century, has no place in a legal system concerned with promoting an image of the state as governing indirectly, therapeutically, and performatively representing "the way things officially are and ought to be."[155]

CONCLUSION

In Timothy Kaufman-Osborn's essay, "What the Law Must Not Hear: On Capital Punishment and the Voice of Pain," he quotes Karl Mayer, "An execution is not a complex verbal event."[156] We understand Meyer's meaning, though it seems, in light of the complexities habeas corpus petitioners have to undergo to get their death sentences reviewed by the Supreme Court, somewhat naive. Jordan Steiker gives an excellent overview of the procedural morass that is habeas corpus.

> A typical decision will briefly recite the facts of the crime and the inmate's constitutional allegations. The bulk of the opinion, though, will address whether the inmate timely filed the petition, exhausted state remedies, avoided all state procedural defaults (or offered some persuasive reason for overlooking the defaults), and adequately developed a factual record in state court. If by some good luck the inmate's claim survives these inquiries, the decision will turn to the "merits," which does not mean exactly what the term suggests. The court will first decide if relief is barred by its nonretroactivity doctrine. In a federal habeas proceeding, a federal court generally cannot grant relief if the inmate seeks the benefit of "new" law, even if the court believes the inmate's claims are compelling in light of prevailing constitutional norms. If, by some luck, the inmate is seeking only the application of well-established constitutional law, the federal court will then get to the crux of the matter: whether the state court's decision was unreasonable. Instead of asking whether the state court's decision was correct according to the federal court's best understanding of the Constitution, the court will undertake the largely anthropological task of determining whether the state court judge remained within the community of respectable interpreters of the federal Constitution.[157]

An execution can be quite simple, even in language, but Steiker's description of the habeas corpus process makes this unlikely. State-sanctioned executions in this particular federal system are never simple, legally speaking, and rarely painless, as Kaufman-Osborn demonstrates in his retelling of the electrocution of Allen Lee Davis. The Florida Supreme Court filtered Davis' blood through legal discourse. The blood that dripped from Davis' face during the execution is contained by the state Supreme Court's language that Davis' nosebleed "began before the electrical current was applied to him." Davis' pain is bracketed by the court's understanding that discomfort is part of the execution process.[158] State-sanctioned death in the United States is a complex verbal event. Dangerousness is the thing said and not said. It appears in movement, in childhood, in all manner of actions. Nothing is as it appears, and the Court, because of its tortured understanding of habeas corpus' mission, made worse by the cases dealing with future dangerousness, has made it so.

SIX

Habeas Corpus and the
Narratives of Terrorism, 1996–2004

Of all the antiterrorism initiatives now before the Senate, the one
that bears most directly on the Oklahoma City tragedy is habeas
corpus reform.

—Robert Dole, in Martin, "The Comprehensive
Terrorism Prevention Act of 1995"

The criminal goes free, if he must, but it is the law that sets
him free.

—*Mapp* v. *Ohio*

T HE WRIT OF HABEAS CORPUS, once defined by a statute passed by the same
Congress that drafted the Fourteenth Amendment, is now governed by the
Antiterrorism and Effective Death Penalty Act of 1996 (AEDPA). On April
24, 1996, just five days after the first anniversary of the bombing of the Alfred
P. Murrah Federal Building in Oklahoma City, Oklahoma, President Bill
Clinton signed the AEDPA into law.[1] Senator Robert Dole of Kansas had
introduced the bill in the Senate, then called the Omnibus Counterterrorism
Act of 1995.[2] In the House of Representatives, Henry Hyde, then the chairman of the Judiciary Committee, said: "Habeas corpus is tied up with terrorism because when a terrorist is convicted of mass killings, we want to make
sure that terrorist ultimately and reasonably has the sentence imposed on him
or her."[3] Congressman Hyde left unsaid, though it is more than clear, that if

habeas corpus is available, it could upset any sentence imposed on terrorists. Like the Supreme Court, Congressman Hyde reversed the writ's historical legacy. Rather than stressing habeas' capacity to expand individual liberty and check unlawful confinement, the congressional narrative emanating from the debate over the AEDPA focused on the postconviction problem of a writ that can free the guilty.

A CONGRESSIONAL NARRATIVE ON TERRORISM

With terrorism on the national political agenda by the mid-1990s, concerns over state court determinations of guilt easily evaporated as the prime reason for limiting habeas corpus review. The discourse of guilt and danger, which grew out of the weaknesses of the federalism defense, now had free reign. Indeed, the extent to which Congress wanted to retract habeas corpus protections for prisoners through a terrorism bill was a topic of extensive debate between the two parties during the mid-1990s.[4] Senator Orrin Hatch, a Republican from Utah, made the habeas corpus-terrorism connection clear by concentrating on habeas' ability to allow convicted criminals to petition for relief on "technical" issues of law, rather than on the substance of guilt or innocence. In fact, the senator from Utah had long been a critic of federal habeas corpus relief and had sponsored or supported numerous bills to restrict state prisoner access to the writ during his career, "only to see his proposals dropped from every successive anticrime measure."[5]

In the Senate debate, Senator Hatch used the imagery, which the Supreme Court had created in the 1970s, when it exchanged federalism for tales of individual brutality and future dangerousness, of habeas corpus as a legal technicality not worthy of constitutional consideration for convicted criminals. The Supreme Court's narrative of violence had made its way into the halls of Congress, as images of violent criminals-cum-terrorists abusing the system were front and center over the legacy of Oklahoma City. Necessarily, Senator Hatch omitted the federalism problem from the habeas petitioner's claim and focused on the inconvenience habeas corpus poses for the administration of justice in terms of future appeals and the doubt the writ casts on jury determinations of guilt. He wanted to impress upon the American public the degree to which habeas corpus and terrorism are intertwined, not just as legal matters but also in language, in light of events in Oklahoma City, the shooting down of an American airplane over Lockerbie, Scotland, in 1988, and the first attack against the World Trade Center on February 26, 1993.[6] Refraining from using the traditional tropes involved in habeas cases— brutal murderers, repeat offenders, and sexual predators—Senator Hatch nevertheless kept close to the same language used in any murder trial that comes before a federal court on a habeas corpus petition, raising the specter of courts releasing terrorists on constitutionally suspect grounds and of terrorists delaying their death sentences by constant petitioning. Senator Hatch said on the Senate floor, "The American people do not want to witness the spectacle of these terrorists abusing our judicial system and delaying the imposition of a just sentence by filing appeal after meritless appeal."[7]

The idea that habeas corpus is a drain on federal judicial resources is not new. "It has been settled since *Ex parte Royall*," Chief Justice William Rehnquist wrote in *Stewart v. Martinez-Villareal* (1998), "that a state prisoner must normally exhaust available state judicial remedies before a federal court will entertain his petition for habeas corpus."[8] Nor is it unknown to Congress that successive habeas petitions greatly vex various justices on the Supreme Court. In *McCleskey v. Zant* (1991), the Court defined "abuse of the writ" (also known as successive petitions) as striking at the heart of the finality doctrine. The purpose of preventing "abuse of the writ," Justice Anthony Kennedy wrote, is to "lessen the injury to a State that results through reexamination of a state conviction on a ground that the State did not have the opportunity to address at a prior, appropriate time; and both doctrines seek to vindicate the State's interest in the finality of its criminal judgments."[9]

These two cases (and there are many cases like these) helped Congress frame the debate over habeas restriction in the mid-1990s, by emphasizing the judicial burdens habeas imposes on state courts and the danger habeas corpus poses to the smooth administration of justice. What seems clear, however, is that the Supreme Court, even by the late 1980s, was not content with confining its criticisms of habeas corpus to the judiciary. The Supreme Court's road to restricting the writ of habeas corpus in the legislative arena began in June 1988, when Chief Justice Rehnquist appointed former Supreme Court Justice Lewis Powell, a longtime critic of federal habeas relief for state prisoners, the chair of the Ad Hoc Committee on Federal Habeas Corpus in Capital Cases. The Powell Committee included four federal district and appellate court judges from the fifth (Louisiana, Mississippi, and Texas) and eleventh circuits (Alabama, Georgia, and Florida). In July 1989, these six states held 40 percent of the nation's death row inmates.[10] The two principal findings of the Powell Committee were as follows: (1) that the present system of federal habeas review fosters delay in the movement of habeas appeals from the state to the federal courts; and (2) that there is a "pressing need for qualified counsel to represent inmates in collateral review." To rectify these problems, the Powell Committee proposed to Congress that "Capital cases should be subject to one complete and fair course of collateral review in the state and federal system, free from the time pressure of impending execution, and with the assistance of competent counsel for the defendant. When this review has concluded, litigation should end."[11] Although the Powell Committee's recommendations were not the last word on habeas corpus reform (both the Reagan Administration's

Justice Department and the American Bar Association put forth proposals in Congress), Congress accepted many of the Powell Committee's recommendations to limit prisoner access to the writ, which it put into the AEDPA, most notably the one-year time period to file habeas petitions. Alexander Rundlet suggests that the motivation for adding habeas provisions to antiterrorist legislation came not from Congress alone but from the chief justice, who was a vocal supporter of the Powell Committee's proposed reforms.[12] "As a comprehensive bill to combat terrorism," Rundlet writes, the AEDPA lacks "many of the provisions that were designed to aid law enforcement in the growing war against terrorism. The background of terrorism, however, served to push the [habeas corpus] measures through both houses of Congress."[13]

The AEDPA's four main features, regarding habeas procedures, are (1) it imposes a one-year limit on filing habeas petitions; previously, there was no deadline (AEDPA sec. 101);[14] (2) habeas petitioners have only one chance for federal review, except in extraordinary circumstances; previously, there were no limits on the number of habeas filings a state prisoner could make (AEDPA sec. 106);[15] (3) it establishes an "opt-in" provision for states to provide counsel (AEDPA sec. 106). In other words, "the opt-in provisions are a quid pro quo. If a state provides counsel, the opportunities of state prisoners for federal review are reduced, thus removing roadblocks to a state's effective and expeditious use of the death penalty."[16] If a state does not opt in, and none have,[17] then the filing deadline for habeas review expands from 180 days after final state court affirmance to 360 days. The failure of any state to "opt in," including those states with the largest death rows, indicates that the states have weighed the costs and the benefits of Congress' reform of habeas procedures and have determined that they are not troubled by the one-year limit; nor, it seems, do the states want to invest the time and financial resources it would take to provide counsel for death row inmates. At the least, the states' reluctance to partake of Congress' gift to speed up executions demonstrates a disconnect between the states' understanding of time delays, the right to counsel, and the death penalty and the understanding of congressmen and Supreme Court justices regarding the administrative problems of habeas corpus. According to Rundlet, "The opt-in provisions require a significant expenditure of effort and resources from the States as a precondition to improve, create, and regulate the competency standards of post-conviction defender systems. This expenditure, when compared with the ease and economy of maintaining the status quo, serves as a disincentive [to the states] that outweighs the persuasive force of the finality benefits offered."[18] Politically, the failure to provide counsel in exchange for a speedier execution date "reflects how readily fairness was sacrificed in Congress in favor of federalism arguments";[19] and (4) "a determination of a factual issue made by a State court shall be presumed to be correct. The applicant shall have the burden of rebutting the presumption of correctness by clear and convincing evidence" (AEDPA sec. 104).[20]

Prior to the AEDPA, federal habeas courts were free to arrive at an independent judgment on the issues presented in habeas corpus petitions. Now, under section 2254(1), a federal court must allow the state court's judgment to stand "unless the adjudication of the claim '(1) resulted in a decision that was contrary to, or involved an unreasonable application of, clearly established federal law, as determined by the Supreme Court . . . ; or (2) resulted in a decision that was based on an unreasonable determination of the facts in light of the evidence presented in the State court proceeding.'"[21] Chief Justice Rehnquist wrote that a federal habeas court could grant relief under the "unreasonable application" clause "if the state court correctly identifies the governing legal principle" from prior Court decisions "but unreasonably applies [them] to the facts of the particular case."[22] This understanding of the "unreasonable application" clause does not make it easier for federal courts to grant the writ. As the Court made clear in *Tyler* v. *Cain*[23] (2001):

> [The Antiterrorism and Effective Death Penalty Act of 1996] greatly restricts the power of federal courts to award relief to state prisoners who file second or successive habeas corpus applications. If the prisoner asserts a claim that he has already presented in a previous federal habeas petition, the claim must be dismissed in all cases. And if the prisoner asserts a claim that was not presented in a previous petition, the claim must be dismissed unless it falls within one of two narrow exceptions. One of these exceptions is for claims predicated on newly discovered facts that call into question the accuracy of a guilty verdict. The other is for certain claims relying on new rules of constitutional law.[24]

All in all, the AEDPA does not leave a lot of room for state prisoners to make their case for unlawful confinement.[25] Justice O'Connor made the difference between pre-AEDPA habeas corpus and post-AEDPA habeas corpus clear, writing in *Williams* v. *Taylor* (2000):

> If today's case were governed by the federal habeas statute prior to Congress' enactment of AEDPA in 1996, I would agree with Justice Stevens that Williams' petition for habeas relief must be granted if we, in our independent judgment, were to conclude that his Sixth Amendment right to effective assistance of counsel was violated. . . . [But] Williams' case is *not* governed by the pre-1996 version of the habeas statute. Because he filed his petition in December 1997, Williams' case is governed by the statute as amended by AEDPA. . . . Accordingly, for Williams to obtain federal habeas relief, he must first demonstrate that his case satisfies the condition set by §2254(d)(1). That provision modifies the role of federal habeas courts in reviewing petitions filed by state prisoners.[26]

The AEDPA's habeas limitations are difficult to get around, and federal deference to state court factfinding will not be easy to overcome, despite Justice John Paul Stevens' point that the word *deference* does not appear in the AEDPA.[27]

For the more conservative members of the Rehnquist Court, this development is not unwelcome. One of the most important habeas provisions of the AEDPA (2254(d)(1)) forbids a federal court from granting relief if the state court's judgment of the state prisoner's claim was "reasonable," even if the decision was erroneous. The AEDPA grants the federal courts the power to issue habeas corpus if the state court's decision was "contrary to . . . clearly established Federal law, as determined by the Supreme Court," and if the state court's decision "involved an unreasonable application of clearly established Federal law," as interpreted by the Supreme Court. In fact, if a federal court finds a meritorious claim in an unexhausted petition, the court must withhold judgment and send the petitioner back to state court to complete his appeal, thereby doing exactly what Justices Powell and O'Connor have long warned against: extending the time period the petitioner undergoes from conviction to execution. Yet the Court's most vocal habeas critics have welcomed these changes. "Principles of exhaustion," Justice Anthony Kennedy wrote in *Williams* v. *Taylor* (2000), "are premised upon recognition by Congress and the Court that state judiciaries have the duty and competence to vindicate rights secured by the Constitution in state criminal proceedings."[28] The congressionally mandated exhaustion requirement comports, Justice O'Connor wrote in *Duncan* v. *Walker* (2001), with the "AEDPA's purpose to further the principles of comity, finality, and federalism."[29] For Justice Clarence Thomas, congressional intent over AEDPA is clear. "Congress enacted AEDPA to reduce delays in the executions of state and federal criminal sentences, particularly in capital cases."[30] "In the interest of finality," Justice Kennedy wrote in *Miller-El* v. *Cockrell* (2003), "AEDPA constrains a federal court's power to disturb state-court convictions."[31] According to Justice Antonin Scalia, the passage of the AEDPA enacted a regime change, putting the finishing touches on the remnants of Warren-era habeas jurisprudence. In a 1998 habeas corpus case that arose under the AEDPA, Scalia wrote, "As hard as it may be for the Court to swallow, in yesterday's enactment of AEDPA Congress curbed our prodigality with the Great Writ."[32] In passing a law directed at foreign and domestic acts of violence against U.S. citizens and buildings, Congress codified substantial portions of the Supreme Court's habeas jurisprudence since the late nineteenth century that limit the rights of state prisoners to gain access to the federal courts and contest their confinements on constitutional grounds.[33]

Although the Supreme Court has been the unchallenged manufacturer of the idea that habeas corpus is a threat to state sovereignty for over one hundred years, Congress can be an effective producer of legal meaning.[34] Moreover, despite the fact that Congress follows the Court's lead on habeas reform, the AEDPA is Congress' most forceful attempt to restrict the rights of state prisoners who attack their convictions in federal court. But as a terrorism measure, the act is weak and porous. The AEDPA, for example, does not make an attack against a federal building such as the Murrah building a terrorist act unless it is committed by a foreign power. Larry Yackle, a prominent critic of the Rehnquist Court's habeas decisions, considers the AEDPA "not well drafted" and says its habeas corpus provisions bear "the influence of various bills that were fiercely debated [in Congress] for nearly forty years."[35] The AEDPA, which expands the government's jurisdiction over anyone attempting to commit an act of terrorism against the United States, does not ban so-called cop killer bullets. Nor does the act ban the use of firearms by terrorists, such as machine guns, sawed-off shotguns, and explosive devices. The act prohibits fundraising to aid terrorists (AEDPA sec. 303) but does not enhance the government's wiretapping powers over suspected terrorists. It is also without provisions to enlist the military "in cases involving biological and chemical weapons," and it failed to lengthen the "statute of limitations on firearms violations"[36] (AEDPA sec. 501). But what the act does clearly is alter habeas corpus procedures for state prisoners attacking their convictions in federal courts. As Senator Joseph Biden said, the AEDPA is "a habeas corpus bill with a little terrorism thrown in."[37]

The AEDPA gave voice to a congressional narrative on habeas corpus and prisoners' rights restrictions that had been festering in the legislative branch for almost forty years. The AEDPA's focus is directed more toward voters' perception of the weaknesses of the criminal justice system (as well as the "activism" of federal courts) than a reasoned response to an actual terrorist threat on American soil.[38] More the result of a politically timed response to "panic" over increasing crime rates, the AEDPA is emblematic of domestic politics in the 1990s that emphasized "get tough" crime measures, such as President Bill Clinton's push for one hundred thousand police officers on city streets, California's "three strikes" legislation, the rise of laws named after victims, such as "Megan's law," and the federal government's war on drugs.[39] According to Ann Chih Lin, President Clinton's success in reframing the crime debate for the Democratic Party during the 1990s had the effect of making it possible for "latent factions within both parties to jockey with the issue of power; for interest groups to bargain with the parties for policies that would advance their cause; and for states and cities to make a claim on federal assistance for a set of distinctly local concerns." The result, Lin suggests, is that there will be a "new crop of crime debates: a perennial one over the reach of government into the regulation of private behavior and a nascent one over the political challenges of devolution."[40] Indeed, the outcome of almost two generations of congressional deliberations over crime and the politics of habeas corpus exemplifies this dichotomy in American politics. The AEDPA produced relatively little that was new, a lot that was symbolic, and some that was harmful to individuals' civil liberties.[41]

If, by 1996, the impetus for habeas reform was terrorism, the framework was criminal justice. For the Court and Congress, the modern construction of the terrorist fits the same profile the public holds of the criminal: the thug, the predator, the dangerous individual, the uncontrollably mentally ill individual, the racialized threat to personal and national security.[42] Justice Kennedy, for example, categorized the fear of releasing aliens slated for deportation into the general population (before September 11, 2001) in terms of the terrorist threat they may pose to the security of the United States. The problem of enemy aliens, like crime itself, is everpresent in post-1996 case law and does not recede by mere confinement. According to Kennedy: "Underworld and terrorist links are subtle and may be overseas, beyond our jurisdiction to impose felony charges."[43] What binds the twin concepts of terrorist and criminal in law is the concern over the (potential) victim,[44] the ready-made reason for the police power, expressed as the need to punish those who choose not to control themselves or as the necessity to scale back liberal permissiveness on the criminal justice front. We have, then, an act principally directed at terrorism but that largely codifies the Supreme Court's counternarrative habeas regime in similar codings and images, first put into effect in the early 1970s, against the backlash of *Fay* v. *Noia* (1963). In 1996, Congress reentered the habeas debate to codify, not alter, the Supreme Court's restrictive habeas decisions from the early 1970s to the mid-1990s.

Substantively, the AEDPA reorients our vision of habeas corpus away from a writ directed at arbitrary executive action and toward prisoners who are looking for any available technicality to get out of jail. The AEDPA, then, both builds on the past and upsets it. As the quotes from Justices Kennedy, O'Connor, Thomas, and Scalia demonstrate, the writ, despite the intervention of AEDPA, still functions as before, mired in the legal profession's nineteenth-century conceptions of federal-state comity and deference. State prisoners will ask for the writ, because they believe that their trials were unfair (though there will be fewer petitions), and the Supreme Court will continue to deny it, in language the Court has used since 1886.[45] But, significantly, the AEDPA will displace the individual rights narrative that made habeas corpus serve the ends of individual justice, a narrative that, of course, has largely disappeared from the Supreme Court's language since the late 1970s.[46] Moreover, habeas provisions encased in a terrorism law will discourage habeas' mainstream supporters in Congress and delegitimize sympathetic members of liberal elite groups outside of Congress. The association of habeas corpus with terrorism will, at the least, perpetuate the image that the writ of habeas corpus is not the way out of prison. The Supreme Court's labeling of habeas petitioners as convicted criminals and "brutal" murderers who commit crimes in a "brutal and callous fashion,"[47] repeated within the halls of Congress and encased in legislation, can only harden public opinion on the question of habeas corpus. As Isaac Balbus once wrote, "once the process of criminalization has begun," "moderate and partially sympathetic members of the elite are likely to find it politically impossible to support the cause of 'criminals.'"[48]

THE OTHER HABEAS CORPUS

How did a writ, whose origins lay in the monarchical arrests of subjects unwilling to loan King Charles I money for war, come to occupy a place in the debate about terrorism?[49] The answer is that the Supreme Court has cut the writ in two: a writ that exists in speech and is tied to constitutional law by Article I, section 9 (habeas corpus I), and a writ that exists by congressional action, created by statute in 1867 (habeas corpus II). Despite its dormancy, habeas corpus I is alive, always ready to attack unlawful executive action; habeas corpus II is a relic of Reconstruction, a nuisance that interferes with the administration of criminal justice and capital punishment. Habeas corpus II causes trouble between levels of government and requires federal judicial supervision and the use of balancing tests; habeas corpus I exists in speech and is celebrated as the "great writ of liberty," but it has no content because it is so rarely used. For some unarticulated reason, habeas corpus I is always pregnant with possibilities—executive detention is hidden but foreboding; habeas corpus II remains an irritant, a reminder that the states were once abusers of civil liberties. With the war on terrorism, habeas corpus I has reentered the political arena. What does this mean for habeas corpus II? Is habeas corpus I antithetical or complementary to habeas corpus II? How will the Supreme Court's opinions that have arisen from the war on terrorism in *Hamdi* v. *Rumsfeld* and *Rasul* v. *Bush* effect habeas corpus II, if at all?

Despite the presence of two habeas', one in service against executive detention in its classical form (habeas corpus I), the other operating postconviction against state arrests (habeas corpus II), there is no real divergence in either habeas' goal of freeing the unlawfully detained. The writ, both in its statutory construction as a method of "second-level review," that is, after conviction, and under Article I, section 9 of the Constitution, is concerned with arbitrary detentions, which began as executive detentions and became known, by extension of the separation of powers, as judicial detentions. Alexander Hamilton made this clear in *The Federalist*: "Arbitrary impeachments, arbitrary methods of prosecuting pretended offenses, and arbitrary punishments upon arbitrary convictions, have ever appeared to me to be the great engines of judicial despotism; and these have all relation to criminal proceedings. The trial by jury in criminal cases, aided by the habeas-corpus act, seems therefore to be alone concerned in the question."[50] Habeas corpus I and II highlight the threat of unlawful detention. Neither posits a universal idea of imprisonment that attaches only to Presidents Abraham Lincoln and George W. Bush but excludes governors or local police chiefs. Nor do the two habeas' privilege one way of understanding detention—with or without trial, pre- or postconviction; rather, the writ attacks unlawful confinement at its source. Habeas corpus, given voice by a detainee, searches for executive action that conflicts with individual movement, regardless of the governmental level that ordered the detention.

The only alteration in habeas' direction (but not its purpose) came after the Civil War, when Congress expanded the writ's jurisdiction to cover "all persons" unlawfully detained and not just those with clear-cut federal questions, as the Judiciary Act of 1789 had done. Changed circumstances merited changing avenues for appeal to the federal judiciary. The 1867 act was an adaptation of the writ to the abolition of slavery and greater federal control and supervision over state action through the Fourteenth Amendment. But habeas corpus' focus remained on the power to deny arrest, final judgment, and sentence, all of which come within habeas' traditional power (habeas corpus I). At the end of Reconstruction, and at the height of industrialization and the corporation-as-person jurisprudence of the federal judiciary, the problem of federalism became part of habeas' legacy, an addition to the narrative of unlawful confinement that first supplemented then supplanted the older, antistatist narrative tradition, causing the storyline of habeas corpus and arbitrary executive detention[51] to detour into preserving state judgments in criminal cases. Not only did the writ's new direction create multiple psychological and criminological discourses concerning deference, respect, finality, and federalism, but it squeezed out the individual's complaint against unlawful detention, forcing the habeas petitioner to focus on her crime, the victim, and her level of remorse. *Ex parte Royall* set in motion the process of criminalizing habeas petitioners.

It therefore serves no purpose to ignore that nineteenth-century federalism concerns divided habeas in two, launching a favored discourse that attacks executive detention because it fit with the dominant antistatist narrative of the founding era and a secondary understanding of habeas corpus that explicitly argues that the 1867 act created a separate habeas corpus doctrine that requires deference and is subject to political pressure.[52] However constitutionally troubling this view is, it should be stressed that proponents of states' rights and advocates of the death penalty have taken habeas corpus onto a different path.[53] But dwelling on this diversion at the expense of downgrading the writ's profound power seems equally unnecessary. There may be striations in habeas corpus law, but the grooves do not tear habeas corpus apart—it attacks executive detentions, only at two levels, one in the form of state actions that may violate a citizen's constitutional rights regarding arrest, trial, and confinement (with a federalism narrative thrown in that need not be dispositive, as Brennan showed in *Fay*), the other against presidential directives that detain citizens and noncitizens without any chance of appeal (that narrative stands almost alone, almost unimpaired, unless there is a declared war).

What is clear is that, regardless of the source, constitutional or statutory, the writ acts as a vessel of speech for those who have been silenced by internment. For this reason, habeas corpus is called "the great writ of liberty," not because it protects citizens from the arbitrary actions of governmental officials operating under the law of necessity and not the rule of law (the writ has no power to preempt executive decisions), but because it guarantees that executive actions regarding arrests will be tested in courts of law.[54] Not confined by jurisdictional niceties when life is at stake, the writ presupposes a dialogue between separate but equal departments of government, the executive and the judiciary but adds the voice of the convicted, replacing the institutional dialogue that exists between state and federal courts with a cross-current that flows through the separation of powers, obfuscating any clear line created by political scientists and historians that tries to establish which branch and which level of government best protects the people's liberty. Should not a writ designed to end arbitrary arrests and confinement evade the strictures of judicial formalism? Habeas corpus argues for itself, for the bodies of the detained. It requires open courts, evidentiary testimony, qualified lawyers, and the right to speak. "There is no room for niggardly restrictions when questions relating to [habeas'] availability are raised."[55]

Rather than focusing on the writ as an invitation for institutional redundancy, as legal functionalists in the 1950s saw it, my focus throughout has been on the writ's function as speech, a plea on behalf of the detained that calls into question the government's authority to arrest those who lack power within society, a point all too often ignored among habeas commentators. Habeas corpus is a preservative of individual liberty that exists in suspense in language, waiting to be called in to speak on behalf of the unlawfully detained.[56]

The idea that habeas corpus is a counternarrative to executive authority is also the Supreme Court's understanding in *Ex parte Milligan* (1866).[57] In that case, Lambdin P. Milligan, a citizen of the United States and a resident of Indiana, was arrested in Indiana on October 5, 1864, by the military commandant of the District of Indiana for conspiracy, inciting insurrection, disloyal practices, and violation of the laws of war. He was tried by a military tribunal rather than in a civil court, which was open. Milligan was sentenced to be hanged and was held in a military prison. He sued for a writ of habeas corpus in the Supreme Court (after the Circuit Court for the District of Indiana denied his habeas petition). President Lincoln, however, had suspended the writ partially in 1861, then throughout the United States in 1862 and again in 1863, the last time with Congress passing a habeas corpus law that ratified Lincoln's actions and indemnified soldiers against lawsuits. Despite this, the Court granted the writ and held—to be sure, after Lincoln's death—that as long as federal district courts are open, a person not accused of a military crime, not part of the insurrection against the United States, and not living in an area controlled by the military cannot be tried in military courts. *Milligan* does not hold that habeas corpus cannot be suspended; it is silent on Lincoln's suspension of an Article I power.[58] Nor does *Milligan* hold that the military cannot arrest civilians during rebellions. The case is directed to the trial of civilians by military tribunals during wartime when other, nonmilitary, options are available.

Given the writ's constitutional language, which is not tied to considerations of federalism, deference, and crime control but to the separation of powers and the meaning of rebellion, it would seem unwise for any president not in a situation involving "rebellion" or "invasion" to question the writ's reach. "At its historical core," Justice John Paul Stevens wrote in *INS* v. *St. Cyr* (2001), "the writ of habeas corpus has served as a means of reviewing the legality of executive detention, and it is in that context that its protections have been strongest."[59]

Woodrow Wilson was the first president since Lincoln to systematically interfere with civil rights, but he did not entertain habeas restrictions as a method to intimidate the alien population during World War I, as no rebellion occurred on U.S. soil. Nor did Wilson set up military tribunals to try those accused of sedition.[60] Unlike Lincoln, Wilson, following America's entry into World War I, relied on civil courts to try sedition cases and Congress to pass the several laws that restricted the speech and activities of both American citizens and non-Americans, such as the Espionage Act and the Sedition Act (1917), the Trading-with-the-Enemy Act (1917), the Threats Against the President Act (1917), and the Alien Act (1918). Wilson did, however, create by executive decree the Committee on Public Information and a Board of Censorship, both of which had broad authority to torment dissenters and deter antiwar sentiment.[61] Despite the democratic stamp of approval Congress gave the president, the developing legal doctrine of free speech incurred a serious setback during Wilson's administration.[62] In the oft-quoted words of Zechariah Chafee:

> It became criminal to advocate heavier taxation instead of bond issues, to state that conscription was unconstitutional though the Supreme Court had not yet held it valid, to say that the sinking of merchant vessels was legal, to urge that a referendum should have preceded our declaration of war, to say that war was contrary to the teachings of Christ. . . . [The Wilson administration has] made it impossible for an opponent of the war to write an article or even a letter in a newspaper of general circulation because it will be read in some training camp where it might cause insubordination or interfere with military success.[63]

Lincoln might have stretched the meaning of executive power in ways that Wilson could only admire, but Lincoln lacked what Wilson had: a cadre of lawyers in the Department of Justice (not in existence during Lincoln's presidency), a bureaucratic apparatus that combined police functions and intelligence gathering capable of "hunting reds" and anarchists, put in place during Theodore Roosevelt's administration, and a functioning Congress willing to give the president broad authority to uproot subversion.[64] "The war," Kathleen Kennedy writes, "permanently changed the tempo and character of the anti-radical crusade. Unlike the pre-war years, wartime repression used federal troops and judicial trials and committed the state to a permanent program whose goal was the destruction of domestic subversion."[65]

The passage of sedition, espionage, and trading with the enemy acts during World War I raised the specter of "enemy aliens."[66] Concerns about sabotage prompted the Wilson administration to ask Congress to restrict alien enemies' movements. Alien enemies were prevented from owning firearms; coming within a hundred yards of canals, wharfs, warehouses and railroad terminals; and warned against acts of treason. Despite initial reluctance to restrict civil liberties, Wilson was soon persuaded that action needed to be taken. "I am in a hurry," the president said, "to have a line-up, and let the men who are thinking first of other countries stand on one side, and all those that are for America first, last, and all the time, on the other side."[67]

The Wilson administration arrested over one hundred enemy aliens within the first month of the passage of the Espionage Act of 1917.[68] The administration also placed broad restrictions on the publication of foreign language newspapers and censored communication between the United States and foreign countries. The administration made it a crime to make false statements that interfered with the success of the military; to interfere with national production necessary for the conduct of the war; to show contempt for the form of government; to display the enemy's flag; and to favor by word or act the cause of any country with which the United States was at war."[69] All told, there were over one thousand convictions in federal courts under the Espionage Act.[70] Various war protestors served time in jail, the most prominent among them being the union leader "Big" Bill Haywood, the anarchist publisher Victor Berger, and union organizer and presidential candidate Eugene V. Debs, all for advocating socialism and for protesting the war effort. President Wilson, at J. Edgar Hoover's promptings, also had the anarchists Emma Goldman and Alexander Berkman deported to Russia (though Goldman was born in Lithuania) for their criticisms of the war and opposition to the draft.[71] Overall, these decrees and statutes created negotiating room for courts to determine the permissible limits of speech and behavior during wartime,[72] but they left untouched the individual's right to petition courts on habeas corpus, and civil courts were kept open and used.

Alien enemies is a term of law that first appeared at the end of John Adams' administration, though it is vague and lacks the legal specificity and clarity used to describe the term *prisoners of war*, which is governed by the Geneva Convention.[73] The Federalists in Congress passed "An Act Respecting Alien Enemies"

(1798), which is still in existence.[74] Section 1 of the act states that during a "declared war between the United States and any foreign nation or government . . . any natives, citizens, denizens, or subjects of the hostile nation or government . . . who shall be within the United States, and not actually naturalized, shall be liable to be apprehended, restrained, secured and removed, as alien enemies." "Alien enemy" refers to a person living in the United States but who has the nationality of the country at war with the U.S. In American law, alien enemies have the right to sue "until carried away by the President."[75] Enemy aliens do have a right to petition for habeas corpus, provided they reside in the United States or are under the jurisdiction of an American official and have not been tried and convicted by a military commission.[76] Federal courts can review "the construction and validity of the [governing detention] statute" and "whether war has been declared, whether the detainee is an alien, and whether the detainee is among the 'natives, citizens, denizens, or subjects of the hostile nation,' within the meaning" of the Alien Enemies Act of 1798, but cannot review "the merits of the Executive's discretionary decision whether to detain or expel an enemy alien."[77] If the First World War brought attention to the legal problem of alien enemies, the Second World War provided the federal courts with the opportunity to judge actual executive detention of "enemy combatants" by military commissions.

The term *enemy combatants* encompasses both Americans and non-American residents of the United States. *Ex parte Quirin* (1942) stands for the proposition that enemy combatants can be tried by military commissions created by executive decree, regardless of whether they are American citizens. Military commissions are neither courts nor tribunals. In *Ex parte Milligan*, David Dudley Field characterized military commissions as an "advisory board of officers, convened for the purpose of informing the conscience of the commanding officer, in cases where he might act for himself if he chose."[78] Commissioners on military tribunals are not independent judges but military officers under the jurisdiction of the secretary of defense. During the Second World War, President Franklin Roosevelt was careful not to abuse this power. "The only persons who were treated as enemy combatants pursuant to Proclamation No. 2561 [detaining Japanese Americans on the West Coast] were members of the German military who had been captured after landing on U.S. beaches from German submarines."[79] All told, the U.S. government classified only ten persons as enemy combatants throughout the Second World War, and only one was an American citizen.

The Supreme Court took the case of the Nazi saboteurs in special session because eight German agents had landed on the U.S. mainland in June 1942 for the purposes of espionage and sabotage, and President Roosevelt wanted the Court's imprimatur on his decision to try these men not in civilian courts or by court martial but in secret and by military tribunal. The facts are both peculiar and important.[80] Of the eight men who came ashore and were captured, two had American citizenship, Ernest Peter Burger and Herbert Hans

Haupt. Burger was a naturalized citizen but forfeited his citizenship by fighting for the Germans, leaving Haupt as the only American to be classified as an enemy combatant. Subsequently, Roosevelt issued two proclamations, one denying to those who commit sabotage or espionage access to U.S. courts, and the other creating a military commission to try the eight men. Roosevelt called for the military tribunal to be governed by the "laws of war" and not the Articles of War.[81] The distinction was crucial. The laws of war are governed by the common law of war, whereas the Articles of War are codified by statute and would have provided the accused with greater legal protections. According to Louis Fisher, "Had Roosevelt cited the 'Articles of War,' he would have triggered the statutory procedures established by Congress for courts-martial."[82] Also, the governing statute on sabotage had a maximum penalty of thirty years in prison. A military tribunal could sentence defendants to death. One other important difference between a military tribunal and a court martial is that a court martial requires unanimity for a death sentence, whereas the president called for the military tribunal to have two-thirds of the members vote for conviction. Within the first week of the capture, Roosevelt issued Proclamation 2561, entitled "Denying Certain Enemies Access to the Courts of the United States."[83] The military trial was conducted in secret, largely to prevent the public from becoming aware of how easily eight Nazi saboteurs infiltrated the United States. Roosevelt feared even a court martial could release information to the public as well as provide the petitioners with greater legal protections, such as the rules of evidence, and force the jury to establish guilt beyond a reasonable doubt. In what can only be characterized as a judicial gift, the Supreme Court, after the eight enemy combatants had already been tried and sentenced, and six had been executed, rejected the petitioners' habeas corpus plea. Ernest Peter Burger and George John Dasch were initially sentenced to death, but Roosevelt (at Attorney General Francis Biddle's urging) commuted Burger's sentence to life imprisonment and Dasch's to thirty years. (Dasch had turned himself in and helped capture the remaining seven.)

The Court was not concerned with the guilt or innocence of the eight defendants, only the jurisdiction of the military tribunal to try the defendants. The Court's opinion was unanimous.[84] Chief Justice Harlan Fiske Stone held that the eight men were unlawful combatants, having entered the United States in German military uniforms but shed them as they moved inland. As such, they were not "entitled to the status of prisoners of war" but were offenders "against the law of war." Moreover, they were not only liable "to capture and detention as prisoners" but also were "subject to trial and punishment by military tribunals for acts which render their belligerency unlawful."[85] The Court did not consider the question whether the president could establish military tribunals without congressional authorization, and *Quirin* does not give "the president carte blanche unilaterally to create an alternative military system of criminal justice for suspicious aliens captured abroad."[86] The critical point in

Quirin was the congressional declaration of war. "For here Congress has authorized trial of offenses against the law of war before such commissions."[87] *Ex parte Quirin* is far from clear regarding by what procedures the government can try enemy combatants. *Ex parte Milligan*, of course, provided the Court with a problem the Court chose not to address, particularly insofar as *Milligan* stands for the idea that if civilian courts are open, they should be used.

The Stone Court acknowledged that Milligan could not be tried by military tribunal. Chief Justice Stone was diplomatic, trying to strike a balance between the rights of the accused and military necessity. He stated, "Constitutional safeguards for the protection of all who are charged with offenses are not to be disregarded in order to inflict merited punishment on some who are guilty." But it is obvious that the military commission had only one purpose: to find the defendants guilty and sentence them to death without concerns over procedures and appeals. Thus the chief justice also held that *Milligan* was not applicable to the *Quirin* petitioners because Milligan was a war protester, not an "enemy combatant," which sufficiently distinguished *Milligan* from *Quirin*. (Milligan was a member of a secret organization opposed to the Civil War and clearly could have been classified as such.) Said Stone, "But the detention and trial of petitioners—ordered by the President in the declared exercise of his powers as Commander in Chief of the Army in time of war and of grave public danger—are not to be set aside by the courts without the clear conviction that they are in conflict with the Constitution or laws of Congress constitutionally enacted."[88]

Quirin holds that Roosevelt's authority to have the prisoners tried by military commission was not because of the president's inherent executive power or with the president's powers under the commander-in-chief clause but because Congress explicitly granted the president authority under the Articles of War to wage war and protect the United States.[89] In this sense, despite the breadth of the opinion, collapsing the distinction between Americans and non-Americans for purposes of trial by military commission, *Quirin* is not similar to *Milligan*.[90] But *Quirin* also has a lot of holes in it. The Court's opinion in *Quirin*, for example, did not "distinguish between enemy soldiers who forfeit the right to be treated as prisoners of war by failing to distinguish themselves as belligerents, as the petitioners had done, and civilians who commit hostile acts during war without having the right to participate in combat."[91] Although both types of persons are "unlawful combatants," the law treats them differently.[92] *Quirin*, then, does not rest on solid constitutional ground in any discussion of war detainees. *Quirin* is also completely politicized and therefore ill equipped to provide a just measure of support for future enemy combatants.

Roosevelt wanted the Court in *Quirin* to supply a narrative of events, a way of telling the American people what happens to enemy combatants who invade U.S. territory and how the rule of law was upheld, despite the fact that the Court was in the dark regarding the military tribunal's trial procedures.[93] Moreover, Justices Frank Murphy, Felix Frankfurter, James F. Byrnes (who was working for the Roosevelt administration while sitting on the Court), Hugo Black, Owen Roberts, and Chief Justice Harlan Fiske Stone (who wrote the majority opinion and whose son was a member of the defense) all had contact with either the prosecution or defense counsel, something that would not be acceptable today. (Murphy, a reserve army lieutenant colonel, appeared in Court in military uniform before recusing himself.) *Quirin* is also problematic because Roosevelt guided the *Quirin* decision from the start. Attorney General Francis Biddle told the justices, apparently at Roosevelt's request: "I won't hand them over to any United States marshal armed with a writ of habeas corpus. Understand?"[94] There were rumors, moreover, that Roosevelt wanted the saboteurs executed regardless of any judicial outcome. The president feared a public trial, was concerned about the standards of guilt a court martial would engender, and knew that the facts were not as J. Edgar Hoover had publicly stated. According to Jonathan Turley, "The [Roosevelt] Administration made it clear [to the justices] that it would not tolerate any judicial interference with its intent to execute the men."[95]

Justice Robert Jackson once wrote that war "exposes the relative vulnerability of the alien's status."[96] But what if the war is not declared, and the alien's status is one of long residence within the United States—what kind of security is the alien accorded? How qualified are detention orders to be? Must they have congressional approval? What, if any, are the limits of executive power in wartime? How long are wars supposed to last? As long as there is a separation of powers among branches of government to ensure that power is dispersed throughout the governmental system, and a separation between state and society, to ensure a space for the free discussion of ideas and the free movement of peoples, then detention can only last as long as the emergency is in operation, assuming, of course, that the end of engagement is quantifiable. But what if it is not? This is the main problem with the war on terrorism. Lacking a formal declaration of war against an aggressor state and a way to frame a peace treaty between the United States and Al Qaeda, no one knows when the "war on terrorism" is officially over. Unlike previous wars, the status of the detained, then, is uncertain and subject to arbitrary rules and procedures. In this darkness, this gray area, violations of the laws of war, including torture, becomes acceptable policy.[97] Military commissions, in fact, are historically linked to wartime,[98] and so far, no war against Al Qaeda has been declared. To the extent, then, that military commissions displace open federal courts, their reason for existing is legally dubious and poses a serious threat to due process concerns, including habeas corpus.[99] Moreover, despite the emphasis placed on the commander-in-chief clause as a grant of authority to the president by both Presidents Lincoln and Bush, Congress has the authority under Article I, section 8, to "provide for organizing, arming, and disciplining the militia, and for governing such part of them as may be employed in the service of the United States," as well as constituting "tribunals inferior to the Supreme Court" and defining and punishing "offenses against the law of nations." Whatever conflict may exist between proponents of executive power and their adversaries, it is clear is that the executive does not get to decide when an emergency exists without congressional oversight and judicial scrutiny.[100]

The president, however, does get to define national security because of his ability to control foreign affairs and therefore to frame the issue in such manner as to make emergency powers turn toward the executive and not the legislature.[101] But "security is like liberty in that many are the crimes committed in its name,"[102] and the problem of judicial deference to executive authority during wartime is everpresent. Are courts to be trusted to exercise review against executive actions taken in the name of national security? *Ex parte Milligan* says yes, as does *Youngstown Sheet & Tube* v. *Sawyer*; *Ex parte Quirin* says no.

HABEAS CORPUS AND THE "FOUR CORNERS OF THE EARTH"

What, then, is the status of habeas corpus I during the war on terrorism, and what are the implications for habeas corpus II? The Court in the three cases that originated from Guantánamo Bay, Cuba (*Hamdi*, *Rasul*, and *Rumsfeld* v. *Padilla*), was not concerned with federalism or with innocence, as such, the traditional concerns of habeas corpus II. Though favorable to habeas corpus, the narrative thrust of the opinions in these cases is the same as before: concerns over future dangerousness, jurisdiction, guilt, and unlawful confinement. Maybe the question should be reversed: how much has habeas corpus II influenced habeas corpus I? The Court's opinions in *Hamdi* and *Rasul* clearly try to "balance" the rights of the individual against the statements of the government about the need for security, thus mimicking the Court's language in habeas corpus II–type cases, which engage questions of the individual's degree of liberty and the state's concern with safety. In this sense, *Hamdi* and *Rasul* are exactly of a piece with the Court's rulings in habeas cases dealing with crime, though significantly, the language is more flowery and more celebratory of habeas' history than in habeas corpus II cases.

Yaser Hamdi filed a habeas corpus petition challenging the legality of his confinement in the Norfolk Naval Brig, in Norfolk, Virginia. The gist of his appeal was that he was not a member either of Al Qaeda or the Taliban, and therefore he could not be classified as an "enemy combatant." United States military forces captured Hamdi in Afghanistan, in a "zone of active combat" against U.S. military forces.[103] The president had ordered U.S. military forces into Afghanistan following the attack against the United States on September 11, 2001. On September 18, 2001, Congress authorized the president "[t]o use all necessary and appropriate force against those nations, organizations, or persons he determines planned, authorized, committed, or aided the terrorist attacks." The authorization is known as the Authorization for Use of Military Force (AUMF).[104] Order V authorizes the trial of any individual by military commission. The secretary of defense is directed to issue rules for the procedures for trial, which he did on March 21, 2002.[105] Conviction can be had by a vote of two-thirds of the members of the tribunal, and defendants are prohibited from appealing the tribunal's decision.

Hamdi is an American citizen. He was born in Louisiana but raised in Saudi Arabia. When captured in Afghanistan, Hamdi was transported first to Guantánamo Bay, Cuba, then to the naval brig in Norfolk. Hamdi's father filed the writ of habeas corpus on his behalf, alleging that Hamdi is a U.S. citizen residing in Afghanistan and is entitled to the same privileges and immunities as any U.S. citizen. He asked the court to order the government to cease interrogating him, that his detention was in violation of his Fifth and Fourteenth Amendment rights, and that he was entitled to rebut the charges against him.

The government asserted that Hamdi was an enemy combatant, a fighter with Al Qaeda, which the fourth circuit court of appeals accepted. "Because it is undisputed," Chief Judge J. Harvie Wilkinson wrote for the majority, "that Hamdi was captured in a zone of active combat in a foreign theater of conflict, we hold that the submitted declaration is a sufficient basis upon which to conclude that the commander in chief has constitutionally detained Hamdi pursuant to the war powers entrusted to him by the United States Constitution."[106] Judge Wilkinson's opinion was largely based on deference to the executive branch's understanding of Hamdi's status. Citing *Quirin*, the fourth circuit court of appeals held that the president gets his power to detain enemy combatants from the commander in chief clause of Article II and congressional approval of the president's actions, post–September 11, 2001. "These powers likewise extend to the executive's decision to deport or detain enemies during the duration of hostilities."[107] But more than just creating a large space for the president to act during wartime, the court of appeals' decision turned on the importance of deference that such situations create. "The deference that flows from the explicit enumeration of powers protects liberty as much as the explicit enumeration of rights. . . . For the judicial branch to trespass upon the exercise of the warmaking powers would be an infringement of the right to self-determination and self-governance at a time when the care of the common defense is most critical."[108]

The court of appeals' constricted understanding both of judicial review and the separation of powers is perplexing, especially in light of Justice Robert Jackson's view of the importance of judicial oversight of executive decisions, particularly during wartime, in *Youngstown Sheet & Tube* v. *Sawyer*. There, Justice Jackson created a three-part test for determining the limits of executive power. If the president acts according to an expressed grant of authority from Congress, then "his authority is at its maximum," Jackson wrote. If the president acts on his own powers, in a "zone of twilight in which he and Congress may have concurrent authority," then the president's power is uncertain but not without limitations. Finally, "when the president takes measures incompatible with the expressed or implied will of Congress, his power is at its lowest ebb."[109] Jackson believed that President Truman's action during the Korean War, seizing the steel mills as a matter of national security, belonged to category three.

Although Jackson's test is not a perfect fit with enemy combatants, it does provide a framework to judge executive action during wartime. There is also precedent for judicial scrutiny of executive actions in the four detention cases arising out of Roosevelt's Executive Order 9066 to send Japanese Americans into concentration camps during World War II.[110] The Supreme Court upheld the convictions in three cases based on congressional grants of authority to the president, but not in a fourth. In *Ex parte Endo*, the Court held that Mitsuye Endo should be released because it found that Congress had not authorized her detention. All told, about two-thirds of the interned were American citizens. The congressional declaration of war and the congressional ratification of Executive Order 9066, which set up the internment policy, helped the Court defend the president's action. But Mitsuye Endo was being held by a civilian agency, the War Relocation Authority, and not by the military, which clearly separated this case from *Milligan* and *Quirin*. In any event, the Supreme Court, when it decided Hamdi's case, overturned Judge Wilkinson's expansive understanding of executive power and limited understanding of deference.

Justice Sandra O'Connor wrote the plurality opinion for the Court. The threshold question in *Hamdi*, she wrote, "is whether the Executive has the authority to detain citizens who qualify as 'enemy combatants.'"[111] The Bush administration's argument was that congressional authority is unnecessary for the president to determine who is and who is not an enemy combatant. Such power flows through Article II. The Court found it unnecessary to investigate this claim, however, because the government's backup argument was that Congress authorized presidential power in the Authorization for Use of Military Force, which the Court accepted as legitimate. The only question, then, for the Court to answer was the narrow one: "whether the detention of citizens falling within" the definition of enemy combatants "is authorized."[112] An enemy combatant is one who is engaged in armed conflict against the United States. The AUMF authorizes the president to use "all necessary and appropriate force" against "nations, organizations, or persons" associated with the events of September 11, 2001. The Court accepted that anyone caught in the theater of war is an enemy combatant. (Hamdi disputed that he is an enemy combatant.) Because of *Quirin*, "There is no bar to the Nation's holding one of its own citizens as an enemy combatant."[113] Consequently, O'Connor's plurality opinion brushed aside that the AUMF does not speak of detention. The plurality also ignored the problem that enemy combatants are usually considered such by reference to being a soldier in an enemy state's army, which Hamdi is not.

Hamdi argued that he was being indefinitely detained, in violation of 18 U.S.C. section 4001, which repealed the 1950 Emergency Detention Act and which requires congressional authorization for the detention of American citizens by the executive. The Emergency Detention Act, which was Title II of the McCarran Internal Security Act of 1950, gave the president the power to detain both Americans and non-Americans, including resident aliens, engaged in espionage and sabotage in the event of a war or emergency. The act did not suspend habeas corpus, and it "limited detention to those individuals who had been active in subversive organizations since January 1, 1949 . . . and restricted apprehension to actual invasion, insurrection, or a declaration of war."[114] Although the detention act had a clause in it protecting a detainee's right to petition for habeas corpus, it is unclear whether the president's declaration that an emergency exists could override that clause. Richard Longakre suggests that the habeas provision would be operative "only to determine whether a person was being held by a tribunal possessing clear statutory jurisdiction," thus effacing the writ's power to investigate the cause of detention.[115]

But in 1971, Congress explicitly repealed the Emergency Detention Act. (In 1976, Congress repealed Roosevelt's Executive Order 9066, making its demise retroactive to the end of hostilities in May 1945.) The purpose of 18 U.S.C. section 4001 is to "(1) restrict the imprisonment or other detention of citizens of the U.S. to situations in which statutory authority for their incarceration exists and (2) to repeal the Emergency Detention Act of 1950 which both authorizes the establishment of concentration camps and imposes certain conditions on their use."[116] Section 4001(a) states, "No citizen shall be imprisoned or otherwise detained by the United States except pursuant to an Act of Congress."

Having accepted the government's position on detaining American citizens because of *Quirin*, the plurality turned its attention to the limits of due process in such situations. Justice O'Connor is famous for balancing habeas corpus against federalism concerns. Here, however, no such issue arose. She accepted the government's position regarding its power to detain American citizens and its criticisms of section 4001, which she balanced with a concern for not letting the government have final say on the length and quality of the detention. Not unlike her habeas corpus opinions from crime cases, O'Connor's opinion in *Hamdi* was not without its bow to the government's position. Her opinion allows the detainees to be tried by "combatant status" review tribunals, which excludes the right to an attorney and places the burden of proof on the detainee.[117] Yet her rhetoric was foursquare on the side of habeas corpus as a remedy for unlawful confinement. For O'Connor, the Court "long since made clear that a state of war is not a blank check for the President when it comes to the rights of the Nation's citizens."[118] This clarity extends to habeas corpus under Article I, a point shared by Justice Scalia in dissent. "Absent suspension," O'Connor writes, "the writ of habeas corpus remains available to every individual detained within the United States."[119] Although the government argued that Hamdi's detention occurred in combat, where habeas corpus does not lie, and the fourth circuit court of appeals upheld that notion, the Supreme Court plurality weighed the interests of the government against those of the detainees and held that "the risk of erroneous deprivation of a citizen's liberty in the absence of sufficient process here is very real."[120]

Despite the plurality's criticism of the government's position asking for absolute control over enemy combatants and the possibility for indefinite detention in the long war against terrorism, Justices Scalia and Stevens dissented, though they agreed with the plurality that the court of appeals' decision should be reversed. Justice Scalia was adamant that the government had only two choices for Hamdi, an American citizen. Either he is to be tried in federal court on treason charges, as occurred during World War I, or the government explicitly declares a rebellion and suspends habeas corpus. Scalia's opinion is both a history lesson on habeas corpus before the Fourteenth Amendment and a warning to the Court not to stray too far from common law principles. Scalia sees a closer connection between *Hamdi* and *Milligan* than O'Connor does and, like Justice Frankfurter, regards *Quirin* as "not the Court's finest hour." He considers the First World War's civil treatment of American traitors to be closer to the way Hamdi ought to be treated than the majority does.[121] Finally, Scalia is dismissive of the government's argument that the AUMF is an authorization for detention because what the government is asking for is a suspension of the writ of habeas corpus. Scalia provides us with a clear understanding of habeas corpus I, which he sees as unconcerned with extracurricular legal rules.

> The Suspension Clause of the Constitution, which carefully circumscribes the conditions under which the writ can be withheld, would be a sham if it could be evaded by congressional prescription of requirements other than the common-law requirement of committal for criminal prosecution that render the writ, though available, unavailable. If the Suspension Clause does not guarantee the citizen that he will either be tried or released, unless the conditions for suspending the writ exist and the grave action of suspending the writ has been taken; if it merely guarantees the citizen that he will not be detained unless Congress by ordinary legislation says he can be detained, it guarantees him very little indeed.[122]

This is a striking passage, but not because it is inconsistent with Scalia's jurisprudence; his reliance on the common law proves it clearly is not.[123] The question is: why not extend such unrestrained language to the writ in criminal cases? Is the detention any less burdensome? The language of the Habeas Corpus Act of 1867 and its statutory provisions (up until the AEDPA) are just as expansive and just as protective of civil liberty as habeas corpus under Article I. Has the AEDPA constrained habeas corpus II while leaving habeas corpus I untouched? Up until now, the Court's argument has been that habeas corpus II is restrained by conceptions of federalism and murderous guilt, which the AEDPA codifies (more the former than the latter). Scalia's argument, so forcefully on the side of habeas corpus I, makes it seem as though there is no chance for habeas corpus II to compare itself to its constitutional cousin. Insofar as *Hamdi* is correctly decided, what I fear from Scalia's opinion (and O'Connor's dicta) is that it will divert attention away from the problems that cause habeas corpus to be called for in the first instance, such as inequality, racism, and the lack of resources the poor have to combat their detentions, because it is so celebratory of the writ's power in history but does not link the writ to systemic problems, the way *Fay* or *Townsend* v. *Sain* did. Instead, Justice Scalia has created a gap in habeas corpus where only executive detention robs the detainee of any legal rights. Given the history of state court decisions that uphold all kinds of constitutional violations, from biased juries to poor counsel to abusive police tactics,[124] is the necessity of habeas corpus II any less urgent simply because it involves a state court's judgment that the accused is guilty?

Functionally, the government believes the same about Hamdi as Georgia did of Frank, Furman, Gregg, and McCleskey and North Carolina with Brown, Speller, and the two Daniels. Does not the history of habeas corpus II reveal the record of inconsistent and biased jury determinations of guilt and the problem of effective state appellate review? Is individual liberty any less threatened by state judgments that ignore constitutional obligations than by presidential detentions that do the same? "Errors that undermine confidence in the fundamental fairness of the state adjudication certainly justify the issuance of the federal writ," Justice Stevens wrote in *Williams* v. *Taylor*.[125] Why, then, contain habeas corpus in one set of cases and not another, when the problem, as Justice Frankfurter explained in *Sunal* v. *Large*,[126] is the same? "The very nature of the writ demands that it be administered with the initiative and flexibility essential to insure that miscarriages of justice within its reach are surfaced and corrected," Justice Abe Fortas wrote in *Harris* v. *Nelson*[127] (1969).

To be sure, there are limits to Scalia's dissent in *Hamdi*. His protection of the writ applies only to those Americans detained "within the territorial jurisdiction of a federal court," which is why he dissents in *Rasul*. In *Rasul* v. *Bush*, Scalia returns to his role as a critic of providing habeas corpus to criminals. *Rasul* v. *Bush* raised the question "whether United States courts lack jurisdiction to consider challenges to the legality of the detention of foreign nationals captured abroad in connection with hostilities and incarcerated at the

Guantánamo Bay Naval Base, Cuba."[128] *Hamdi* involved an American asking for habeas corpus, which does not seem like a difficult decision, even with *Quirin* as precedent. In *Hamdi*, either *Quirin* or *Milligan* controlled (and the Court's plurality sides with *Quirin*, up to a point) with some concerns over the meaning of section 4001 and congressional approval of the detention of American citizens.[129] On the one hand, with the exception of Justice Thomas' call for deference whenever the executive arrests combatants in a war, *Hamdi* reached a clear majority in favor of granting the writ. On the other hand, *Rasul* involves two Australians and twelve Kuwaiti citizens asking for the writ because they are subject to U.S. control over their movements, as they were being held in a foreign country but within a naval base controlled by the United States since 1903. *Rasul* is governed by *Johnson* v. *Eisentrager*, another case coming out of World War II.

In *Eisentrager*, twenty-one German nationals asked the district court in Washington, D.C. for habeas corpus. They were captured in China and held by U.S. forces for violating the laws of war, in particular, engaging in military activity after hostilities had ceased. The U.S. Army took them into custody, and they were tried by military commission, where they were found guilty of war crimes in Nanking. They were repatriated to Germany to serve out their sentences. The habeas petition alleged that the prisoners were being held in violation of Articles I and III of the Constitution and the Fifth Amendment. The district court denied the writ, but the court of appeals reversed, holding that even enemy aliens, being held under the authority of the U.S. government, are entitled to the writ. The Supreme Court was confronted with a perplexing question: whether "enemy aliens" are entitled to petition for habeas corpus when they have never lived in the United States, were captured outside of the territory of the United States, were tried and convicted by a military commission operating outside the United States, and remain imprisoned outside the United States. Justice Robert Jackson found *Quirin* not to apply because those enemy combatants were being held in the United States. Nor does the language of the Fifth Amendment, referring to persons and not citizens as those entitled to due process, aid their claim for habeas corpus. Justice Jackson thought that the court of appeals' argument in favor of the petitioners "would extend coverage of our Constitution to nonresident alien enemies denied to resident alien enemies."[130] Such a construction, he wrote, would confer Fifth Amendment rights "on all the world." The resident enemy alien has limited rights in the United States. Courts can determine if the detainee is subject to the Alien Enemy Act but will "not inquire into any other issue as to his internment."[131]

The Court in *Rasul* rejected the district court's dismissal of the petitioners' plea for habeas corpus, which rested on the *Eisentrager* ruling. *Rasul* is similar to *Eisentrager*. The issue in *Rasul* is "whether the habeas statute confers a right to judicial review of the legality of Executive detention of aliens in a territory over which the United States exercises plenary and exclusive jurisdiction, but not 'ultimate sovereignty.'"[132] *Eisentrager*, then, does not strictly apply to *Rasul* because the detainees were not nationals of countries at war with the United States. Moreover, unlike *Eisentrager*, the detainees in *Rasul* had never been "afforded access to any tribunal, much less charged with and convicted of wrongdoing."[133] They also disputed that they were enemy combatants. The question is whether the executive can have war detainees held in a jurisdictional "zone of twilight" for the purposes of not treating war prisoners with the requirements of due process.

This is an old trick in habeas corpus. Seventeenth-century British monarchs would move prisoners from one jurisdiction to another, hoping either to find a sympathetic judge who would deny the writ or to avoid a judge who would grant it. In fact, the British often moved prisoners offshore, beyond the reach of the judiciary.[134] (The Court dealt with the question of jurisdiction and "forum shopping" in *Rumsfeld* v. *Padilla*, where the Court held that Padilla's habeas petition was directed at the wrong person and in the wrong jurisdiction. The dissent thought that the question Padilla raised—Padilla is an American citizen being held without Fifth Amendment protections by the U.S. military—was too important to dismiss on a jurisdictional technicality.) In *Rasul*, however, the Court recognized Guantánamo Bay Naval Brig as being part of the United States.[135] The Court's ruling relied on the language of the habeas statute (28 U.S.C. section 2241), which states that federal district courts have the power to hear applications for habeas corpus by any person held "in violation of the Constitution or laws or treaties of the United States." The United States holds Guantánamo Bay, Cuba, by treaty. Section 2241 is the "direct ancestor"[136] of the Habeas Corpus Act of 1867, and as such, "It is impossible to widen this jurisdiction."[137] Once the facts of *Eisentrager* were separated from *Rasul*, the Court's opinion had to turn on habeas' availability. It is worth remembering that the writ does not operate against the detainee but against the person holding the detainee. Could the writ reach Cuba by way of the person responsible for Rasul's detention? The plain meaning of the habeas statute implicates a global reach for the writ. Because the habeas corpus statute speaks of persons, not citizens, and such persons are under the direct control of American military personnel, Justice Stevens held, for the Court, that "aliens held at the base, no less than American citizens, are entitled to federal courts' authority under section 2241."[138]

If habeas corpus reaches Cuba, how far can it go? Justice Scalia, as pointed out above, sees two writs that diverge in narrative form, one based on common law, the other statutory. Although both cases involved 28 U.S.C. section 2241, *Hamdi* is the common law writ, *Rasul* the statutory. Hamdi gets Scalia's vote (as a strident dissent); Rasul does not. The Court in *Rasul*, according to Justice Scalia, has gone too far. "Respective jurisdictions," in his view, do not reach beyond the jurisdictional borders of the United States. The Court in *Eisentrager* knew as much: "Nothing in the text of the Constitution extends such a right, nor does anything in our statutes."[139] For Scalia, then, *Rasul* overrules *Eisentrager* by implication. By extending the jurisdiction of federal habeas courts "beyond the sovereign territory of the United States" the Court extends habeas corpus "to the four corners of the earth,"[140] which is quite an accomplishment given the limitations on the writ established in the AEDPA.

CONCLUSION

Why did Justice Scalia favor habeas corpus in *Hamdi* but not in *Rasul*? Although both cases have the same pedigree—the capture of combatants in a war zone and confinement in a jurisdiction sufficiently not part of the United States as to call into question any appeal to habeas corpus—there are differences. Hamdi appeals to habeas corpus as an American citizen; Rasul does not. Not only does Hamdi ask for habeas corpus, but he may be detained in violation of section 4001(a). For detentions of Americans to be legal, congressional authorization is required, which has not been given. Hamdi may also be held in violation of the third Geneva Convention.[141] So what of habeas corpus II?

Rasul links habeas corpus I and II. The detention is by the executive during war, the remedy is by section 2241. Scalia makes much of the distinction between citizens and aliens, but I believe there is more to it than that. The two decisions, though both based on habeas corpus as a statute, are connected to different narratives. Justice Scalia, on the one hand, caught up in the common law notion of habeas corpus, sees Hamdi's case in mythic terms, as a liberating action against unlawful confinement during war. *Rasul*, on the other hand, goes too far in extending habeas corpus to noncitizens, bringing in questions of cost, timing, and judicial aggravation, problems often associated with habeas corpus II. This is not to suggest that Scalia sees the writ as without force; he clearly says that Hamdi should be granted the writ. But it seems to me that, in his dissent in *Hamdi*, Scalia's defense of habeas corpus is aimed at a symbolic understanding of the writ's power, not a jurisdictional one, and therefore is profound only at a narrative level but cannot reach down to the body of the incarcerated. Lacking this mythic component, the implications for habeas corpus II are almost zero.

The decision in *Hamdi* appeals to the mythic writ; *Rasul* to the "narrow but important question whether the United States courts lack jurisdiction to consider challenges to the legality of the detention of foreign nationals captured abroad in connection with hostilities and incarcerated at the Guantánamo Bay Naval Base, Cuba."[142] If there are two forms of habeas, one common law the other statutory, do they operate on a horizontal plane, extending along a continuum that stretches from arbitrary executive power at the presidential level to arbitrary executive power at the state level? With *Rasul*, habeas corpus has been split again, this time along a vertical plane, extending up and down the Western Hemisphere, wherever American military power places the flag.[143] Both notions seem consistent with habeas corpus' mission.

Justice Stevens sees the writ operating horizontally.[144] O'Connor's opinion in *Hamdi* suggests that she also sees the writ this way, though she is tortured over it because the ramifications in both instances trouble her. Her question is never: is the petitioner entitled to the writ? but to what extent can the institution being attacked absorb the blow? She regards the writ as a constant thorn in the side of institutional norms, as her willingness to allow the government to try those held in Guantánamo by an "appropriately authorized and properly constituted"[145] military commission demonstrates. With O'Connor's help, over the course of forty years, the Court has "shifted the focus of federal habeas corpus review" from "the preservation of constitutional rights to a fact-based inquiry into the habeas petitioner's guilt or innocence."[146] Her plurality opinion in *Hamdi* does not go that far, but it does not foreclose future considerations of guilt or dangerousness, either.

It is not out of some antiquarian desire that I see habeas corpus as an "unceasing contest between personal liberty and government oppression,"[147] which borrows the language of habeas corpus I but constitutionalizes habeas corpus II. Rather, a writ designed to attack unlawful and arbitrary executive action should not be so restricted in its understanding of the operations of criminal law that it cannot free a man whose will has been overborne by local police tactics. Such a writ is no writ of liberty at all. "For its function has been to provide a prompt and efficacious remedy for whatever society deems to be intolerable restraints."[148] Justice Brennan's language in *Fay* v. *Noia* is as applicable to Rasul or Hamdi as it was to Noia. But a writ that is tied to a terrorism act does not leave much room for hope that it will once again be extended to all prisoners held in violation of the laws of the United States. Although the Guantánamo cases were a victory for habeas corpus, the victory was for a certain understanding of the writ, one that does not apply to the vast majority of habeas applicants. While the Guantánamo cases certainly restrain executive action, the cases that have arisen under the AEDPA have had a far more detrimental effect on habeas corpus. That understanding of habeas corpus remains tied to a conception of federalism and dangerousness that elides the problem of unequal justice in the United States. However unconscionable "enemy combatants" are being treated, it is important not to lose sight of the fact that it took nine years for Rubin "Hurricane" Carter to hear the words, "The writ of habeas corpus has been granted." But Carter's case may not have been favorably decided had it happened after the passage of the AEDPA. The AEDPA seriously undercuts any chance a prisoner has to have his or her case heard in a federal court. In this sense, then, Carter's warning about the writ's prospects are valid. The "Writ of Habeas Corpus," he wrote, "the one federal check on abuses at the State Court level, the one life affirming jewel in the crown of thorns we know as the criminal justice system, is being threatened with extinction."[149]

SEVEN

Conclusion

The law wishes to have a formal existence.
—Stanley Fish, "The Law Wishes
to Have a Formal Existence"

From the beginning of this government, the criminal's body has belonged to the state. That relationship has been markedly unbalanced. The prisoner, with barely any rights, goes up against "the expert adversary, the government"[1] in a battle she cannot win because she is marked as a danger to society even before her petition for relief reaches a federal habeas court; her crime already classified as "vicious," her murder instantly categorized as "violent."[2]

Because habeas corpus today is often used by death-row inmates, more often than not the criminal's legal unveiling as a constitutional person serves instead to reveal an unworthy holder of civil rights. Important procedural questions regarding jury, police, and prosecutorial bias fade into the background of the judicial investigation and are replaced by a legal calculus based on the criminal's propensity for violence, his criminal record, and vivid descriptions of his deeds and the nature of his crime. Narratives of violence replace the law's dispassionate inquiry into the merits of punishment. Thus, Justice Harry Blackmun "chooses," Justice Antonin Scalia wrote in *Callins v. Collins* (1993), as the case in which he will say that he will no longer "tinker with the machinery of death," the case of "the murder of a man ripped by a bullet suddenly and unexpectedly, with no opportunity to prepare himself and his affairs, and left to bleed to death on the floor of a tavern."

The death-by-injection which Justice Blackmun describes looks pretty desirable next to that. It looks even better next to some of the other cases currently before us which Justice Blackmun did not select as the vehicle for his announcement that the death penalty is always unconstitutional—for example, the case of the 11-year old girl raped by four men and then killed by stuffing her panties down her throat. How enviable a quiet death by lethal injection compared with that![3]

As in so many contemporary habeas decisions, this case highlights the Rehnquist Court's concerns with governmental limits and the more personal appeal to individual safety that deeply influences the legal outcome of its habeas cases, despite habeas' legacy in the Anglo-American legal tradition as "the single most important procedural device for protecting individual liberty."[4]

The United States Supreme Court, after creating the federalism problem in *Ex parte Royall* (1886), a federal habeas corpus case with no federal-state issues, slowly moved away from that idea and concentrated on the criminal and his or her actions. *Royall* began the Court's merger of the institutional with the discursive as reasons to deny habeas corpus. From the midtwentieth century on, federalism became a useful supplement to the Court's overall understanding of the historic rights of the states to prosecute criminals free from federal supervision. By the end of the 1960s, as the criminal came to be seen as a threat to public safety and not just as a particular individual seeking relief from local injustice, the language of the Court's habeas decisions hardened, and federalism performed the function of a prop for a doctrine that lacked constitutional moorings sufficient to reject a habeas application. In other words, it was more important for the justices to demonstrate that habeas petitioners were not only convicted criminals but that their violent actions made them potentially dangerous in the future than to settle on a clear definition of federalism. Federalism, understood as a defense of state prerogative where the Constitution is silent, is of hardly any significance in these latter-day cases, as the narrative dynamic at play is quite descriptive of the crimes committed and intentionally tilted toward public opinion.

ON THE MEANING OF FINALITY

Coleman v. *Thompson* (1991) merits the attention of those interested in federalism and criminal justice because it is the Court's clearest statement that finality is a narrative trope the Court uses to denigrate either claims of innocence or charges that a state has ignored fundamental procedural protections. In a capital case in which a man's contention of unconstitutional state confinement was denied a federal hearing because of the late filing of an appeal, Justice Sandra O'Connor, writing for the Court, began her opinion with these words: "This is a case about federalism. It concerns the respect that federal courts owe the States and the States' procedural rules when reviewing the claims of state prisoners in federal habeas corpus."[5]

Roger Keith Coleman was convicted of rape and murder in Virginia and sentenced to death. The Supreme Court denied certiorari in 1984. His state postconviction petition raised numerous federal constitutional claims not raised on direct appeal. After an evidentiary hearing, the state court ruled against Coleman's claims. The court entered final judgment on September 4, 1986. Coleman then filed a notice of appeal on October 7, 1986, thirty-three days after the entry of final judgment. He also filed a petition of appeal with the Virginia Supreme Court, and the state filed a countermotion to dismiss. Virginia argued that Coleman's petition was three days late and thus in violation of state procedures. In May 1987, the Virginia Supreme Court ruled in favor of the state. The United States Supreme Court again denied certiorari.

In Felix Frankfurter's dissent in *Daniels* v. *Allen* (1953), he asked whether a denial of federal review by the Supreme Court because of an inadvertent procedural default "is an act so arbitrary and so cruel in its operation, considering that life is at stake, that in the circumstances of this case it constitutes a denial of due process in its rudimentary procedural aspect." The underlying reason for denying relief, Frankfurter stated, "is the jejune abstraction that habeas corpus cannot be used for an appeal."[6]

That abstraction, and many more, is the ground upon which the Supreme Court has developed, over the past thirty years, its finality, procedural default, and exhaustion rules. Indeed, it is how the Court has defined federalism. *Fay* v. *Noia*, O'Connor stated in *Coleman*, "was based on a conception of federal/state relations that undervalued the importance of state procedural rules."[7] She argued that habeas corpus imposes serious costs on states that are ignored by habeas petitions. "When a federal habeas court considers the federal claims of a prisoner in state custody for independent and adequate state law reasons, it is the state that must respond. It is the state that pays the price in terms of the uncertainty and delay addressed to the enforcement of its criminal laws. It is the state that must retry the petitioner if the federal courts reverse his conviction."[8] Yet O'Connor ignored Noia's and Coleman's stories. It is Noia, after all, who remained in prison; it is Noia who did not get his day in federal court. And it was Coleman who was executed because of attorney error. *Fay*—and *Coleman*—can only be understood in the context of a history of state procedural rules that have intentionally thwarted state prisoners' constitutional claims on habeas corpus.

Why did O'Connor consider this a case "about federalism" when a man's life was at stake? Beyond a certain respect for Supreme Court doctrines limiting federal habeas review, she offered no reason why the federal judiciary should refrain from exercising its constitutionally mandated power to hear state prisoner claims alleging constitutional error. She cast federalism not as an expression of local liberty but as a test of a prisoner's willingness to endure a lengthy appellate process.

Justice Harry Blackmun pierced the veil of the Court's federalism decisions by noting the multiple and arbitrary meanings the Court has given to federalism over the years. "Federalism; comity; state sovereignty; preservation of state resources; certainty," he wrote in dissent. "The Court today continues its crusade to erect petty procedural barriers in the path of any state prisoner seeking review of his federal constitutional claims."[9] Justice Blackmun focused on what O'Connor failed to mention: Coleman's "right to a criminal proceeding free from constitutional defect."[10] The Court's decision, he wrote, marks a "crusade to erect petty procedural barriers in the path of any state prisoner seeking review of his federal constitutional claims."[11] O'Connor rejected this assertion but failed to articulate a ground for her states' rights argument. "State courts presumably have a dignitary interest in seeing that their state laws are not ignored by a federal habeas court." Individual, procedural errors, she asserted, have substantive effects on state policy, not the other way around. "By filing late," she wrote, "Coleman defaulted his entire state collateral appeal."[12]

By filing late, Coleman went to his death. O'Connor failed to define federalism beyond the affront habeas corpus gives to state judges' dignity. She provided no basis for a reasoned critique or rebuttal of her claims that attorney errors implicate federalism. *Coleman* v. *Thompson* is the Court's strongest effort to return habeas corpus to its nineteenth-century roots. Without saying more, a case that allows a state to sentence a man to death without a federal hearing is not a case "about federalism." O'Connor does not make the case for federal deference or state traditions on criminal justice. The narrative of Coleman's murderous behavior is too important to ignore. *Coleman* v. *Thompson* is a story about power.

CONCLUSION

The history of habeas corpus in the United States is of a limited rise (1787 to 1867) and a precipitous fall (1886 to 1915) and of a substantive but patchwork rise (1923 to 1969) and of a substantive and patterned fall (1970 to 1996) that continues to this day.

Periodizing the history of habeas corpus in the United States calls into question the mythic characterizations of habeas corpus as the "great writ of liberty," the grand narrative tradition that puts individual liberty in the future (but not out of reach, as *Hamdi* shows) and racism, discrimination, and due process violations in the past. But as *Coleman* shows, the Supreme Court has made habeas corpus and federalism into one thing, a narrative merging of comity concerns and the truncated rights of prisoners from before the era of incorporation. The present is conspicuously absent. It is in fact clear that the Supreme Court and Congress consider the writ to pose a greater threat to the states' interest in capital punishment rather than as a material support for individual liberty. And the perception of this threat transcends habeas' narrative power to set free convicted murderers. Increasingly less reliant on formal, institutional mechanisms to restrain habeas petitioners, the Court has invoked what is underneath the petition: the established guilt and the murderous behavior, the brutality of the crime and the remorselessness of the defendant. Habeas corpus' ability to serve as a legal protection against unlawful and arbitrary confinement is in serious doubt.

If the law wants habeas corpus to have a formal existence, grounded in state law and custom, then the federal and state courts are going to have to cease categorizing the habeas petitioner as a "dangerous sociopath and a human 'time bomb.'"[13] By relying on these narratives of brutality, the Supreme Court has formalized what previously was unformed, the petitioner's character. It has replaced the idea that the states have primary responsibility to govern society with the notion that habeas petitioners are convicted murderers, and the states have the right to control that behavior. These stories of violence, moreover, are sufficiently embedded within the public's understanding of crime that it is unnecessary for the Court's narratives to function as traditional narratives do, with a beginning, a middle, and an end. Instead, as Peter Brooks makes clear, the Court's narratives start "at the end of the story, which is there from the beginning, transforming events into indicia of their finality, their making sense in terms of their outcome."[14]

One effect of this work has been to document how the Supreme Court has relied, from decade to decade, less on federalism as a structure to uphold convictions and more on narratives of violence to fine tune the deeply embedded structural situation of those who argue for their freedom from the disadvantaged point of being in a prison cell. But what is most fascinating about this study of the Court's use of narratives of violence is how seamlessly the Court has reversed the established point of the writ's storytelling, without being explicit about its mission. Marie-Christine Leps has noted that narratives played a key role in the development of scientific discourse in the nineteenth century, "for they intervened whenever dogmatic or enthymematical discourse could no longer reason what had to be demonstrated: at that moment, short stories would take over and function as the direct manifestation of reality."[15] The Supreme Court's narratives of violence do just this: recognizing the limits of state sovereignty once the Fourteenth Amendment applied to the states, the narratives found a way to bleed through the very structures of criminal justice administration, overwhelming the rigid standards the Court itself had created that prevent people like Roger Keith Coleman from gaining access to a federal habeas court. The reliance on narratives of violence demonstrates the inflexibility of the Court's understanding of federalism and institutional protections when attacked by convicted criminals on their own terms. The Court's narratives of violence exist to buttress the law's desire to execute criminals.

If, as lore has it, the first writers were accountants, then writing is a taking of accounts, and court cases are preternaturally disposed toward narratives. But the plaintiff's problem is not his description of reality.[16] It is that he does not have final say on determining the outcome of his story. He is not the author of his text. Courts decide meaning; they contextualize it, and thereby expand or retract from the original. The entire history of habeas corpus has been defined by the Court's editing of petitioners' claims against the states.

By the 1970s, the Court was invoking narratives regularly in criminal cases, but to limit not to enhance the application of the Bill of Rights, to deny not to grant the petitioner's claims. What bothers Justice Clarence Thomas about Charles Foster's petition for certiorari, for example, is that it redirects moral indignation away from the brutal facts of the murder and toward the state's unconstitutional treatment of Foster, who asks for relief from twenty-seven years on death row, but does not mention that he "slit Julian Lanier's throat, dragged him into bushes, and then, when petitioner realized that he could hear Lanier breathing, cut his spine."[17] What this proves—if anything—is that "brutality" is an empty vessel, jargon. First used to describe Sheriff Screws' behavior toward a black man whom he handcuffed to a pole and beat to within an inch of his life, it is now used by the justices against habeas petitioners to describe their crimes, to bring out into the open the loss of innocent life, and to cover over the constitutional claims of all habeas petitioners. The point is the same; the direction is all too easily reversed.

It therefore behooves constitutional scholars interested in capital punishment to pay more attention to the language of violence and of form as they appear in Supreme Court opinions. It involves paying closer attention not just to the narratives of "justice" and "violence" that permeate Supreme Court opinions but also to the narratives of structure, the reification of the past, the stress on administration, the emphasis on institutions as authoritative devices to limit and restrict individual movement. Suits against prison officials or postconviction appeals that challenge state court rulings provide a lens through which to view how institutions respond to challenges to their authority. Studying habeas corpus over time highlights the plurality of jurisdictional powers that struggle for control over the movement of prisoners and underscores the problem of administering justice in a federal republic. Those looking for a way to understand capital punishment jurisprudence need to pay closer attention to the language of the Supreme Court's habeas corpus decisions and to the long-term effects of congressional inactivity on prisoners' rights claims. As long as habeas corpus remains a right that prisoners have to be heard, "to argue and present evidence,"[18] then the burden of foreclosing that right must rest with the government. For prisoners to be free from that expert adversary, only an analysis of the government's narrative constructions of crime and punishment can reveal the depths to which the government is willing to go to deny that right to speak.

Notes

INTRODUCTION

1. *Harris* v. *Nelson*, 394 U.S. 286, 290–92 (1969).

2. Gerald Neuman, "Habeas Corpus, Executive Detention, and the Removal of Aliens," *Columbia Law Review* 98:961, 1057 (1998); Jordan Steiker, "Incorporating the Suspension Clause: Is There a Constitutional Right to Federal Habeas Corpus for State Prisoners?" *Michigan Law Review* 92:862 (1994); *INS* v. *St. Cyr*, 533 U.S. 289 (2001).

3. Act of Feb. 5, 1867, ch. 27, 14 Stat. 385.

4. *Hurtado* v. *California*, 110 U.S. 516 (1884).

5. Pub. L. No. 104–32, § 106(b)(3)(E), 110 Stat. 1214, 1221 (1996) (amending 28 U.S.C. § 2244(b) (1994)).

6. *Rasul* v. *Bush*, 124 S.Ct. 2686, 2707 (2004).

7. In *Fay* v. *Noia*, 372 U.S. 391, 400–01 (1963), Justice Brennan characterized habeas corpus as an "unceasing contest between personal liberty and government oppression." Chief Justice John Marshall said, in *Ex parte Watkins*, 28 U.S. 193, 201 (1830): "The writ of habeas corpus is a high prerogative writ, known to the common law, the great object of which is the liberation of those who may be imprisoned without sufficient cause"; William Wiecek, *The Sources of Antislavery Constitutionalism in America, 1760–1848* (Ithaca: Cornell University Press, 1977), p. 157, n. 24: "The writ of habeas corpus is the single most important procedural device for protecting individual liberty in the Anglo-American legal tradition"; Maxwell Cohen, "Some Considerations on the Origins of Habeas Corpus," *The Canadian Bar Review* 16:92 (1938); Zechariah Chafee, *How Human Rights Got into the Constitution* (Boston: Boston University Press, 1952), chapter 3; A. V. Dicey, *Introduction to the Study of the Law of the Constitution* (London: Macmillan, 1961), 10th ed., chapter 5; E.C.S. Wade and G. Godfrey Philips, *Constitutional Law* (London: Longmans, 1960), 6th ed., chapter 35; Jordan Steiker, "Habeas Exceptionalism," *Texas Law Review* 78:1703 (2000).

8. *Fay* at 399.

9. Maxwell Cohen, "Some Considerations on the Origin of Habeas Corpus," *Canadian Bar Review* 16:92 (1938).

10. This is *res judicata*. William F. Duker, *A Constitutional History of Habeas Corpus* (Westport: Greenwood Press, 1980), pp. 5–6.

11. Delmar Karlen, *Anglo-American Criminal Justice* (New York: Oxford University Press, 1967), pp. 217–19; Daniel Kobil, "The Quality of Mercy Strained: Wresting the Pardoning Power from the King," *University of Texas Law Review* 69:569 (1991).

12. Maxwell Cohen, "Habeas Corpus Cum Causa—The Emergence of the Modern Writ-I," The *Canadian Bar Review* 18:10 (1940).

13. Susan Bandes, "Simple Murder: A Comment on the Legality of Executing the Innocent," *Buffalo Law Review* 44:501, 503 (1996).

14. William Wiecek, "*Murdoch v. Memphis*: Section 25 of the 1789 Judiciary Act and Judicial Federalism," Maeva Marcus, ed., *Origins of the Federal Judiciary: Essays on the Judiciary Act of 1789* (New York: Oxford University Press, 1992); Martin J. Sklar, *The Corporate Reconstruction of American Capitalism, 1890–1916: The Market, the Law, and Politics* (Cambridge: Cambridge University Press, 1988).

15. Robert Putnam, *Making Democracy Work: Civic Traditions in Modern Italy* (Princeton: Princeton University Press, 1993), p. 8; Kathleen Thelen and Sven Steinmo, "Historical Institutionalism in Comparative Politics," Sven Steinmo, Kathleen Thelen, and Frank Longstreth, eds., *Structuring Politics: Historical Institutionalism in Comparative Analysis* (Cambridge: Cambridge University Press, 1992).

16. Robert Cover and Alexander Aleinikoff, "Dialectical Federalism: Habeas Corpus and the Court," *Yale Law Journal* 86:1019 (1977).

17. *Brown v. Allen*, 344 U.S. 443, 498 (1953).

18. *Furman v. Georgia*, 408 U.S. 238, 270, 444 (1972).

19. *Gregg v. Georgia*, 428 U.S. 153, 175 (1976).

20. *Coleman v. Thompson*, 501 U.S. 722 (1991).

21. *Vasquez v. Hillery*, 474 U.S. 254, 260, 267–68 (1986).

22. Duker, *A Constitutional History of Habeas Corpus*, p. 8.

23. Jordan Steiker, "Restructuring Post-Conviction Review of Federal Constitutional Claims Raised by State Prisoners: Confronting the New Face of Excessive Proceduralism," *University of Chicago Legal Forum* 13:315 (1998).

24. Richard Pacelle Jr., *The Transformation of the Supreme Court's Agenda: From the New Deal to the Reagan Administration* (Boulder: Westview, 1991), pp. 12–17.

25. Stephen Skowronek, *Building the New American State: The Expansion of National Administrative Capacities, 1877–1920* (Cambridge: Cambridge University Press, 1982), p. 27.

26. Paul Bator, "Finality in Criminal Law and Federal Habeas Corpus for State Prisoners," *Harvard Law Review* 76:441 (1963); Henry J. Friendly, "Is Innocence Irrelevant? Collateral Attack on Criminal Judgments," *University of Chicago Law Review* 38:142 (1970).

27. Sue Davis, *Justice Rehnquist and the Constitution* (Princeton: Princeton University Press, 1989), pp. 165–73.

28. A constitutional technicality is known as harmless error and would be a conviction that was "tainted by a constitutional violation" but did not have a "substantial and injurious effect or influence in determining the jury's verdict." *Brecht* v. *Abrahamson*, 507 U.S. 69, 644 (1993); *Kotteakos* v. *United States*, 328 U.S. 750, 776 (1946).

29. Michael Reagan and John Sanzone, *The New Federalism* (New York: Oxford University Press, 1981), 2d edition, p. 18.

30. Thelen and Steinmo, "Historical Institutionalism in Comparative Politics," p. 2.

31. *Frank* v. *Magnum*, 237 U.S. 309 (1915); *Moore* v. *Dempsey*, 261 U.S. 86 (1923); *Brown* v. *Allen*, 344 U.S. 443 (1953).

32. *Fay* at 402.

33. Thelen and Steinmo, "Historical Institutionalism in Comparative Politics," p. 15.

34. *National League of Cities* v. *Usery*, 426 U.S. 833 (1976); *Garcia* v. *San Antonio Metropolitan Transit Authority*, 469 U.S. 528 (1985); *Withrow* v. *Williams*, 507 U.S. 680 (1993).

35. *South Carolina* v. *Gathers*, 490 U.S. 805, 815 (1989).

36. *Burger* v. *Kemp*, 483 U.S. 776, 815 (1987).

37. Jean-Francois Lyotard, *The Postmodern Condition: A Report on Knowledge*, Brian Massumi, trans. (Minneapolis: University of Minnesota Press, 1984), p. xxiii.

38. Pierre Schlag, *The Enchantment of Reason* (Durham: Duke University Press, 1998), p. 133.

39. *State of Louisiana ex rel. Francis* v. *Resweber*, 329 U.S. 459, 471 (1947).

40. *Resweber* at 481 (n. 2).

41. *Resweber* at 472–73.

42. Henry J. Abraham, *The Judicial Process: An Introductory Analysis of the Courts of the United States, England, and France* (New York: Oxford University Press, 1986), 5th edition, p. 217.

43. Henry Giroux, Colin Lankshear, Peter McLaren, and Michael Peters, *Counternarratives: Cultural Studies and Critical Pedagogies in Postmodern Spaces* (London: Routledge,1996), p. 2.

44. *Brown* at 557–58.

45. *South Carolina* at 816–17.

46. *O'Dell* v. *Netherland*, 521 U.S. 151, 153–54 (1997).

47. *O'Dell* at 154.

48. *Screws* v. *United States*, 325 U.S. 91 (1945); *Robles* v. *Prince George's County, Maryland*, 302 F.3d 262 (2002): "Plaintiff Nelson Robles claims that police officers Antonio DeBarros and James Rozar violated his state and federal constitutional rights by tying him to a metal pole in a deserted parking lot and abandoning him there for approximately 10 minutes." *Robles* v. *Prince George's County, Maryland*, 308 F.3d 437 (2002); *Chavez* v. *Martinez*, 538 U.S. 760 (2003).

49. *Gregg* v. *Georgia*, 428 U.S. 227, 229 (1976).

50. *O'Dell* at 168, 170.

51. *O'Dell* at 169, n. 1.

52. Mark Brown and John Pratt, "Introduction," Mark Brown and John Pratt, eds., *Dangerous Offenders: Punishment & Social Order* (London: Routledge, 2000), p. 4.

53. *Hepburn* v. *Griswold*, 8 Wall. 608 (1870); *Loan Association* v. *Topeka*, 87 U.S. 655 (1875); *In re Kemmler*, 136 U.S. 436 (1890).

54. *Ex parte Royall*, 117 U.S. 241 (1886); *Lockyer* v. *Andrade*, 538 U.S. 62 (2003).

55. *County of Santa Clara* v. *Southern Pacific Railroad*, 118 U.S. 394 (1886).

56. *Lockyer* v. *Andrade*, 538 U.S. 62 (2003).

CHAPTER 1

1. *Frank* v. *Magnum*, 237 U.S. 309 (1915).

2. This fact spilled over into the postwar period as well. *The Civil Rights Cases*, 109 U.S. 3 (1883). The antebellum state cannot be considered "weak" if the Supreme Court's decisions regarding commerce and the effect of these decisions on economic development are considered. Felix Frankfurter, *The Commerce Clause under Marshall, Taney and Waite* (Chicago: Quadrangle Books, 1964); Felix Frankfurter and James Landis, "The Business of the Supreme Court of the United States—A Study in the Federal Judicial System," *Harvard Law Review* 38:1005, 1008 (1925); Rudolph Bell, *Party and Faction in American Politics: The House of Representatives, 1789–1801* (Westport: Greenwood, 1973), chapters 2 and 3; Stephen Skowronek, *Building a New American State: The Expansion of National Administrative Capacities, 1877–1920* (Cambridge: Cambridge University Press, 1982), chapters 1 and 2.

3. Leonard White, *The Jacksonians: A Study in Administrative History, 1829–1861* (New York: Free Press, 1954), pp. 512–16; Jonathan Pincus, *Pressure Groups, Politics and Antebellum Tariffs* (New York: Columbia University Press, 1977); Edward Stanwood, *American Tariffs in the Nineteenth Century* (Boston: Houghton Mifflin, 1903).

4. Act of February 4, 1815, 3 Stat. 195; Act of March 3, 1815, 3 Stat 231; Act of March 3, 1817, 3 Stat. 396, extending removal provisions. Patricia Allen Lucie, *Freedom and Federalism: Congress and Courts, 1861–1866* (New York: Garland, 1986), p. 156; Felix Frankfurter and James Landis, *The Business of the Supreme Court: A Study in the Federal Judicial System* (New York: Macmillan, 1928), p. 11, n. 22.

5. *Congressional Globe*, 22d Congress, 1st session (Jan. 28, 1833), p. 245.

6. *Congressional Globe*, 22d Congress, 1st session (Jan. 31, 1833), p. 293. The final vote in the House of Representatives, on March 1, 1833, was 149 to 48 in favor of the bill. *Congressional Globe*, 22d Congress, 1st session (Feb. 20, 1833), p. 1755.

7. *Congressional Globe*, 27th Congress, 2d session (appendix), pp. 255–59 (May 9, 1842).

8. *Congressional Globe*, 27th Congress, 2d session (appendix), p. 953 (Aug. 26, 1842).

9. *Congressional Globe*, 27th Congress, 2d session (appendix), p. 955 (Aug. 26, 1842).

10. Lucie, *Freedom and Federalism*, p. 64; *Congressional Globe*, 37th Congress, 3d session, p. 536 (Jan. 27. 1863).

11. Act of August 29, 1842, c. 257, 5 Stat. 539–40; William F. Duker, *A Constitutional History of Habeas Corpus* (Westport: Greenwood, 1980), pp. 188–89.

12. *Congressional Globe*, 27th Congress, 2d session (appendix), p. 953 (Aug. 26, 1842).

13. *Congressional Globe* 27th Congress, 2d session (appendix), p. 957 (August 26,1842).

14. Abraham Lincoln, *Speeches and Writings, 1859–1865* (Library of America, 1989), vol. 2, pp. 237, 246 ff.

15. Act of March 3, 1863, 12 Stat. 756.

16. *Congressional Globe*, 37th Congress, 3d session; on Delaware, see debate on Dec. 24, 1862, pp. 162–64; on Kentucky, see pp. 159–61.

17. Lucie, *Freedom and Federalism*, p. 56; *Congressional Globe*, 37th Congress, 3d session, pp. 534–35 (Jan. 27, 1863).

18. *Congressional Globe*, 37th Congress, 3d session, p. 217 (Jan. 7, 1863).

19. *Congressional Record*, 37th Congress, 3d session, p. 534 (Jan. 27, 1863).

20. Dall Forsythe, *Taxation and Political Change in the Young Nation, 1789–1833* (New York: Columbia University Press, 1977), pp. 80–81; William Chambers, "Parties and Nation-Building in America," Joseph LaPalombara and Myron Weiner, eds., *Political Parties and Political Development* (Princeton: Princeton University Press, 1966); Lee Benson, *The Concept of Jacksonian Democracy: New York as a Test Case* (New York: Antheneum, 1965), chapter 3.

21. Act of 1789, c. 20, sec. 14, 1 Stat. 81.

22. *Ex parte Watkins*, 3 Pet. 193 (1836).

23. *Ex parte Dorr*, 3 How. 193 (1845).

24. Charles Warren, "New Light on the History of the Federal Judiciary Act of 1789," *Harvard Law Review* 37:49, 91 (1923). The difference between an appeal to a higher court and removal is that appeals are limited to a review of the law in question; facts are not subject to review on appeal as a sign of respect to the jury. A removal begins a new trial, and the "extraordinary" writs of certiorari, mandamus, and habeas corpus allow review of both facts and law. Wilfred Ritz, *Rewriting the History of the Judiciary Act of 1789: Exposing Myths, Challenging Premises, and Using New Evidence*, Wythe Holt and L. H. LaRue, eds. (Norman: University of Oklahoma Press, 1990), pp. 40–41, 66–70.

25. The acts in question: Act of Feb. 4, 1815 (removal), c. 31, 3 Stat. 105; Act of March 3, 1815 (same), c. 94, 3 Stat. 231; Act of March 3, 1817 (same), c. 109, 3 Stat. 396; Act of March 2, 1833 (removal and habeas corpus), c. 57, 4 Stat. 632; Act of Aug. 23, 1842 (habeas corpus), c. 188, 5 Stat. 516; Act of March 3, 1863 (habeas corpus), c. 81, 12 Stat. 755; Act of March 7, 1864 (same), c. 20, 13 Stat. 14; Act of Jan. 13, 1866 (both), c. 184 Stat. 98; Act of May 11, 1866 (both), c. 80, 14 Stat. 46; Act of Feb. 5,

1867 (habeas corpus), c. 27, 14 Stat. 385. The debates in 1863 specifically refer to the 1815 removal statute. *Congressional Globe*, 37th Congress, 3d session (Jan. 27, 1863), p. 534.

26. Dallin H. Oaks, "Habeas Corpus in the States—1776–1865," *University of Chicago Law Review* 32: 243, 247, 249–52 (1964–1965).

27. Eric Freedman, "Just Because John Marshall Said It, Does not Make It So: *Ex parte Bollman* and the Illusory Prohibition on the Federal Writ of Habeas Corpus for State Prisoners in the Judiciary Act of 1789," *Alabama Law Review* 51: 531 (1999–2000).

28. *Ex parte Bollman*, 8 U.S. 75 (1807).

29. *Bollman* at 93, 94.

30. Ritz, *Rewriting the History*, chapter 6, and Wythe Holt, "'To Establish Justice': Politics, the Judiciary Act of 1789, and the Invention of the Federal Courts," *Duke Law Journal* 1989:1421 (1989); Joel Silbey, ed., *National Development and Sectional Crises, 1815–1860* (New York: Random House, 1970); Laurent Frantz, "Congressional Power to Enforce the Fourteenth Amendment against Private Acts," *Yale Law Journal* 73:1353 (1964).

31. 1 Stat. 96, Res. 2 (Sept. 23, 1789); Leonard White, *The Federalists: A Study in Administrative History* (New York: Macmillan, 1948), p. 402.

32. Act of March 3, 1825, 4 Stat. 115; Dwight F. Henderson, *Congress, Courts, and Criminals: The Development of Federal Criminal Law, 1801–1829* (Westport: Greenwood, 1985), pp. 9, 37.

33. Ritz, *Rewriting the History*, p. 106.

34. Warren, "New Light on the History of the Federal Judiciary Act of 1789," p. 53. The provisions of the first Judiciary Act satisfied neither party, Warren wrote, "though they pleased the Anti-federalists more than the Federalists." Holt, "'To Establish Justice,'" pp. 1515–17.

35. Act of March 3, 1875, 18 Stat. 470; Act of Feb. 6, 1889, 25 Stat. 655; Act of March 3, 1891, 26 Stat. 826. *Ex parte Wilson*, 114 U.S. 417 (1885); *Ex parte Siebold*, 100 U.S. 371 (1879).

36. Act of March 3, 1875, 18 Stat. 470.

37. Frankfurter and Landis, *The Business of the Supreme Court*, p. 109. "For a full hundred years, there was no right of appeal to the Supreme Court in criminal cases. Until 1889 even issues of life or death could reach that Court only upon a certificate of division of opinion."

38. Calvin Jillson, "Patterns and Periodicity in American National Politics," Lawrence Dodd and Calvin Jillson, eds., *The Dynamics of American Politics: Approaches and Interpretations* (Boulder: Westview, 1994), p. 27; Robert Putnam, *Making Democracy Work: Civic Traditions in Modern Italy* (Princeton: Princeton University Press, 1993), pp. 7, 8.

39. Karen Orren, *Belated Feudalism: Labor, the Law and Liberal Development in the United States* (Cambridge: Cambridge University Press, 1991), chapter 2.

40. *Calderon v. Thompson*, 523 U.S. 538, 555–56 (1998).

41. Daniel Elazar, *American Federalism: A View from the States* (New York: Harper and Row, 1984), 3d ed., p. 3.

42. Alexander Hamilton, James Madison, and John Jay, *The Federalist Papers*, introduction by Clinton Rossiter (New York: New American Library, 1961), no. 1, p. 33.

43. *McGautha* v. *California*, 402 U.S. 183, 247 (1971).

44. Jesse Choper, *Judicial Review and the National Political Process: A Functional Reconsideration of the Role of the Supreme Court* (Chicago: University of Chicago Press, 1980).

45. Andrew Hammel, "Diabolical Federalism: A Functional Critique and Proposed Reconstruction of Death Penalty Federal Habeas," *American Criminal Law Review* 39(1):1 (2002); *Printz* v. *U.S.*, 521 U.S. 898 (1997); *U.S.* v. *Morrison*, 529 U.S. 598 (2000).

46. James Madison used "partly national, partly federal" in *Federalist* 39. Tocqueville, too, had no word for the peculiar compound republic he visited. Alexis de Tocqueville, *Democracy in America* (New York: HarperPerennial, 1988), George Lawrence, trans., J. P. Mayer, ed., volume I, chapters 5 and 8. As a judicial term, *federalism* had no meaning until Felix Frankfurter first used it in 1939. Michael Collins, "Whose Federalism?" *Constitutional Commentary* 9:75 (1992).

47. *U.S.* v. *Cruikshank*, 92 U.S. 542 (1876); *U.S.* v. *Harris*, 106 U.S. 629 (1883); Pamela Brandwein, *Reconstructing Reconstruction: The Supreme Court and the Production of Historical Truth* (Durham: Duke University Press, 1999).

48. *Brown* v. *Allen*, 344 U.S. 443, 540 (1953).

49. See the discussion of this in the next chapter. *Ex parte Royall*, 117 U.S. 241 (1886); *Santa Clara County* v. *Southern Pacific Railroad*, 118 U.S. 394 (1886).

50. *Knapp* v. *Schweitzer*, 357 U.S. 371, 379 (1958).

51. *Hurtado* v. *California*, 110 U.S. 516 (1884); *In re Kemmler*, 136 U.S. 436 (1890); *Chicago, Burlington, & Quincy Railroad* v. *Chicago*, 166 U.S. 226 (1897).

52. *Wheeling Steel Corporation* v. *Glander*, 337 U.S.562, 579–80 (1949).

53. Carl Mayer, "Personalizing the Impersonal: Corporations and the Bill of Rights," *Hastings Law Journal* 41:577, 589, n. 61 (1990).

54. Mayer, "Personalizing the Impersonal," p. 644 (appendix I).

55. Mayer, "Personalizing the Impersonal," p. 589.

56. Richard T. Ely, *Property and Contract in their Relations to the Distributions of Wealth* (Macmillan, 1922 [1914]), vol 2, pp. 662–79; Howard Gillman, *The Constitution Besieged: The Rise and Demise of Lochner Era Police Powers Jurisprudence* (Durham: Duke University Press, 1993).

57. *Hepburn* v. *Griswold*, 75 U.S. 603 (1870); *Legal Tender Cases*, 79 U.S. 457 (1870).

58. *Loan Association* v. *Topeka*, 87 U.S. 655 (1875).

59 *Munn* v. *Illinois*, 94 U.S. 113, 146 (1877); *Mugler* v. *Kansas*, 123 U.S. 623 (1887).

60. *Allgeyer* v. *Louisiana*, 165 U.S. 578 (1897).

61. *Lochner* v. *New York*, 198 U.S. 45 (1905).

62. *Davidson* v. *New Orleans*, 96 U.S. 97, 104 (1878).

63. Frankfurter and Landis, *The Business of the Supreme Court*, pp. 88–89.

64. Frankfurter and Landis, *The Business of the Supreme Court*, p. 88.

65. Arnold Paul, *Conservative Crisis and the Rule of Law: Attitudes of Bar and Bench, 1877–95* (Ithaca: Cornell University Press, 1960).

66. Richard Franklin Bensel, *Sectionalism and American Political Development: 1880–1980* (Madison: University of Wisconsin Press, 1984), chapter 3.

67. *Congressional Globe*, 39th Congress, 1st session (Dec. 19, 1865) p. 87. The Judiciary Committee of the House of Representatives was directed to "inquire and report to the House, as soon as practicable, by bill or otherwise, what legislation is necessary to enable the courts of the United States to enforce the freedom of the wives and children of soldiers of the United States under the joint resolution of March 3, 1865, and also to enforce the liberty of all persons under the operation of the constitutional amendment abolishing slavery." *Congressional Globe*, 39th Congress, 1st session (Jan. 8, 1866), p. 136; *Congressional Globe*, 39th Congress, 1st session (July 25, 1866), pp. 4151; and *Congressional Globe*, 39th Congress, 1st session (July 27, 1866), pp. 4228–30.

68. The impeachment of President Andrew Johnson demonstrated Congress' strength and executive weakness. Eric McKitrick, *Andrew Johnson and Reconstruction* (Chicago: University of Chicago Press, 1960).

69. Robert Kaczorowski, *The Nationalization of Civil Rights: Constitutional Theory and Practice in a Racist Society, 1866–1883* (New York: Garland, 1987), chapter 3; William Wiecek, "The Great Writ and Reconstruction: The Habeas Corpus Act of 1867," *Journal of Southern History* 36:530, 538 (Nov. 1970); Philip S. Paludan, *A Covenant with Death: The Constitution, Law, and Equality in the Civil War Era* (Urbana: University of Illinois Press, 1975), pp. 85–108.

70. Donald Zeigler, "Twins Separated at Birth: A Comparative History of the Civil and Criminal Arising under Jurisdiction of the Federal Courts and Some Proposals for Change," *Vermont Law Review* 19:673 (1995).

71. Paul Bator, "Finality in Criminal Law and Federal Habeas Corpus for State Prisoners," *Harvard Law Review* 76:441 (1963); Lewis Mayers, "The Habeas Corpus Act of 1867: The Supreme Court as Legal Historian," *University of Chicago Law Review* 33:31 (1965); Raoul Berger, "Incorporation of the Bill of Rights: A Reply to Michael Curtis' Response," *Ohio State Law Journal* 44:1 (1983); Charles Fairman, "Does the Fourteenth Amendment Incorporate the Bill of Rights? The Original Understanding," *Stanford Law Review* 2:5 (1949).

72. Frantz, "Congressional Power to Enforce the Fourteenth Amendment against Private Acts," p. 1356.

73. The term *police power* comes from Chief Justice John Marshall in *Brown* v. *Maryland*, 12 Wheaton 419 (1827); *Willson* v. *Black-Bird Marsh Co.*, 2 Peters 245 (1829); *Mayor of the City of New York* v. *Miln*, 11 Peters 102 (1937); *Cooley* v. *Board of Wardens*, 12 Howard 299 (1851); Ruth Locke Roettinger, *The Supreme Court and State Police Power* (Washington, D.C.: Public Affairs, 1957).

74. *Ashcraft* v. *Tennessee*, 322 U.S. 143, 158 (1944).

75. Tony Freyer, "The Federal Courts, Localism, and the National Economy, 1865–1900," *Business History Review* 38:343 (1979).

76. Charles Warren, *The Supreme Court in United States History* (Boston: Little, Brown, 1926), vol. II, p. 608.

77. James W. Ely Jr., *The Guardian of Every Other Right: A Constitutional History of Property Rights* (New York: Oxford University Press, 1997), 2d ed., p. 3.

78. Harold Hyman, "Up from Dred Scott; Down to Slaughterhouse: Inventive Interim Judicial Protections for Property in Reconstruction America," Ellen Frankel Paul and Howard Dickman, eds., *Liberty, Property, and Government: Constitutional Interpretation before the New Deal* (Albany: State University of New York Press, 1989).

79. Act of 1885, 23 Stat. 437; *Ex parte McCardle*, 73 U.S. (6 Wall.) 318 (1867) and *Ex parte McCardle*, 74 U.S. (7 Wall.) 506 (1868); Warren, *The Supreme Court in United States History*, vol. 2, chapter 35; William Van Alstyne, "A Critical Guide to *Ex parte McCardle*," *Arizona Law Review* 15:229 (1973); Leonard Ratner, "Majoritarian Constraints on Judicial Review: Congressional Control of Supreme Court Jurisdiction," *Villanova Law Review* 27:929 (1982); Ratner, "Congressional Power over the Appellate Jurisdiction of the Supreme Court," *University of Pennsylvania Law Review* 157:109 (1960); Gerald Gunther, "Congressional Power to Curtail Federal Court Jurisdiction: An Opinionated Guide to the Ongoing Debate," *Stanford Law Review* 36:895 (1984); *Congressional Globe*, 40th Congress, 2d session, pt. 2 (March 12, 1868), pp. 1859–60; *Congressional Globe*, 40th Congress, 2d session, pt. 3 (March 27, 1868), pp. 2163, 2165. Eric Foner, *Reconstruction: America's Unfinished Business, 1863–1877* (New York: Harper and Row, 1988), p. 33; Michael Les Benedict, *The Impeachment and Trial of Andrew Johnson* (New York: Norton, 1973); *Ex parte Yerger*, 75 U.S. 85 (1868). *Ex parte Yerger* was a more sophisticated use of the Court's power to maintain its habeas jurisdiction in light of the repealing legislation. The Court's decision in *Yerger*, upholding the power of a general appellate habeas review, muted the effect of the 1868 Act and allowed the Court to continue hearing habeas cases throughout its appellate suspension. As Stanley Kutler has demonstrated, the Supreme Court was not part of the walking wounded following the Civil War; rather, it played a "creative and determinative role" in the development of the postwar United States. Stanley Kutler, *Judicial Power and Reconstruction Politics* (Chicago: University of Chicago Press, 1968), p. 6.

80. "The Supreme Court had no jurisdiction of a writ of error from a circuit court in a criminal case." See Frankfurter Landis, *The Business of the Supreme Court*, p. 79, n. 107. *U.S.* v. *More*, 3 Cranch 159 (1805).

81. By 1874, the end of Reconstruction was already in sight. The Congress that had passed the 1875 Removal Act also sponsored a bill to limit removal legislation. After the 1876 election, the Republicans' hold on Congress weakened. Their strength would not be the same until the realignment of 1896. C. Vann Woodward, *Reunion and Reaction: The Compromise of 1877 and the End of Reconstruction* (Boston: Little, Brown, 1966); Frankfurter and Landis, *The Business of the Supreme Court*, pp. 88–89.

82. Warren, *The Supreme Court in United States History*, vol. 2, p. 485: "The acquittal of President Johnson, in May, 1868, broke the power of the radicals"; Eric Foner, *Reconstruction*, chapter 9, esp. pp. 424–59; William Gillette, *Retreat from Reconstruction, 1869–1879* (Baton Rouge: Louisiana State University Press, 1979), chapter 1; Henry Adams, "The Session, 1869–1879," George Hochfield, ed., *The Great Secession Winter of 1860–61 and Other Essays* (New York: Barnes, 1958).

83. Wiecek, "The Great Writ," p. 543.

84. Warren, *The Supreme Court in United States History*, vol. 2, p. 687, quoting Seymour Thompson, "Abuses of the Writ of Habeas Corpus," *American Law Review* 18:1 (1884).

85. Act of March 3, 1885, amending section 764 of Rev. Stat.; *Congressional Globe*, 48th Congress, 2d session, passes Senate (March 3, 1885), pp. 2480–81; Howard Jay Graham, *Everyman's Constitution: Historical Essays on the Fourteenth Amendment, the "Conspiracy Theory," and American Constitutionalism* (Madison: State Historical Society of Wisconsin, 1968), p. 141, n. 114; Wiecek, "The Great Writ," p. 545.

86. Act of March 3, 1875, 18 Stat. 470.

87. Warren, *The Supreme Court in United States History*, vol. 2, p. 684.

88. A law passed in 1889 had inadvertently increased the Court's jurisdiction over criminal cases, but it was repealed two years later. Frankfurter and Landis, *The Business of the Supreme Court*, pp. 109–22.

89. *Ex parte Parks*, 93 U.S. 18 (1876).

90. *Ex parte Lange*, 85 U.S. 163 (1873).

91. *Parks* at 23. The Supreme Court dropped the jurisdiction standard in *Waley* v. *Johnston*, 316 U.S. 101 (1942).

92. *Parks* at 22.

93. *Ex parte Siebold*, 100 U.S. 371 (1880); *Ex parte Clarke*, 100 U.S. 399 (1880).

94. *Siebold* at 375–77.

95. *Siebold* at 391–92.

96. Michael Les Benedict, "Laissez-Faire and Liberty: A Re-evaluation of the Meaning and Origins of Laissez-Faire Constitutionalism," *Law and History Review* 3:293 (1985); Kennedy, *Race, Crime, and the Law*, chapter 9.

97. Oliver Wendell Holmes, "The Path of the Law," Richard Posner, ed., *The Essential Holmes: Selections from the Letters, Speeches, Judicial Opinions, and Other Writings of Oliver Wendell Holmes* (Chicago: University of Chicago Press, 1992); Morton White, *Social Thought in America: The Revolt Against Formalism* (Boston: Beacon, 1947), chapter 5; Dorothy Ross, *The Origins of American Social Science* (Cambridge: Cambridge University Press, 1991), chapters 8 and 9.

98. Other important cases decided by the Court prior to the restoration of its jurisdiction include *Ex parte Crouch*, 112 U.S. 178 (1884); *Ex parte Bigelow*, 113 U.S. 328 (1885); and *Ex parte Wilson*, 114 U.S. 417 (1885). In *Crouch* at 180, on a habeas challenge attacking not only the jurisdiction of the committing court but also a constitutional provision, the Court stated, "The office of a writ of habeas corpus is neither to correct such errors, nor to take the prisoner away from the court which holds him for trial."

99. *Covell* v. *Heyman*, 111 U.S. 176 (1884).

100. *Royall* at 252, citing *Covell* at 182.

101. *Allgeyer* v. *Louisiana*, 165 U.S. 578 (1897); *Lochner* v. *New York*, 198 U.S. 45 (1905); *Adair* v. *United States*, 208 U.S. 161 (1908); *Coppage* v. *Kansas*, 236 U.S. 1 (1915).

102. Daniel Meador, *Habeas Corpus and Magna Carta: Dualism of Power and Liberty* (Charlottesville: University of Virginia Press, 1966), p. 5.

103. Frankfurter and Landis, *The Business of the Supreme Court*, pp. 101–02.

104. Act of Feb. 6, 1889, 25 Stat. 655.

105. Frankfurter and Landis, *The Business of the Supreme Court*, p. 109.

106. Act of March 3, 1891, 26 Stat. 826.

107. Frankfurter and Landis, *The Business of the Supreme Court*, pp. 101–02.

108. Frankfurter and Landis, *The Business of the Supreme Court*, p. 119.

109. Warren, *The Supreme Court in United States History*, vol. 2, p. 694.

110. *In re Wood*, 140 U.S. 278 (1890); *In re Shibuya Jugiro*, 140 U.S. 291 (1891); *Ex parte Frederich*, 149 U.S. 70 (1893); *Andrews* v. *Swarts*, 156 U.S. 272 (1894).

111. *Ex parte Siebold*, 100 U.S. 371 (1880); *Ex parte Curtis* 106 U.S. 371 (1882); *Ex parte Carryl*, 106 U.S. 521 (1882); *Ex parte Bigelow*, 113 U.S. 328 (1884); *Ex parte Yarbrough*, 110 U.S. 651 (1883); *Ex parte Wilson*, 114 U.S. 417 (1884); *Ex parte Royall*, 117 U.S. 241 (1885); *In re Snow*, 120 U.S. 274 (1887); *In re Coy*, 127 U.S. 731 (1887); *In re Wright, petitioner*, 134 U.S. 136 (1889); *Stevens* v. *Fuller*, 136 U.S. 468 (1889); *In re Kemmler*, 136 U.S. 436 (1890).

112. *Ex parte Frederich* at 76.

113. *Drury* v. *Lewis*, 200 U.S. 1 (1906); *In re Lincoln*, 202 U.S. 178 (1905); *Koizo* v. *Henry*, 211 U.S. 146 (1908); *Toy Toy* v. *Hopkins*, 212 U.S. 542 (1908); *Harlan* v. *McGourin*, 218 U.S. 442 (1908); *Hyde* v. *Shine*, 199 U.S. 84 (1904); *Tinsley* v. *Treat*, 205 U.S. 20 (1906). In *In re Snow*, 120 U.S. 274 (1887), *Hans Nielsen, petitioner*, 131 U.S. 176 (1888), and *In re Loney*, 134 U.S. 372 (1889), where habeas was issued, "the grounds were such as attacked the validity of the judgments, and the objections sustained were such as rendered the judgment not merely erroneous, but void."

114. *Harlan* at 448.

115. *Maxwell* v. *Dow*, 176 U.S. 581, 603 (1900). Over Justice Harlan's dissent, the Court stated that "trial by jury has never been affirmed to be a necessary requisite of due process of law."

116. *Holden* v. *Hardy*, 198 U.S. 366 (1898).

117. *Twining* v. *New Jersey*, 21 U.S. 78 (1908).

118. *In re Converse*, 137 U.S. 624, 632 (1891).

119. *Maxwell* at 603; *Caldwell* v. *Texas*, 137 U.S. 692 (1891); *Leeper* v. *Texas*, 139 U.S 462 (1891).

120. *Henry* v. *Henkel*, 235 U.S. 219, 228 (1914).

121. *Henry* at 228.

122. Felix Frankfurter, "Distribution of Judicial Power between United States and State Courts," *Cornell Law Quarterly* 13:499, 523 (1928).

123. *Royall* at 251.

124. *The Federalist*, no. 43; *Marbury* v. *Madison*, 1 Cranch 137 (1803).

125. The Leo Frank case is well documented. Steve Oney, *And the Dead Shall Rise: The Murder of Mary Phagan and the Lynching of Leo Frank* (New York: Pantheon 2003); Robert Seitz Frey and Nancy Thompson Frey, *The Silent and the Damned: The Murder of Mary Phagan and the Lynching of Leo Frank* (New York: Cooper Square, 2002); Albert Lindemann, *The Jew Accused: Three Anti-Semitic Affairs: Dreyfus, Beilis, Frank, 1894–1915* (Cambridge: Cambridge University Press, 1991); Leonard Dinnerstein, *The Leo Frank Case* (Athens: University of Georgia Press, 1987); Eric Freedman, "Leo Frank Lives: Untangling the Historical Roots of Meaningful Federal Habeas Corpus Review of State Convictions," *Alabama Law Review* 51:1467 (2000); Nancy MacLean, "The Leo Frank Case Reconsidered: Gender and Sexual Politics in the Making of Reactionary Populism," *Journal of American History* 78:917 (Dec. 1991); Eugene Levy, "Is the Jew a White Man? Press Reaction to the Leo Frank Case, 1913–1915" *Phylon* 35(2):212 (1974).

126. In an agreement between Frank's attorneys and the trial court judge, Frank was allowed to remain in his cell for his own protection when the verdict was read. Though this was later claimed to be a denial of Frank's due process rights, it was not included in the initial petition for a new trial. *Frank* at 316.

127. Dinnerstein, *The Leo Frank Case*, chapter 2. Frank's attorneys then filed for a new trial based on new evidence.

128. *Frank* at 325. One, that the disorder "in and about the courtroom" constituted mob domination, which influenced both judge and jury to convict Frank, and thus constituted a due process violation under the Fourteenth Amendment. Two, that neither Frank nor his counsel had the right to waive his presence at the reading of the verdict. Three, his absence at that stage constituted a due process violation. Four, Frank's attorneys' failure to allege new grounds for a new trial in their first motion "did not deprive [Frank] of the right to afterwards attack the judgment as a nullity." And five, that the Georgia Supreme Court's verdict in light of Frank's absence "was available on the motion for a new trial and under proper practice ought to have been then taken, and because not then taken could not be relied upon as a ground for setting aside the verdict as a nullity and was itself in conflict with the Constitution" as an ex post facto law because "it departs from the practice settled by previous decisions of the same court."

120. *Twining* at 92.

130. *Twining* at 100.

132. *Twining* at 197, 110, and 111. *Hovey* v. *Elliot*, 167 U.S. 409 (1897); *Roller* v. *Holly*, 176 U.S. 398 (1900).

133. *Frank* at 326.

134. *Frank* at 327 (italics added).

135. *Frank* at 331.

136. *Frank* at 328; *McKane* v. *Durston*, 153 U.S. 684 (1893); *Andrews* v. *Swartz*, 156 U.S. 272 (1894).

137. *Frank* at 332.

138. *Frank* at 332–33.

139. *Frank* at 333.

140. *Frank* at 329.

141. *Frank* at 347.

142. *Frank* at 346.

143. Fred Perry Powers, "Recent Centralizing Tendencies in the Supreme Court," *Political Science Quarterly* 5(3):389 (Sept. 1890).

CHAPTER 2

1. Ian Hacking, *Mad Travelers: Reflections on the Reality of Transient Mental Illness* (Charlottesville: University Press of Virginia, 1998), p. 48.

2. Robert Louis Stevenson, *Dr. Jekyll and Mr. Hyde and Other Stories* (London: Penguin, 1979 [1886]), p. 82.

3. *County of Santa Clara* v. *Southern Pacific Railroad*, 118 U.S. 394 (1886).

4. *Ex parte Royall*, 117 U.S. 241 (1886).

5. Alan Hunt and Gary Wickham, *Foucault and Law: Towards a Sociology of Law as Governance* (London: Pluto, 1998 [1994]), p. 95.

6. Phillipa Rothfield, "Bodies and Subjects: Medical Ethics and Feminism," Paul Komesaroff, ed., *Troubled Bodies: Critical Perspectives on Postmodernism, Medical Ethics, and the Body* (Durham: Duke University Press, 1995), p. 181.

7. David Armstrong, "Bodies of Knowledge/Knowledge of Bodies," Colin Jones and Roy Porter, eds., *Reassessing Foucault: Power, Medicine and the Body* (London: Routledge, 1998), p. 22.

8. James Willard Hurst, *Law and the Conditions of Freedom in the Nineteenth-Century United States* (Madison: University of Wisconsin Press, 1956), p. 6.

9. Martin Sklar, *The Corporate Reconstruction of American Capitalism, 1890–1916: The Market, the Law, and Politics* (Cambridge: Cambridge University Press, 1988), p. 51.

10. Sklar, *The Corporate Reconstruction of American Capitalism*, p. 2; Alan Hunt, "Marxism, Law, Legal Theory and Jurisprudence," Peter Fitzpatrick, ed., *Dangerous Supplements: Resistance and Renewal in Jurisprudence* (Durham: Duke University Press, 1991).

11. Michel Foucault, *Discipline and Punish: The Birth of the Prison* (New York: Vintage Books, 1977 [1979]), p. 194.

12. Alan Sekula, "The Body and the Archive," *October* 30:3 (Winter 1986); Carl Mayer, "Personalizing the Impersonal: Corporations and the Bill of Rights," *Hastings Law Journal* 41:577 (1990).

13. Gary Burchell, "Peculiar Interests: Civil Society and Governing 'The System of Natural Liberty,'" Gary Burchell, Colin Gordon, and Peter Miller, eds., *The Foucault Effect: Studies in Governmentality* (Chicago: University of Chicago Press, 1991), p. 119.

14. Michel Foucault, "Truth and Power," Colin Gordon, ed., *Power/Knowledge: Selected Interviews and Other Writings, 1972–1977* (New York: Pantheon Books, 1980), p. 117.

15. Morton Horwitz, *The Transformation of American Law, 1870–1960: The Crisis of Legal Orthodoxy* (New York: Oxford University Press, 1992); Gary Mark, "The Personification of the Business Corporation in American Law," *University of Chicago Law Review* 54:1141 (1987).

16. Michel Foucault, *The Order of Things: An Archeology of the Human Sciences* (New York: Vintage Books, 1970 [1994]), p. 319.

17. Alan Hyde, *Bodies of Law* (Princeton: Princeton University Press, 1997), p. 6.

18. David Garland, *Punishment and Modern Society: A Study in Social Theory* (Chicago: University of Chicago Press, 1990), p. 143.

19. Maxwell Cohen, "Habeas Corpus Cum Causa—The Emergence of the Modern Writ-I," *The Canadian Bar Review* 18:10 (1940); Cohen, "Habeas Corpus Cum Causa—The Emergence of the Modern Writ-II," *The Canadian Bar Review* 18:172 (1940).

20. *Royall* at 251.

21. Paul Bator, "Finality in Criminal Law and Federal Habeas Corpus for State Prisoners," *Harvard Law Review* 76(3):441, 479, n. 88 (1963).

22. Antiterrorism and Effective Death Penalty Act of 1996, Pub. L. No. 104–132, 110 Stat. 1214 (1996). Marshall Hartman and Jeanette Nyden, "Habeas Corpus and the New Federalism after the Anti-Terrorism and Effective Death Penalty Act of 1996," *The John Marshall Law Review* 30:337 (1997).

23. Thomas Byrnes, *1886: Professional Criminals of America* (New York: Lyons, 2000 [1886]), p. x.

24. Karen Halttunen, *Confidence Men and Painted Women: A Study of Middle-Class Culture in America, 1830–1870* (New Haven: Yale University Press, 1982); Joachim Schlör, *Nights in the Big City* (London: Reaktion Books, 1998).

25. Simon Cole, *Suspect Identities: A History of Fingerprinting and Criminal Identification* (Cambridge: Harvard University Press, 2001), p. 21.

26. Charles Fairman, *Reconstruction and Reunion, 1864–88* (New York: Macmillan, 1987 (in two parts)), p. 715; J. T. Moore, "Black Militancy in Readjuster Virginia, 1879–1883," *Journal of Southern History* 41(2):167 (1975).

27. David Currie, "The Constitution in the Supreme Court: The Interpretation of Economic Interests, 1889–1910," *University of Chicago Law Review* 52:324 (1985); *Royall* v. *Virginia*, 116 U.S. 572 (1886).

28. William Royall, *History of the Virginia Debt Controversy: The Negro's Vicious Influence in Politics* (Richmond: West, 1909), p. 101; Royall, *Some Reminiscences* (New York: Neale, 1897).

29. Thomas Porter, *The Rise of Statistical Thinking, 1820–1900* (Princeton: Princeton University Press, 1988).

30. Dr. Laurent, "Physiognomy of the Insane," *The Journal of Insanity* 20(2):216 (October 1863).

31. John Torpey, *The Invention of the Passport: Surveillance, Citizenship and the State* (Cambridge: Cambridge University Press, 1999); David Johnson, *Illegal Tender: Counterfeiting and the Secret Service in Nineteenth-Century America* (Washington, D.C.: The Smithsonian Institution Press, 1995).

32. Hunt and Wickham, *Foucault and Law*, p. 67.

33. Foucault, *Discipline and Punish*, p. 23.

34. Matt Matsuda, *The Memory of the Modern* (New York: Oxford University Press, 1996), pp. 121–23.

35. Sekula, *The Body and the Archive*, p. 9.

36. Byrnes, *Professional Criminals*, p. 55.

37. Eugenia Parry, *Crime Album Stories: Paris, 1886–1902* (Zurich: Scalo, 2000); Charles Rosenberg, *The Trial of the Assassin Guiteau: Psychiatry and Law in the Gilded Age* (Chicago: University of Chicago Press, 1968).

38. Matsuda, *The Memory of the Modern*, p. 124; Carroll Smith-Rosenberg, *Disorderly Conduct: Visions of Gender in Victorian America* (Oxford: Oxford University Press, 1986), pp. 90–108.

39. Thomas Cochran, *Railroad Leaders, 1845–1890: The Business Mind in Action* (Cambridge: Harvard University Press, 1953), p. 1.

40. Francis Galton, *Finger prints* (London: Macmillan, 1892); Alphonse Bertillon, *Signaletic Instructions, including the Theory and Practice of Anthropometrical Identification* (Chicago: Werner, 1896).

41. Cole, *Suspect Identities*, p. 37.

42. François Crouzet, *The First Industrialists* (Cambridge: Cambridge University Press, 1985), p. 4.

43. Crouzet, *The First Industrialists*, pp. 2–8.

44. Hubert Dreyfus and Paul Rabinow, *Michel Foucault: Beyond Structuralism and Hermeneutics* (Chicago: University of Chicago Press, 1982), p. 153.

45. John Diggins, *The Promise of Pragmatism: Modernism and the Crisis of Knowledge and Authority* (Chicago: University of Chicago Press, 1994), p. 376.

46. David Walker Howe, *Making the American Self: Jonathan Edwards to Abraham Lincoln* (Cambridge: Harvard University Press, 1997), p. 254.

47. Howe, *Making the American Self*, p. 8.

48. *County of Santa Clara v. Southern Pacific Railroad*, 118 U.S. 394, 396 (1886).

49. *Dartmouth College v. Woodward*, 17 U.S. 518, 613 (1819); J. S. Davis, *Essays in the Earlier History of American Corporations* (Cambridge: Harvard University Press, 1917).

50. *Bank of the United States v. Deveaux*, 9 U.S. 61 (1809).

51. *Bank of the United States v. Deveaux* at 86–87.

52. Mark, "The Personification of the Business Corporation," p. 1451; Stuart Schane, "The Corporation Is a Person: The Language of a Legal Fiction," *Tulane Law Review* 61:563, 573–74 (1987).

53. Hurst, *Law and the Conditions of Freedom*, p. 15; *Charles River Bridge Co. v. Warren Bridge Co.*, 36 U.S. 420 (1837).

54. Mark Barkelay and Rogers Smith, "The One Best System? A Political Analy-

sis of Neoclassical Institutional Perspectives on the Modern Corporation," William Samuels and Arthur Miller, eds., *Corporations and Society: Power and Responsibility* (Westport: Greenwood, 1987), p. 90.

55. David Millon, "Theories of the Corporation," *Duke Law Journal* 1990: 201, 207 (1990).

56. Millon, "Theories of the Corporation," p. 208.

57. Barkelay and Smith, "The One Best System?" p. 101.

58. *Bank of Augusta* v. *Earle*, 38 U.S. 519 (1839).

59. James Willard Hurst, *The Legitimacy of the Business Corporation in the Law of the United States, 1780–1970* (Charlottesville: University Press of Virginia, 1970), p. 64.

60. Hurst, *The Legitimacy of the Business Corporation*, pp. 64, 65.

61. Mark, "The Personification of the Business Corporation," p. 1458.

62. Mark, "The Personification of the Business Corporation," p. 1456.

63. William G. Roy, *Socializing Capital: The Rise of the Large Industrial Corporation in America* (Princeton: Princeton University Press, 1997), pp. 10–11.

64. Roy, *Socializing Capital*, p. 11.

65. Roy, *Socializing Capital*, p. 155.

66. Olivier Zunz, *Making America Corporate, 1870–1920* (Chicago: University of Chicago Press, 1990), pp. 52–53, 56.

67. Arthur Chandler, *The Visible Hand: The Managerial Revolution in American Business* (Cambridge: Belknap, 1977).

68. Zunz, *Making America Corporate*, p. 7.

69. Louis Galambos, *The Public Image of Big Business in America, 1880–1940: A Quantitative Study in Social Change* (Baltimore: Johns Hopkins University Press, 1975), p. 76.

70. *The Slaughterhouse Cases*, 83 U.S. 36 (1873); *Munn* v. *Illinois*, 94 U.S. 113 (1877).

71. *The Railroad Tax Cases*, 13 F. 722 C.C.D. Cal. (1882).

72. *The Railroad Tax Cases* at 737, 743.

73. Schane, "The Corporation Is a Person," p. 574.

74. *The Railroad Tax Cases* at 743–44; italics added.

75. John Flynn, "The Jurisprudence of Corporate Personhood: The Misuse of a Legal Concept," Samuels and Miller, eds., *Corporations and Society: Power and Responsibility*, p. 139.

76. Pierre Schlag, "The Problem of the Subject," *Texas Law Review* 69:1627, 1639 (1991).

77. Flynn, "The Jurisprudence of Corporate Personhood," p. 138.

CHAPTER 3

1. *Ex parte Siebold*, 100 U.S. 371, 375 (1879): "But the general rule is, that a conviction and sentence by a court of competent jurisdiction is lawful cause of imprisonment, and no relief can be given by habeas corpus."

2. *Brown* v. *Allen*, 344 U.S. 443, 486 (1953).

3. *Powell* v. *Alabama*, 287 U.S. 45 (1932); *Palko* v. *Connecticut*, 302 U.S. 319 (1937).

4. Alan Hunt and Gary Wickham, *Foucault and Law: Towards a Sociology of Law as Governance* (London: Pluto, 1998 [1994]), p. 8.

5. *Ashcraft* v. *Tennessee*, 322 U.S. 143, 152 (1944).

6. *Ashcraft* at 157.

7. *Ashcraft* at 157.

8. Patricia Ewick and Susan Silbey, "Subversive Stories and Hegemonic Tales: Toward a Sociology of Narrative," *Law & Society Review* 29(2):197 (1995).

9. Rosemary Coombe, "Contingent Articulations: A Critical Cultural Studies of Law," Austin Sarat and Thomas Kearns, eds., *Law in the Domains of Culture* (Ann Arbor: University of Michigan Press, 2000), p. 54.

10. *Ex parte Royall*, 117 U.S. 254 (1886); *Munn* v. *Illinois*, 94 U.S. 113 (1877); *In re Kemmler*, 136 U.S. 436 (1890); *Lochner* v. *New York*, 198 U.S. 45 (1905); *Muller* v. *Oregon*, 208 U.S. 412 (1908); Arthur Miller, *The Supreme Court and American Capitalism* (New York: Free Press, 1968).

11. Lawrence Friedman, *Crime and Punishment in American History* (New York: Basic Books, 1993), p. 50.

12. *Moore* v. *Dempsey*, 261 U.S. 86, 93 (1923).

13. *Brown* at 485.

14. *Carter* v. *Rafferty*, 781 U.S. F.2d 993, 996 (1986).

15. Joseph Hoffmann and William Stuntz, "Habeas after the Revolution," *Supreme Court Review* 1993:65 (1993).

16. *Screws* v. *U.S.*, 325 U.S. 91, 144–45 (1945).

17. *Fay* v. *Noia*, 372 U.S. 391 (1963); *White* v. *Texas*, 310 U.S. 530 (1940); *Lee* v. *Mississippi*, 332 U.S. 742 (1948); *Malinski* v. *New York*, 324 U.S. 401 (1945); *Brown* v. *Allen*, 344 U.S. 443, 1953; *Lisenba* v. *California*, 314 U.S. 219, 1941; *Chambers* v. *Florida*, 309 U.S. 227 (1940); *Brown* v. *Mississippi*, 297 U.S. 278 (1936); *Powell* v. *Alabama*, 287 U.S. 45 (1932).

18. *Ward* v. *Texas*, 316 U.S. 547, 551–52 (1942).

19. *Ward* at 550.

20. *Ward* at 551, 552.

21. *Ward* at 555.

22. *Adamson* v. *California*, 332 U.S. 46 (1947); *Brown* v. *Allen*, 344 U.S. 443 (1953).

23. Anne Barron, "Legal Discourse and the Colonisation of the Self in the Modern State," Anthony Carty, ed., *Post-Modern Law: Enlightenment, Revolution and the Death of Man* (Edinburgh: Edinburgh University Press, 1990), p. 119.

24. *Moore* v. *Dempsey*, 261 U.S. 86 (1923); *Screws* v. *United States*, 325 U.S. 91 (1945).

25. Phillip J. Cooper, *Hard Judicial Choices: Federal District Court Judges and State and Local Officials* (New York: Oxford University Press, 1988); Malcolm Feely and

Edward Rubin, *Judicial Policymaking and the Modern State: How the Courts Reformed America's Prisons* (Cambridge: Cambridge University Press, 1998).

26. *Coleman* v. *Thompson*, 501 U.S. 722 (1991); *Wainwright* v. *Sykes*, 433 U.S. 72 (1977).

27. *Culombe* v. *Connecticut*, 367 U.S. 568, 636 (1961).

28. The quote is from Rosa Luxemburg, regarding the 103 volumes of the Verein fur Sozialpolitik. Dietrich Rueschemeyer and Theda Skocpol, "Conclusion," Dietrich Rueschemeyer and Theda Skocpol, eds., *States, Social Knowledge, and the Origins of Modern Social Policies* (Princeton: Princeton University Press, 1996), p. 301.

29. Sara Knox, *Murder: A Tale of Modern American Life* (Durham: Duke University Press, 1998), p. 17.

30. Michel Foucault, "The Dangerous Individual," Lawrence Kritzman, ed., *Politics, Philosophy, Culture: Interviews and Other Writings, 1977–1984* (London: Routledge, 1988), p. 140.

31. Paul Boyer, *Urban Masses and Moral Order in America, 1820–1920* (Cambridge: Harvard University Press, 1978); Sander Gilman, *Difference and Pathology: Stereotypes of Sexuality, Race, and Madness* (Ithaca: Cornell University Press, 1985); Charles Rosenberg, *The Trial of the Assassin Guiteau: Psychiatry and the Law in the Gilded Age* (Chicago: The University of Chicago Press, 1968 [1989]).

32. Foucault, "The Dangerous Individual," p. 135.

33. Pliny Earle, "On the Causes of Insanity," *American Journal of Insanity* 4(3):185 (1848); G. Boody, "On the Study of the Palate," *American Journal of Insanity* 52(4):541 (1896); Boody, "The Degenerate Jaw," *American Journal of Insanity* 52(3):281 (1896); W. Krauss, "The Stigmata of Degeneration," *American Journal of Insanity* 55(1):55 (1898); Carlos MacDonald, "The Trial, Execution, Autopsy and Mental Status of Leon F. Czolgosz, Alias Fred Newman, the Assassin of President McKinley, with a report of the post-mortem examination by Edward A. Spitzka," *American Journal of Insanity* 58(3):26 (1902); Orpheus Everts, "Criminal Responsibility of the Insane," *American Journal of Insanity* 40(4):440 (1884).

34. W. McCorn, "Degeneration in Criminals as Shown by the Bertillon System of Measurement and Photographs," *American Journal of Insanity* 52(1) (1896); William Morrison, "The Study of Crime," *Mind* 1(4):489 (1892); Morrison, "The Juvenile Offender, and the Conditions Which Produce Him," *International Journal of Ethics* 5(2):162 (1895).

35. Thomas Byrnes, *1886: Professional Criminals of America* (New York: Lyons, 2000 [1886]).

36. *Brown* v. *Mississippi*, 297 U.S. 278, 281–82 (1936).

37. *Sunal* v. *Large*, 332 U.S. 174 (1947).

38. *Sunal* at 189.

39. 28 U.S.C. sections 2241–54

40. Paul Bator, "Finality in Criminal Law and Federal Habeas Corpus for State Prisoners," *Harvard Law Review* 76:441 (1963).

41. Ronnie Nichols, "Conspirators or Victims? A Survey of Black Leadership in the Riots," *Arkansas Review: A Journal of Delta Studies* 32(2):123 (2001); Griffin Stock-

ley, "The Legal Proceedings of the Arkansas Race Massacres of 1919 and the Evidence of the Plot to Kill Planters," *Arkansas Review: A Journal of Delta Studies* 32(2):141 (2001).

42. J. S. Waterman and E. E. Overton, "The Aftermath of *Moore* v. *Dempsey*," *St. Louis University Law Review* 18:117 (1933); Richard Cortner, *A Mob Intent on Death: The NAACP and the Arkansas Riot Cases* (Middletown: Wesleyan University Press, 1988); Randall Kennedy, *Race, Crime, and the Law* (New York: Pantheon Books, 1997), p. 95.

43. Waterman and Overton, "The Aftermath of Moore," pp. 118, 119.

44. Stockley, "The Legal Proceedings of the Arkansas Race Massacre," p. 142; *Moore* at 89.

45. *Moore* at 90.

46. *Moore* at 92.

47. *Frank* v. *Magnum*, 237 U.S. 309, 326 (1915).

48. *Moore* at 91.

49. *Moore* at 86.

50. *Moore* at 89.

51. *Knewel* v. *Egan*, 268 U.S. 442, 446–47 (1925), holding that the judgments of state courts in criminal cases will not be reviewed on habeas corpus "merely because some right under the Constitution of the United States is alleged to have been denied to the person convicted." *Mooney* v. *Holohan*, 294 U.S. 103, 112, 115 (1935); *Davis* v. *Burke*, 179 U.S. 399 (1900); *Urquhart* v. *Brown*, 205 U.S. 179 (1907); *U.S. ex rel. Kennedy* v. *Tyler*, 269 U.S. 13 (1925); *New York ex rel. Bryant* v. *Zimmerman*, 278 U.S. 63 (1928).

52. Robert Cover, "The Origins of Judicial Activism in the Protection of Minorities," *Yale Law Journal* 91:1287, 1306 (1982). Cover writes that Holmes, in a letter to Harold Laski, asked why Laski was not as exercised over Moore as he was with Sacco and Vanzetti. "I cannot but ask myself why this so much greater interest in red than black." Kennedy, *Race, Crime, and the Law*, p. 100.

53. Kennedy, *Race, Crime, and the Law*, p. 94.

54. In *U.S. ex rel. Kennedy* v. *Tyler*, 269 U.S. 13, 18–19 (1925), the Court acknowledged that it had allowed bypass of state exhaustion rules only three times, all considered exceptional cases: *In re Neagle*, 135 U.S. 1 (1890); *In re Loney*, 134 U.S. 372 (1890); and *Wildenhaus's case*, 120 U.S. 1 (1887). See also *Frisbie* v. *Collins*, 342 U.S. 519 (1952).

55. 28 U.S.C. 1257 (1958).

56. Curtis Reitz, "Federal Habeas Corpus: Impact of an Abortive State Proceeding," *Harvard Law Review* 74:1315, 1538 (1961); Felix Frankfurter and James Landis, "The Supreme Court under the Judiciary Act of 1925," *Harvard Law Review* 42:1, 11 (1928); O. John Rogge and Murray Gordon, "Habeas Corpus, Civil Rights, and the Federal System," *The University of Chicago Law Review* 20:509, 511 (1953).

57. *Rochin* v. *California*, 342 U.S. 165, 172 (1952).

58. Stanley Friedelbaum, "Independent State Grounds: Contemporary Invitations to Judicial Activism," Mary Cornelia Porter and G. Alan Tarr, eds., *State Supreme Courts: Policymakers in the Federal System* (Westport: Greenwood, 1982), chapter 2.

59. *Herb* v. *Pitcairn*, 324 U.S. 117, 125–26 (1945). The origins of the independent and adequate state ground doctrine go back to *Murdock* v. *City of Memphis*, 87 U.S. 590 (1875).

60. Reitz, "Federal Habeas Corpus," pp. 1329, 1343.

61. Reitz, " Federal Habeas Corpus," p. 1341.

62. Barbie Zelizer, *Covering the Body: The Kennedy Assassination, the Media, and the Shaping of Collective Memory* (Chicago: University of Chicago Press, 1992), p. 33.

63. Michael Klarman, "The Racial Origins of Modern Criminal Procedure," *Michigan Law Review* 99:48 (2000–2001); Klarman, "Race and the Court in the Progressive Era," *Vanderbilt Law Review* 51:881 (May 1998).

64. *Culombe* at 636.

65. *Culombe* at 640.

66. *Powell* v. *Alabama*, 287 U.S. 45 (1932).

67. Powell's reach was restricted to the facts of the case. In *Gideon* v. *Wainwright*, 372 U.S. 335 (1963), the Court applied the Sixth Amendment to state defendants.

68. *Powell* at 67.

69. *Powell* at 65.

70. *Powell* at 68.

71. *Powell* at 57.

72. *Powell* at 60.

73. *Powell* at 60.

74. *Palko* v. *Connecticut*, 302 U.S. 319, 325 (1937).

75. *Palko* at 327, citing *Moore* v. *Dempsey* and *Mooney* v. *Holohan*.

76. *Palko* at 327.

77. *Johnson* v. *Zerbst*, 304 U.S. 458 (1938).

78. *Zerbst* at 464; *Aetna Insurance Co.* v. *Kennedy*, 301 U.S. 389 (1937).

79. *Zerbst* at 465–66.

80. *Mooney* v. *Holohan*, 294 U.S. 103 (1935).

81. *Zerbst* at 465.

82. *Zerbst* at 466; *Frank* at 331.

83. *Walker* v. *Johnston*, 312 U.S. 275 (1941).

84. *Waley* v. *Johnston*, 316 U.S. 101 (1942).

85. *Smith* v. *O'Grady*, 312 U.S. 329, 331–32 (1941).

86. *Chambers* v. *Florida*, 309 U.S. 227 (1940).

87. *Chambers* at 236, n.8.

88. *Chambers* at 238.

89. *Chambers* at 240–41.

90. *Lisenba* v. *California*, 314 U.S. 219 (1941).

91. *Hysler* v. *Florida*, 315 U.S. 411 (1942). For a summary of the Court's confession cases, see *Spano* v. *N.Y.*, 360 U.S. 315 (1959), n. 2.

92. *Wade* v. *Mayo*, 334 U.S. 672 (1948).

93. *Darr* v. *Burford*, 339 U.S. 200 (1950).

94. *Brown* v. *Allen*, 344 U.S. 443 (1953).

95. Hearings before Subcommittee No. 1, Committee of the Judiciary, H.R., 80th Congress, 1st session (March 7, 1947).

96. Clarence Galston, "An Introduction to the New Federal Judicial Code," *Federal Rules Decisions* 8:201, 205 (1948).

97. Rogge and Gordon, "Habeas Corpus, Civil Rights, and the Federal System," p. 523.

98. *Ex parte Hawk*, 321 U.S. 114 (1944).

99. *Hawk* at 116.

100. *Hawk* at 116–17; italics added.

101. *Hawk* at 118, citing *Salinger* v. *Loisel*, 265 U.S. 224 (1924).

102. William Speck, "Statistics on Federal Habeas Corpus," *Ohio State Law Journal* 10:337 (1949).

103. Speck, "Statistics on Federal Habeas Corpus," table 3. A federal question is distinct from other types of habeas corpus appeals, such as deportation issues or cases where the U.S. government is a defendant are here excluded. Federal questions range from due process violations in general to particular constitutional claims, such as lack of counsel, coercion of confessions, and the like.

104. Louis Goodman, "Use and Abuse of the Writ of Habeas Corpus," *Federal Rules Decisions* 7:313, 315 (1947).

105. *Hawk* at 118. See also *House* v. *Mayo*, 324 U.S. 42 (1945); *White* v. *Ragen*, 324 U.S. 760 (1945); *Hawk* v. *Olson*, 326 U.S. 271 (1945).

106. *Wade* at 689.

107. *Wade* at 677.

108. *Wade* at 681.

109. Bator, "Finality," p. 454.

110. *Wade* at 692.

111. *Wade* at 692.

112. Justice Reed further held that eliminating certiorari from the "normal paths of review" would result in an "extravagant exercise of federal jurisdiction [which] would furnish another technique of delay in a criminal system which often permits long periods of time to elapse between sentencing and execution of sentence." *Wade* at 692.

113. *Darr* v. *Burford*, 339 U.S. 200 (1950).

114. *Darr* at 228.

115. *Darr* at 208–10.

116. *Darr* at 217–18.

117. *Darr* at 217.

118. *Darr* at 220.

119. *Darr* at 226.

120. Gordon, "An Introduction to the New Federal Judicial Code"; John J. Parker, "Limiting the Abuse of Habeas Corpus," *Federal Rules Decisions* 8:171 (1948); Goodman, "Use and Abuse of the Writ of Habeas Corpus"; Herbert Wechsler, "Federal Jurisdiction and the Revision of the Judicial Code," *Law and Contemporary Problems* 13:216 (1948).

121. 28 U.S.C. 2254(a) and (b).

122. *Darr* at 235–37.

123. Parker, "Limiting the Abuse," p. 176.

124. Goodman, "Use and Abuse," p. 315. United States district judge Louis Goodman found that, from 1937 to 1947, 180 inmates at Alcatraz had filed 368 petitions for habeas corpus. This would seem to mean that, on average, each inmate filed two petitions. In fact, according to judge Goodman, "117 inmates filed one petition each. The remaining 63 filed 251 petitions." The most petitions filed by one inmate was 16.

125. Parker, "Limiting the Abuse," p. 178.

126. Parker, "Limiting the Abuse," p. 177.

127. *Brown v. Allen*, 344 U.S. 443 (1953).

128. *Brown v. Allen* is case no. 32; *Speller v. Allen*, case no. 22; *Daniels v. Allen*, case no. 20.

129. *Brown* at 548–49.

130. *Speller v. Allen* is similar. He, too, was found guilty of rape and sentenced to death. *Daniels*, however, is slightly different. He was found guilty of murder. The trial judge gave Daniels and one other convicted with him (also named Daniels) sixty days to serve a statement of the case on appeal. The statement was filed on the sixty-first day. Daniels was denied an appeal. The Supreme Court upheld the conviction.

131. *Waley v. Johnston*, 316 U.S. 101, 104–05 (1942): "[T]he use of the writ in the federal courts to test the constitutional validity of a conviction for crime is not restricted to those cases where the judgment of conviction is void for want of jurisdiction of the trial court to render it. It extends also to those exceptional cases where the conviction has been in disregard of the constitutional rights of the accused."

132. *Brown* at 491.

133. Parker, "Limiting the Abuse," p. 178.

134. *Brown* at 487.

135. *Brown* at 498.

136. *Brown* at 501.

137. *Brown* at 498.

138. *Brown* at 533–36.

139. Bator, "Finality," p. 506.

140. O. John Rogge and Murray Gordon, "Habeas Corpus, Civil Rights and the Federal System," *University of Chicago Law Review*, 20:509 (1953). The authors were counsel to Daniels in *Daniels v. Allen*.

141. *Brown* at 535.

142. *Brown* at 535.

143. *Brown* at 540–41.

144. Bator, "Finality," p. 452.

145. *Brown* at 540; *McNally v. Hill*, 293 U.S. 131, 136–38 (1934).

146. *Brown* at 540; italics added.

147. *Brown* at 544.

148. Larry Yackle, *Reclaiming the Federal Courts* (Cambridge: Harvard University Press, 1994), p. 27.

149. *Brown* at 557–58.

150. *Brown* at 558.

CHAPTER 4

1. *Palko* v. *Connecticut*, 302 U.S. 319 (1937).

2. *Wolf* v. *Colorado*, 338 U.S. 25 (1949).

3. *Mapp* v. *Ohio*, 367 U.S. 643, 655 (1961).

4. *Weeks* v. *United States*, 232 U.S. 383 (1914).

5. *Mapp* at 679, 682.

6. *Gideon* v. *Wainwright*, 371 U.S. 335 (1963).

7. *Miranda* v. *Arizona*, 384 U.S. 436 (1966).

8. *Culombe* v. *Connecticut*, 367 U.S. 568 (1961).

9. *Fay* v. *Noia*, 372 U.S. 391 (1963).

10. *Planned Parenthood of Southeastern Pa.* v. *Casey*, 505 U.S. 833, 943 (1992). Emphasizing the individual component to the "right to privacy," Justice Blackmun wrote: "I am 83 years old. I cannot remain on this Court forever, and when I do step down, the confirmation process for my successor well may focus on the issue before us today. That, I regret, may be exactly where the choice between the two worlds will be made."

11. *Desist* v. *United States*, 394 U.S. 244, 261 (1969).

12. *Desist* at 253; *Michigan* v. *Tucker*, 417 U.S. 433 (1974).

13. *Kaufman* v. *United States*, 394 U.S. 217 (1969).

14. Henry Friendly, "Is Innocence Irrelevant? Collateral Attack on Criminal Judgments," *University of Chicago Law Review* 38:142 (1970).

15. *Benton* v. *Maryland*, 395 U.S.784 (1969).

16. Ronald Flagg, "*Stone* v. *Powell* and the New Federalism: A Challenge to Congress," *Harvard Journal of Legislation* 14:152 (1976).

17. *Stone* v. *Powell*, 428 U.S. 465, 494, n. 35 (1976).

18. Jeffrey Henig, *Public Policy and Federalism: Issues in State and Local Politics* (New York: St. Martin's, 1985), p. 16.

19. Richard McGee, *Prisons and Politics* (Lexington, MA: Lexington Books, 1981); Bruce Jackson, *Law and Disorder: Criminal Justice in America* (Urbana: University of Illinois Press, 1984); *To Establish Justice, To Insure Domestic Tranquility, Final Report of the National Commission on the Causes and Prevention of Violence* (Washington, D.C.: U.S. Government Printing Office, 1969).

20. *Chicago, Burlington, & Quincy R.R. Co.* v. *Chicago*, 166 U.S. 226 (1897).

21. *Fiske* v. *Kansas*, 274 U.S. 380 (1927); *Gitlow* v. *New York*, 268 U.S. 652 (1925) (speech and press); *DeJonge* v. *Oregon*, 299 U.S. 353 (1937) (assembly); *Shelton* v. *Tucker*, 364 U.S. 479 (1960) (freedom of association).

22. *Mapp* v. *Ohio*, 367 U.S. 643 (1961).

23. *Robinson* v. *California*, 370 U.S. 660 (1962).

24. *Sanders* v. *United States*, 372 U.S. 1 (1963), a federal habeas corpus case.

25. *Malloy* v. *Hogan*, 378 U.S. 1 (1964).

26. *Klopfer* v. *North Carolina*, 386 U.S. 213 (1967). The right to a public trial was established in *In re Oliver*, 333 U.S. 257 (1948).

27. *Pointer* v. *Texas*, 380 U.S. 400 (1967).

28. *Washington* v. *Texas*, 388 U.S. 14 (1967).

29. *Duncan* v. *Louisiana*, 391 U.S. 145 (1968).

30. *Palko* v. *Connecticut*, 302 U.S. 145 (1937); *Bruton* v. *U.S.*, 391 U.S. 123 (1968); *Katz* v. *U.S.*, 389 U.S. 347 (1967) (warrantless searches are unconstitutional); *Mempha* v. *Ray*, 389 U.S. 128 (1967) (right to counsel at sentencing); *Stoval* v. *Denno*, 388 U.S. 293 (1967) (due process protection against unreliable evidence); *Gilbert* v. *California*, 388 U.S. 263 (1967) (right to counsel at postindictment lineup); *Massiah* v. *U.S.*, 377 U.S. 201 (1964) (right to counsel); *White* v. *Maryland*, 373 U.S. 59 (1963) (right to counsel at preliminary hearing in capital case); *Douglas* v. *California*, 372 U.S. 353 (1963) (right to counsel for indigents on first appeal as of right); *Hamilton* v. *Alabama*, 368 U.S. 52 (1961) (right to counsel at arraignment).

31. Philip Kurland, *Politics, the Constitution, and the Warren Court* (Chicago: University of Chicago Press, 1970), p. 96.

32. Kurland, *The Warren Court*, p. 58.

33. Kurland, *The Warren Court*, p. 60.

34. *Brown* v. *Mississippi*, 297 U.S. 278, 285 (1936).

35. Anthony Amsterdam and Jerome Bruner, *Minding the Law* (Cambridge: Harvard University Press, 2000), chapter 2, "On Categories."

36. Stephen Skowronek, *The Politics Presidents Make: Leadership from John Adams to Bill Clinton* (Cambridge: Harvard University Press, 1993), p. 15.

37. *Schneckloth* v. *Bustamonte*, 412 U.S. 218 (1973).

38. *Schneckloth* at 253.

39. *Schneckloth* at 264.

40. *Schneckloth* at 259.

41. *Johnson* v. *Massachusetts*, 390 U.S. 511 (1968).

42. *Johnson* at 513–14.

43. *Brown* v. *Mississippi*, 297 U.S. 278 (1936); *Lisenba* v. *California*, 314 U.S. 219 (1941); *Chambers* v. *Florida*, 309 U.S. 227 (1940); *White* v. *Texas*, 310 U.S. 530 (1940); *Ward* v. *Texas*, 316 U.S. 547 (1942); *Ashcraft* v. *Tennessee*, 322 U.S. 143 (1944); *Malinski* v. *New York*, 324 U.S. 401 (1945); *Lee* v. *Mississippi*, 332 U.S. 742 (1948); *Leyra* v. *Denno*, 347 U.S. 556 (1954); *Herman* v. *Claudy*, 350 U.S. 116 (1956); *Payne* v. *Arkansas*, 356 U.S. 560 (1958).

44. *Thomas* v. *Arizona*, 356 U.S. 390 (1958).

45. *Rochin* v. *California*, 342 U.S. 165 (1952).

46. *Culombe* at 576.

47. *Leyra* at 556.

48. *Leyra* at 584.

49. In *Culombe* at 604–05, Frankfurter writes, "The notion of 'voluntariness' is itself an amphibian. It purports at once to describe an internal psychic state and to characterize that state for legal purposes."

50. *Frank v. Magnum*, 237 U.S. 306, 346 (1915).

51. *Fay* at 437.

52. Abraham Sofaer, "Federal Habeas Corpus for State Prisoners: The Isolation Principle," *New York University Law Review* 39:78 (1964).

53. *Fay* at 422, 430–31.

54. *Fay* at 398–99, italics in original.

55. *Fay* at 399.

56. *Fay* at 464.

57. *Johnson v. Zerbst*, 304 U.S. 458, 464 (1938); Curtis Reitz, "Federal Habeas Corpus: Impact of an Abortive State Proceeding," *Harvard Law Review* 74:1315, 1336 (1961).

58. *Fay* at 439.

59. *Fay* at 440.

60. *Fay* at 439.

61. *Fay* at 439; Larry Yackle, *Postconviction Remedies* (Rochester: Lawyers Cooperative, 1981), p. 310.

62. *Herb v. Pitcairn*, 324 U.S. 117 (1945).

63. Reitz, "Federal Habeas Corpus," p. 1341. Stanley Friedelbaum, "Independent State Grounds: Contemporary Invitation to Judicial Activism," Mary Cornelia Porter and G. Alan Tarr, eds., *State Supreme Courts: Policymakers in the Federal System* (Westport: Greenwood, 1982).

64. *Ex parte Lange*, 85 U.S. 163 (1873); *Ex parte Siebold*, 100 U.S. 371 (1880); *Waley v. Johnston*, 316 U.S. 101 (1942).

65. *Ex parte Royall*, 117 U.S. 241 (1886).

66. Friedelbaum, "Independent State Grounds," p. 24.

67. William J. Brennan, "Federal Habeas Corpus and State Prisoners: An Exercise in Federalism," *Utah Law Review* 7:423, 436 (1961).

68. Reitz, "Federal Habeas Corpus," p. 1342.

69. *Fay* at 418.

70. *Fay* at 441.

71. *Fay* at 402, 465–66. Henry Hart, "Foreword: The Time Chart of the Justices," *Harvard Law Review* 73:84, 118 (1959).

72. 28 U.S.C. 2241(c)(1).

73. *Townsend v. Sain*, 372 U.S. 293 (1963).

74. *Townsend* at 309.

75. *Townsend* at 311–12.

76. *Brown v. Allen*, 344 U.S. 443, 505 (1953).

77. *Thomas v. Arizona*, 356 U.S. 390 (1958); *Rogers v. Richmond*, 357 U.S. 220 (1958); Note, "Habeas Corpus: Developments since *Brown v. Allen*: A Survey and Analysis," *Northwestern University Law Review* 53:765 (1959); Comment, "Federal

Habeas Corpus Review of State Convictions: An Interplay of Appellate Ambiguity and District Court Discretion," *Yale Law Journal* 68:98 (1958).

78. *Townsend* at 320.

79. *Townsend* at 314.

80. *Townsend* at 297–99.

81. *Townsend* at 300–01.

82. *Townsend* at 315.

83. *Townsend* at 316.

84. *Townsend* at 311–12.

85. *Fay* at 454.

86. *Fay* at 460.

87. *Fay* at 462.

88. Graham Hughes, "Sandbagging Constitutional Rights: Federal Habeas Corpus and the Procedural Default Principle," *New York University Review of Law & Social Change* 16:321, 333 (1987–88).

89. The 2255 petition was filed without counsel, and the only claim was ineffective counsel at trial. At the hearing, Kaufman, with counsel, alleged supplementary claims, including illegal search of his vehicle.

90. *Kaufman* at 224; Jacob Landynski, *Search and Seizure and the Supreme Court: A Study in Constitutional Interpretation* (Baltimore: Johns Hopkins University Press, 1966); Francis Allen, "Federalism and the Fourth Amendment: A Requiem for *Wolf*," *The Supreme Court Review* 1961:1 (1961).

91. *Kaufman* at 228.

92. *Schneckloth* v. *Bustamonte*, 412 U.S. 218, 251 (1973); *Kaufman* at 224.

93. *Kaufman* at 219.

94. *Kaufman* at 232.

95. *Kaufman* at 232.

96. *Kaufman* at 236. "Surely, it cannot be said of Kaufman, an admitted armed robber, that he is a person whom 'society has grievously wronged' and for whom belated liberation is little enough compensation."

97. *Kaufman* at 242.

98. *McGautha* v. *California*, 402 U.S. 183, 195–96 (1971).

99. *McGautha* at 247.

100. *Wainwright* v. *Sykes*, 433 U.S. 72 (1977).

101. Gary Peller, "In Defense of Federal Habeas Corpus Relitigation," *Harvard Civil Rights-Civil Liberties Law Review* 16:579 (1982).

102. Henry Friendly, "Is Innocence Irrelevant? Collateral Attack on Criminal Judgments," *University of Chicago Law Review* 38:142 (1970).

103. Friendly, "Innocence," p. 160.

104. Friendly, "Innocence," p. 142, 154–56.

105. Friendly, "Innocence," p. 160.

106. *Brady* v. *United States*, 397 U.S. 742 (1970); *McMann* v. *Richardson*, 397 U.S. 759 (1970); *Parker* v. *North Carolina*, 397 U.S. 790 (1970); *McMann* at 760; Richard

Michael, "The 'New Federalism and the Burger Court's Deference to the States in Federal Habeas Proceedings," *Iowa Law Review* 64:233 (1979).

107. *Brady* at 747; italics added.

108. *McMann* at 772.

109. *McGautha* at 234.

110. *McMann* at 772.

111. *McMann* at 766.

112. *Tollett* v. *Henderson*, 411 U.S. 258 (1976).

113. *Tollett* at 259–60.

114. *Tollett* at 266; *McMann* at 771.

115. *Chambers* at 240.

116. *Parker* v. *North Carolina*, 390, 790, 801 (1970).

117. *Tollett* at 267; *Lefkowitz* v. *Newsome*, 420 U.S. 283 (1975).

118. Larry Yackle, *Postconviction Remedies* (Rochester: Lawyers Cooperative, 1981), section 80, p. 321; section 102, p. 400.

119. *Miranda* v. *Arizona*, 384 U.S. 436, 457 (1966).

120. Elaine Scarry, *The Body in Pain: The Making and Unmaking of the World* (New York: Oxford University Press, 1985), p. 35.

121. Michel Foucault, *The History of Sexuality: An Introduction*, volume I (New York: Vintage, 1978 [1990]), pp. 61–62.

122. Peter Brooks, *Troubling Confessions: Speaking Guilt in Law and Literature* (Chicago: University of Chicago Press, 2000), p. 87.

123. *Stone* v. *Powell*, 428 U.S. 465 (1976).

124. *Kaufman* at 239.

125. *Stone* at 490.

126. *Stone* at 477–79.

127. *Stone* at 486.

128. *Schneckloth* at 491, n. 31; *Stone* at 489.

129. *Elkins* v. *United States*, 364 U.S. 206, 217 (1960).

130. *Rogers* v. *Richmond*, 365 U.S. 535, 540–41 (1961); Louis Lusky, *By What Right? A Commentary on the Supreme Court's Power to Revise the Constitution* (Charlottesville: Michie, 1975), p. 156.

131. *Rogers* at 544.

132. Charles Weisselberg, "Evidentiary Hearings in Federal Habeas Corpus Cases," *Brigham Young University Law Review* 1990:131, 168 (1990).

133. *Francis* v. *Henderson*, 425 U.S. 537, 539 (1976).

134. *Francis* at 541.

135. *Francis* at 542.

136. *Sykes* at 88–90.

137. *Sykes* at 87.

138. *Davis* v. *United States*, 411 U.S. 233 (1973).

139. *Murdock* v. *Memphis*, 87 U.S. 590 (1875).

140. *Sykes* at 81.

141. *Fay* at 399–426.

142. Glenn Pierce and Michael Radelet, "The Role and Consequences of the Death Penalty in American Politics," *New York University Review of Law & Social Change* 18:711 (1990–91); Sam Boyte, "Federal Habeas Corpus after *Stone* v. *Powell*: A Remedy for the Arguably Innocent?" *University of Richmond Law Review* 11:291 (1977); Alfred Hill, "The Forfeiture of Constitutional Rights in Criminal Cases," *Columbia Law Review* 78:1050 (1978); Frank Remington, "Restricting Access to Federal Habeas Corpus: Justice Sacrificed on the Alters of Expediency, Federalism and Deterrence," *New York University Review of Law & Social Change* 16:339 (1987–88).

143. Anthony Paduano and Clive A. S. Smith, "The Unconscionability of Sub-Minimum Wages Paid Appointed Counsel in Capital Cases," *Rutgers University Law Review* 43:281 (1991); Michael Mello and Donna Duffy, "Suspending Justice: The Unconstitutionality of the Proposed Six-Month Time Limit on the Filing of Habeas Corpus Petitions by State Death Row Inmates," *New York University Review of Law & Social Change* 18:451 (1990–91).

144. *Murray* v. *Giarranto*, 492 U.S. 1 (1989); *McFarland* v. *Scott*, 512 U.S. 849 (1994); Michael Mello, "Is There a Federal Constitutional Right to Counsel in Capital Postconviction Proceedings?" *Journal of Criminal Law & Criminology* 79:1065 (1989).

145. Hughes, "Sandbagging Constitutional Rights," p. 333.

146. *Rose* v. *Mitchell*, 443 U.S. 545 (1979).

147. *Rose* at 582.

CHAPTER 5

1. *Lee* v. *Mississippi*, 332 U.S. 742 (1948).

2. *Sawyer* v. *Whitley*, 505 U.S. 333, 336 (1992).

3. *Sawyer* v. *Smith*, 497 U.S. 227, 229–30 (1990).

4. *United States* v. *Carolene Products*, 304 U.S. 144, 53 (1938).

5. Richard Cortner, *A Mob Intent on Death: The NAACP and the Arkansas Riot Cases* (Middletown: Wesleyan University Press, 1988); Cortner, *The Iron Horse and the Constitution: The Railroads and the Transformation of the Fourteenth Amendment* (Westport: Greenwood, 1993); Laura Kalman, *The Strange Career of Legal Liberalism* (New Haven: Yale University Press, 1998).

6. *Escobedo* v. *Illinois*, 378 U.S. 478 (1964).

7. *Miranda* v. *Arizona*, 384 U.S. 436, 457 (1966).

8. Richard A. Michael, "The 'New' Federalism and the Burger Court's Deference to the States in Federal Habeas Proceedings," *Iowa Law Review* 64:233 (1979); *Stone* v. *Powell*, 428 U.S. 465 (1976); Henry Friendly, "Is Innocence Irrelevant?" Collateral Attack on Criminal Judgments," *University of Chicago Law Review* 38:142 (1970); Gary Peller, "In Defense of Federal Habeas Corpus Relitigation," *Harvard Civil Rights-Civil Liberties Law Review* 16:579 (1982).

9. *Wainwright* v. *Sykes*, 433 U.S. 72 (1977); Comment, "Habeas Corpus—The Supreme Court Defines the *Wainwright* v. *Sykes* 'Cause' and 'Prejudice' Standard," *Wake Forest Law Review* 19:441 (1983).

10. Larry Yackle, *Postconviction Remedies* (Rochester: Lawyers Cooperative, 1981), secs. 54 and 55. Comity derives from the law of nations. *Hilton* v. *Guyot*, 159 U.S. 113, 164 (1895).

11. Paul Bator, "Finality in Criminal Law and Federal Habeas Corpus for State Prisoners," *Harvard Law Review* 76:441 (1963); Robert Cover and T. Alexander Aleinikoff, "Dialectal Federalism: Habeas Corpus and the Court," *Yale Law Journal* 86:1035 (1977).

12. *Sykes* at 87.

13. *Sumner* v. *Mata*, 449 U.S. 539, 549–51: "A writ issued at the behest of a petitioner under [the habeas statute] 28 U.S.C. 2254 is in effect overturning either the factual or legal conclusion reached by the state-court system under the judgment of which the petitioner stands convicted, and friction is a likely result."

14. *Rose* v. *Lundy*, 455 U.S. 509 (1982).

15. *Engle* v. *Isaac*, 456 U.S. 107 (1982).

16. *Teague* v. *Lane*, 489 U.S. 288 (1989).

17. *Penry* v. *Lynaugh*, 492 U.S. 302 (1989).

18. *Sykes* at 92.

19. *Sykes* at 116.

20. *Engle* at 111–19.

21. *Engle* at 127–28.

22. *Engel* at 134; italics added.

23. *Engel* at 134.

24. *Engel* at 134–35. Why "plain error" does not apply to collateral attacks, and the adequate and independent state ground rule does, was never made explicit. The only reason can be that the former would benefit habeas petitioners, and the latter would not. Rule 12(b)(2) of the Federal Rules of Criminal Procedure defines the "cause and prejudice" standard. Under that rule, failure to follow specified procedures constitutes cause for waiver. The purpose of judicial inquiry into cause is not to "ascertain whether a waiver occurred; rather, its function [is] to determine whether a waiver should be excused."

25. The number of state prisoners more than doubled between 1981 and 1991. *Habeas Corpus in State and Federal Courts* (Williamsburg, VA: National Center for State Courts, 1994), p. 14.

26. *Schneckloth* v. *Bustamonte*, 412 U.S. 218, 263 (1973).

27. *Sanders* v. *United States*, 373 U.S. 1, 16 (1963).

28. *Kuhlmann* v. *Wilson*, 477 U.S. 436 (1986).

29. *Murray* v. *Carrier*, 477 U.S. 478 (1986).

30. *Smith* v. *Murray*, 477 U.S. 527 (1986).

31. *Herrera* v. *Collins*, 506 U.S. 390, 439 (1993); italics added.

32. *Kuhlmann* at 439–40.

33. *United States* v. *Henry*, 447 U.S. 264 (1980).

34. *Massiah* v. *United States*, 377 U.S. 201 (1964).

35. In *Sanders* v. *United States*, 373 U.S. 1, 16 (1963), the Court defined a successive petition as one that raises identical grounds as the previously rejected petition. "Even if the same ground was rejected on the merits of a prior application, it is open to the applicant to show that the ends of justice would be served by permitting the redetermination of the ground."

36. *Kuhlmann* at 446–47; *Schneckloth* v. *Bustamonte*, 412 U.S. 218 (1973).

37. *Kuhlmann* at 450.

38. *Kuhlmann* at 452.

39. *Herrera* v. *Collins*, 506 U.S. 390, 419 (1993).

40. *Herrera* at 399–400.

41. *Kuhlmann* at 454, 456; italics added.

42. Sandra Day O'Connor, "Trends in the Relationship between the Federal and State Courts from the Perspective of a State Court Judge," *William & Mary Law Review* 22:801, 815 (1981).

43. *Murray* v. *Carrier*, 477 U.S. 478, 487, quoting *Engle* at 129.

44. *Carrier* at 488.

45. *Carrier* at 492; italics added.

46. *Carrier* at 499.

47. *Carrier* at 495–96.

48. *Smith* v. *Murray*, 477 U.S. 527, 541 (1986).

49. *Linkletter* v. *Walker*, 381 U.S. 618, 641 (1965).

50. *Mapp* v. *Ohio*, 367 U.S. 643 (1961).

51. *Desist* v. *United States*, 394 U.S. 244 (1969).

52. *Mackey* v. *United States*, 401 U.S. 667 (1971).

53. *Mackey* at 675; *Desist* at 256.

54. *Teague* at 309.

55. *Mackey* at 692–93, quoting *Palko* v. *Connecticut*, 302 U.S. 319, 325 (1932).

56. *Desist* at 262.

57. *Mackey* at 687.

58. *Teague* at 316; italics in original.

59. *Penry* v. *Lynaugh*, 492 U.S. 302 (1989).

60. *Penry* at 340.

61. *Teague* at 300.

62. *Linkletter* at 629.

63. *Schneckloth* v. *Bustamonte*, 420 U.S. 283 (1973); *Stone* v. *Powell*, 428 U.S. 465 (1976); *Wainwright* v. *Sykes*, 433 U.S. 72 (1977); *Murray* v. *Carrier*, 477 U.S. 478 (1986).

64. *Teague* at 301; italics in original.

65. James Liebman, "More Than 'Slightly Retro': The Rehnquist Court's Rout of Habeas Corpus Jurisdiction in *Teague* v. *Lane*," *New York University Review of Law & Social Change* 18:537, 551 (1990–91); italics added.

66. *Teague* at 300–01.

67. *Teague* at 307, quoting *Mackey* at 692.

68. *Teague* at 314.

69. *Teague* at 311.

70. *Benton* v. *Maryland*, 395 U.S. 784 (1969).

71. *Teague* at 312.

72. *Teague* at 314; *Rose* v. *Lundy*, 455 U.S. 544 (1982).

73. Emily F. Reed, *The Penry Penalty: Capital Punishment and Offenders with Mental Retardation* (Lanham, Md.: University Press of America, 1993).

74. *Lockett* v. *Ohio*, 438 U.S. 586 (1978).

75. *Eddings* v. *Oklahoma*, 455 U.S. 104 (1982).

76. *Penry* at 315. In Texas, for a jury to impose the death penalty, it must answer "yes" to the following questions: (1) whether the conduct of the defendant that caused the death of the deceased was committed deliberately and with the reasonable expectation that the death of the deceased or another would result; (2) whether there is a probability that the defendant would commit criminal acts of violence that would constitute a continuing threat to society; and (3) if raised by the evidence, whether the conduct of the defendant in killing the deceased was unreasonable in response to the provocation, if any, by the deceased. *Penry* at 310.

77. *Jurek* v. *Texas*, 428 U.S. 262 (1976).

78. *Gregg* v. *Georgia*, 428 U.S. 153 (1976); *Proffitt* v. *Florida*, 428 U.S. 242 (1976); *Woodson* v. *North Carolina*, 428 U.S. 280 (1976).

79. *Penry* at 319.

80. *Ford* v. *Wainwright*, 477 U.S. 399 (1986), upheld the common law notion against the execution of the insane. *Ford* was decided after *Penry*'s conviction, hence for Penry to benefit from *Ford*, it would have to have been declared retroactive. O'Connor thought applying *Ford* to *Penry* would constitute a new rule.

81. *Penry* at 340.

82. *Penry* at 328.

83. *Penry* at 329.

84. *Penry* at 330.

85. *Coker* v. *Georgia*, 433 U.S. 584 (1977).

86. *Penry* at 330.

87. *Penry* at 340.

88. *Sawyer* v. *Smith*, 497 U.S. 227 (1990).

89. *Sawyer* at 234; italics added.

90. Peter Brooks, *Troubling Confessions: Speaking Guilt in Law and Literature* (Chicago: University of Chicago Press, 2000), p. 77.

91. *Atkins* v. *Virginia*, 536 U.S. 304, 338 (2002).

92. Rosemary Coombe, "Finding and Losing One's Self in the Topoi: Placing and Displacing the Postmodern Subject in Law," *Law & Society Review* 29(4):599, 600 (1995).

93. *Thompson* v. *Oklahoma*, 487 U.S. 815 (1988).

94. *Thompson* at 819.

95. *Thompson* at 859–60.

96. *Franklin* v. *Lynaugh*, 487 U.S. 164 (1988); *California* v. *Brown*, 479 U.S. 538 (1987).

97. *Thompson* at 860–61.

98. *Booth* v. *Maryland*, 482 U.S. 496 (1987).

99. *Payne* v. *Tennessee*, 501 U.S. 808 (1991).

100. *Payne* at 815–16.

101. *South Carolina* v. *Gathers*, 490 U.S. 805 (1989).

102. *Booth* at 507.

103. Michel Foucault, *The History of Sexuality: An Introduction*, volume 1 (New York: Vintage Books, 1990), p. 144.

104. *Payne* at 825.

105. Kristin Bumiller, *The Civil Rights Society: The Social Construction of Victims* (Baltimore: Johns Hopkins University Press, 1988).

106. *Kansas* v. *Hendricks*, 521 U.S. 346, 352 (1997).

107. *Arave* v. *Creech*, 507 U.S. 463 (1993).

108. *Arave* at 465.

109. *Arave* at 469.

110. *Arave* at 472; Samuel Thumma and Jeffrey Kirchmeier, "The Lexicon Has Become a Fortress: The United States Supreme Court's Use of Dictionaries," *Buffalo Law Review* 47:229 (1999); *NEA* v. *Finley*, 524 U.S. 569, 591–93 (1998).

111. *Arave* at 473.

112. *Arave* at 473–74.

113. *Estelle* v. *Smith*, 451 U.S. 454, 457–58 (1981).

114. *Hammett* v. *Texas*, 448 U.S. 725 (1980).

115. In 1995, Dr. Grigson was expelled from the American Psychiatric Association "for arriving at psychiatric diagnoses without first having examined the individuals in question." "Lawyers Call for Changes in Death Penalty in Texas" (Source: Associated Press, October 15, 2000). Aclu.org/DeathPenalty/DeathPenalty.cfm?ID=7742&c=62 (accessed January 16, 2003). Edward Lazarus, *Closed Chambers: The First Eyewitness Account of the Epic Struggles Inside the Supreme Court* (New York: Times Books, 1998), p. 151, writes that defendants received death sentences in 115 of the 124 cases in which Dr. Grigson was involved.

116. *Estelle* at 464–65.

117. *Estelle* at 465.

118. *Estelle* at 464.

119. Edward Spitzka, *Insanity: Its Classification, Diagnosis and Treatment* (New York: Arno, 1887 [1973]), p. 99.

120. Carlos MacDonald, "The Trial, Execution, Autopsy and Mental Status of Leon F. Czolgosz, Alias Fred Nieman, the Assassin of President McKinley, with a Report of the Post-Mortem Examination by Edward A. Spitzka," *American Journal of Insanity*, 58(3):26 (1901).

121. Joseph Hoffmann and William Stuntz, "Habeas After the Revolution," *Supreme Court Review* 1993: 65.

122. *Ramdass* v. *Angelone*, 530 U.S. 156 (2000).

123. *Shafer* v. *South Carolina*, 532 U.S. 36 (2001).

124. *Kelly* v. *South Carolina*, 534 U.S. 246 (2002).

125. *Kelly* at 732.

126. *Simmons* v. *South Carolina*, 512 U.S. 154 (1994).

127. *Simmons* at 156.

128. *Simmons* at 160.

129. *Simmons* at 157.

130. *Simmons* at 162.

131. *Simmons* at 163.

132. *Simmons* at 163.

133. *Simmons* at 163.

134. *Ramdass* at 159.

135. *Ramdass* at 160.

136. *Ramdass* at 171.

137. *Ramdass* at 161, 162.

138. *Ramdass* at 162.

139. *Ramdass* at 157.

140. *Ramdass* at 170.

141. *Ramdass* at 171.

142. *Ramdass* at 196.

143. *Shafer* at 39.

144. *Kelly* at 248.

145. *Kelly* at 249.

146. *Kelly* at 250.

147. *Kelly* at 250.

148. *Kelly* at 246.

149. *Kelly* at 247.

150. *Kelly* at 252.

151. Kelly at 254–55.

152. Pat O'Malley, "Risk Societies and the Government of Crime," Mark Brown and John Pratt, eds., *Dangerous Offenders: Punishment and Social Order* (London: Routledge, 2000), p. 21.

153. O'Malley, "Risk Societies and the Government of Crime," p. 21.

154. Michel Foucault, "The Dangerous Individual," Lawrence Kritzman, ed., *Politics, Philosophy, Culture: Interviews and Other Writings, 1977–1984* (London: Routledge, 1998).

155. David Garland, *Punishment and Modern Society: A Study in Social Theory* (Chicago: University of Chicago Press, 1990), p. 265.

156. Timothy Kaufman-Osborn, "What the Law Must Not Hear: On Capital Punishment and the Voice of Pain," Austin Sarat, ed., *Pain, Death, and the Law* (Ann

Arbor: University of Michigan Press, 2001), p. 78; Robert Cover, "The Bonds of Constitutional Interpretation: Of the Word, the Deed, and the Role," *Georgia Law Review* 20:815 (1985–1986).

157. Jordan Steiker, "Restructuring Post-Conviction Review of Federal Constitutional Claims Raised by State Prisoners: Confronting the New Face of Excessive Proceduralism," *University of Chicago Legal Forum* 1998: 315, 316 (1998).

158. Kaufman-Osborn, "What the Law Must Not Hear," p. 85.

CHAPTER 6

1. The Antiterrorism and Effective Death Penalty Act of 1996, Pub. L. 104–132, passed the Senate by a vote of 91–8 (Republicans: 51–1; Democrats: 40–7). The House of Representatives passed the bill 293–133 (Republicans: 186–46; Democrats: 105–86). *Congressional Quarterly Weekly Report*, April 20, 1996, pp. 1076, 1082.

2. Holly Idelson, "Republican Crime Bills Head for House Floor," *Congressional Quarterly Weekly Report*, February 4, 1995, p. 367; Idelson, "Anti-Terrorist Measure Heads to House Floor," *Congressional Quarterly Weekly Report*, June 24, 1995, p. 1848.

3. Quoted in Alexander Rundlet, "Opting for Death: State Responses to the AEDPA's Opt-in Provisions and the Need for a Right to Post-Conviction Counsel," *University of Pennsylvania Journal of Constitutional Law* 1:661, 702, n. 227 (1999).

4. Representative Henry Hyde framed the habeas corpus-terrorism issue in partisan terms. He said that the Democrats "are very concerned about the rights of the accused. We [the Republicans] are very concerned about the rights of society and the victim." Holly Idelson, "House GOP Crime Bills Win Easy Passage," *Congressional Quarterly Weekly Report*, February 11, 1995, p. 457.

5. David Cole and James X. Dempsey, *Terrorism and the Constitution: Sacrificing Civil Liberties in the Name of National Security* (New York: New Press, 2002), p. 114.

6. See the remarks of Senators Biden and Hatch in Thomas Martin, "The Comprehensive Terrorism Prevention Act of 1995," *Seton Hall Legislative Journal* 20:201, 215, n. 68 (1996).

7. Karen Marshall, "Finding Time for Federal Habeas Corpus: *Carey* v. *Saffold*," *University of Akron Law Review* 37:549, 560, n. 61 (2004). *Stewart* v. *Martinez-Villareal*, 523 U.S. 627, 647–48 (1998), focuses on the problem of successive petitions and the ramifications for federal-state relations.

8. *Martinez-Villareal* at 644.

9. *McCleskey* v. *Zant*, 499 U.S. 467, 493 (1991). Congress defines "abuse of the writ" as follows: "A second or successive petition may be dismissed if the judge finds that it fails to allege new or different grounds for relief and the prior determination was on the merits or, if new and different grounds are alleged, the judge finds that the failure of the petitioner to assert those grounds in a prior petition constituted an abuse of the writ." 28 U.S.C. 2254 Rule 9(b).

10. Vivian Berger, "Justice Delayed or Justice Denied?—A Comment on Recent

Proposals to Reform Death Penalty Habeas Corpus," *Columbia University Law Review* 90:1665, 1674, n. 62 (1990).

11. "Habeas Corpus Reform." Hearings Before the Committee of the Judiciary, United States Senate, 101st Congress, 1st and 2d sessions (Nov. 8, 1989; Feb. 21, 1990); Lewis Powell, "Capital Punishment," *Harvard Law Review* 102:1035 (1988–1989).

12. Rundlet, "Opting for Death," p. 696; *Saffle* v. *Parks*, 494 U.S. 484 (1990); *Butler* v. *McKellar*, 494 U.S. 407 (1990); Cary Federman, "Who Has the Body? The Paths to Habeas Corpus Reform," *The Prison Journal*, 84(3): 317 (2004).

13. Rundlet, "Opting for Death," p. 702.

14. *Artuz* v. *Bennett*, 531 U.S. 4 (2000); *Carey* v. *Saffold*, 536 U.S. 214 (2002).

15. *Castro* v. *U.S.*, 540 U.S. 375 (2003), a federal habeas corpus case dealing with successive petitions.

16. Burke Kappler, "Small Favors: Chapter 154 of the Antiterrorism and Effective Death Penalty Act, the States, and the Right to Counsel," *Journal of Criminal Law and Criminology* (2000), p. 469.

17. Cristina Stummer, "To Be or Not to Be: Opt-In Status under the Antiterrorism and Effective Death Penalty Act," *Vermont Law Review* 25:603, 608 (2001).

18. Rundlet, "Opting for Death," p. 688.

19. Rundlet, "Opting for Death," p. 699.

20. *Williams* v. *Taylor*, 529 U.S. 420, 435 (2000).

21. Marshall Hartmann and Jeanette Nyden, "Habeas Corpus and the New Federalism After the Anti-Terrorism and Effective Death Penalty Act of 1996," *The John Marshall Law Review* 30(2):337, 355–56 (1997).

22. *Bell* v. *Cone*, 535 U.S. 685, 694 (2002).

23. *Tyler* v. *Cain*, 533 U.S. 656 (2001).

24. *Tyler* at 661–62.

25. *O'Sullivan* v. *Boerckel*, 526 U.S. 838 (1999).

26. *Williams* v. *Taylor*, 529 U.S. 362, 402–03 (2000).

27. Justice Stevens, in *Williams* v. *Taylor*, 529 U.S. 362, 379 (2000), writes that despite the deference requirement, "A construction of AEDPA that would require the federal courts to cede this authority to the courts of the States would be inconsistent with the practice that federal judges traditionally followed in discharging their duties under Article III of the Constitution."

28. *Williams* v. Taylor, 529 U.S. 420, 435, 436 (2000).

29. *Duncan* v. *Walker*, 533 U.S. 167, 168 (2001); *Williams* v. *Taylor*, 529 U.S. 420, 435, 436.

30. *Woodford* v. *Garceau*, 538 U.S. 202, 206 (2003).

31. *Miller-El* v. *Cockrell*, 537 U.S. 322, 326 (2003).

32. *Martinez-Villareal* at 648 (1998).

33. *Rose* v. *Lundy*, 455 U.S. 509, 510, 520 (1982); *Brecht* v. *Abrahamson*, 507 U.S. 619, 623 (1993); Richard Pierce, "The Due Process Counterrevolution of the 1990s? *Columbia Law Review* 90:1973 (1996); Sharad Sushil Khandelwal, "The Path to

Habeas Corpus Narrows: Interpreting 28 U.S.C. section 2254(d)(1)," *Michigan Law Review* 96:434 (1997). It is, however, unclear if the AEDPA includes all restrictive Supreme Court cases since *Wainwright* v. *Sykes.*

34. Congress codified the Supreme Court's exhaustion rule in *Ex parte Hawk,* 321 U.S. 114 (1944) and the abuse of the writ doctrine from *Sanders* v. *U.S.,* 373 U.S. 1 (1963). Congress extended the right to counsel for indigent capital defendants using habeas corpus to get review in federal courts. The Supreme Court has not been as generous. Anti-Drug Abuse Act of 1988, Pub.L. No. 100–690, 102 Stat. 4181 (1988); *Murray* v. *Giarratano,* 492 U.S. 1 (1989). In *Miller* v. *Fenton,* 474 U.S. 104, 111 (1985), the Supreme Court admitted that a previous version of section 2254, governing state habeas applicants, "was an almost verbatim codification of the standards delineated in *Townsend* v. *Sain,* for determining when a district court must hold an evidentiary hearing before acting on a habeas petition." For a list of congressional codifications of post-*Wainwright* v. *Sykes* cases, see Powell, "Capital Punishment," p. 1042, n. 44.

35. Larry Yackle, "A Primer on the New Habeas Statute," *Buffalo Law Review* 44:381 (1996); Mark Tushnet, "'The King of France with Forty Thousand Men': *Felker* v. *Turpin* and the Supreme Court's Deliberative Processes," *Supreme Court Review* (1996), p. 163; Andrea Kochan, "The Antiterrorism and Effective Death Penalty Act of 1996: Habeas Corpus Reform?" *Journal of Urban and Contemporary Law* 52:399 (1997).

36. Roberta Smith, "America Tries to Come to Terms with Terrorism: The United States' Anti-Terrorism and Effective Death Penalty Act of 1996 v. British Anti-Terrorism Law and International Response," *Cardozo Journal of International and Comparative Law* 5:249, 269 (1997).

37. Peter Sessions, "Swift Justice? Imposing a Statute of Limitations on the Federal Habeas Corpus Petitions of State Prisoners," *Southern California Law Review* 70:1515, 1542, n. 155 (1997).

38. Presumably, the U.S.A. Patriot Act 2001 rectifies AEDPA's oversights. Regarding judicial activism, see Philip Kurland, *Politics, the Constitution, and the Warren Court* (Chicago: University of Chicago Press, 1970); Herbert Wechsler, "Toward Neutral Principles of Constitutional Law," *Harvard Law Review* 73:1 (1959); Robert Bork, *The Tempting of America: The Political Seduction of the Law* (New York: Free Press, 1997), p. 78; Phillip Cooper, *Hard Judicial Choices: Federal District Court Judges and State and Local Officials* (New York: Oxford University Press, 1998); Donald Horowitz, *The Courts and Social Policy* (Washington, D.C.: Brookings Institution, 1977); Malcolm Feeley and Edward Rubin, *Judicial Policy Making and the Modern State: How the Courts Reformed America's Prisons* (Cambridge: Cambridge University Press, 1998).

39. Mark Tushnet and Larry Yackle, "Symbolic Statutes and Real Laws: The Pathologies of the Antiterrorism and Effective Death Penalty Act and the Prison Litigation Reform Act," *Duke Law Journal* 47:1 (1997); Lord Windlesham, *Politics, Punishment, and Populism* (New York: Oxford University Press, 1998); Michael Vitiello, "Three Strikes: Can We Return to Rationality?" *Journal of Criminal Law and Criminology* 87:395 (1997); Theodore Caplow and Jonathan Simon, "Understanding Prison

Policy and Population Trends," Michael Tonry and Joan Petersilia, eds., *Prisons* (Chicago: University of Chicago Press, 1999).

40. Ann Chih Lin, "The Troubled Success of Crime Policy," Margaret Weir, ed., *The Social Divide: Political Parties and the Future of Activist Government* (Washington, D.C.: Brookings Institution, 1998), p. 353.

41. The AEDPA seems to have eliminated *Teague* v. *Lane's* two exceptions for considering retroactivity. The AEDPA most likely prevents federal courts from considering retroactive application of a constitutional rule. As bad as the *Teague* decision was for state prisoners, this situation seems to be worse. Alan Chen, "Shadow Law: Reasonable Unreasonableness, Habeas Theory, and the Nature of Legal Rules," *Buffalo Criminal Law Review* 2:535 (1999). Justice Stevens' majority opinion in *Williams* v. *Taylor,* 529 U.S. 362, 379–90 (2000) suggests that AEDPA codified *Teague's* non-retroactivity ruling.

42. David Garland, *The Culture of Control: Crime and Social Order in Contemporary Society* (Chicago: University of Chicago Press, 2001), p. 102; Lorna A. Rhodes, *Total Confinement: Madness and Reason in the Maximum Security Prison* (Berkeley: University of California Press, 2004), chapter 2; Mark Seltzer, *Serial Killers: Death and Life in America's Wound Culture* (New York: Routledge, 1998); Jeffroy Clymer, "The 1886 Chicago Haymarket Bombing and the Rhetoric of Terrorism in America," *The Yale Journal of Criticism* 15(2):315 (2002); Ryan Simmons, "What Is a Terrorist? Contemporary Authorship, the Unabomber, and *Mao II,*" *Modern Fiction Studies* 45(3): 675 (1999); Jasbir Puar and Amit Rai, "Monster, Terrorist, Fag: The War on Terrorism and the Production of Docile Bodies," *Social Text* 20(3): 117 (2002).

43. *Zadvydas* v. *Davis,* 533 U.S. 678, 714 (2001).

44. Title 2 of the AEDPA is called "Justice for Victims." On the role of the victim in criminal law, Markus Dirk Dubber, "The Victim in American Penal Law: A Systematic Overview," *Buffalo Criminal Law Review* 3:3 (1999), and Cornelius Prittwitz," The Resurrection of the Victim in Penal Theory," *Buffalo Criminal Law Review* 3:109 (1999).

45. *Woodford* v. *Garceau,* 538 U.S. 202, 208 (2003); *Lindh* v. *Murphy,* 521 U.S. 320 (1996). See the conflicting narrative accounts of *Royall's* legacy in *O'Sullivan* v. *Boerckel,* 526 U.S. 838 (1999), by Justice O'Connor (at 842 ff.) in the majority, and Justice Stevens (at 850 ff.) in the dissent.

46. Stephen Bright, "Is Fairness Irrelevant? The Evisceration of Federal Habeas Corpus Review and Limits on the Ability of State Courts to Protect Fundamental Rights," *Washington and Lee Law Review* 54:1 (1997).

47. *Woodford* v. *Garceau* at 204; *Vasquez* v. *Hillery,* 474 U.S. 254, 255 (1986); *Bell* v. *Cone* at 690, 698.

48. Isaac Balbus, *The Dialectics of Legal Repression: Black Rebels before the American Criminal Courts* (New York: Russell Sage Foundation, 1973), p. 12.

49. *Darnel's Case,* or the case of the Five Knights (1627), began when Charles I forced the knights to lend him money. They refused and were held without bail. The knights unsuccessfully petitioned the King's Bench for habeas corpus. When Parlia-

ment was recalled, it overturned the precedent, and in 1641, passed the Habeas Corpus Act of 1641, which limited the king's power to arbitrarily arrest his own subjects. J. A. Guy, "The Origins of the Petition of Right Reconsidered," *The Historical Journal* 25(2):289 (1982).

50. *The Federalist Papers*, Clinton Rossiter, ed. (New York: New American Library, 1961), no. 83, p. 499; Mark Neely Jr., *The Fate of Liberty: Abraham Lincoln and Civil Liberties* (New York: Oxford University Press, 1991), pp. 120–24.

51. *Ex parte Bollman*, 4 Cranch 75 (1807); *Luther v. Borden*, 48 U.S. 1 (1849).

52. "Report to the Attorney General on Federal Habeas Corpus Review of State Judgments," Office of Legal Policy, Department of Justice (May 27, 1988).

53. *Sumner v. Mata*, 449 U.S. 539 (1981).

54. *Ex parte Milligan*, 71 U.S. 2 (1866).

55. *Hirota v. MacArthur*, 338 U.S. 197, 201 (1948).

56. *Moore v. Dempsey*, 281 U.S. 86 (1923); *Townsend v. Sain*, 373 U.S. 293 (1963); *Gideon v. Wainwright*, 372 U.S. 335 (1963).

57. *Ex parte Milligan*, 71 U.S. 2 (1866); Kenneth Stampp, "The *Milligan* Case and the Election of 1864 in Indiana," *The Mississippi Valley Historical Review* 31(1): 41 (1944).

58. But *Ex parte Merryman*, 17 F.Cas. 144 (1861), is not.

59. *INS v. St. Cyr*, 533 U.S. 289, 301 (2001).

60. Military tribunals were used throughout the Civil War, in thousands of instances. Neely, *The Fate of Liberty*, pp. 176–77; Sheldon Glueck, "By What Tribunal Shall War Offenders Be Tried?" *University of Nebraska Law Review* 24(2):143 (1945); Harold Kaplan, "Constitutional Limitations on Trials by Military Commissions," *University of Pennsylvania Law Review* 92(2):119 (1943–1944); Kaplan, "Constitutional Limitations on Trials by Military Commissions," *University of Pennsylvania Law Review* 92(2):272 (1943–1944); F. Granville Munson, "The Arguments in the Saboteur Trial," *University of Pennsylvania Law Review* 91:239 (1942–1943).

61. Act of June 15, 1917, ch. 30, title I (sec. 3) and title XII, 40 Stat. 219, amended by Act of May 16, 1918, ch. 75, 40 Stat. 553–54, reenacted by Act of March 3, 1921, chapter 136, 41 Stat 1539, current version codified at 18 U.S.C. section 2388; Trading with the Enemy Act, Act of October 6, 1917, chapter 106, 40 Stat. 411 (1917). On Wilson's seizure of property, which Congress conferred on him, see *Youngstown Sheet & Tube Co. v. Sawyer*, 343 U.S. 579, 611 (1952); *Schenck v. U.S.*, 249 U.S. 47 (1919); *Masses Publishing Co. v. Patten*, 244 Fed. 535 (S.D.N.Y. 1917); *Debs v. U.S.*, 249 U.S. 211 (1919); William Preston, *Aliens and Dissenters: Federal Suppression of Radicals, 1903–1933* (New York: Harper Torchbooks, 1963); Cedric Larson and James Mock, "The Lost Files of the Creel Committee of 1917–19," *The Public Opinion Quarterly*, 22(2):262 (1942); Howard C. Hill, "The Americanization Movement," *The American Journal of Sociology*, 24(6):609 (1919).

62. David Rabban, *Free Speech in Its Forgotten Years* (New York: Cambridge University Press, 1997), chapter 7; Thomas Carroll, "Freedom of Speech and of the Press in War Time: The Espionage Act," *Michigan Law Review* 17(8): 621 (1918–1919);

Robert Cushman, "Some Constitutional Problems of Civil Liberty," *Boston University Law Review* 23:335 (1943); Kenneth O'Reilly, "The Roosevelt Administration and Black America: Federal Surveillance Policy and Civil Rights During the New Deal and World War II Years," *Phylon* 48(1):12 (1987).

63. Zechariah Chafee, *Free Speech in the United States* (Cambridge: Harvard University Press, 1942), pp. 51–52.

64. David Williams, "The Bureau of Investigation and Its Critics, 1919–1921: The Origin of Federal Political Surveillance," *The Journal of American History* 68(3):560 (1981); Robert Ward, "The Origin and Activities of the National Security League, 1914–1919," *The Mississippi Valley Historical Review* 47(1):51 (1960); Sidney Fine, "Anarchism and the Assassination of McKinley," *The American Historical Review* 60(4):777; Charles McCormick, *Seeing Reds: Federal Surveillance of Radicals in the Pittsburgh Mill District, 1917–1921* (Pittsburgh: University of Pittsburgh Press, 1990); *Ex parte Vallandigham*, 68 U.S. 243 (1864); James G. Randall, *Constitutional Problems under Lincoln* (Urbana: University of Illinois Press, 1997); Neely, *The Fate of Liberty*, pp. 196–97; Frank Klement, *The Limits of Dissent: Clement L. Vallandigham & the Civil War* (New York: Fordham University Press, 1998).

65. Kathleen Kennedy, *Disloyal Mothers and Scurrilous Citizens: Women and Subversion During World War I* (Bloomington: Indiana University Press, 1999), p. xv; W. A. Dunning, "Disloyalty in Two Wars," *The American Historical Review* 24(4):625 (1919).

66. James W. Garner, "Treatment of Enemy Aliens," *The American Journal of International Law*," 12:27 (1918); Robert M. W. Kempner, "The Enemy Alien Problem in the Present War," *The American Journal of International Law* 34(3):443 (1940); Edmund Morgan, "Court-Martial Jurisdiction Over Non-Military Personnel Under the Articles of War," *Minnesota Law Review* 4(2):79 (1919–1920); Edwin Borchard, "The Right of Alien Enemies to Sue in Our Courts," *Yale Law Journal* 27:104 (1917–1918); John Higham, *Strangers in the Land: Patterns of American Nativism, 1860–1925* (New York: Atheneum, 1971).

67. Quoted in Paul Murphy, *World War I and the Origin of Civil Liberties in the United States* (New York: Norton, 1979), p. 52. Donald Johnson, "Wilson, Burleson, and Censorship in the First World War," *The Journal of Southern History* 28:46 (1962); J. Malcolm Smith and Cornelius P. Cotter, "Freedom and Authority in the Amphibial State," *Midwest Journal of Political Science* 1(1):40, 41–43 (1957).

68. W. C. Hunter, "Alien Rights in the United States During Wartime," *Michigan Law Review* 17:33, 39 (1918–1919).

69. Carl Brent Swisher, "Civil Liberties in War Time," *Political Science Quarterly* 55:321, 326 (1940).

70. Harry Scheiber, *The Wilson Administration and Civil Liberties, 1917–1921* (Ithaca: Cornell University Press, 1960), appendix.

71. Emma Goldman, *My Further Disillusionment in Russia* (New York: Doubelday, 1924); Alice Wexler, *Emma Goldman in Exile: From the Russian Revolution to the Spanish Civil War* (Boston: Beacon, 1989).

72. *Schenck* v. *U.S.*, 249 U.S. 47 (1919); *Abrams* v. *U.S.*, 250 U.S. 616 (1919) *Debs* v. *U.S.*, 249 U.S. 211 (1919).

73. Office of the High Commissioner for Human Rights: http://www.unhchr.ch/html/menu3/b/91.htm.

74. An Act Respecting Alien Enemies, section 1, 1 Stat. 577 (Approved July 6, 1798); Marshall Smesler, "George Washington and the Alien and Sedition Acts," *The American Historical Review* 59(2):322 (1954).

75. Edwin M. Borchard, "The Right of Alien Enemies to Sue in Our Courts," *Yale Law Journal* 27:104, 108 (1917–1918); Robert Wilson, "Treatment of Civilian Alien Enemies," *The American Journal of International Law* 37(1):30 (1943).

76. Military commissions do not exercise judicial power under the meaning of Article III, section 2, which could restrict applications for habeas corpus. *Hirota* v. *MacArthur*, 338 U.S. 197, 200 (1948). W. C. Hunter writes that the only case to come before the courts questioning the constitutionality of Wilson's proclamation under the Alien Act was on a petition for habeas corpus. Hunter, "Alien Rights in the United States," p. 41; *Johnson* v. *Eisentrager*, 339 U.S. 763 (1950); *Rasul* v. *Bush*, 124 S.Ct. 2686 (2004).

77. Gerald Neuman, "Habeas Corpus, Executive Detention, and the Removal of Aliens," *Columbia Law Review* 98:961, 994 (1998); Burrus Carnahan, "Lincoln, Lieber and the Laws of War: The Origins and Limits of the Principle of Military Necessity," *The American Journal of International Law* 92(2):213 (1998).

78. *Ex parte Milligan*, 71 U.S. 2, 47 (1866).

79. Jennifer Elsea, "Detention of American Citizens as Enemy Combatants." CRS Report for Congress (updated March 15, 2004), http://www.fas.org/irp/crs/RL31724.pdf (accessed October 19, 2004).

80. Robert Cushman, "The Case of the Nazi Saboteurs," *The American Political Science Review* 36(6):1082 (1942); Jonathan Turley, "Tribunals and Tribulations: The Antithetical Elements of Military Governance in a Madisonian Democracy," *George Washington Law Review* 70: 649, 736 (2002); Louis Fisher, *Nazi Saboteurs on Trial: A Military Tribunal and American Law* (Lawrence: University of Kansas Press, 2003).

81. Jennifer Elsea, "Terrorism and the Law of War: Trying Terrorists as War Criminals before Military Commissions." CRS Report for Congress, http://www.fpc.state.gov/documents/organization/7951.pdf (accessed October 8, 2004); Charles Barber, "Trial of Unlawful Enemy Combatants," *Cornell Law Quarterly* 29:53, 70 ff. (1943–1944).

82. Louis Fisher, "Military Tribunals: The *Quirin* Precedent." CRS Report for Congress, p. 5, www.fas.org/irp/crs/RC31340.pdf (accessed October 8, 2004).

83. The proclamation can be found at 7 Fed. Reg. 5101 (1942).

84. The Court issued a per curiam opinion upholding the government's case on July 31, 1942, and in October published its opinion. Fisher, "Military Tribunals: The *Quirin* Precedent," p. 12.

85. *Ex parte Quirin* 317 U.S. 1, 31 (1942); Cushman, "The Case of the Nazi Saboteurs," p. 1086.

86. Harold Hongju Koh, "The Case against Military Commissions," *The American Journal of International Law* 96(2):337, 340 (2002).

87. *Ex parte Quirin* at 29.

88. *Ex parte Quirin* at 25, 45. According to Turley, "Tribunals and Tribulations," the Chief Justice, in a private letter, wrote: "I distinguish Milligan on the ground that, whether or not Milligan violated the law of war, the petitioners clearly did," p. 740.

89. *Ex parte Quirin* at 26, 27.

90. In *Ex parte Vallandigham*, a Civil War case, the Supreme Court rejected Clement L. Vallandigham's claim that the Court had jurisdiction to review the decisions of military tribunals during the Civil War. The Court upheld the arrest of the Democratic politician for antiwar speeches during the Civil War on the ground that the president had the authority by the nature of his executive position during wartime to arrest Vallandigham.

91. Elsea, "Detention of American Citizens," p. 9.

92. Jennifer Elsea, "Treatment of 'Battlefield Detainees' in the War on Terrorism." CRS Report for Congress (updated September 17, 2003), http://www.fas.org/irp/crs/RL31367.pdf.

93. According to Fisher, "Military Tribunals: The *Quirin* Precedent," p. 12, Stone worried about the Court's reputation once the real facts of the case became known. "If the decision should be in their favor it would leave the present Court in the unenviable position of having stood by and allowed six to go to their death without making it plain to all concerned—including the President—that it had left undecided a question on which counsel strongly relied to secure petitioners' liberty."

94. Turley, "Tribunals and Tribulations," p. 738.

95. Turley, "Tribunals and Tribulations: The Antithetical Elements of Military Governance in a Madisonian Democracy," p. 738; Michael Dobbs, *Saboteurs: The Nazi Raid on America* (New York: Knopf, 2004).

96. *Johnson v. Eisentrager*, 339 U.S. 763, 771 (1950).

97. The Constitution Project, "Report on Post-9/11 Detentions," http://www.watchingjustice.org/pub/doc_286/Const%20Proj.pdf (accessed September 24, 2004); "The Road to Abu Ghraib," Human Rights Watch, http://www.hrw.org/reports/2004/usa0604 (accessed September 24, 2004); Office of the United Nations High Commissioner for Human Rights, "Convention against Torture and Other Cruel, Inhuman or Degrading Treatment or Punishment (http://www.unhchr.ch/html/menu3/b/h_cat39.htm); Tim Golden, "After Terror: A Secret Rewriting of Military Law," *The New York Times*, October 24, 2004, A1; Tim Golden, "Administration Officials Split over Stalled Military Tribunals," *The New York Times*, October 25, 2004, A1.

98. A. Wigfall Green, "The Military Commission," *The American Journal of International Law* 42(4):832 (1948).

99. Joan Fitzpatrick, "Jurisdiction of Military Commissions and the Ambiguous War on Terrorism," *The American Journal of International Law* 96(2):345; Neal Katyal and Laurence Tribe, "Waging War, Deciding Guilt: Trying the Military Tribunals," *Yale Law Journal* 111:1259 (2002).

100. *Youngstown Sheet & Tube Co.* v. *Sawyer*, 343 U.S. 579 (1952); *Home Building & Loan Association* v. *Blaisdell*, 290 U.S. 398 (1934); Clinton Rossiter, *Constitutional Dictatorship* (New York: Harcourt, Brace, and World, 1963); Stephen Vladeck, "The Detention Power," *Yale Law and Policy Review* 22:153, 164 (2004).

101. Harold Hongju Koh, *The National Security Constitution: Sharing Power After the Iran-Contra Affair* (New Haven: Yale University Press, 1990), chapter 5.

102. *Knauff* v. *Shaughnessy*, 338 U.S. 537, 551 (1950).

103. *Hamdi* v. *Rumsfeld*, 316 F.3d 450, 459 (4th Cir. 2003). This case is known as *Hamdi* III. *Hamdi* v. *Rumsfeld*, 294 F.3d 598 (4th Cir.2002) ("*Hamdi* I") and *Hamdi* v. *Rumsfeld*, 296 F.3d 278 (4th Cir.2002) ("*Hamdi* II").

104. Authorization for Use of Military Force, Pub.L.No. 107–40, 115 Stat. 224 (Sept. 18, 2001).

105. The Department of Defense's Military Order can be found at http://www.defenselink.mil/news/Mar2002/d20020321ord.pdf.

106. *Hamdi* III at 459.

107. *Hamdi* III at 463.

108. *Hamdi* III at 463.

109. *Youngstown*, pp. 636–38.

110. Act of March 21, 1942, Pub. L. No. 77–503, ch. 191, 56 Stat. 173 did not officially authorize President Roosevelt's detention order, though it criminalized disobedience of the order. The act of March 21, 1943, was repealed by the Act of June 25, 1948, Pub. L. No. 80–772, ch. 645, sec. 21, 62 Stat. 683, 868. *Hirabayashi* v. *U.S.*, 320 U.S. 81 (1943); *Yasui* v. *U.S.*, 320 U.S. 115 (1943); *Korematsu* v. *U.S.*, 323 U.S. 214 (1944); and *Ex parte Endo*, 323 U.S. 283 (1944); Maisie Conrat, *Executive Order 9066: The Internment of 111,000 Japanese Americans* (California Historical Society, 1972); Greg Robinson, *By Order of the President: FDR and the Internment of Japanese Americans* (Cambridge: Harvard University Press, 2003).

111. *Hamdi* v. *Rumsfeld*, 124 S. Ct. 2633, 2639 (2004).

112. *Hamdi* v. *Rumsfeld* at 2639.

113. *Hamdi* v. *Rumsfeld* at 2640.

114. Athan Theoharis, "The Truman Administration and the Decline of Civil Liberties: The FBI's Success in Securing Authorization for a Preventive Detention Program," *The Journal of American History* 64(4):1010, 1021 (1978).

115. Richard Longaker, "Emergency Detention: The Generation Gap, 1950–1971," *The Western Political Quarterly* 27(3):395, 399 (1974); Cornelius Cotter and J. Malcolm Smith, "An American Paradox: The Emergency Detention Act of 1950," *The Journal of Politics* 19(1):20 (1957).

116. Legislative History to 18 U.S.C. section 4001, P.L. 92–128 (House Report No. 92–116, Senate Report No. 92–304, Congressional Record, vol. 117 (1971)). Passed the House of Representatives, September 14, 1971, the Senate, September 16, 1971, http://www.cwsl.edu/content/benner/18USC4001LegislativeHistory.pdf (accessed October 8, 2004).

117. *Hamdi* v. *Rumsfeld* at 2643; Neil Lewis, "Guantanamo Prisoners Getting

Their Day, but Hardly in Court," *The New York Times*, November 8, 2004, p. A1.

118. *Hamdi* v. *Rumsfeld* at 2650.

119. *Hamdi* v . *Rumsfeld* at 2643.

120. *Hamdi* v . *Rumsfeld* at 2647.

121. Terrorists, both foreign and domestic, including foreign leaders, have been tried by federal courts. *U.S.* v. *McVeigh*, 153 F.3d 1166 (1998); *U.S.* v. *McVeigh*, 157 F.3d 809 (1998); *U.S.* v. *McVeigh*, 9 Fed. Appx. 980 (10th Cir. 2001); *United States of America* v. *John Lindh*, plea agreement in the United States District Court for the Eastern District of Virginia (http://news.findlaw.com/hdocs/docs/lindh/uslindh71502pleaag. pdf); *United States of America* v. *Salameh*, 261 F.3d 271 (2001); *U.S.* v. *Noreiga*, 683 F. Supp. 1373 (S.D. Fla. 1988); *U.S.* v. *Moussaoui*, 382 F.3d 452 (2004).

122. *Hamdi* v. *Rumsfeld* at 2672.

123. Antonin Scalia, *A Matter of Interpretation: Federal Courts and the Law* (Princeton: Princeton University Press, 1998); *Arizona* v. *Evans*, 480 U.S. 321 (1987); David Sklansky, "The Fourth Amendment and Common Law," *Columbia Law Review* 100:1739 (2000).

124. James Liebman, Jeffrey Fagan, and Valerie West, "A Broken System: Error Rates in Capital Cases, 1973–1995," http://www2.law.columbia.edu/instructionalservices/liebman/; James Liebman, Jeffrey Fagan, Valerie West, Andrew Gelman, Garth Davies, and Alexander Kiss, "A Broken System Part II: Why There Is So Much Error in Capital Cases and What Can Be Done about It," http://www2.law.columbia.edu/brokensystem2/index2.html.

125. *Williams* v. *Taylor*, 529 U.S. 362, 375 (2000).

126. *Sunal* v. *Large*, 332 U.S. 174 (1947).

127. *Harris* v. *Nelson*, 394 U.S. 286, 291 (1969).

128. *Rasul* v. *Bush*, 124 S. Ct. 2686, 2690 (2004).

129. Stephen Vladeck, "A Small Problem of Precedent: 18 U.S.C. 4001(a) and the Detention of U.S. Citizen 'Enemy Combatants,'" *Yale Law Journal* 112:961 (2003).

130. *Eisentrager* at 763.

131. *Eisentrager* at 775.

132. *Rasul* v. *Bush* at 2693.

133. *Rasul* v. *Bush* at 2688.

134. Habeas Corpus Act of 1679, paragraph XII (31 Car. 2, c. 2, 27 May 1679); Peter Linebaugh and Marcus Rediker, *The Many-Headed Hydra: Sailors, Slaves, Commoners, and the Hidden History of the Revolutionary Atlantic* (Boston: Beacon, 2001); Harold Hongju Koh, "America's Offshore Refugee Camps," *University of Richmond Law Review* 29:139 (1994–1995).

135. Brief of Amici Curiae Bipartisan Coalition of National and International Nongovernmental Organizations in Support of Petitioners (*Rasul* v. *Bush*), p. 8 (n. 4), http://www.jenner.com/files/tbl_s69NewsDocumentOrder/FileUpload500/81/AmiciCuriae_Bipartisan_Coalition_National_International_%20Non_Govt_Org.pdf.

136. Brief of Amici Curiae Bipartisan Coalition (*Rasul* v. *Bush*), p. 13.

137. *Ex parte McCardle*, 73 U.S. 318, 326 (1868).

138. *Rasul* v. *Bush* at 2696.

139. *Rasul* v. *Bush* at 2694; *Eisentrager* at 768.

140. *Rasul* v. *Bush* at 2706.

141. *Hamdi* v. *Rumsfeld* at 2658 ff.

142. *Rasul* v. *Bush* at 2690.

143. *Al Odah* v. *United States of America*, 321 F.3d 1134 (2003); *Hirota* v. *MacArthur*, 338 U.S. 197 (1948).

144. *Padilla* v. *Rumsfeld*, 124 S.Ct. 2711, 2729–30 (2004).

145. *Hamdi* v. *Rumsfeld* at 2651.

146. *Herrera* v. *Collins*, 506 U.S. 390, 437 (1993).

147. *Fay* v. *Noia*, 372 U.S. 391, 400 (1963).

148. *Fay* at 401–02.

149. Rubin Carter, "Keynote Address," *Santa Clara Law Review* 35:425, 430 (1994–1995).

CHAPTER 7

1. *McNeil* v. *Wisconsin*, 501 U.S.171, 177 (1991).

2. *Moran* v. *Burbine*, 475 U.S. 412, 436 (1986).

3. *Callins* v. *Collins*, 510 U.S. 1141, 1142–43, 1145 (1991).

4. William Wiecek, *The Sources of Antislavery Constitutionalism in America, 1760–1848* (Ithaca: Cornell University Press, 1977), p. 157, n. 24.

5. *Coleman* v. *Thompson*, 511 U.S. 722, 726 (1991).

6. *Brown* v. *Allen*, 344 U.S. 443, 588 (1953).

7. *Coleman* at 750.

8. *Coleman* at 738–39.

9. *Coleman* at 758.

10. *Coleman* at 758.

11. *Coleman* at 758–59.

12. *Coleman* at 738, 749.

13. *Carter* v. *Rafferty*, 781 F.2d 993, 995 (1986).

14. Peter Brooks, "The Law as Narrative and Rhetoric," Peter Brooks and Paul Gewirtz, eds., *Law's Stories: Narrative and Rhetoric in the Law* (New Haven: Yale University Press, 1996), p. 19.

15. Marie-Christine Leps, *Apprehending the Criminal: The Production of Deviance in Nineteenth-Century Discourse* (Durham: Duke University Press, 1992), p. 56.

16. Catherine MacKinnon, "Law's Stories as Reality and Politics," Brooks and Gewirtz, eds., *Law's Stories*, p. 233.

17. *Foster* v. *Florida*, 123 S.Ct. 470, 471 (2002).

18. *Townsend* v. *Sain*, 372 U.S. 293, 312 (1963).

Index

Abelman v. *Booth*, ix
Abraham, Henry, 15
Act Respecting Alien Enemies,
    169–170, 180
Adams, John, 169
Adamson v. *California*, 83, 97, 113
Ad Hoc Committee on Federal Habeas
    Corpus in Capital Cases (Powell
    Committee), 159–160
alien enemies, 164, 169–170, 180
Allgeyer v. *Louisiana*, 30
Al Qaeda 3, 173–175
American Journal of Insanity, 74
anthropometry, 53, 75, 149
Antiterrorism and Effective Death
    Penalty Act (1996), xi, 3, 6, 20,
    157–158, 160–164, 179, 182–183
Arave v. *Creech*, 147
Arwood, Frances, 126–127
Ashcraft v. *Tennessee*, 65, 88, 102, 104,
    128
Atkins, Daryl Renard, 142
Atkins v. *Virginia*, 142, 146
Authorization for Use of Military Force
    (AUMF), 174–178

Balbus, Isaac, 164
Bank of Augusta v. *Earle*, 57

Bank of the United States v. *Deveaux*, 56
Barkelay, Mark, 57
Barron v. *Baltimore*, ix
Bator, Paul, 50, 86, 90, 123
Benton v. *Maryland*, 100, 138
Berger, Victor, 169
Berkman, Alexander, 169
Biden, Joe, 163
Biddle, Francis, 171, 173
Bill of Rights, 12, 27, 35, 37, 48, 50, 64,
    67, 70, 81, 83, 93, 96–97, 100, 103,
    112–113, 123, 128, 135–137, 190. *See
    also* Constitution
Black, Hugo, x, 28–29, 65, 72, 83, 87,
    89, 97–98, 101–103, 106, 113–115,
    119–120, 135, 173
Blackmun, Harry, 132, 150, 185–186,
    188
Board of Censorship, 168
Bonino, Frank, 105
Boone, Jack, 110
Booth v. *Maryland*, 145–146
Bradley, Joseph, 1, 29, 33–34
Brady v. *United States*, 116–118
Brennan, William, x, 7, 12, 14, 77, 99,
    101, 103–109, 111–115, 120,
    122–123, 130, 143, 166, 183
Brewer, David, 29

Brooks, Peter, 119, 142, 189

Brown, Malcolm "Possum," 144

Brown v. *Allen*, x, 9, 65, 67–68, 71, 76, 79, 84–85, 88–94, 96–97, 109, 112–113, 122, 128, 136, 138, 141, 152

Brown v. *Maryland*, 29

Brown v. *Mississippi*, 75–76, 82, 102, 129, 130, 144, 146

Burger, Ernest Peter, 170–171

Burger, Warren, 98, 101–102, 125, 129. *See also* Supreme Court

Burton, Harold, 14, 86, 103

Bush, George W., 165, 173

Byrnes, James, 70, 173

Byrnes, Thomas, 51, 55

Calderon v. *Thompson*, 27

Callins v. *Collins*, 185

capital punishment. *See* death penalty

Cardozo, Benjamin, 82, 96, 138

Carter, Ruben "Hurricane," 1, 183

Chafee, Zechariah, 168

Chambers v. *Florida*, 83, 103, 118, 128

Charles I, 165

Civil Rights Act 1866, 32

Civil War, ix, 2–3, 5, 19, 21, 23–27, 31, 51, 166

Clinton, Bill, 157, 163

Coker v. *Georgia*, 140

Coleman, Roger Keith, 187–189

Coleman v. *Thompson*, x, 17, 125, 150, 152, 186–188

Cominto, Santo, 105

Committee on Public Information, 168

common law, 5, 20, 25, 49, 82, 101, 120, 137, 171, 178, 181

Congress, ix–xi, 1, 3, 5, 21–26, 28–33, 77, 79, 85, 87, 90, 137, 158–160, 162, 164, 166, 168–169, 172–174, 176–177, 188, 190; on criminal law, 25; radical Republicans, 28, 31. *See also* writ of habeas corpus

Constitution, x, 2–3, 5, 9–10, 12, 27, 30, 34–35, 39, 52–53, 55, 57, 60, 66, 68, 82, 87, 91, 100, 102, 121, 137, 154, 165, 168, 173, 175, 178, 180–181, 186; due process, 3, 5–7, 11–12, 16, 18–19, 27–30, 33, 36–38, 40–44, 48, 59, 63, 65–66, 70, 72, 75, 77–78, 80–83, 89, 92, 95–97, 99, 103, 135, 143, 146, 150, 152, 181, 188; as fundamental fairness, 12, 100, 127; equal protection, 29, 71, 96; first amendment, 97, 99; fourth amendment, x, 15–16, 29, 64, 96–97, 99, 113–114, 120, 128; fifth amendment, 15–16, 28–29, 64, 67, 82, 96–97, 100, 128, 175, 180; sixth amendment, 15–16, 27, 29, 64, 81–83, 97, 99–100, 123, 128, 161; eighth amendment, 15–16, 28, 64, 67, 97, 99, 128, 139–140; thirteenth amendment, 32; fourteenth amendment x, 5–6, 8–9, 11, 16, 18–19, 26–30, 32, 36–37, 41, 46–48, 55, 58–60, 64–67, 70, 74, 76, 78, 82–83, 90–91, 93, 95–96, 98–99, 101–102, 104, 127–128, 135, 143, 150, 166, 175, 189; fifteenth amendment, 28

Coombe, Rosemary, 66, 142

corporations, 9, 19, 29, 46, 54–60, 65, 100; as persons, 9, 19, 35, 46–49, 52, 54–57, 59–61, 66

County of Santa Clara v. *Southern Pacific Railroad*, 9, 19, 29, 46–49, 60–61, 81, 101

Covell v. *Heyman*, 36

Crampton v. *Ohio*, 115

Creech, Thomas, 147

Crouzet, François, 54

Culombe v. *Connecticut*, 73, 95–96, 102, 119, 128

Culombe, Arthur, 73, 102–103

Czolgosz, Leon, 74

Daniels v. *Allen*, 64, 92–93, 105, 112, 187

Darr v. *Burford*, 84–88
Dartmouth College v. *Woodward*, 56
Dasch, George John, 171
Davis, Allen Lee, 155
Davis v. *United States*, 123
death penalty, 7, 9–10, 14–15, 17, 27, 39, 77, 89, 105, 115, 137, 139–141, 143, 146–147, 150, 159–161, 167, 171, 190
Debs, Eugene V., 169
Declaration of Independence, 81
De Meerlerr v. *Michigan*, 138
Democratic Party, 23, 163
Desist v. *United States* 98, 136
Dr. Jekyll and Mr. Hyde, 46, 55
Dole, Robert, 157
Douglas, William, 28, 72, 83, 87, 89, 101–102, 115, 117–118
Duker, William, 23
Duncan v. *Louisiana*, 100
Duncan v. *Walker*, 162

Eddings v. *Oklahoma*, 139–140
Elazar, Daniel, 27
Emergency Detention Act, 177. *See also* Internal Security Act
Endo, Mitsuye, 176
enemy aliens. *See* alien enemies
enemy combatants, 170–172, 174, 176, 178, 181, 183
Engle v. *Isaac*, 130–132
Escobedo, Danny, 128
Espionage Act, 168–169
Estelle v. *Smith*, 148
Ex parte Bollman, 25
Ex parte Bridges, 1
Ex parte Endo, 176
Ex parte Hawk, 84–85, 87–88
Ex parte Lange, 34
Ex parte Milligan, 167–168, 170, 172, 174, 176, 178, 180
Ex parte Parks, 34
Ex parte Quirin, 170–178, 180

Ex parte Royall, x, 9, 19, 30, 35, 38, 46–48, 50–52, 60–61, 82, 84, 87, 92, 101, 107, 121, 130, 159, 166, 186
Ex parte Siebold, 34
Ex parte Watkins, 24

Fay v. *Noia*, x–xi, 19, 85, 97–99, 103–109, 111–116, 118, 120–123, 129, 135, 143, 164, 166, 179, 183, 187
federal courts ix, xi, 1–3, 5, 8–10, 12–13, 22–24, 26, 31–34, 36–37, 39–41, 44, 47, 50, 56, 60, 66, 68–69, 80, 82–86, 88–89, 91, 93–94, 101, 104–105, 108–112, 121–122, 127, 130, 133, 138, 161–162, 167–170, 178–179
federalism, xi, 2, 6–7, 9–13, 15–16, 19–21, 26–30, 32–36, 39, 48–50, 61, 63, 67, 69–70, 76, 79–80, 87, 90, 92, 96, 98–104, 106, 112–113, 115–116, 119–122, 124–126, 129–132, 134, 136–137, 141, 144, 150, 155, 158, 162, 166, 178–179, 183, 186–190; defined, 33; federal-state comity, 2–3, 12, 15, 19, 27, 32, 36, 39, 48, 64, 70, 94, 96–97, 103–104, 106–108, 113–114, 122, 129, 131–132, 137, 140, 154, 162, 164, 166, 188; federal-state conflict, 39, 86, 104–107, 111; federal-state relations, 13, 16–18, 30–32, 34, 39, 41–43, 47, 70, 73, 92, 101, 104, 107, 113, 124, 187; finality, 2–3, 27–28, 36, 76, 90–93, 123, 127, 129, 131–134, 137, 141, 159, 162, 166, 186, 188, 190; state sovereignty, 23, 36, 48, 65, 188; states rights, 28, 86, 94, 104
Felker v. *Turpin*, xi
Field, David Dudley, 170
Field, Stephen, 29–30, 57–60
Fish, Stanley, 185
Fisher, Louis, 171
Flynn, John, 60

Ford v. *Wainwright*, 140
formalism. *See* legal formalism
Fortas, Abe, 179
Foster, Charles, 190
Foucault, Michel, 1, 49, 74
Francis v. *Henderson*, 121–123
Francis, Willie, 14–15
Frank, Leo, 19, 21, 39, 40–42, 44, 179.
    See also *Frank* v. *Magnum*
Frankfurter, Felix, 7, 14, 69, 72–73,
    87–90, 92–94, 96–97, 101–103, 106,
    109, 119, 121, 173, 178–179, 187
Frank v. *Magnum*, x, 21, 38–44, 76–78,
    83, 89, 93, 97, 109, 141
Frantz, Laurent, 32
Friedman, Lawrence, 66
Friendly, Henry, 116, 132
Fuller, Melville, 38. *See also* Supreme
    Court
Furman v. *Georgia*, 7
future dangerousness, 17–18, 20, 66–67,
    75, 125, 129, 141–142, 146–155, 174,
    183

Galambos, Louis, 58
Garfield, James, 74
Geneva Convention, 169, 182
Gideon, Clarence, 128
Gideon v. *Wainwright*, x, 96, 99, 123
Gilded Age, 9–10, 28, 49, 51–54, 66, 100
Gitlow v. *New York*, 97
Goldman, Emma, 169
Goodman, Louis, 85
Gordon, Murray, 90
Gregg v. *Georgia*, 7, 143
Grigson, James, 148–149
Guantánamo Bay, Cuba, 2, 20, 174–175,
    180–183
Guiteau, Charles, 74
habeas corpus. *See* writ of habeas corpus
Hacking, Ian, 45
Hamdi v. *Rumsfeld*, 165, 174–180,
    182–183, 188

Hamdi, Yaser, 174–179, 182
Hamilton, Alexander, 165
Harlan, John Marshall (I), 36
Harlan, John Marshall (II), 98, 104, 112,
    115, 136–138, 140
Harris v. *Nelson*, 179
Hatch, Orrin, 158–159
Haupt, Herbert Hans, 170–171
Herb v. *Pitcairn*, 80, 106
Herrera, Lionel Torres, 133
Herrera v. *Collins*, 132–133
Heywood, Bill, 169
Holden v. *Hardy*, 38
Holmes, Oliver Wendell, x, 5–6, 42–43,
    78–79, 94, 97, 109
Hoover, J. Edgar, 169, 173
Hughes, Charles Evans, 42, 75–76, 82.
    See also Supreme Court
Hunt, Alan, 65
Hurst, J. Willard, 57
Hurtado v. *California*, 36, 81
Hyde, Alan, 45, 49
Hyde, Henry, 157–158
Hysler v. *Florida*, 83

Immigration and Naturalization Service v.
    St. Cyr, 168
industrial revolution, 47, 54
Ingersoll, Charles, 22–23
Internal Security Act (18 U.S.C. 4001),
    177, 180, 182

Jackson, Robert, 3, 65, 67–69, 82,
    86–87, 90–93, 173, 175–176, 180
Jackson v. *Denno*, 117
Japanese, detention of, 170, 176
Jensen, David, 147
Johnson v. *Eisentrager*, 3, 180–182
Johnson v. *Massachusetts*, 102
Johnson v. *Zerbst*, 82–83
Judiciary Acts: act of 1789, ix, 2, 23–25,
    34, 166; act of 1875, 26, 33–34; act
    of 1885, 33; act of 1889, 26, 37; act

of 1891, 37; act of 1916, 79; act of
    1925, 79
Jurek v. *Texas* 139, 151

Kansas v. *Hendricks*, 154
Kaufman v. *United States*, x, 98–99,
    113–114, 120–121, 135
Kayani, Mohammed, 151–152
Keene, Charles, 144–145
Kelly, Billy, 153
Kelly v. *South Carolina*, 150, 152–153
Kemmler, William, 30, 38
Kennedy, Anthony, 27, 126, 141,
    150–151, 159, 162, 164
Kennedy, Kathleen, 169
Klarman, Michael, 80
Klopfer v. *North Carolina*, 100
Kuhlmann v. *Wilson*, 132–134
Kurland, Philip, 100

Lane, Charles, 126
Lanier, Julian, 190
Lee, Benny, 133
Lee v. *Mississippi*, 126
legal formalism, 8, 35, 41, 81, 107,
    167
legal functionalism, 10, 49, 71–72, 137,
    167
legal realism, 5–6, 10, 14, 16, 19–20, 32,
    35, 41–42, 68, 72, 101, 106, 120
Leps, Marie Christine, 189
Leyra v. *Denno*, 102–103
Lin, Ann Chih, 163
Lincoln, Abraham, 2, 23, 63, 165,
    167–168, 173
Linkletter v. *Walker*, 135–137
Lisenba v. *California*, 83
Loan Association v. *Topeka*, 30
Lochner v. *New York*, 37, 40, 101
Lockett v. *Ohio*, 139–140, 146
Louisiana v. *Resweber*, 14
Longakre, Richard, 176
Lyotard, Jean-François, 15

Mackey v. *United States*, 136–137
Magna Carta, 3–4
Malloy v. *Hogan*, 100
Mapp, Dollree, 128, 136
Mapp v. *Ohio*, 96, 98, 128, 135–136,
    157
Marbury v. *Madison*, 11
Marbury, William, 11
Mark, Gary, 57
Marshall, John, 11, 24–25, 29, 55–56.
    See also Supreme Court
Marshall, Thurgood, 102
Massiah v. *United States*, 133
Maudsley, Henry, 63
Maxwell v. *Dow*, 38
McCleskey v. *Zant*, 159
McGautha v. *California*, 115, 117–118
McKinley, William, 74
McLeod, Alexander, 22
McMann v. *Richardson*, 117
McReynolds, James, 67
McVeigh, Timothy, 3
Meyer, Carl, 29
Meyer, Karl, 154
military tribunals, 167–168, 170–174,
    180, 183
Miller-El v. *Cockrell*, 162
Miller, Samuel, 29, 30
Milligan, Lambdin, 167, 172
Minton, Sherman, 103
Miranda, Ernesto, 128
Miranda v. *Arizona*, 96, 98, 100, 119,
    125
Moody, William, 40
Mooney v. *Holohan*, 83, 85, 138
Moore, Frank, 78, 80
Moore v. *Dempsey*, x, 67, 77–80, 82–83,
    89, 93–94, 97–98, 138
Munn v. *Illinois*, 30, 58
Murdock v. *Memphis*, 122
Murphy, Frank, 72, 101–102, 126,
    173
Murray v. *Carrier*, 132, 134

Nesbitt, Eric, 142
New Deal, 15–16, 29, 72, 76, 127. *See also* Supreme Court
Nichols, Terry, 3
Nixon, Richard, 98, 115
Noia, Charles, 103, 105–106, 112, 116

Oaks, Dallin, 25
O'Connor, Sandra Day, xi, 7, 10, 13, 16–17, 73, 131–132, 134, 136–140, 143, 147–148, 150, 161–162, 164, 176–178, 183, 186–188
O'Dell, Joseph Roger, 17
O'Dell v. *Netherland*, 17–18
Omnibus Counterterrorism Act, 157
Osborn, Timothy-Kaufman, 154–155

Padilla, José, 181
Palko v. *Connecticut*, 82, 96, 98, 100, 138–139
Parker, John J., 88
Payne, Pervis Tyrone, 146
Payne v. *Tennessee*, 146
Peckham, Rufus, 29–30
Penry, Johnny Paul, 139–140
Penry v. *Lynaugh*, xi, 125, 130, 135, 137, 139–141
Phagan, Mary, 39
phrenology, 53, 75
Pitney, Mahlon, 40–41
Pointer v. *Texas*, 100
Powell, Lewis, x, 7, 10, 99, 101–102, 114, 119–121, 123, 133–134, 159, 160
Powell, Lloyd, 119–120
Powell v. *Alabama*, 72, 81
Professional Criminals of America, 51
progressive era, 65, 102
Railroad Tax Cases, 58–59
Ramdass, Bobbie Lee, 151–152
Ramdass v. *Angelone*, 150–152
Rasul, Shafiq, 181
Rasul v. *Bush*, 3, 165, 174, 179–183

Reagan Administration, 159–160
Reconstruction, x, 2–3, 26, 28, 40, 43, 98, 122, 166
Reed, Stanley, 86–87, 89, 103
Rehnquist, William, 73, 101–102, 117, 122–123, 125–126, 129, 159, 161. *See also* Supreme Court
Reitz, Curtis, 80, 107
Republican Party, 23
Roberts, Owen, 15, 173
Robinson v. *California*, 99
Rochin v. *California*, 102, 106
Rogers v. *Richmond*, 121
Rogge, O. John, 90
Roosevelt, Franklin Delano, 15, 171–173; court-packing plan, 15; Executive Order 9066, 176–177; Proclamation 2561, 170–171
Roosevelt, Theodore, 169
Rose v. *Lundy*, 130
Rose v. *Mitchell*, 124
Rothfield, Philippa, 47
Roy, William, 58
Royall, William, 9, 11, 15, 47, 51–53, 60, 91
Rumsfeld v. *Padilla*, 174, 181
Rundlet, Alexander, 160
Rutledge, Wiley, 72, 77, 101–102

Sanders v. *United States*, 99, 134
Sawyer, Robert, 127
Sawyer v. *Smith*, 126–127, 141
Sawyer v. *Whitley*, 126
Scalia, Antonin, 3, 142, 143–145, 148, 150, 153–154, 162, 164, 178–179, 182, 185
Schartner, Helen, 16
Schlag, Pierre, vi, 14
Schneckloth v. *Bustamonte*, 101, 114
Scorcese, Martin, 142
Screws v. *United States*, 69, 106, 190
Sedition Act, 168
Sekula, Allan 53

Shafer v. *South Carolina*, 150, 152–153
Shano, Cynthia, 126–127
Simmons v. *South Carolina*, 17, 150–153
Skowronek, Stephen, 9
Slaughterhouse Cases, The, 33, 58
Smith, Ernest Benjamin, 148
Smith, Rogers, 57
Smith v. *Murray*, 132, 135
Sofaer, Abraham, 104
Souter, David, 153
South Carolina v. *Gathers*, 13, 146
State v. *Robinson*, 130
Steiker, Jordan, 154
Stevens, John Paul, 17, 135, 143–144,
    152, 162, 168, 178–179, 183
Stevenson, Robert Louis, 46
Stewart, Potter, 7, 121
Stewart v. *Martinez-Villareal*, 159
Stone, Harlan Fiske, 171–172
Stone v. *Powell*, x, 113, 116, 120–121,
    123, 135, 139
Sunal v. *Large*, 179
Supreme Court, ix, 1–3, 6, 9–10, 12–16,
    20, 24, 26–29, 31–33, 35–44, 46–51,
    53–56, 61, 64–66, 68–74, 76–77,
    79–87, 89–90, 92–101, 105–106,
    108–109, 112–113, 115–117, 119,
    120–123, 125, 127, 129–135,
    137–142, 145–154, 159, 162,
    164–165, 170–172, 174, 176, 180,
    186–190; Burger Court, 18, 20,
    97–99, 102–104, 106, 113, 118–119,
    120–123, 125, 129–130, 132, 135,
    137; Fuller Court, 38; Hughes Court,
    29, 64, 69; New Deal Court, 15–16,
    19, 70–74, 77, 102, 118, 128;
    Rehnquist Court, 10, 16–18, 72, 103,
    125–126, 128–130, 132, 136–137,
    140–141, 143–144, 148–150, 159,
    162–163, 186; Stone Court,
    171–172; Taney Court, 57; Vinson
    Court, 86; Warren Court, 6, 10,
    16–19, 29, 48, 64, 88, 96–99, 100,
    102–104, 111, 114–115, 118, 124,
    128–129, 135–136, 141, 150
Sutherland, George, 81–82
Sweeten (Sheriff), 70

Taney, Roger, 29, 57. *See also* Supreme
    Court
Teague v. *Lane*, xi, 17, 125, 130,
    135–139, 141
terrorism 3, 157–158, 160, 163–165,
    173, 183
Thomas, Clarence, 17–18, 150, 162,
    164, 180, 190
Thomas v. *Arizona*, 102
Thompson v. *Oklahoma*, 143–146
Thompson, William Wayne, 143–145
Threats Against the President Act, 168
Tollett v. *Henderson*, 117–118, 122
Townsend v. *Sain*, 99, 108–118, 179
Townsend, Charles, 109–111
Trading-with-the-Enemy Act, 168–169
Truman, Harry, 176
Turley, Jonathan, 173
Turner v. *Murray*, 1
Twining v. *New Jersey*, 38, 40–41
Tyler v. *Cain*, 161

United States v. *Carolene Products*, 127
United States v. *Henry*, 133

Van Buren, Martin, 22
Vasquez v. *Hillery*, 7
Vinson, Fred, 86. *See also* Supreme
    Court
victim impact statements, 16, 145
Vivet, Louis, 45

Wade v. *Mayo*, 84–88
Wainwright v. *Sykes*, 116, 122–123, 129,
    130, 135
Waite, Morrison, 29, 38
Waley v. *Johnston*, 83
Walker v. *Johnston*, 83

Ward v. *Texas*, 70–71
War of 1812, 4, 22
Warren, Charles, 34
Warren, Earl, x, 73, 98–101, 109–113,
    115, 117, 119, 162. *See also* Supreme
    Court
Washington v. *Texas*, 100
Weems v. *United States*, 21
Weisselberg, Charles, 121
Wheeling Steel Corporation v. *Glander*, 28
Wickham, Gary, 65
Wilkinson, J. Harvie, 175–176
Wilson, Woodrow, 168–169
Williams v. *Taylor*, 161–162, 179
Wolf v. *Colorado*, 96
World Trade Center, 158
World War I, 5, 38, 168–169, 178
World War II, 65, 170, 176, 180
writ of habeas corpus: act of 1641, 24;
    act of 1679, 24–25; act of 1815
    (removal), 22–24, 33, 42, 63; act of
    1833, 22–23; act of 1842, 22–23; act
    of 1863, 23; act of 1867, ix, 2–3, 21,
    24, 26, 28, 30–32, 36, 39, 41, 43, 69,
    80, 86, 90, 167, 179, 181; act of 1948
    (18 U.S. C., sections 2241–2255), 87,
    88, 108, 113, 133, 161–162, 181–182;
    abuse of, 88, 133, 159; adequate and
    independent state ground rule,
    79–80, 105–107; appellate review, 41;
    Britain, use in, 3–5, 8, 37, 47, 107;
    cause and prejudice, 116, 121–124,
    129–132, 134–135; collateral attack,
    ix, 8, 116, 121; common law, mean-
    ing of, 5, 25; Congress on, 32–33, 37,
    77, 79, 84, 87–88, 157–165, 173;
    conservatives, views on, 8–10, 16;
    Constitution, mentioned in, 2, 17,
    168, 178; contemporaneous objection
    rule, 122; defined, ix, 1; deference,
    role of, 34, 36, 39, 42, 86; deliberate
    bypass, 105–106, 122, 134–135;
    exhaustion doctrine, 35–36, 38–40,
    43–44, 84–86, 88, 94, 105, 162;
    Federalist Papers, mentioned in, 165;
    formal process, 5; guilt and inno-
    cence, 113–118, 120–121, 132, 134,
    174; habeas corpus I, 20, 165–166,
    174, 178–179, 182–183, 188; habeas
    corpus II, 20, 165–166, 174, 179,
    182–183, 188; human right, 4; isola-
    tion principle, 103–104, 107, 112;
    jurisdiction standard, 31, 34, 36–38,
    40–41, 43, 44, 70, 89–90; liberals,
    views on, 8–9; Magna Carta, 23, 37;
    narrative, 6–9, 11–18, 30, 35, 39, 42,
    47, 49, 61, 64–83, 91–97, 107,
    109–111, 119, 124–129, 142–155,
    157–165, 174–175, 185–190; new
    rule, 137–140; plain error rule, 131;
    postconviction remedy, 2, 79, 113;
    procedural default, 123, 134, 188;
    Reagan Administration, views on,
    160; retroactivity, 130, 135–141;
    sandbagging, 122; as speech,
    109–111, 114, 119, 190; Supreme
    Court, views on, x–xi, 7, 10, 12, 16,
    19–21, 25–30, 32–35, 39, 47, 81–87,
    91–93, 98, 100–105, 115; suspension
    of, ix, 2, 23, 31, 165, 168, 177–178;
    waiver, 117
writ of mandamus, 11

Yackle, Larry, 93, 163
Youngstown Sheet & Tube Co. v. *Sawyer*,
    174–175

Zunz, Olivier, 58